Research Studies in Library Science, No. 12

RESEARCH STUDIES IN LIBRARY SCIENCE

Bohdan S. Wynar, Editor

No. 1.   *Middle Class Attitudes and Public Library Use*. By Charles Evans, with an Introduction by Lawrence Allen.

No. 2.   *Critical Guide to Catholic Reference Books*. By James Patrick McCabe, with an Introduction by Russell E. Bidlack.

No. 3.   *An Analysis of Vocabulary Control in Library of Congress Classification and Subject Headings*. By John Phillip Immroth, with an Introduction by Jay E. Daily.

No. 4.   *Research Methods in Library Science. A Bibliographic Guide*. By Bohdan S. Wynar.

No. 5.   *Library Management: Behavior-Based Personnel Systems. A Framework for Analysis*. By Robert E. Kemper.

No. 6.   *Computerizing the Card Catalog in the University Library: A Survey of User Requirements*. By Richard P. Palmer, with an Introduction by Kenneth R. Shaffer.

No. 7.   *Toward a Philosophy of Educational Librarianship*. By John M. Christ.

No. 8.   *Freedom versus Suppression and Censorship*. By Charles H. Busha, with an Introduction by Peter Hiatt, and a Preface by Allan Pratt.

No. 9.   *The Role of the State Library in Adult Education: A Critical Analysis of Nine Southeastern State Library Agencies*. By Donald D. Foos, with an Introduction by Harold Goldstein.

No. 10.   *The Concept of Main Entry as Represented in the Anglo-American Cataloging Rules. A Critical Appraisal with Some Suggestions: Author Main Entry vs. Title Main Entry*. By M. Nabil Hamdy, with an Introduction by Jay E. Daily.

No. 11.   *Publishing in Switzerland: The Press and the Book Trade*. By Linda S. Kropf.

No. 12.   *Library Science Dissertations, 1925-1972: An Annotated Bibliography*. By Gail A. Schlachter and Dennis Thomison.

Library Science Dissertations, 1925-1972

An Annotated Bibliography

GAIL A. SCHLACHTER

DENNIS THOMISON

1974

LIBRARIES UNLIMITED INC., LITTLETON, COLO.

LIBRARIES UNLIMITED, INC.
P.O. Box 263
Littleton, Colorado 80120

CONTENTS

INTRODUCTION 7

LIBRARY SCIENCE DISSERTATIONS, 1925-1972 9

A STATISTICAL PROFILE OF LIBRARY
SCIENCE DISSERTATIONS, 1925-1972 256

AUTHOR INDEX 263

SUBJECT INDEX 271

INTRODUCTION

Background

The antecedents of this work date back to 1956 when the Research Committee of the Association of American Library Schools recognized the need for a central listing of library science dissertations. Under the direction of Dr. Martha Boaz, Dean of the School of Library Science at the University of Southern California, the Committee assembled an annotated bibliography of 224 doctoral studies relating to library science completed at the Graduate Library School of the University of Chicago between 1925 and 1950 and at other accredited library schools between 1951 and 1959. The bibliography was completed by Nathan M. Cohen, Barbara Denison and Jessie Boehlert and published under the title *Library Science Dissertations, 1925-1959: An Annotated Bibliography of Doctoral Studies.*

Since 1960, there has been an enormously accelerated output of library science dissertations. In the past 12 years—as a result of increased professional interest, job demands and federal funding—more library science doctoral studies were completed than in the 35 years between the first dissertation relating to librarianship in 1925 and the completion of the Research Committee's compilation in 1960.

There has not been, however, a corresponding increase in the bibliographic control of this research. It is ironic that librarianship—a field which places such a great emphasis on information storage and retrieval—should have such poor access to the scholarly literature of its own field. There is no one central location where a researcher can secure complete and accurate information on doctoral studies that relate to library science. Instead, the researcher must use a combination of current bibliographic listings, such as those in *Dissertation Abstracts International, Library Literature,* and *Library Quarterly.* Neither individually nor totally do these tools offer a complete record of research done in the field of librarianship. It is to begin to fill this gap that the present publication was compiled.

Scope

The bibliography was compiled from listings in *Dissertation Abstracts International, Library Literature, Library Quarterly, Library Science Dissertations* and David H. Eyman's pamphlet *Doctoral Dissertations in Library Science* (Ann Arbor, Michigan, Xerox University Microfilms, 1973). An attempt was made to locate in the five sources those doctoral studies which were either accepted by library schools or concerned with areas bearing a close relationship to the field of librarianship (e.g., communications, information services, education, etc.) and completed between 1925 and 1972.

Whenever possible, annotations were prepared—delineating purpose, procedure, findings, conclusions and recommendations—by drawing on existing abstracts, requesting author-prepared annotations, or using the original dissertations. For some studies, however, it was not possible to obtain either abstracts or the original dissertations. Nevertheless, these studies are included, without annotations, in the bibliography and, when sufficient information is available, in the statistical summaries, in order to present as complete a picture as possible of research in librarianship.

Bibliographic information given for each citation includes the name of the author, degree received, school attended, year completed, and complete title of the study. In addition, number of pages (when available) and University Microfilms' *Dissertation Abstracts International* order number (where appropriate) are given.

Arrangement

The basic arrangement of the bibliography is chronological by date of completion, in order to show the development of library science research and the areas emphasized during different time periods. Within each year, the arrangement is alphabetical by author. The work also includes a statistical description of the dissertations. Using cross tabular and chi-square analysis, an investigation is made of the relationship between the sex of the author, degree received, institution attended, year completed, and research methodology employed. The publication is concluded with author and detailed subject indexes.

Acknowledgements

In addition to acknowledging our indebtedness to those individuals mentioned above, we would like to express our gratitude to Dr. R. David Weber of the University of Southern California, Mr. Robert S. Miles of Long Beach City College, and the staff of the Social Science Research Institute at the University of Southern California for assistance in the completion of this bibliography.

Library Science Dissertations,

1925-1972

1. Tai, Tse-Chien (Ph.D., State University of Iowa, 1925). **Professional education for librarianship.**

PURPOSE: The purpose of the study was to review and analyze the development of libraries and library education from a broad historical point of view, and to propose a program for library education.

PROCEDURE: The historical method was the basic approach used in this study.

FINDINGS: The author presented the factors that have influenced the development of libraries, and the relationship of these factors to the character of professional education for librarianship. The origin and development of library schools in Europe and the United States are studied critically. A proposal for the establishment of a library school at the State University of Iowa was included.

2. Koos, Frank Hermann (Ed.D., Columbia University, Teachers College, 1927). **State participation in public school library service.**

PURPOSE: The purpose of the study was to identify and analyze the activities of those government agencies authorized by law to give library service to public school libraries.

PROCEDURE: The data were collected from legal codes and session laws of the states, reports of commissions and other agencies, state courses of study, correspondence, and library literature.

FINDINGS: A detailed analysis is given of state statutory provisions relating to school libraries, state education departments, state libraries and commissions, and other agencies. Materials, such as book lists, standards, and reports, are also analyzed.

RECOMMENDATIONS: The author recommended that leadership in this field should be exercised by the state departments of education, and that state programs should be given adequate financial support.

3. Rosenlof, George W. (Ed.D., Columbia University, Teachers College, 1928). **The teachers college library.**

PURPOSE: The purpose of the study was to examine the library collections of teachers' colleges in the United States, with a view towards proposing new standards. PROCEDURE: The author examined collections, administration, staff, and budgets of teachers' colleges and normal schools in the United States.
RECOMMENDATIONS: The author suggested the following standards for teachers' college libraries: a minimum of 25,000 volumes and 150 periodical subscriptions; provisions for separate training-school libraries, separate textbook libraries, sufficient qualified personnel, and a certain percentage of the total college budget allocated to the library.

1930

4. Upton, Eleanor Stuart (Ph.D., University of Chicago, 1930). **A guide to sources of seventeenth century history in selected reports of the Historical Manuscripts Commission of Great Britain.**
PURPOSE: The purpose of the study was to provide an access to the important historical source materials in the Historical Manuscripts Commission of Great Britain reports.
PROCEDURE: The author provided a subject indexing of the source materials in private collections in England and Wales, as listed in the reports of the Commission.
FINDINGS: The study covers political, military, social, economic, cultural, and ecclesiastical aspects of life in England, Wales, and the British colonies.

1931

5. Condit, Lester David (Ph.D., University of Chicago, 1931). **Studies in Roman printing type of the fifteenth century.**
PURPOSE: The purpose of the study was to identify a new approach to the problem of identifying early printed books by their type.
PROCEDURE: The protractor was used to measure the basic angles of uppercase letters M, N, V, A, and Z. Certain other type measurements were also taken.

6. Kwei, John Chi Ber (Ph.D., University of Chicago, 1931). **Bibliographical and administrative problems arising from the incorporation of Chinese books in American libraries.**
PURPOSE: The purpose of the study was to describe the major collections of Chinese books in the United States and Canada, to analyze the physical characteristics of Chinese books, and to discuss how they may be prepared for use in American libraries.

PROCEDURE: The data were collected from the printed literature, correspondence, visits to the collections described, and from practical experience.

FINDINGS: The data revealed that Chinese books differ widely from a bibliographic standpoint from volumes of European origin because of basic differences in language, physical characteristics, and bibliographic conventions. The two methods of handling Chinese books in American libraries are studied: grouping them together and classifying them independently of publications in Occidental languages, or interfiling them by subject together with non-Chinese publications.

7. Swindler, Robert Earl (Ph.D., University of Virginia, 1931). **The high school library and reading problems in the social studies with particular reference to United States history.**

PURPOSE: The purpose of the study was to make a qualitative study of the holdings in social studies (mainly of United States history) in a selected group of junior and senior high school libraries.

PROCEDURE: The principal research tool used was the questionnaire, with information gathered from 347 school systems.

FINDINGS: Among the findings are the following: an adequate number of social science books was found in only a small number of the schools studied; inadequately trained library staffs indicated that there was a need for more trained librarians and for more courses in library science; a great many of the books included in the social science collections were not suited for the students in the schools; and the quality of social studies collections in Southern school libraries was considerably below the average for the country.

1932

---

8. Akers, Susan Grey (Ph.D., University of Chicago, 1932). **Relation between theory and practice of cataloging: with special reference to courses in cataloging in library schools.**

PURPOSE: The purpose of the study was to compare the cataloging practices of librarians with the theory that is taught in library school courses in cataloging, classification, and subject headings.

PROCEDURE: The information was collected from a checklist returned by 83 catalog librarians in 69 libraries throughout the United States and by 12 instructors in accredited library schools. This checklist was composed of subjects listed in topical outlines for first-year cataloging classes and other courses of 12 accredited library schools.

FINDINGS: The majority of the respondents (60 percent) agreed on 92 topics relating to cataloging *per se*, and on 21 topics relating to the organization and administration of a catalog department.

CONCLUSIONS: The author concluded that all 113 topics should be included in a basic cataloging course.

9. Boney, Cecil De Witt (Ed.D., Columbia University, Teachers College, 1932).
A study of library reading in the primary grades.
PURPOSE: The purpose of the study was to examine the objectives for reading
programs, their origins, and the techniques used in conducting them.
PROCEDURE: The author used the following methods to obtain the necessary
information: a search of the literature, a study of course outlines, and a questionnaire
completed by 254 teachers in various sections of the United States.
FINDINGS: The following findings were determined from the study: (1) the typical
reading program attempts to develop strong motives for and permanent interest in
reading, and to offer rich and varied experience; (2) it is essential that supervised
periods for reading are provided; (3) the conduct of reading programs should be
shared by teachers and children; (4) book reports should be voluntary; (5) children
should be encouraged to read books outside of the classroom.

10. Carnovsky, Leon (Ph.D., University of Chicago, 1932). **The reading needs of
typical student groups; with special attention to factors contributing to the
satisfaction of reading interests.**
PURPOSE: The author's purpose was to determine relationships between nonfiction
reading interests and the actual reading of students at the University of Chicago.
PROCEDURE: A checklist of books, mostly recent, was compiled by the author.
Students in the study were then asked to indicate which of these books they had
read, whether or not they had been read in connection with school work, and where
the students had obtained the books.
FINDINGS: The results of the study indicated suggestive rather than definitive
findings. Books representing topics of low or high interest were widely read when
such titles were extensively advertised, widely accessible, readable, and written by
well-known authors. At least one of these factors must be present in addition to
interest if the book is to be widely read. The differing interests between men and
women students carried over to their actual reading.

11. Willoughby, Edwin Elliott (Ph.D., University of Chicago, 1932). **The printing
of the first folio of Shakespeare.**
PURPOSE: The author's purpose was to investigate the history behind the printing
of the first Shakespeare folio.
FINDINGS: The investigation determined that the printing of the first folio was
done at two different times. The first run apparently was done about August-October
1621 and produced all of the comedies except *The Winter's Tale*, plus *King John*,
and the first two pages of *Richard II*. The second run, one year and a half later,
included the remaining history plays, the tragedies, the preliminary matter, *Troilus
and Cressida*, and *The Winter's Tale*.

12. Adams, A. Elwood (Ed.D., University of Southern California, 1933). **The use of the school library by teachers and pupils in junior and senior high schools.**
PURPOSE: The purpose was to study the nature and extent of school library use by pupils and teachers.
PROCEDURE: A sample population of 24 representative junior and senior high schools was selected. A canvass was made of "expert judgments" regarding the purpose of a school library and the place it should occupy in an educational institution. Libraries were evaluated in terms of their traditional functions, such as the acquisition and organization of library materials, instruction in their use, availability of reference materials, etc.
FINDINGS: The general finding of the author was that the libraries studied performed these functions only partially.
RECOMMENDATIONS: The following recommendations were made as a result of the study: the school library should extend its hours both before and after school; a free reading program should be initiated; cooperation should exist between the librarian and the teachers and between the school and the public library; and instruction in library use should be given to all pupils.

13. Emerson, Wallace LeRoy (Ph.D., University of Southern California, 1933). **A study of secondary school libraries in the United States from the standpoint of educational administration.**
PURPOSE: The purpose of the study was to analyze secondary school and junior college libraries in relation to policies and practices of the state department of education, training of librarians, and library conditions.
PROCEDURE: The data were gathered from library school catalogs, and from questionnaires returned by 50 junior colleges, 208 junior high school libraries, and 47 state departments of education, as well as 645 questionnaires sent to secondary school principals.
FINDINGS: The following are among the findings reported by the author: in general, state departments of education have not formulated functional objectives for the library; in relation to existing standards, the support of the library in junior high schools seems fairly adequate, less so in high schools, and least adequate in junior colleges; adequate and definite policies do not seem to govern the selection of books; the physical facilities of all three groups are inadequate, with the junior colleges in the poorest condition; 67.5 percent of high school librarians, 65 percent of junior high school librarians, and 54.5 percent of junior college librarians received their education at accredited high schools.

14. Hirschstein, Bertha T. (Ph.D., New York University, 1933). **A sociological study of a public library in an interstitial area.**
PURPOSE: The purpose of the study was to investigate the activities and clientele of the Aguilar Branch of the New York Public Library, undertaken as part of a larger study of a Boys' club in East Harlem.

PROCEDURE: The following methods were used in obtaining the data: study of library circulation and registration records, interviews, and examination of the pertinent literature.

FINDINGS: Among the findings were the following: the ratio of circulation to book stock remained almost constant over a period of years, although the circulation of Italian books increased; distance from the library seemed to be a prime factor in determining its use; in this area, people over 21 years read more than those under 21; delinquent boys read more fiction than did the whole population studied; and there was a great similarity between the reading habits of boys' club members and those of nonmembers.

15. Taam, Cheuk-Woon (Ph.D., University of Chicago, 1933). **The development of Chinese libraries under the Ch'ing Dynasty, 1644-1911.** 107p.

PURPOSE: The purpose of the study was to show the development of libraries prior to, and the progress during, the Ch'ing Dynasty.

PROCEDURE: The historical method of research was used, utilizing both primary and secondary sources.

FINDINGS: The legacy from the Ming Dynasty was described in terms of the intellectual climate and the book collections. The imperial libraries are discussed in detail. The development of four important personal libraries established after the Taiping Rebellion is shown.

CONCLUSIONS: The author concluded that the development of libraries during the 267 years overshadowed the library achievement of all the previous dynasties combined.

1934

---

16. Joeckel, Carleton Bruns (Ph.D., University of Chicago, 1934). **The government of the American public library.** 393p.

PURPOSE: The purpose of the study was to describe and evaluate the role of the public library in the government of the United States. The author included the legal forms and types of governmental organization of public libraries, and their relation to the political units to which they are attached or which they serve.

PROCEDURE: Data were gathered from 310 public libraries serving populations of more than 30,000. Some consideration was also given to public libraries in smaller communities.

FINDINGS: There is a discussion of improvements in library legislation, including the concept of uniformity, federal relations, and federal aid. There is also consideration of the various forms of libraries, such as the school-district public libraries and the large-unit systems of service.

17. Kelly, Grace Osgood (Ph.D., University of Chicago, 1934). **The classification of books in terms of use with some regard to the advantages of the subject-catalog.**

PURPOSE: The purpose of the study was to try to determine whether the subject catalog or the classification assigned to books is of greater help to library users.
PROCEDURE: The sources of information in this study were the catalogs of the University of Chicago Library, the Library of Congress, the Massachusetts State Library, and the Library of Northwestern University.
FINDINGS: The author included information on the historical situation with regard to classification, and included ways in which libraries have met the need for availability of subject matter. The 13 elements which affect adversely the usefulness of the classified arrangement of books are analyzed in detail.
CONCLUSIONS: The author concluded that the flexibility of the subject catalog, as opposed to the unavoidable rigidity of classification, makes it the better arrangement for indicating subject resources of a library.

18. McDiarmid, Errett Weir, Jr. (Ph.D., University of Chicago, 1934). **Conditions affecting use of the college library.**
PURPOSE: The purpose of the study was to develop a procedure for estimating and analyzing student use of college libraries.
PROCEDURE: The data were gathered from circulation records and other records provided by seven North Central colleges.
FINDINGS: Among the findings were the following: (1) library use is consistently high in the humanities and the social sciences; (2) women read more than men do; (3) upperclassmen borrow more library materials than do freshmen and sophomores; (4) good students borrow more books than do the poor students; (5) libraries with good book collections and adequate funds are used more often than are others.

19. Rood, Helen Martin (Ph.D., University of Chicago, 1934). **Nationalism in children's literature.**
PURPOSE: The purpose of the study was to test the thesis that the popularity of children's books in the international market is influenced by the number of "nationalist symbols" included in them. A nationalist symbol is defined as a word or phrase considered to be patriotic by inhabitants of the country in which or about which the book is written.
PROCEDURE: The popularity of 24 selected titles, measured by bookstore sales and library circulation in 16 European countries and the United States, is related to incidence of 52 nationalist symbols.
CONCLUSIONS: The author has stated the following conclusions based on the study: the chance that a child's book will reach an international market is greater if the book has a small number of nationalist symbols; dialect makes a children's book unpopular abroad; expressions of hostility towards a nation in a book will restrict the popularity of the book in that nation; war books for children are most popular in those nations spending the most on national defense; to have the best expectation of a wide foreign market, a children's book should deal first with social and economic situations, then with situations rich in patriotic symbols.

20. Shores, Louis (Ph.D., George Peabody College for Teachers, 1934). **Origins of the American college library, 1638-1800.** 290p.
PURPOSE: The purpose was to describe the development of the college library during the Colonial and Revolutionary periods, as well as to evaluate its contribution to colonial higher education.

PROCEDURE: Nine libraries were studied: Harvard, William and Mary, Yale, Princeton, Columbia, Pennsylvania, Brown, Rutgers, and Dartmouth. Information was obtained from the published histories of colonial education, from visits to the libraries, and from primary and secondary sources of information about the colleges.

FINDINGS: The study revealed the great importance which the colonial college placed on the library and its collection of books. This carried over to the position of the librarian, who was chosen for scholarly ability. Rules relating to the ordering, cataloging, and classifying of books were carefully worked out. The book collections were all very small, with the largest being 12,000 volumes.

1935

---

21. Danton, Joseph Periam (Ph.D., University of Chicago, 1935). **The selection of books for college libraries: an examination of certain factors which affect excellence of selection.**
PURPOSE: The purpose of the study was to determine the effect of librarians, faculty, and book fund policies on the quality of book selection in liberal arts college libraries.
PROCEDURE: The author used Charles B. Shaw's *A List of Books for College Libraries* as a basis for formulation of a book selection quality index, and index numbers were assigned to 86 college libraries having collections of less than 50,000 volumes. Information about the book selection practices and factors influencing them was obtained through questionnaires and correspondence. This information was supplemented by personal visits to 11 libraries with the highest index numbers and 13 with the lowest.
FINDINGS: Librarians in the high-index libraries, compared with those in the low, had more general and professional education, more library experience, more responsibility and time to devote to book selection, greater facility in the use of book selection aids, and more control over the book budget. Similarly, the faculty in the high-index group spent more time on library book selection, had better educations, and made use of more selection aids.

22. Foster, Jeannette Howard (Ph.D., University of Chicago, 1935). **An experiment in classifying fiction based on the characteristics of its readers.**
PURPOSE: The author's purpose was to devise a classification scheme for fiction which was based on key data about fiction readers.
PROCEDURE: The reading records of 15,285 people were analyzed. Works of the 254 most-read fiction authors were tabulated according to 15 subject classes, and 6 quality levels. The tabulations were correlated with such data about the readers as age, sex, education, and occupation.
CONCLUSIONS: The study indicated that such a classification system might be more meaningful if the number of subject classes were reduced to 10. Further research is needed into the reasons people read the way they do.

23. Stieg, Lewis Francis (Ph.D., University of Chicago, 1935). **An introduction to paleography for librarians.**

PURPOSE: The purpose of the study was to discuss the basic principles involved in deciphering and reading medieval and ancient manuscripts.

FINDINGS: The study disclosed that the bibliographic apparatus for paleography is inadequate. The author also suggests that a student first read a manuscript through rapidly in order to gather the meaning of the document as a whole, disregarding unintelligible portions on the first reading. Other suggestions for reading manuscripts are given, according to problems of decipherment and problems of interpretation.

24. Wellard, James Howard (Ph.D., University of Chicago, 1935). **Bases for a theory of book selection.**

PURPOSE: The purpose of the study was to attempt to formulate a social theory of book selection for public libraries.

FINDINGS: The study reviewed the historical background of social attitudes toward public library development in England and the United States. It considers the literary and sociopsychological aspects of book selection as well as standards of social value.

CONCLUSIONS: The author has concluded that book selection must be related to full realization of the place of the library in the community to be served.

1936

---

25. Little, Evelyn Steel (Ph.D., University of Michigan, 1936). **Homer and Theocritus in English translation: a critical bibliography designed as a guide for librarians in the choice of editions for the general reader.**

PURPOSE: The purpose of the study was to develop a critical bibliography of translations of Homer and Theocritus in terms of the best editions for librarians to buy for the general reader.

PROCEDURE: The author commented critically on translations published between 1470 and 1935, and listed in the catalogs of the British Museum, the Library of Congress, and seven other large libraries, as well as in the trade bibliographies.

FINDINGS: The author has specified the best translations of the works of Homer and Theocritus.

26. Miller, Robert Alexander (Ph.D., University of Chicago, 1936). **Cost accounting for libraries: a technique for determining the labor costs of acquisition and cataloguing work.** 193p.

PURPOSE: The purpose of the study was to develop a method for obtaining library cost data for purposes of administrative evaluation and planning.

PROCEDURE: The study involved the cataloging and acquisitions department of one large university library, presumed to be representative. The study was eight weeks in duration.

FINDINGS: Through the use of timesheets, the various routines and operations were analyzed. The cost of each operation was then determined for comparative purposes. Included were suggestions for the simplification of routines that would reduce costs.

27. Purdy, George Flint (Ph.D., University of Chicago, 1936). **A study of the status of the public library in Middle-Western society.** 140p.
PURPOSE: The purpose of the study was to compare the public library resources of seven Midwestern states with the distribution of other reading materials, and with economic and educational factors.
PROCEDURE: The characteristics of seven states (Illinois, Indiana, Iowa, Michigan, Minnesota, Ohio, and Wisconsin) were studied. Of the sample of 254 counties studied, 154 were selected at random, and 100 according to whether they served a rural or an urban population.
FINDINGS: The study showed that in general, counties having relatively advanced library development rated high in urbanization, wealth, secondary school enrollment, and number of radios, general magazines, and daily newspapers. Wealth appeared to be the most important condition for library development, but it accounted for only a little more than half of the variations in library service.

1937

---

28. Ellsworth, Ralph Eugene (Ph.D., University of Chicago, 1937). **The distribution of books and magazines in selected communities.** 88p.
PURPOSE: The purpose of the study was to determine the relative importance of the various distribution agencies in supplying different types of printed materials to a sample of readers.
PROCEDURE: In obtaining the data, both the questionnaire and interview techniques were used.
FINDINGS: The study demonstrated that public libraries were the main suppliers of books in the sample, with almost 45 percent; for magazines, subscriptions were the main sources, with 39 percent. It was further pointed out that half the users of the public library are students, and that there is a direct correlation between the amount of library use and the level of education.
RECOMMENDATIONS: The author has suggested that public libraries should devote a greater effort toward supplying good reference service and good literature to the public.

29. Reed, Lulu Ruth (Ph.D., University of Chicago, 1937). **A test of students' competence to use the library.** 290p.
PURPOSE: The purpose of the study was to devise tests to determine student competence in the use of college, high school, and elementary school libraries.
PROCEDURE: Reference librarians at the University of Chicago Library, and faculty and selected students at the Graduate Library School were interviewed.

PROCEDURE (cont'd): Preliminary drafts of the tests were taken by groups of high school and college students.

FINDINGS: Five aspects of test reliability were considered: objectivity, length, sampling of subject matter, selection of schools, and statistical measure. The students tested displayed greater ability in locating specific books than in using reference books effectively.

30. Wilson, Eugene Holt (Ph.D., University of Illinois, 1937). **Preprofessional background of students in a library school.**

PURPOSE: The purpose of the study was to consider the preprofessional background of library school students in relation to their scholastic success.

PROCEDURE: The data were collected from the records of 808 library science students at the University of Illinois between 1926-27 and 1935-36.

FINDINGS: The "typical" student was described as an unmarried woman, 26 years of age, with a middle-class social, economic, and cultural background, and with somewhat better than average undergraduate grades. Students with some library experience tend to achieve a slightly higher degree of success in library school than do those without. Other factors, such as undergraduate grades, amount of preparation in French and German, type of college attended, and undergraduate major seem to have little effect on library school achievement.

1938

---

31. Kramer, Sidney David (Ph.D., University of Chicago, 1938). **Stone & Kimball, 1893-97, and Herbert S. Stone & Company, 1896-1905: studies in publishing history.** 126p.

PURPOSE: The purpose of the study was to present a history and bibliography of the publishing activities of the two men connected with the two publishing firms.

PROCEDURE: The historical method was the basic approach used in this study.

FINDINGS: Many of the leading authors of the day were contributors to Stone and Kimball's literary magazine called *The Chapbook*: Thomas Bailey Aldrich, Stephen Crane, Eugene Field, Henry James, and Robert Louis Stevenson. They published books by Edmund Gosse, Ibsen, Poe, Henry James, and George Bernard Shaw. Background material on the "little magazines" of the period is included, as well as a complete bibliography of the discovered publications of the two firms.

32. Leidner, Sister M. Dorothy (Ph.D., Fordham University, 1938). **Libraries in Catholic secondary schools: a study based on the secondary schools in the Diocese of Brooklyn.**

PURPOSE: The purpose of the study was to examine the secondary school libraries in the Brooklyn Diocese in relation to the various standards and to library practice elsewhere.

PROCEDURE: The data were obtained through questionnaires and from personal visits to the school libraries.

FINDINGS: Among the findings of the study are the following: there was a shortage of adequately trained personnel in the libraries; most of the schools had separate library facilities, and most of these rooms had an adequate seating capacity; the book and materials collections were adequately balanced; more than half of the schools surveyed had regular allocations for materials, while the rest received funds as needed; library instruction is given on a regular basis by the librarians in over two-thirds of the schools; many techniques have been used by librarians to stimulate library usage.

33. Richardson, Mary C. (Ed.D., New York University, 1938). **Implementing a building for the Library and the Library School Department of the State Normal School at Geneseo, New York, in terms of the curricula offered.**
PURPOSE: The purpose of the paper was to analyze Geneseo's need for a new combined library/library school building, and to present plans intended to act as a guide for this and other small teachers' colleges.
PROCEDURE: The study is based on personal observation, correspondence with experts in the field and a survey of the literature.
FINDINGS: The study reviews the place of the library in the academic environment, analyzes the library building according to the needs of its staff and clientele, examines the requirements of the Library School Department at Geneseo, and presents basic principles that support the basic contention that a new building is needed.

1939

---

34. Alvarez, Robert Smyth (Ph.D., University of Chicago, 1939). **Qualifications of heads of libraries in cities of over ten thousand population in the seven north-central states.** 192p.
PURPOSE: The purpose of the study was to analyze the educational qualifications and experience of head librarians in relation to their professional capabilities and rate of advancement.
PROCEDURE: The data were collected from biographical sources and from a questionnaire returned by the directors of 189 (of 241) public libraries in Illinois, Indiana, Iowa, Michigan, Minnesota, Ohio, and Wisconsin.
FINDINGS: The data revealed that the qualifications of chief librarians are only slightly better than those of the average member of the library profession. This suggests that administrators owe their rise to intangible factors and qualities that are difficult to measure. In Wisconsin, a state that has a librarian certification law, the salaries and educational preparation of head librarians are better than in states that do not have such a law.

35. Butler, Helen Louise (Ph.D., University of Chicago, 1939). **An inquiry into the statement of motives by readers.** 117p.
PURPOSE: The purpose of the study was to discover the reasons why people read books.

PROCEDURE: The author prepared lists of 134 purposes that might be satisfied by books, and distributed them to readers in the Rochester, New York, Public Library. A total of 1,427 returns were analyzed.

FINDINGS: In general, fiction books were read for recreation, fine arts books were used in connection with hobbies, and business and science books were read for occupational purposes. In all fields the dominating motives for reading appeared to be for information, recreation, aesthetic appreciation, and critical understanding of the effect produced by the book.

RECOMMENDATIONS: The author suggests that further research be done to identify the "occasions" that cause people to read a particular book on a particular subject.

36. Cecil, Henry LeRoy (Ed. D., New York University, 1939). **An interpretive study of library service for the school superintendent.**

PURPOSE: The purpose of the study was to review the history of school library service, interpret its importance, and analyze current administrative practices.

PROCEDURE: The data were derived from a survey of the literature of the field, and from questionnaires sent to superintendents of schools and librarians in public and school libraries.

FINDINGS: The author reported the following among the findings: permissive legislation for the establishment of school libraries has been enacted by 29 states, while 15 states have enacted mandatory legislation; 20 percent of the central libraries in 67 cities are public libraries serving both schools and the general public; and 47 percent of the 3,278 schools represented in the study have central libraries.

CONCLUSIONS: Among the conclusions of the study are the following statements: the school library was found to be recognized as an integral part of the school organization; state-wide supervision of school library service is the most effective; and there is a nationwide need for generous support of school libraries from the state governments.

37. Gleason, Eliza Atkins (Ph.D., University of Chicago, 1939). **The government and administration of public library service to Negroes in the South.** 173p.

PURPOSE: The purpose of the study was to trace the history and development of library service to Negroes in the South.

PROCEDURE: The following sources were used to supply the data: published materials, correspondence with state library agencies, records of the American Library Association, and personal observation.

FINDINGS: The following findings were reported by the author: the Negro population in the South received far less public library service than did the white population; Negro library service was most often found in wealthy areas and in large urban centers; the separate-but-equal doctrine created special problems in low economic areas; statistics for Negro library service were rated as unsatisfactory.

38. Lane, Robert Frederick (Ph.D., University of Chicago, 1939). **The place of American university presses in publishing.** 527p.

PURPOSE: The purpose of the study was to trace the rise and development of the university press in the United States, and to determine the status of university presses in publishing.

PROCEDURE: Information for the study was obtained from printed sources and from correspondence with publishers.

FINDINGS: The information indicated that the support presses receive from their universities is meagre and haphazard. A number of factors, including support from departments, resulted in the publication of materials of local concern only.

CONCLUSIONS: The author has concluded from the study that the influence of university presses is not widespread. This was based on book production during the sample year of 1935, when only 55 percent of the 812 titles were reviewed, and only about one-half were copyrighted.

39. Spencer, Gwladys (Ph.D., University of Chicago, 1939). **The Chicago Public Library: origins and backgrounds.** 470p.

PURPOSE: The purpose of the study was to present the history of the Chicago Public Library, including the background of Chicago and library legislation in Illinois.

PROCEDURE: The historical method of research was used, with data being derived from primary and secondary sources, interviews, and correspondence.

FINDINGS: The founding of the Chicago Public Library was stimulated by the following factors: the strong civic improvement which followed the great fire of 1871; the passage of a free public library act in Illinois in 1872; and substantial gifts from England and other European countries.

1940

40. Axe, Fred Warren (Ed.D., University of Southern California, 1940). **A technique for making secondary school library apportionments on the basis of relative need.**

PURPOSE: The purpose of the study was to develop and describe a technique for measuring and comparing the book fund needs of secondary schools.

PROCEDURE: The data were obtained from official records and from questionnaires sent to junior and senior high schools in Los Angeles.

CONCLUSIONS: On the basis of the study the author concluded that the most valid measure of need for library book funds is the number of pupil-periods of social studies offered by the schools. If accurate data are not available, weighted average daily attendance may serve as the measure.

1941

41. Berelson, Bernard Reuben (Ph.D., University of Chicago, 1941). **Content emphasis, recognition, and agreement: an analysis of the role of communications in**

determining public opinion.
PURPOSE: The purpose of the study was to determine the extent of influence of newspapers, radio, magazines, and conversation on public opinion.
PROCEDURE: The study was based on interviews with two representative groups in a small Midwest county, and content analysis of selected public communications. The 1940 presidential campaign provided the issues that were considered in this study.
CONCLUSIONS: The author reached the following conclusions as a result of this study: (1) people are aware of the arguments emphasized by communications media; (2) they tend to accept arguments that support their own pre-judgments; and (3) they will also accept persuasive or appealing arguments found in public communications.

42. Brown, Howard Washington (Ph.D., University of Pennsylvania, 1941). **A study of methods and practices in supplying library service to public elementary schools in the United States.**
PURPOSE: The purpose of the study was to determine the methods and practices followed by elementary school librarians in American cities with a population of 10,000 or more.
PROCEDURE: The basic research instrument used was the questionnaire, returned by 631 superintendents of school systems.
FINDINGS: The study revealed that of the schools studied, 65 percent have classroom collections only, 16 percent have centralized libraries only, and 19 percent have both types of facilities. In those schools with centralized libraries serving enrollments of less than 500, the average number of volumes is 1,309; for those over 500, the average number of volumes is 1,936. These averages are more than twice as high as those schools which have classroom collections only.
CONCLUSIONS: The author has concluded that the collections in these school libraries include many "inappropriate" books. This was based on the fact that only 33 percent of the books in the small libraries and 43 percent of those in the large libraries are listed in the *Children's Catalog.*

43. Deily, Robert Howard (Ph.D., University of Chicago, 1941). **Public library expenditures in cities of over 100,000 population in relation to municipal expenditures and economic ability.** 272p.
PURPOSE: The purpose of the study was to test the assumption that the economic ability of cities affects public library expenditures more than any other factors.
PROCEDURE: The hypothesis was tested by comparing the 1937 public library expenditures of 95 large cities with their expenditures for municipal operation in general and their economic ability.
CONCLUSIONS: From the information gathered, the author offered the following conclusions: levels of municipal expenditure and economic ability tend to correspond; a similar correlation exists between economic ability and library expenditures; and municipal expenditure per capita is likely to be a more valid measure for library expenditure than the theoretical concept of "economic ability."

44. Herdman, Margaret May (Ph.D., University of Chicago, 1941). **The public library in depression.** 116p.
PURPOSE: The purpose of the study was to describe the effects of the Great

PURPOSE (cont'd): Depression on public libraries in order to provide data to assist in the planning and administration of libraries.

PROCEDURE: A sample of 150 libraries provided information for the period 1930 to 1935, primarily in the areas of circulation and book budgets.

FINDINGS: The information revealed that as employment declined during the period covered, library circulation rose, and as employment began to increase, circulation declined. The study also considered such influences as book sales, rental libraries, radios, and motion pictures.

45. Lancaster, John Herrold (Ph.D., Columbia University, 1941). **The use of the library by student teachers.** 138p.

PURPOSE: The primary purpose of the study was to determine how institutions preparing secondary school teachers could stimulate more effective use of the library by their students.

PROCEDURE: Data were collected from 31 small and medium-sized colleges, universities, and teachers' colleges accredited by the North Central Association of Colleges and Secondary Schools. The author discussed four considerations: knowledge of library tools and materials, as shown by tests given 952 student teachers; the use made of libraries, based on 548 use records; the relationship of certain given factors to students' use of the library and ways of making the library more effective in colleges preparing teachers.

FINDINGS: The following findings and suggestions were included: many student teachers should devote more time to study and reading; collections were inadequate in many of these libraries studied, and the study environment needed to be improved in some; the students demonstrated important weaknesses in their knowledge of library resources and skills.

46. McCarthy, Stephen Anthony (Ph.D., University of Chicago, 1941). **America in the 1880's: a bibliographical study of intellectual and cultural development.**

PURPOSE: The purpose of the study was to examine the developments in higher education and the subject matter of nonfiction books reviewed during the 1880's, as a measure of the cultural and intellectual climate of the decade.

PROCEDURE: The study was based on a literature search and analysis of book reviews that appeared in *Atlantic Monthly, Critic, Dial, Nation,* and *North American Review.*

FINDINGS: It was during this period that the following developments were taking place in higher education: the adoption of the election system of course selection; an emphasis on modern foreign languages, science, and social science instead of the classics; the lowering of entrance requirements, resulting in increased enrollments; and the expansion of graduate education and higher education for women. The reviews studied showed that biographical and historical works were most numerous at this time. The largest body of literature in the social sciences was in the field of economics. In philosophy, the German idealists were being reprinted and discussed; in literature, books were devoted to controversies over new discoveries and theories in science.

47. Tauber, Maurice Falcolm (Ph.D., University of Chicago, 1941). **Reclassification and recataloging in college and university libraries.** 356p.

PURPOSE: The purpose of the study was to consider the value of classification in

PURPOSE (cont'd): academic libraries from a historical and practical point of view. The reasons for reclassification in an academic library are discussed in detail.
PROCEDURE: The author studied 60 United States and Canadian college and university libraries that had changed, or were changing, to the Library of Congress classification. Historical information is also given on how policies of systematic arrangement were influenced by various groups.
FINDINGS: The author analyzed the validity of reasons for reclassification and recataloging in light of the nature of existing catalogs, the strengths and weaknesses of the systems that were discarded, needs of the libraries' various clienteles, problems of administration, and cost factors.
CONCLUSIONS: The author concluded that some commonly accepted reasons for reclassification and recataloging are not particularly valid.

48. Veit, Fritz (Ph.D., University of Chicago, 1941). **State supervision of public libraries, with special emphasis on the organization and functions of state library extension agencies.** 230p.
PURPOSE: The purpose of the study was to investigate the organization and activities of state library extension agencies as they relate to the supervision of public libraries.
PROCEDURE: The data were gathered from a literature search and from questionnaires sent to state library agencies by the U.S. Office of Education.
FINDINGS: The following results were indicated by the information in the study: (1) the state library agencies were generally responsible for popularizing the library concept throughout their states; (2) state library agency personnel frequently are no better qualified than the library staffs they are supposed to supervise; (3) state agencies help to keep smaller libraries alive, but they seldom attempt to create large library units; (4) few agency chiefs are aware of the potentialities of the state grants-in-aid and state grants are not adequate to meet the agencies' objectives; cooperation between the state library extension agencies and other state agencies for library service is meagre; the states are able to exert considerable influence over libraries in various ways.

1942

49. Carter, Mary Duncan (Ph.D., University of Chicago, 1942). **A survey of Montreal library facilities and a proposed plan for a library system.** 180p.
PURPOSE: The purpose of the study was to examine the library facilities in Montreal, and to recommend a plan for development of a public library system.
PROCEDURE: The study was based on primary and secondary sources.
FINDINGS: The study disclosed the information that the four independent library systems serving the public in the greater Montreal area compare unfavorably with libraries in American cities of similar size. Circulation of materials, staffs, budgets, and collections are small, and since the libraries do not cooperate with one another, they do not offer the benefits of a system.

RECOMMENDATIONS: The author proposed a plan for gradual integration of existing libraries into the nucleus of a system, with centralization of administrative control. Specific functions would be delimited in light of particular facilities, resources, and locations of the particular libraries. With the addition of new public libraries in other areas, adequate library service for Montreal could in time become a reality.

50. Goldhor, Herbert (Ph.D., University of Chicago, 1942). **The selection of employees in large civil service and non-civil service public libraries.**
PURPOSE: The purpose of the study was to examine the effect which civil service regulations had upon the selection of employees in public libraries.
PROCEDURE: The data were collected for the years 1937-41 through visits to the public libraries of six cities having populations over 200,000. In Los Angeles, Oakland, and St. Paul, the public libraries were regulated by civil service, while the libraries in Detroit, Portland, and Providence were not. Twenty principles of public personnel administration, formulated in terms of a career service, were used as criteria for the evaluation of employee selection policies.
FINDINGS: The data indicated that superior libraries of both types are applying approved principles of personnel administration in their selection of employees. The main disadvantages of civil service libraries are the residence requirement and the fact that the qualifying examinations are held only in those cities where the libraries are located; the main advantage is their use of objective examination procedures.
CONCLUSIONS: The author concluded that more attention must be paid to personnel procedures if a career service is to be developed in librarianship.

51. Heflin, Harry B. (Ph.D., University of Pittsburgh, 1942). **The purposes, organization, functioning, and adequacy of elementary school libraries in North Carolina.**
PURPOSE: The purpose of the study was to evaluate the libraries of elementary schools in North Carolina in terms of the standards of that state. As part of the project, the North Carolina standards were compared with the elementary school library standards of seven states having state school library supervisors.
PROCEDURE: The survey method was used, involving 232 white elementary schools in North Carolina.
FINDINGS: The study revealed that very few of the states surveyed had definite standards enforced by their state department of education. Only two states require that instruction in library usage be given to elementary school pupils. The evaluation of North Carolina elementary school libraries showed that the number of books is satisfactory in all but the small schools; however, dictionaries are lacking in many schools, and encyclopedias are often lacking in the small schools. The selection and training of librarians seems to be inadequate, and elementary school library practice in general leaves much to be desired in North Carolina.

52. Jensen, Elmer A. (Ed.D., University of Missouri, 1942). **A study of high school libraries and library services in the first class high schools of Missouri.**
PURPOSE: The purpose of the study was to describe and evaluate the library resources and services of Missouri high schools.
PROCEDURE: Data were gathered from the following sources: review of the

PROCEDURE (cont'd): educational literature, official reports, and questionnaires completed by 278 librarians, 259 principals, 222 teachers, and 2,493 students in Missouri high schools.

FINDINGS: The author reported the following findings: the accrediting agencies have a direct influence on library facilities; the technical training of librarians is very meagre; largely because libraries were not provided for when buildings were planned, the housing of school libraries is inadequate; pupils make good use of existing facilities; and principals seem to be more aware of library needs than either teachers or librarians.

53. Logsdon, Richard Henry (Ph.D., University of Chicago, 1942). **The instructional literature of sociology and the administration of college library book collections.** 101p.

PURPOSE: The purpose of the study was to examine the instructional literature of sociology over a 40-year period to establish criteria for use in administration of college library book collections.

PROCEDURE: A sample of 88 books by 51 authors or author-groups, cited in various sources as textbooks used in introductory courses in sociology, formed the basis for the study.

FINDINGS: Among the findings of the study are the following: there is a lack of agreement among instructors as to the best textbooks for the introductory courses in sociology; books cited by the instructors cover a wide range of subjects in addition to sociology; and only a few titles maintain their usefulness over long periods of time.

CONCLUSIONS: The author formed the following conclusions as a result of the study: college librarians should expect that a large part of their sociology collection will become rapidly obsolete; processing and maintenance costs should be studied in relation to the brief span of usefulness of sociology books; and that the role of the librarian in the selection of sociology books is not likely to be significant, since the choice of materials in a given course depends on the instructor.

54. Merritt, Leroy Charles (Ph.D., University of Chicago, 1942). **The United States government as publisher.** 209p.

PURPOSE: The purpose of the study was to determine the scope and subject content of government publishing, and to trace the trends from 1900 to 1940.

PROCEDURE: The study was based on the October issues of the *Monthly Catalog of United States Government Publications* for selected years from 1900 to 1940, and on data from official reports.

FINDINGS: While expenditures of the Government Printing Office were five times greater in 1940 than they were in 1900, during this period they dropped from about 1 percent of total government expenditures to 1/4 of 1 percent. The largest number of government publications were designed to serve the purposes of individuals and special groups. The greater part of the subject content was concerned with basic responsibilities of government; second in quantity was business, while the area of public utilities ranked third.

55. Muller, Robert Hans (Ph.D., University of Chicago, 1942). **Social stratification in magazine fiction and its relations to socioeconomic status of readers.** 109p.

PURPOSE: The purpose of the study was to explore the relationship between the status of magazine fiction characters and that of magazine readers.

PROCEDURE: The study was based on an analysis of 269 fictional characters who have appeared in 72 stories in six magazines (*Ladies Home Journal, Saturday Evening Post, True Story, Liberty, Love Story*, and *Story*), and on data furnished by McCall Corporation about the economic status of readers of five of these magazines.

FINDINGS: The author noted a positive relationship between the social standing of characters in the magazine stories and the socioeconomic level of the readers. In the low-income groups, magazine sales seem to be increased by stories about social climbers, who are generally characterized by charm, romance, perseverance, hard work, willpower, and self-education. In magazines purchased largely by high-income readers, talent and personality are emphasized as the attributes leading to upward social movement.

56. Stallmann, Esther Laverne (Ph.D., University of Chicago, 1942). **Public library service to public school children: its administration in large American cities.**

PURPOSE: The purpose of the study was to describe the patterns of organization, personnel, leadership, and finance in public library service to public schools in American cities.

PROCEDURE: The data were gathered from a literature review and from personal observation. The study included 42 cities with populations of over 200,000.

FINDINGS: The author reported the following findings: (1) definite objectives for service to children have been formulated by very few public libraries; (2) through a number of means, public libraries give service to schools; (3) in general, library administrators are opposed to housing public library branches in school buildings; (4) most school libraries are administered by school systems; (5) children's librarians and supervisors show a surprising lack of formal training; (6) in some cities it is impossible to build a career within the children's department of the public library because the top salary is too close to the beginning salary.

57. Stanford, Edward Barrett (Ph.D., University of Chicago, 1942). **Library extension under the W.P.A.: an appraisal of an experiment in Federal aid.** 284p.

PURPOSE: The purpose of the study was to describe and evaluate library extension under the W.P.A.

PROCEDURE: The historical method of research was used in this study.

FINDINGS: An essentially sound pattern was developed for library assistance and extension by the federal government under the W.P.A., although the primary objective of the program was to provide work for needy persons. Data are given on employment provided, finances, and materials.

CONCLUSIONS: The author has concluded that the results achieved by the W.P.A. in library extension were notable, especially in view of the fact that the primary purpose was in the provision of work for needy persons.

58. Van Male, John Edward (Ph.D., University of Chicago, 1942). **The state as librarian: a study of the co-ordination of library services in Wisconsin.**

PURPOSE: The purpose of the study was to describe and evaluate the six Wisconsin state library agencies in terms of the user.

PROCEDURE: The author surveyed 400 library users in eight small Wisconsin communities.

FINDINGS: The use of the state library was divided as follows: 30 percent by students for educational purposes, 28 percent was professional, 20 percent served group needs, and 20 percent was related to personal activities and interests. Users requesting specific books received better service than did those who made requests by subject. Those who made subject requests received better service if special collections or services in the subject area were available at the state libraries.

1943

---

59. Cross, Neal Miller (Ed.D., Stanford University, 1943). **Evaluating the use of school library books according to the needs of the student and the philosophy of the school.**
PURPOSE: The purpose of the study was to devise a method for evaluating use of books in a school library in terms of the philosophy of the school.
PROCEDURE: The data were derived from a series of questionnaires and interviews with students and faculty at the Menlo School and Junior College at Menlo Park, California.
FINDINGS: The students' own interests and reading guidance were the two factors that were found to influence students' leisure reading of books judged to be "valuable" or "desirable" by the faculty. Techniques such as allowing free reading time in English classes and providing special collections in reading laboratories did not lead to significantly better leisure reading.

60. Gosnell, Charles Francis (Ph.D., New York University, 1943). **The rate of obsolescence in college library book collections as determined by an analysis of three select lists of books for college libraries.**
PURPOSE: The purpose of the study was to determine the rate of obsolescence of college library books and to develop a statistical method to help compute it.
PROCEDURE: The data were gathered from a review of the literature and from an analysis of two bibliographies useful in building library collections: Charles B. Shaw's *A List of Books for College Libraries* and Foster E. Mohrhardt's *A List of Books for Junior College Libraries.*
FINDINGS: The author analyzed the titles listed according to publication date, and plotted exponential curves to assist in determining their obsolescence rate.

61. Phelps, Rose Bernice (Ph.D., University of Chicago, 1943). **The effects of organizational patterns on reference service in three typical metropolitan libraries: Boston, St. Louis, and Los Angeles.** 302p.
PURPOSE: The purpose of the study was to examine the organizational patterns of three public libraries to determine which pattern provides the most efficient reference service.
PROCEDURE: The St. Louis Public Library represented the functional pattern, the Los Angeles Public Library the subject department, and the Boston Public Library the "mixed." The services and costs of reference facilities of the three libraries were analyzed.

FINDINGS: The data indicated that organization by subject departments offers the best reference service at the least cost, while the functional gives the poorest service. The mixed type is the most expensive.

62. Phillips, Thomas Edward (Ed.D., Rutgers University, 1943). **Study of the non-technical preparation of 100 librarians in the accredited high schools of New Jersey.**
PURPOSE: The purpose of the study was to determine the professional applicability of content of education courses required for New Jersey school librarians.
PROCEDURE: A questionnaire based on published literature and on statements prepared by 50 recognized authorities in the school library field was sent to 100 librarians in accredited New Jersey high schools.
FINDINGS: Among the findings reported by the author are the following: (1) all of the librarians reported giving some instruction in use of the library; (2) the librarians reported that the most helpful education courses were those that dealt with guidance and personnel; (3) the least helpful courses were those that dealt with the history of education and measurements and statistics; (4) librarians who were prepared for certain types of activities performed them more often than did those who had not received such preparation.

1944

---

63. Eaton, Andrew Jackson (Ph.D., University of Chicago, 1944). **Current political science publications in five Chicago libraries: a study of coverage, duplication, and omission.** 262p.
PURPOSE: The purpose of the study was to examine the patterns of acquisition and distribution of political science books among five Chicago libraries.
PROCEDURE: The acquisitions in political science of the Chicago Public Library, John Crerar Library, Newberry Library, Northwestern University Library, and the University of Chicago Library were compared. For purposes of comparison, the holdings of the New York Public Library were listed.
FINDINGS: Among the findings are the following: that in 1937 the libraries acquired 46 percent of all the new books in political science published in France, Germany, Italy, England, and the United States; the libraries purchased 53 percent of those books reviewed in outstanding political science journals; 71 percent of the books published in English were purchased; and 23 percent of those published in foreign languages were purchased. Considerable duplication of acquisitions among the five libraries was noted. Similarly, the study noted that there were substantial gaps among the five libraries' combined holdings.

64. Rankin, Marie (Ph.D., Columbia University, Teachers College, 1944). **Children's interests in library books of fiction.** 146p.
PURPOSE: The purpose of the author was to determine the features that affect the popularity of fiction among young adolescents.

PROCEDURE: Circulation data were collected in eight different public library agencies for books published between 1920 and 1940. Other information was obtained through interviews and observation of junior high school children in experimental situations, and from one-paragraph compositions on "How I select a good book to read just for fun."

FINDINGS: The data revealed that stories of careers for girls proved to be the most popular, with sea adventures next. Only one Newbery Medal winner was found on the list of the 10 most popular books.

CONCLUSIONS: The author concludes that for the young adolescent the story, preferably on a theme of current interest, is the most important element.

65. Shera, Jesse Hauk (Ph.D., University of Chicago, 1944). **Foundations of the public library: the origins of the library movement in New England, 1629-1855.** 341p.

PURPOSE: The purpose of the study was to trace the growth of the movement in New England that culminated in the establishment of the first public library, and to delineate some of the factors that influenced its development.

PROCEDURE: The historical method was used, based on primary and secondary sources.

CONCLUSIONS: The author concluded that the public library was a product of its environment at a time when the economic capacity of cities became sufficient to support such an institution.

66. Spain, Frances Lander (Ph.D., University of Chicago, 1944). **Libraries of South Carolina: their origins and early history, 1700-1830.** 174p.

PURPOSE: The purpose of the study was to trace the early history of South Carolina libraries in the context of social and economic conditions.

PROCEDURE: The historical method was used, and was based on both primary and secondary sources.

FINDINGS: The study showed that all libraries but the Provincial were privately owned and supported by subscription societies. A strong influence for the establishment of the libraries was the English background of the settlers. There was a close association among the church, school, and library; library societies developed in communities having a well-established economy, a sense of permanency, and a cultured society.

67. Swank, Raynard Coe (Ph.D., University of Chicago, 1944). **The organization of library materials for research in English literature.** 253p.

PURPOSE: The purpose of the study was to describe critically the various means of organization in English literature research collections.

PROCEDURE: The author analyzed the 108 doctoral dissertations in English literature produced at the University of Chicago between 1930 and 1942.

FINDINGS: Six types of studies were identified in the group of 108 dissertations; the most appropriate bibliographical arrangement for each type was discussed, and the effectiveness of the Library of Congress modification in use at the University of Chicago was compared with that of various bibliographies.

CONCLUSIONS: The author suggested the following conclusions as a result of the study: (1) bibliographies produce better results than do the library catalog and shelf classification taken separately or together; (2) although bibliographies

CONCLUSIONS (cont'd): supplement these two library tools, the latter do not supplement the bibliographies in any important way; (3) the library catalog and the shelf classification to a large extent duplicate each other.

68. Wu, Kwang Tsing (Ph.D., University of Chicago, 1944). **Scholarship, book production, and libraries in China (618-1644).** 291p.
PURPOSE: The purpose of the study was to trace the development of book production and libraries from 618 to 1644.
PROCEDURE: The historical method of research was used, employing both primary and secondary sources.
FINDINGS: The data indicated that there were three major factors which influenced the spread of learning, the increase in book production, and the development of libraries during this period: (1) the predominance of Confucian scholarship; (2) the rising prestige of the literati; and (3) the powerful effect of the civil service system, which required applicants to pass written examinations. The imperial libraries showed a similar pattern in their histories. At the beginning of a dynasty, there was an intensive effort at building book collections; as time went on, the efforts slackened and in some cases ceased. By the end of the dynasty, many books were destroyed as a result of the warfare.

1945

---

69. Ditzion, Sidney H. (Ph.D., Columbia University, 1945). **Arsenals of a democratic culture: a social history of the American public library movement in New England and the Middle States from 1850 to 1900.** 263p.
PURPOSE: The purpose of the study was to describe the foundations of the public library movement in the United States.
PROCEDURE: The historical method of research was used in this study.
FINDINGS: The cultural background of the library movement is described, as is the political and social setting. There was a slow transition in New England from the private to the public library.
CONCLUSIONS: The author concludes that both the institution and its methods were conceived as a contribution toward the self-realization of the broad masses of the people.

70. Jones, Virginia Lacy (Ph.D., University of Chicago, 1945). **Problems of Negro public high school libraries in selected Southern cities.** 225p.
PURPOSE: The purpose of this paper was to describe and analyze conditions and problems affecting library service to Negro public high schools in 14 Southern cities.
PROCEDURE: Interviews were conducted with principals, teachers, librarians, and pupils in 20 Negro schools in seven Southern states and with state department of education personnel in charge of public school library service.
FINDINGS: Local socioeconomic conditions affecting school and school library conditions were reflected in adequate planning at the state level. There was

FINDINGS (cont'd): insufficient financial support at both state and local levels. There was a lack of educational philosophy and definition of objectives at the local level.
RECOMMENDATIONS: Federal aid should be given to these libraries. There should also be a revision of present local and state policies regarding distribution of tax funds to Negro and white schools.

71. Martin, Lowell Arthur (Ph.D., University of Chicago, 1945). **The desirable minimum size of public library units.** 206p.
PURPOSE: The purpose of the study was to determine the point in public library service at which resource advantages of the large unit and personal service advantages of the small unit coincide.
PROCEDURE: The author studied 60 Midwestern city public libraries located. outside of metropolitan areas and serving populations ranging from 5,000 to 75,000. Collections were evaluated, specialized professional assistance was determined, and the organization of materials was checked. These characteristics were evaluated by means of questionnaires, personal visits, and by comparing holdings with various published booklists.
FINDINGS: The findings indicated that minimum adequate library service is seldom achieved by libraries serving populations under 50,000. An even larger population base is required for rural library service at a minimum adequate level.

72. Powers, Sister Mary Luella (Ph.D., University of Chicago, 1945). **The contribution of American Catholic commercial publishers, 1930-42.** 169p.
PURPOSE: The purpose of the study was to determine the contribution of the Catholic press to American intellectual, social, and political life in the 20th century.
PROCEDURE: The study evaluated the output of 13 American Catholic book trade publishers during 1932-42. Three techniques were used: (1) the titles by prominent Catholic authors issued by general publishers between 1940 and 1942 (105) were compared with those published by 13 Catholic firms (64) and by other Catholic publishers (41); (2) the titles selected by the Catholic Book Club: 129 were issued by general publishers, and 34 by Catholic publishers; (3) and 1,002 book reviews that appeared in Catholic periodicals for 1940-41 were studied.
CONCLUSIONS: The author concluded that although the Catholic press during this period produced an impressive and commendable body of religious literature which would not otherwise be available to American Catholics, they did not contribute in a vital manner to the intellectual, social, and political life of twentieth century America.

73. Stone, John Paul (Ph.D., University of Chicago, 1945). **Regional union catalogs: a study of services actual and potential.**
PURPOSE: The author's purpose in doing the study was to describe and evaluate the usefulness of regional union library catalogs and bibliographic centers in inter-library lending, cataloging, order work, and other regional and national bibliographic services.
PROCEDURE: The data were derived from an examination of the records of 11 centers during 1940, and from personal interviews.
FINDINGS: Among the findings were the following: (1) 85 percent of the requests received by the centers were for aid in locating books; (2) about 80 percent

FINDINGS (cont'd): of the requests came through libraries, while 20 percent came directly from individuals; (3) the chief users of the centers were college instructors and students, but other individuals not connected with institutions also made extensive use of the centers; (4) the centers serve a useful purpose in helping to determine the division of subject fields for cooperative acquisition programs.

1946

74. Hodgson, James Goodwin (Ph.D., University of Chicago, 1946). **Rural reading matter as provided by land-grant colleges and libraries.**
PURPOSE: The purpose of the study was to examine the rural service of land-grant colleges and public libraries to determine how effective it is and which of the two types of agency provide the more important services to rural areas.
PROCEDURE: The data were gathered from personal visits to 300 rural homes in four counties in Indiana and Illinois, including two counties that have no public library service.
FINDINGS: The three types of materials read by rural families are, in order, newspapers, magazines, and books. Pamphlets furnished by land-grant colleges were used by 59 percent of the farm families and 31 percent of the non-farm families. The subjects of greatest interest were those related to agricultural matters or to home economics. In the two counties that provided public library service, 52 percent of the non-farm and 28 percent of the farm families made use of it. The families of community leaders used the library more frequently than did other families.

75. Powell, Benjamin Edward (Ph.D., University of Chicago, 1946). **The development of libraries in Southern state universities to 1920.** 233p.
PURPOSE: The author's purpose in making the study was to survey the history of state university libraries in Alabama, Georgia, Louisiana, Mississippi, North Carolina, South Carolina, Tennessee, and Virginia.
PROCEDURE: The historical method was used, based on primary and secondary sources.
FINDINGS: The libraries studied were administered by faculty committees until the early 1900's. Even as late as 1920, only 14 professional librarians had been appointed to the eight libraries. Financial support was weak during most of the period of time covered, although the importance of the library was recognized by the universities.

76. Ruffin, Mary Beverley (Ph.D., University of Chicago, 1946). **Types of catalog knowledge needed by non-cataloging library personnel.** 206p.
PURPOSE: The purpose of the study was to determine the types of cataloging knowledge needed by non-cataloging librarians.
PROCEDURE: The data were gathered from a literature search and from a survey of noncatalogers in eight public, school, and college libraries.
FINDINGS: The study indicated that most important to noncatalogers is a

FINDINGS (cont'd): knowledge of how author, title, and subject entries are constructed in terms of the card catalog of the particular institution in which they are employed. Librarians also need other sources for identifying and locating library materials.

CONCLUSIONS: The author concluded that library school courses in cataloging include some irrelevant topics and sometimes omit useful ones. The essentials of a suggested library school course for noncatalogers are summarized.

77. Sabine, Julia Elizabeth (Ph.D., University of Chicago, 1946). **Antecedents of the Newark Public Library.** 169p.

PURPOSE: The purpose of the study was to study the social and cultural background of the city of Newark, of New Jersey, and the other Middle Atlantic states prior to the formation of the Newark Public Library.

PROCEDURE: The historical method was used, based on primary and secondary sources.

FINDINGS: The author has suggested the following factors which led to the founding of the Newark Public Library: the early settlers brought with them the ideals of formal education and self-improvement; the subscription libraries set a precedent by providing at least limited library service; a larger working class, articulate in seeking public education, was stimulated by the expansion of commerce and industry; the Lyceum movement stimulated the urge for self-improvement; there was an increasing demand for wholesome recreation for the children and young people; and the passage of statewide legislation regarding free education, school libraries, and permissive legislation for public libraries.

78. Smith, George Donald (Ph.D., University of Chicago, 1946). **The nature of student reading.** 135p.

PURPOSE: The purpose of the study was to identify the areas in which relationships exist between a student's reading, certain personal characateristics, and academic achievement.

PROCEDURE: The study was based on the literature of the field, test results, and college library reading records for approximately 250 freshmen who entered the University in the autumn quarter of 1936.

FINDINGS: The author reported the following findings from the study: (1) there was a definite relationship between academic achievement and students' curricular reading; (2) there appeared to be a relationship between students' academic achievement and their free nonfiction reading; (3) there appeared to be a relationship between the quality of fiction read and academic success; (4) there appeared to be a relationship between the type or subject matter of fiction read and academic success; (5) there appeared to be a strong tendency for students rating very high on educationally desirable traits to make greater use of curricular materials than do other students who achieve equal academic success; (6) there appeared to be no relationship between student reading and student possession of special aptitudes and abilities.

79. Barnes, Eugene Burdette, Jr. (Ph.D., University of Chicago, 1947). **The international exchange of knowledge in Western Europe, 1680-89.**
PURPOSE: The purpose of the study was to attempt to determine the amount of intellectual exchange among the countries of Western Europe between 1680 and 1689.
PROCEDURE: The procedure followed in the study was to examine the reviews of foreign books appearing in nine periodicals published in France, England, Saxony, and Holland.
FINDINGS: Of the 2,920 titles noted, 1,971 were reviewed by periodicals in countries other than the country of origin. Scientific works circulated more widely than any others.
CONCLUSIONS: The author concluded that, in spite of the rigorous controls and censorship, there was extensive international exchange of knowledge among the countries of Western Europe during this period.

80. Floyd, Grace Hazel (Ph.D., University of Texas, 1947). **Library service in public elementary schools of Texas.**
PURPOSE: The purpose of the study was to survey the nature, scope, and administrative procedures of library service in public elementary schools for white students in Texas.
PROCEDURE: The data were gathered through questionnaires, personal visits, and correspondence. The questionnaires were returned by 240 county superintendents, 577 independent school district superintendents, and 68 tax-supported city libraries.
CONCLUSIONS: The author has offered the following conclusions based on the study: (1) that the financing of school library service is not based on any real plan among school administrators; (2) the major source of library funds is from school boards in the independent school districts, although funds from other sources are not negligible; (3) expenditures, books, personnel, and facilities are all inadequate; (4) the public schools receive invaluable service from the public libraries.

81. Smith, Sidney Butler (Ph.D., University of Chicago, 1947). **The United States government as bibliographer.** 147p.
PURPOSE: The purpose of the study was to analyze the bibliographies issued by the federal government over a 46-year period, in terms of agency production, subjects treated, and usefulness.
PROCEDURE: The data were collected from the published literature, and from the *Monthly Catalog of United States Government Publications* for sample years between 1899 and 1944.
FINDINGS: Among the findings of the study were the following: (1) approximately 5,500 bibliographies were published during the period studied; (2) during the period, the Government Printing Office, the Department of Agriculture, and the Library of Congress led all other agencies in the number of bibliographies published; (3) publication of bibliographies in specific subject areas increased during the period studied; the majority of these were general bibliographies of publications issued by an agency rather than those on specialized subjects.

RECOMMENDATIONS: The following recommendations were suggested in the study: the use of more critical annotations; each bibliography should include an introductory statement that would state the purpose, the quality or completeness of the material included, and the audience for whom it was prepared.

82. Williams, Dorothy Gwendolyn (Ph.D., University of Chicago, 1947). **The treatment of the second Roosevelt administration in three popular magazines.** 123p.

PURPOSE: The purpose of the study was to analyze the contents of three popular magazines to determine their attitudes toward the domestic and foreign policies of the United States during the second Roosevelt administration.

PROCEDURE: The method used in the study was to examine the published literature, and the issues of the *Saturday Evening Post, American Magazine,* and *Reader's Digest* between January 1937 and January 1941.

FINDINGS: The study showed that all three magazines presented attitudes unfavorable to the administration. The *Post*, which devoted about 16 percent of its pages to the administration, was the most vehement and the most consistent in its conservative and isolationist views. The *Digest*, which devoted 10 percent of its pages to the administration, generally objected to the domestic policies but favored the foreign policies of the administration. The *American Magazine* devoted but five percent of its pages to the administration, largely avoided controversy, and generally indicated qualified disapproval of the administration's policies.

1948

---

83. Burke, Redmond Ambrose (Ph.D., University of Chicago, 1948). **The control of reading by the Catholic Church.** 106p.

PURPOSE: The study investigates the role of the Catholic Church in controlling reading material for the layman.

PROCEDURE: The study is based on the documents issued by the Catholic Church which contain regulations concerning the reading of Catholics, the application of these principles in particular cases by the Holy See, the interpretation of these principles by canonists and interviews.

FINDINGS: The Catholic Church has always respected books and maintained a dual policy: (1) to stimulate the reading of good books and (2) to discourage the reading of books that might endanger faith or morals as defined by the Church. The Church policy regarding censorship is reviewed from three viewpoints: *imprimatur* prior to publication; prohibition of books after publication; invocation of penalties against violators. The study includes lists of forbidden authors and titles.

84. Davies, David William (Ph.D., University of Chicago, 1948). **The place of the Elziviers in the social history of the seventeenth century.** 278p.

PURPOSE: The purpose of the study was to trace the activities of the Elzivier family from 1580 to 1712 within the background of the times.

PROCEDURE: The author's method was to use primary and secondary sources, as well as to consult authorities on the subject.

FINDINGS: For more than a century the Elziviers were among the leading European printers, publishers, and booksellers. As university printers, they reflected the times in publishing books which could not be published in countries other than Holland. They were also the publishers of the leading authors of the day.

85. Eaton, Thelma (Ph.D., University of Chicago, 1948). **The wandering printers of Spain and Portugal, 1473-1536.** 317p.

PURPOSE: The purpose of the study was to identify the earliest printers in Spain and Portugal, and to relate their movements and their production of books to the contemporary demand for printed materials.

PROCEDURE: The study was based on a literature search.

FINDINGS: The first Iberian presses were established in those cities which seemed to offer the best financial prospects to the German printers who drifted to the area seeking a living. Since most of the demand for printing at that time came from the Church, it was necessary for the printers to move about in order to obtain business. According to the author, about 60 percent of the books published in the two countries during this period were the products of the wandering printers.

86. Fussler, Herman Howe (Ph.D., University of Chicago, 1948). **Characterisitcs of the research literature used by chemists and physicists in the United States.** 115p.

PURPOSE: The purpose of the study was to examine the character of the research literature of chemistry and physics used in the U.S. over a period of 47 years to determine any trends that might prove to be important to librarians.

PROCEDURE: The procedure was to select a random sampling of citations from the *Physical Review* and the *Journal of the American Chemical Society* for 1899, 1919, 1939, and 1946 for analysis.

CONCLUSIONS: The following conclusions were offered by the author: (1) there was no strong tendency for subject diversification in these fields to change, but there was a strong diversification of titles; (2) indexes and abstracting facilities are necessary because subject classification is not sufficient to bring together all pertinent material; (3) careful selection of a small number of journals can result in acquisition of a substantial portion of the most important references in a given research field.

87. Hammitt, Frances Eleanor (Ph.D., University of Chicago, 1948). **School library legislation in Indiana, Illinois, and Wisconsin: a historical study.** 266p.

PURPOSE: The purpose of the study was to analyze the laws relating to school libraries passed by the general legislatures of the three states.

PROCEDURE: The procedure was to use primary and secondary sources, correspondence, and interviews with state officials in the three states covered in the study.

FINDINGS: The early laws passed by the three states regarding schools provided that libraries be attached, but the laws varied in concept and detail. Furthermore, plans for library service in school districts based on these early laws proved to be unsatisfactory; the libraries declined or disappeared in the decades after 1860. After this period Indiana provided no real legal framework for school libraries. Illinois retained its original statutory provisions, and the expanding powers of local boards of

FINDINGS (cont'd): education carried authority for the establishment of school libraries. Wisconsin resumed the appropriation of school funds for support of small school libraries and enacted laws for their management and regulation.

88. Lancour, Harold (Ed.D., Columbia University, Teachers College, 1948). **A plan for the remodeling of the Cooper Union Library.**
PURPOSE: The purpose of the study was to examine the background and the functions of the library in order to determine the space needs for the future.
PROCEDURE: The data were collected from primary and secondary sources, from consultations with the staff of Cooper Union, and from personal knowledge.
FINDINGS: The library collections are relatively strong in those areas closely related to the curriculum. In other areas, approximately 20 percent of the books could be discarded. The author noted that changes are necessary if the library is to meet the needs of the future.
RECOMMENDATIONS: The following three recommendations were made as a result of the study: (1) a larger amount of space should be assigned to library staff in the non-public areas; (2) the two art libraries should be combined into one library convenient to both the Art Department and the Museum; (3) and a separate engineering library, humanities library, reference library, browsing collection, and seminar library should be created.

89. Morrison, Duncan Grant (Ed.D., University of Washington, 1948). **The relation of the public library to adult education in the state of Washington.**
PURPOSE: The purpose of the study was to examine the extent and influence of public library service to adult education in the state of Washington, and to make recommendations for the improvement of its effectiveness.
PROCEDURE: The data were gathered from a search of the literature, and from interviews conducted by the Washington Public Opinion Laboratory in connection with a survey of leisure time activities.
FINDINGS: The data indicated that only about 20 percent of the adults studied borrowed books from public libraries, although over half of the adults had access to the libraries. Nearly 50 percent of the adults in the state did not know whether adult education services were offered by the public library nearest to them.
RECOMMENDATIONS: The author made the following recommendations as a result of the findings: that the facilities of public libraries should be expanded; that there should be legislation for the establishment of demonstration units; that rural areas should receive more service from bookmobiles and book stations; that there should be additional use of film forums; and that there should be more co-operation with adult education agencies.

90. Qualls, LeRoy Lillard (Ph.D., University of Illinois, 1948). **A study of the economic basis of minimum financial support of public libraries in Illinois.**
PURPOSE: The purpose of the study was to explore the economic and demographic factors to determine the population base required to support minimum public library service.
PROCEDURE: The author studied individual communities and counties in Illinois in terms of statutory tax ceilings for public library support, actual library support, and personal income and property valuations.
FINDINGS: The study indicated that in almost all areas of the state existing

FINDINGS (cont'd): statutory tax rates allow for sufficient revenues to support the minimum per capita library standards. However, few communities are able to make available for public library use the $37,500 required for minimum service because of sparse population and economic conditions.

RECOMMENDATIONS: It was recommended that a library district with a minimum population base of 25,000 be considered the administrative unit for a system.

91. Van Hoesen, Florence Ruth (Ph.D., University of Chicago, 1948). **An analysis of adult reference work in public libraries as an approach to the content of a reference course.** 219p.

PURPOSE: The purpose of the study was to analyze reference questions, as well as the types of people asking them, in an effort to establish a basis for the preparation of a reference course syllabus.

PROCEDURE: A total of 3,596 reference questions asked during 1937 and 1938 in 15 public libraries were analyzed. Libraries in the following systems participated: the Public Library of Cincinnati and Hamilton County, Washington, D.C., Public Library, Los Angeles Public Library, Tampa Public Library, and the Boston Public Library.

FINDINGS: More than half of the questions asked were in the fields of sociology, science, and technology; most questions were of the general information type or were fact questions. At the main libraries the largest percentage of questions were asked by businessmen; at the branches, students asked the most questions. About two-thirds of the professional people and almost half of the skilled workers and business groups asked questions related to their work.

1949

---

92. Asheim, Lester Eugene (Ph.D., University of Chicago, 1949). **From book to film: a comparative analysis of the content of novels and the films based upon them.** 335p.

PURPOSE: The purpose of the study was to show the extent to which book content is changed when a novel is transferred to the screen.

PROCEDURE: The author analyzed the changes made when 24 novels were made into films.

FINDINGS: Among the findings are the following: no matter how much the content is changed, the novel's title is almost always retained in the film version; normal chronological sequence is followed more closely in films than in novels; in 13 of the films, descriptive scenes were at least as prominent as descriptive passages, and sometimes more so; while the amount of action is increased for films, the proportion of violence, brutality and sadism is reduced.

93. Brough, Kenneth J. (Ph.D., Stanford University, 1949). **Evolving conceptions of library service in four American universities: Chicago, Columbia, Harvard, Yale, 1876-1946.**

PURPOSE: The purpose of the study was to describe the evolution of several concepts of library service in four American universities.

PROCEDURE: The basic methodology used was the historical method, utilizing primary sources almost exclusively.

FINDINGS: Until approximately 1876, the main preoccupation of these university libraries was in the collection and its preservation. Since that time the emphasis has been on utilizing the materials and making the collections more accessible. The author also studied the educational preparation and university status of the four chief librarians. The following factors were cited by the author as significant in establishing university librarians on a par with their academic colleagues: increased research in the library field and the development of graduate programs leading to the doctorate; and the development of professional associations for librarians.

94. Harvey, John Frederick (Ph.D., University of Chicago, 1949). **The content characteristics of best-selling novels.** 194p.

PURPOSE: The purpose of the study was to attempt to isolate content features which distinguish best-selling novels published between 1930 and 1946 from similar books that did not sell as well.

PROCEDURE: The author selected 22 best-sellers during the period, and compared them with a sample of "poor sellers."

FINDINGS: The author made three generalizations about the content characteristics of the best-selling novels: (1) emotion and emotionalism as well as sentimentality and sensationalism distinguish the best-seller; (2) simplicity of style or readability promotes sales; (3) a moralizing theme tends to increase sales if the novel is readable and strikes a timely emotional note.

95. Henne, Frances (Ph.D., University of Chicago, 1949). **Preconditional factors affecting the reading of young people.** 414p.

PURPOSE: The purpose of the study was to identify the preconditional factors affecting the reading of high school students, and to analyze their implications for the high school library.

PROCEDURE: The preconditional factors were identified as student characteristics and the availability and accessibility of library materials. The study was based on the literature of the field, data about 2,927 Chicago high school students derived from another study, and nine reading guidance cases.

FINDINGS: The author noted that: each high school student has a unique reading pattern, and generalizations based on group studies at best can be only suggestive; in the typical high school there are many students who do not have a mechanical reading ability adequate for their needs; although some differences are noted, reading habits cannot be precisely differentiated according to the sex of the reader; the school library serves as the principal source of materials needed by high school students; and young people can raise the maturity level of their reading.

RECOMMENDATIONS: The study recommended that school libraries reappraise their programs to stress appropriate selection and accessibility of materials, participation in the developmental reading programs of schools, and systematic reading guidance to supplement that provided in informal programs.

96. Lamb, Natalie (Ed.D., Columbia University, Teachers College, 1949). **A plan for adapting secondary school library service of Bridgeport, Connecticut, to**

a curriculum which includes a required program of general education.

PURPOSE: The purpose of the study was to examine the secondary school curriculum and library service in Bridgeport, and to suggest the revision of both to accommodate a general education program.

PROCEDURE: The data in the study were derived from a literature search, official records, personal knowledge, and questionnaires returned by students, teachers, and librarians.

FINDINGS: The study showed that the libraries in the Bridgeport secondary schools do not meet the American Library Association standards, although they are judged "satisfactory" according to *Evaluative Criteria* (a publication of the Cooperative Study of Secondary School Standards). The study also indicated a need to adopt a functional approach to the curriculum in the secondary schools.

97. Lemley, Dawson Enlo (Ph.D., University of Pittsburgh, 1949). **The development and evaluation of administrative policies and practices in public school library service as evidenced in city school surveys, 1907-1941.**

PURPOSE: The purpose of the study was to analyze the administrative policies and practices in American public schools in order to chart trends in school library service.

PROCEDURE: The information was gathered from 134 selected city school surveys and from the published literature.

FINDINGS: The survey indicated a general correlation between concepts of school library service presented in professional literature and library practices followed over the years. During the early years the attention was focused on problems of recognition of the school library as an integral part of the school, and on such questions as location, space, and facilities. As the concept of the school library became accepted, concern shifted to other areas: collections, services, per student expenditures, and the professional training of school library personnel.

98. McCarty, Pearl Sands (Ed.D., University of Florida, 1949). **Reading interests of Florida secondary school pupils as determined by their book choices in their school libraries.**

PURPOSE: The purpose of the study was to determine the reading interests of Florida students in grades 7 through 12, including implications about the extent of quality reading.

PROCEDURE: The data for the study were gathered from a review of the literature and from the reading records of 4,814 pupils in 15 Florida junior and senior high schools.

FINDINGS: The study indicated the following findings: the students read some very good books not required for school assignments; more than half of the books preferred by the students were published after 1930; 7th to 10th grade boys were most interested in adventure stories, with general fiction their next choice; for 11th and 12th grade boys, this order of preference was reversed; general fiction interested most girls in all grades; interest in the Newbery Medal books was not as great as it should have been, if the prize books actually were the best books of successive years.

99. McMullen, Charles Haynes (Ph.D., University of Chicago, 1949). **The administration of the University of Chicago libraries, 1892-1928.** 204p.

PURPOSE: The purpose of the study was to review the development of the University of Chicago libraries in terms of administration, collections, personnel, finances, etc.

PROCEDURE: The data were gathered from primary and secondary sources, interviews, and correspondence.

FINDINGS: The libraries began as a combination of autonomous departmental agencies with a general circulating library. There was a move toward centralization during this period, but not as fast as at other universities. During the first 18 years Chicago had no head librarian, and from 1910 a trained librarian served as associate to the faculty member who was the chief librarian. At first there was no uniformity of cataloging and classification practices, and when the libraries were unified, all of the books had to be recataloged.

100. Minster, Maud (Ed.D., Pennsylvania State College, 1949). **A study of library facilities, organization, administration, and service, during the term of 1941-42 in 289 secondary school libraries in Pennsylvania where certificated librarians were employed: a survey directed toward the formulation of recommended procedures for secondary school library efficiency.** Order no. 1444.

PURPOSE: The purpose of this study was to investigate Pennsylvania secondary school libraries, directed toward the formulation of recommended practices and procedures.

PROCEDURE: The data were gathered from questionnaires, interviews, site visits, and writings of library leaders.

CONCLUSIONS: The author suggested the following conclusions, based on the data gathered in the study: additional personnel, larger budgets, and additional seating capacities are needed in the secondary school libraries. There is a lack of uniformity in the organization and administration of the libraries.

RECOMMENDATIONS: The following recommendations were made: an advisor to school librarians should be included on the staff of the State Department of Education; librarians in secondary schools should be *ex officio* members of all curriculum committees; and school libraries should be measured against the standards of the National Education Association rather than those established for public libraries.

1950

---

101. Hall, James Herrick (Ed.D., George Washington University, 1950). **Criteria for the administration of library service in Christian education in the independent autonomous church at the local level.**

PURPOSE: The purpose of the study was to formulate tentative standards for administration of church library service, and to develop criteria for measuring practice according to these standards.

PROCEDURE: Information was gathered from the literature of the field, questionnaires completed by librarians in the Southern Baptist Convention, and interviews with library authorities.

FINDINGS: The author has submitted the following criteria to be followed: (1) church library administration should be characterized by sound public and Christian educational principles; (2) sound management practices should be followed to make the library a learning/teaching aids resource center; (3) administrative supervision based upon sound learning/teaching principles should be provided for the improvement of service; (4) adequate provision should be made for the evaluation of church library service. A tentative checklist for use in evaluation of the effectiveness of church library administration is included.

102. McGaw, Howard Franklin (Ed.D., Columbia University, Teachers College, 1950). **Marginal punched cards: their use in college and university libraries.** 237p.

PURPOSE: The purpose of the study was to describe the standard marginal punched card systems, showing how they have been adopted in certain academic libraries to facilitate routine tasks.

PROCEDURE: The author conducted an experiment at Ohio Wesleyan University involving punched card systems. Information about student reading habits was coded and punched into cards for later use in library reports to faculty and administration.

FINDINGS: The principal emphasis in the study was on the McBee Keysort cards, and on circulation routines, which have most often been simplified through punched card applications.

103. Monagan, Roger Thomas (Ed.D., University of Missouri, 1950). **A study of the administration of libraries in the public elementary schools of St. Louis.**

PURPOSE: The purpose of the study was to determine the administrative practices and opinions in St. Louis public elementary school libraries, comparing them with those in other selected schools and those considered desirable by authorities in the field of school librarianship.

PROCEDURE: The data were gathered through a literature search and from questionnaires completed by 101 school librarians in St. Louis and by librarians or principals in 174 selected school libraries representing all states.

FINDINGS: The study indicated that St. Louis school administrators' opinions are similar to those held by school administrators and by authorities on school librarianship. In practice, however, there was a wide divergency between these opinions and actual functioning of the St. Louis school libraries. The only school libraries in the city having full-time librarians are those housing public library branches. In book collections, book selection practices, and library expenditures, the St. Louis schools do not measure up to the accepted standards. However, St. Louis schools have made a greater effort to meet the needs of retarded readers than other schools studied in the sample.

104. Shaw, Ralph Robert (Ph.D., University of Chicago, 1950). **Literary property and the scholar.** 335p.

PURPOSE: The purpose of the study was to examine the United States copyright law, to describe its weaknesses, and to recommend changes.

PROCEDURE: The procedure was to examine American court records.

FINDINGS: The author noted that the principal source of confusion about copyright is the lack of a clear and authoritative statement of what literary property

FINDINGS (cont'd): is, and what is to be protected, for whom, why, and how.
RECOMMENDATIONS: The author made the following suggestions: (1) the
literary property acts and common law need to be restudied and redesigned in
order to achieve intended goals; (2) legislation needs to be passed which will be
clearly understood and which will provide protection to all concerned; (3) the
copyright should be granted only to the author; (4) all unnecessary and non-
discrete terms in copyright law should be eliminated; and (5) there should be provision for a franchise for all public use when the author complies with the requirements of the statute and makes his first public use for profit.

1951

---

105. Collier, Francis Gilman (Ph.D., Harvard University, 1951). **A history of the
American public library movement through 1880.**
PURPOSE: The purpose of the study was to trace the evolution of public libraries
from the subscription services to the municipally owned institutions of today.
PROCEDURE: The historical method was used in this study.
FINDINGS: The study identified the decades of establishment of public libraries
in the United States: 30 during the 1850's, 40 more during the 1860's, and over
140 in the 1870's. There were approximately 200 public libraries in existence in
the United States by 1880. At that time, the states with the most libraries were
Massachusetts, Illinois, and Ohio. The author also stressed three events of 1876 that
contributed a great deal to the crystallization of the idea of public libraries as educational institutions: the founding of the American Library Association, the beginning of *Library Journal* as the first professional library journal, and the issuance by
the U.S. Bureau of Education of its massive report on public libraries.

106. Grady, Marion B. (Ph.D., University of Chicago, 1951). **A comparison of
motion pictures and books as resource materials.** 450p.
PURPOSE: The purpose of the study was to determine the influence and comparative effectiveness of books and educational films as sources of instructional information.
PROCEDURE: This was a 12-week experiment involving two groups of American
history students at Ball State Teachers College at Muncie, Indiana. The control
class of 39 students used only printed materials, while the experimental class
of 43 students used motion pictures in addition to printed materials.
CONCLUSIONS: The findings indicated that the use of films caused a significant
increase in the amount of historical material gained by the students, but did not
noticeably affect their interest in history. Students of relatively low intelligence
seemed to benefit more from the use of films than did those with relatively high
intelligence.

107. Leonard, August Orin (Ed.D., Columbia University, Teachers College, 1951).
**A plan to extend library services for group discussion in the New York Public
Library.**

PURPOSE: The purpose of the study was to investigate the methods of extending services of the New York Public Library to include the conducting of group discussions of current problems.
PROCEDURE: The data were gathered through a literature search, from questionnaires returned by individuals and organizations, from interviews with librarians and community leaders, and from "action-research" involving participation of the author in group discussion activities.
FINDINGS: The author reported the following findings based on the data: (1) lack of time, money, and skill make it difficult for librarians to serve as discussion leaders; (2) while the effectiveness of discussion groups in branch libraries was not demonstrated, such programs can be developed; (3) and community leaders and librarians agree that the library should provide training for group discussion leaders.
RECOMMENDATIONS: The author recommended that the New York Public Library initiate a program for the training of group discussion leaders.

108. McAnally, Arthur M. (Ph.D., University of Chicago, 1951). **Characteristics of materials used in research in United States history.**
PURPOSE: The purpose of the study was to examine and identify the characteristics of research literature used in writing articles, monographs, and books dealing with American history since 1789.
PROCEDURE: The author analyzed the citations occurring in representative historical works published during the years 1903, 1938, and 1948. These results were then compared with the results obtained by similar studies in other fields.
CONCLUSIONS: The author has suggested the following conclusions, based on the findings: (1) cooperative interdependence among libraries and non-library agencies is desirable because vast quantities of rarely used materials must be available to scholars as needed; (2) classification by bits of information or ideas instead of by physical units, or arrangement by broad associations of classified material, with access through bibliographies, should be considered; (3) a divisional organization that serves several of the social sciences is more desirable than one serving history alone; (4) librarians should consider providing physical access to only a limited part of their resources, offering service through bibliographies rather than physical accessibility.

109. McNeal, Archie L. (Ph.D., University of Chicago, 1951). **Rural reading interests: needs related to availability.** 132p.
PURPOSE: The purpose of the study was to survey the reading interests of a rural population in the South served by a regional library program in order to determine how well the facilities satisfy the needs of readers.
PROCEDURE: The survey method was used, covering interviews with 385 men and 455 women in 10 Tennessee counties.
FINDINGS: One problem that was pinpointed by the study was that of reader interests: only 19 percent of the persons interviewed reported that they had read any books at all. Another problem was the accessibility of materials in libraries.

110. Stevens, Rolland Elwell (Ph.D., University of Illinois, 1951). **The use of library materials in doctoral research: a study of the effect of differences in research method.** 149p. Order no. 3151.
PURPOSE: The purpose of the study was to compare the availability of materials

PURPOSE (cont'd): needed for historical research with the availability of materials needed for experimental research.

PROCEDURE: A random sampling of 100 doctoral dissertations in five subject fields prepared at three research libraries between 1930 and 1948 was analyzed for citations.

FINDINGS: The historical research makes demands that cannot be satisfied by a single library, whereas experimental research, which makes use of a smaller body of literature more frequently, often can be supported by a single research collection.

CONCLUSIONS: The cost of maintaining a research library is primarily the cost of supporting historical research. Cooperative specialization and storage library plans should be based on the principle of separation of library materials according to type of research in which they will be useful rather than according to subject field.

1952

---

111. Aldrich, Frederic D. (Ph.D., Western Reserve University, 1952). **History of Ohio public school library legislation.**

PURPOSE: The purpose of the study was to describe the effect on public school library development which legislation had from 1785 to the early 1950's.

PROCEDURE: The historical method was used, including the laws, and the educational and political background literature.

FINDINGS: The legislative distinction between urban and rural school libraries from 1867 to 1900 led to the establishment of school libraries in 98 percent of urban schools, but in only 40 percent of rural schools.

112. Brumbaugh, William Donald (Ed.D., Indiana University, 1952). **Developmental aspects of film library centers in selected colleges and universities from 1942 to 1951.**

PURPOSE: The purpose of the study was to ascertain the patterns in growth of college and university film library centers.

PROCEDURE: The data were collected for the years 1942, 1947, and 1951 to show the developments that had taken place. The research instrument was the questionnaire, returned by 40 institutions of higher education having film library centers.

FINDINGS: The study revealed a strong correlation between the length of service of the director and the expansion of his film library center. The most important element in securing financial support for film library centers and stimulating their growth was found to be the dynamic leadership of the director.

113. Hintz, Carl (Ph.D., University of Chicago, 1952). **Internationalism and scholarship: a comparative study of the research literature used by American, British, French, and German botanists.** 175p.

PURPOSE: The purpose of the study was to try to characterize research literature used by botanists in the four countries by determining national origin of the

PURPOSE (cont'd): literature used in each of the countries, its principle forms, length of time elapsing between publication and use, interrelationships of subject matter in terms of the Library of Congress classification, and most important serial titles in terms of quantitative use.

PROCEDURE: The author analyzed the references cited in selected botanical journals for 1899 and 1939.

FINDINGS: The author reported the following findings: (1) methods and materials of scholarship are international in character; (2) in the research, serial literature predominates; (3) use of national publications exceeds use of those from other countries; (4) the heaviest use of a serial occurs within five years of publication date; (5) there was an increase in specialized journals during the period surveyed.

114. Robinson, Ruth W. (Ph.D., University of Pennsylvania, 1952). **Four community subscription libraries in colonial Pennsylvania: Darling, Hatboro, Lancaster, and Newtown (1743-1790).**

PURPOSE: The purpose of the study was to trace the development of four colonial libraries in Pennsylvania, with emphasis on their founders, organization, and collections.

PROCEDURE: This was a historical study, employing both primary and secondary sources in the collection of information.

FINDINGS: The purpose of the subscription libraries was to insure that the colonists would stay in touch with significant developments in English and European civilizations. A secondary purpose was to collect practical books on such subjects as farming and roadbuilding. An examination of the collections revealed the following areas emphasized (in descending order): *belles lettres*, history and biography, religion, and political science.

CONCLUSIONS: The author has suggested that these libraries helped to create a reading public for literary works, a necessary condition for the evolution of a native American literature.

115. Stewart, Nathaniel (Ed.D., Columbia University, Teachers College, 1952). **Evening session programs in library science.**

PURPOSE: The purpose of the study was twofold: to contribute to an investigation in the administration of part-time education for librarianship, and to examine evening school offerings in library science in New York City, which might be useful to other urban centers.

PROCEDURE: The data were gathered from literature sources, interviews, correspondence, and questionnaires.

FINDINGS: Among the findings of the study were the following: (1) evening programs in library science demonstrate sound administrative practices for safeguarding academic standards; (2) the evening programs make a significant contribution in meeting the needs of library employees; (3) the diverse library school courses offered in New York City provide a guide and pattern for other large urban communities having similar personnel needs.

116. Batchelor, Lillian L. (Ed.D., Columbia University, Teachers College, 1953).
The improvement of the school library program in Philadelphia secondary schools.
PURPOSE: The purpose of the study was to suggest directions in which the future development of Philadelphia high school libraries might be guided.
PROCEDURE: The procedure of the study was to review the literature, review official records, observe school libraries in other large cities, and draw on personal experience as a librarian and supervisor in Philadelphia.
RECOMMENDATIONS: After investigating the Philadelphia high school libraries, the author made the following recommendations, based on the appropriate standards: the book budgets should be increased by 100 to 150 percent; the seating capacity of libraries should be increased by 100 to 200 percent; each school library should have added one to three professional librarians as well as secretarial assistants; and the library should be made available to students and faculty throughout the day.

117. Brodman, Estelle (Ph.D., Columbia University, 1953). **The development of medical bibliography.**
PURPOSE: The purpose of the study was to present a detailed history of the medical bibliography in Western languages since the beginning of printing, including a study of past and current problems in the field.
PROCEDURE: The basic procedure used in this study was the historical method.
FINDINGS: The study was divided into five sections: the infancy of medical bibliography; the development of bibliographic technique in the seventeenth century; the golden age of individual bibliographers; the development of cooperative bibliography; and the present situation. A list of medical bibliographies published in Western languages since 1500 is included as an appendix.

118. Coryell, Gladys A. (Ed.D., University of California at Los Angeles, 1953).
Emerging patterns of elementary school library service in California.
PURPOSE: The purpose of the study was to determine which type of library service to elementary schools in San Diego offers greater potential for provision of optimum service.
PROCEDURE: The data were gathered from a review of the literature, official records, 147 questionnaires completed by teachers and administrators, and five weeks of observation of services and discussions with librarians, administrators, teachers, and students in San Diego. The San Diego schools were selected because they received library service from both the county library and the county superintendent of schools.
FINDINGS: The services and collections were compared in detail in the study. The data indicated that library service under the superintendent of schools has greater potential than under the county library.

119. Jones, Ruth Merrell (Ed.D., Stanford University, 1953). **Selection and use of books in the elementary school library.**
PURPOSE: The purpose of the study was to attempt to determine how the elementary school library can aid in accomplishing the objectives of elementary education through the selection and use of books.
PROCEDURE: The data were gathered through interviews, observation, and correspondence. On the basis of three well-known statements of the objectives of elementary education, the author listed six major points and formulated criteria for the selection of books most appropriate to each.
FINDINGS: The author listed seven ways in which the school library can materially aid in elementary education.

120. Shukla, Champaklal Pranshanker (Ph.D., University of Michigan, 1953). **A study of the publications of the Government of India, with special reference to serial publications.** 175p. Order no. 5732.
PURPOSE: The purpose of the study was to describe the branches of the Indian government, outline their functions, and discuss the important publications that emanate from each of the branches.
PROCEDURE: The survey method of research was used, supplemented by the historical method.
FINDINGS: The study discussed the major groups of publications produced by the government of India. It traced the history of the publication branch and described its present activities.

121. Winger, Howard Woodrow (Ph.D., University of Illinois, 1953). **Regulations relating to the book trade in London from 1357 to 1586.** 257p. Order no. 5250.
PURPOSE: The purpose of the study was to review and evaluate the regulations issued by the Church, the Crown, and the London Stationers' Company for the control of the book trade from 1357 to 1586.
PROCEDURE: The study employed historical research techniques with content analysis.
FINDINGS: The findings indicated that the authorities during this period tried to suppress all books that attacked the essential features of the predominant culture, and vigorously promoted those books that explicitly supported those features. In spite of universal acceptance of the tradition of restraint, the attempt to control the book trade completely according to that tradition resulted in failure.

1954

122. Alford, John D. (Ed.D., University of Wyoming, 1954). **A study of factors related to possible cooperative procedures among film libraries of the Rocky Mountain-Great Plains area.**
PURPOSE: The purpose of the study was to investigate the methods of cooperation that might help film libraries to serve their patrons better.

PROCEDURE: The data were collected from the published literature, interviews, observation of film libraries and their activities, and records and correspondence of film libraries. The study involved 13 college and university film libraries in seven states having 250 or more prints.
FINDINGS: The study indicated that with very little administrative change in individual libraries, it would be feasible to institute many cooperative measures. Regional cooperation would: permit purchase of more specialized and more expensive films; save time in the evaluation of films; create closer cooperation between film producers and the libraries; and aid in the interchange of ideas and professional development of all staffs. The establishment of a central booking office and issuance of a film bulletin would save time and money.

123. Archer, Horace Richard (Ph.D., University of Chicago, 1954). **Some aspects of the acquisition program at the University of Chicago Library: 1892-1928.** 394p.
PURPOSE: The purpose of the study was to trace the development of the library during these formative years.
PROCEDURE: The data in the study were derived from the following sources: the correspondence in the library archives; the president's files; official publications of the library and the university; and records belonging to the library, the comptroller, and other university officials.
CONCLUSIONS: The author concluded that much of what librarians know today was learned from trial-and-error methods of the late nineteenth and early twentieth century.

124. Bidlack, Russell Eugene (Ph.D., University of Michigan, 1954). **The University of Michigan General Library: a history of its beginnings, 1837-1852.** 660p. Order no. 8274.
PURPOSE: The purpose of the study was to trace the founding and early history of the University of Michigan Library.
PROCEDURE: The author used the historical method in this study.
FINDINGS: This work placed special emphasis on the initial collections of books, important acquisitions, and the general method by which the books were arranged. There is a discussion of the administration of one librarian, from 1845 to 1848, including his adoption of Jefferson's classification scheme and the printed catalog of the collection published in 1846.

125. Branscomb, Lewis C., Jr. (Ph.D., University of Chicago, 1954). **A bio-bibliographical study of Ernest Cushing Richardson, 1860-1939.** 143p.
PURPOSE: The purpose of the study was to demonstrate the importance of the work of Ernest Cushing Richardson, one of the major pioneers in American librianship.
PROCEDURE: The author's procedure was to use the historical method, utilizing both primary and secondary sources.
FINDINGS: Richardson's bibliographic work exerted a great deal of influence not only on librarians of his own generation but also on those of today. He suggested the emphasis on scholarly aspects in library education and seemed to believe in two levels of preparation for librarianship. His greatest contribution was in the development of the National Union Catalog into a magnificent bibliographic

FINDINGS (cont'd): tool. The impetus to interlibrary cooperation and to world scholarship which this achievement has made is incalculable.

126. Breen, Mary Frances (Ed.D., University of Buffalo, 1954). **Library instruction in colleges for teacher education in the United States.**
PURPOSE: The purpose of the study was to evaluate programs of library instruction in teacher-education colleges, and to propose a new program for the State University of New York College for Teachers at Buffalo.
PROCEDURE: The data were gathered from a literature review, from library diagnostic tests, from questionnaires returned by 242 (of 262) member colleges of the American Association of Colleges for Teacher Education, and from the author's personal knowledge of conditions at Buffalo.
FINDINGS: Library instruction programs are part of either an orientation course or freshman English in most of the colleges studied. Special instruction for student teachers is offered by 58 libraries. The library is responsible for library instruction in 136 of the schools studied.

127. Kaye, Bernard William (Ed.D., Columbia University, Teachers College, 1954). **The role of the principal in relation to library service in the public elementary schools.**
PURPOSE: The purpose of the study was to review the practices in selected school libraries providing superior service in New York, New Jersey, and Connecticut, and to show how principals have assisted in the development of these libraries.
PROCEDURE: The data were gathered by a search of the literature, personal observation, and interviews with librarians, teachers, principals, superintendents, and students in 54 schools in 30 systems.
FINDINGS: The data showed that the major contributions of the principals to the libraries were: seeking financial support from boards of education and other sources; providing for updating of facilities; promoting professional attitudes and practices in the library; encouraging the use of the library by teachers and students; and promoting closer relationships between schools and public libraries. The most important single element in effective library service, according to the author, is a capable, efficient, full-time librarian.

128. Rothstein, Samuel (Ph.D., University of Illinois, 1954). **The development of reference services in American research libraries.** 281p. Order no. 9128.
PURPOSE: The purpose of the study was to trace the history and development of reference service to the scholar.
FINDINGS: By the time of World War I reference work had been accepted as a central responsibility of both public and university libraries, and was usually delegated to full-time specialized personnel. Prior to this time it was library policy to encourage self-sufficiency at all levels, and scholars expected to receive very little help in doing research. The prejudice against direct information service as a reference department function gradually diminished, and gains were made in the quality of service rendered. A few important experiments in research service, notably the "research librarianships" at Cornell and Pennsylvania, showed that extensive assistance by librarians was practical and useful even for university scholars working in the humanities and social sciences.

129. Sharma, Jagdish Saran (Ph.D., University of Michigan, 1954). **Mahatma Gandhi: a descriptive bibliography.** 529p. Order no. 8408.

PURPOSE: The purpose of the study was to gather and annotate references to works in print by and about Gandhi found in books, periodicals, and society publications.

FINDINGS: The study included a chronology of Gandhi's life (1868-1948), with particular reference to his nonviolent struggle for Indian independence. The bibliography includes 3,376 entries, of which 90 percent are in English.

1955

---

130. Baldwin, Ruth Marie (Ph.D., University of Illinois, 1955). **Alexander Gill the elder, high master of St. Paul's School: an approach to Milton's intellectual development.** 208p. Order no. 13,449.

PURPOSE: The purpose of the study was to trace the educational development of the high master of one of the schools that John Milton attended.

PROCEDURE: The historical method was the basic approach in this study.

FINDINGS: The author has reconstructed the formal education of Alexander Gill, and concluded that his writings reveal a greater knowledge and intimacy with contemporary literature than most men of that time. The likelihood of Milton's being influenced by this "wellspring" of literature suggests that there be further study of Gill.

131. Boaz, Martha Terosse (Ph.D., University of Michigan, 1955). **A qualitative analysis of the criticism of best sellers: a study of the reviews and reviewers of best selling books from 1944 to 1953.** 339p. Order no. 11,243.

PURPOSE: The purpose of the study was to determine the quality of book reviewing during the period, and to determine if the reviews were a form of advertisement for the books which helped to make them so popular.

PROCEDURE: Reviews of ten fiction and ten nonfiction bestsellers for each of ten years were studied. In addition, the author discussed principles and criteria of book reviewing, and included the criteria for evaluating the reviews studied.

FINDINGS: The information collected indicated that most of the reviewers were well qualified to do the reviewing. As a whole, the reviews were quite comprehensive, including all of the points expected in a good review, and useful comparisons with similar publications.

CONCLUSIONS: On the basis of the information collected, the author concluded that the reviews published during this period considered both the positive and negative aspects of the books. In general, the reviews included criticism which would be fairly satisfactory for the average reader.

132. Connolly, Father Brendan, S.J. (Ph.D., University of Chicago, 1955). **The roots of Jesuit librarianship: 1540-1599.** 288p.

PURPOSE: The purpose of the study was to explore the attitudes of Jesuits toward

PURPOSE (cont'd): libraries, books, and reading, from the beginning of the order until the promulgation of *The Plan of Studies* (Ratio Studiorum), which controlled Jesuit education until 1832.

PROCEDURE: The archives of the Order, as well as printed materials, were searched by the author for evidence of library holdings.

FINDINGS: The author has indicated that two major attitudes existed among sixteenth century Jesuits, in a rather uneasy truce: as well-educated men, the Jesuits had a high respect for books and learning; as Catholic priests, living in a period of religious rebellion, they were less concerned with new discoveries than with perpetuating what they were certain to be truths. The author has included transcriptions of records of holdings of five sixteenth century Italian Jesuit college libraries.

133. Covey, Alan Dale (Ed.D., Stanford University, 1955). **Evaluation of college libraries for accreditation purposes.** 450p. Order no. 13,240.

PURPOSE: The purpose of the study was to list and analyze the criteria for evaluating specific libraries in an effort to assist accrediting agencies, administrators, and librarians in appraising libraries and establishing goals.

PROCEDURE: Evaluation and possible improvement of Schedule C, a questionnaire designed to determine the relationship between college libraries and their parent institutions in California, was the principal concern of the study. Library literature was surveyed for criteria, and Schedule C was tested at a number of accredited California teachers' colleges.

CONCLUSIONS: Among the conclusions offered by the author are the following: (1) an institution should be appraised in terms of its success in achieving its own stated objectives and in relation to its social pattern as an agency of higher education; (2) qualitative and quantitative criteria should both be used, but qualitative criteria should be used only as discussion points; (3) the A.L.A. service load formula appears to be the most satisfactory quantitative standard; and (4) the quality of a library staff is indicated by its status within the college.

134. Grimm, Dorothy Fear (Ph.D., University of Pennsylvania, 1955). **A history of the Library Company of Philadelphia, 1731-1835.**

PURPOSE: The purpose of the study was to trace the origin, development, and importance of the Library Company of Philadelphia.

PROCEDURE: The historical method was used in this study.

FINDINGS: According to the author, the heterogeneous religious and political beliefs of its managers during its two centuries of existence assured concern for the welfare of the library, and played an important role in the development of the collection. Events taking place in Philadelphia and in America were reflected in the changes in the library's adminstrative policies. An analysis of the library's holdings during the early years showed a heavy emphasis on science, while the collection in 1835 showed the major holdings to be in literature and history.

135. Leonard, Lloyd Leo (Ed.D., Colorado State College of Education, 1955). **Practices followed in administering elementary school libraries in certain cities in the State of Iowa and the opinions of the school superintendents in these cities concerning those and other practices.**

PURPOSE: The purpose of the study was to determine the current administrative

PURPOSE (cont'd): practices followed in Iowa elementary school libraries, and what the attitudes of school superintendents were toward those practices.

PROCEDURE: The procedure was to survey the elementary school libraries in all county seats and all cities with populations of 2,500 or more. Recommendations of school superintendents concerning school library administration were collected and compared with actual practices and also with the standards of the American Library Association.

FINDINGS: The study indicated that in almost all areas of school library administration, actual practice does not correspond to the convictions of school superintendents. Examples of this difference mentioned concerned centralized libraries, employment of full-time librarians, book budgets, allocations for audiovisual aids, and the education of librarians.

136. Lieberman, Irving (Ed.D., Columbia University, Teachers College, 1955).
Audiovisual instruction in library education. 213p.

PURPOSE: The purpose of the study was to survey audiovisual instruction in library schools during 1953-54, and to outline a guide for the presentation of audiovisual courses.

PROCEDURE: The data were obtained through an analysis of published literature, participation in workshops which discussed this subject, and two years' experience as director of an experimental program of audiovisual instruction at the School of Librarianship of the University of California.

FINDINGS: The data indicated that only four library schools were doing a "good" or "excellent" job of audiovisual instruction. The Carnegie Corporation-sponsored project at the University of California, was described, including details about the curriculum, classroom projects and materials, and a special program of in-service workshops for practicing librarians.

RECOMMENDATIONS: The author recommended the development of a strong audiovisual course structure, integrated with instruction in all library school courses on audiovisual materials and on their organization and use.

137. Voisard, Boyer Warren (Ed.D., University of Southern California, 1955).
Librarian participation in high school programs of curriculum improvement.

PURPOSE: The purpose of the study was to ascertain what high school librarians throughout the country are doing to assist curricular improvement programs, and how they can make their participation in such programs more effective.

PROCEDURE: The data in the study were collected from a survey of the literature, and from questionnaires returned by 318 schools with enrollments of over 1,000 in which curriculum improvement programs are being conducted.

FINDINGS: The study indicated the following findings: as the number of students increases, the adequacy of library staffing diminishes; librarians are most likely to participate in programs for the modification of subject curricula; librarians are often included in committees established to solve specific curriculum problems, but they rarely participate; and the standards concerning book budgets are not being met.

RECOMMENDATIONS: The author made the following recommendations based on the findings of the study: each high school should have established a "friends of the library" committee; librarians should be given more opportunities to participate in the formulation and development of curriculum improvement; and materials centers should be established adjacent to the library in each school.

138. Yenawine, Wayne Stewart (Ph.D., University of Illinois, 1955). **The influence of scholars on research library development at the University of
Illinois.** 294p. Order no. 11,551.
PURPOSE: The purpose of the study was to show the growth in importance of
the research library at the University of Illinois from 1900 to 1930.
PROCEDURE: The historical method was used in the study.
FINDINGS: Several factors gave impetus to the development of the research
library: the redefinition of a university's function, the expansion of the graduate
library school in 1906, strong library leadership, integration of library functions
with research and graduate programs and strong financial support.

1956

---

139. Bonk, Wallace John (Ph.D., University of Michigan 1956). **The printing, pub-
lishing, and bookselling activities of John P. Sheldon and his associates in
Detroit, 1817-1830.** 234p. Order no. 21,150.
PURPOSE: The purpose of the study was to investigate the printing, publishing,
and bookselling activities of John P. Sheldon and his associates in Detroit between
1817 and 1830.
PROCEDURE: The historical method was used in the study. It was concerned
with the *Detroit Gazette*, other publishing by the *Gazette* press and the Detroit
Book Store.
FINDINGS: The *Gazette* was first a nonpartisan newspaper, but became more
political after its editors began to enter politics in 1825. Of the publications un-
covered, more than one-third printed by Sheldon's company were official Territorial publications. In addition, the 593 titles listed for sale by the Detroit Book
Store between 1817 and 1828 present a good picture of what a small bookstore
offered to its community.

140. Dawson, John Minto (Ph.D., University of Chicago, 1956). **The acquisitions
and cataloging of research libraries: a study related to the possibilities for
centralized processing.** 167p.
PURPOSE: The purpose of the study was to investigate monographic acquisitions
of nine university libraries and their cataloging and classification practices in order
to explore possibilities of centralized processing.
PROCEDURE: Library of Congress cards were used without alteration for 2,679
of the 5,142 titles cataloged by the libraries over a two-week period. A sample of
500 titles drawn at random from the 2,463 locally written cards was checked
against the Library of Congress printed cards to determine the extent to which
Library of Congress cards were available but not used.
FINDINGS: There is a generalized acquisition pattern for research libraries, and
the author noted that extensive duplication of titles justified the conclusion that
major economies might be effected by centralized cataloging. Library of Congress
cards were available for 60 percent of the titles cataloged by the libraries.

CONCLUSIONS: The author concluded that since new developments in centralized cataloging will likely be based on the Library of Congress system, its cataloging should be extended to include more titles in foreign languages and should be made available abroad.

141. Harrington, Father John Henry (D.L.S., Columbia University, 1956). **The production and distribution of books in Western Europe to the year 1500.** 193p. Order no. 17,057.
PURPOSE: The purpose of the study was to trace the development of book production and distribution in Europe from the classical period through the fifteenth century in order to determine whether one can apply the term "publishing" to these activities prior to the invention of the movable type.
PROCEDURE: The author's procedure was to use the historical method.
FINDINGS: During the classical period, there was sufficient production and distribution of books to satisfy a rather large market. Until the twelfth century, single and multiple copies of books were available, with the majority of them being produced in the monastic scriptoria. As the universities developed, they also undertook the production of accurate texts and commentaries. According to the author, these activities must be termed "publishing" in the strict sense of the word.
CONCLUSIONS: The author has concluded that the invention of the movable type made possible the rapid duplication of books, but it did not create the book publishing industry. This industry had been in existence for a long time, and the invention was rather an enormous technological advance.

142. Hartin, John Sykes (Ph.D., University of Michigan, 1956). **The Southeastern United States in the novel through 1950: a bibliographic review.** 639p. Order no. 21,667.
PURPOSE: The author's purpose was to describe bibliographically the novels inspired by the 11 Southeastern states.
FINDINGS: The fictional studies relating to the 11 Southeastern states are arranged with consistent information, including the plot, theme, and other features. Authors from all parts of the United States and from several foreign countries are represented.

143. Helfert, Bryan Alois (Ed.D., University of Wyoming, 1956). **An appraisal of elementary school library practices in Wisconsin.**
PURPOSE: The author's purpose in conducting the study was to examine and evaluate elementary school library service in Wisconsin cities of 10,000 or more.
PROCEDURE: The author used three techniques in gathering the data for the study: a search of the literature of the field, a questionnaire that was returned by 116 respondents in 30 cities, and visits to 10 schools that seemed, on the basis of the questionnaire, to have the most adequate library facilities.
CONCLUSIONS: The following conclusions were offered as a result of the study: although many of the libraries studied are inadequately supported, the majority appear to be offering adequate library service; a tendency was noticed to provide a combination of classroom and centralized library service, although many central libraries have been discontinued because the space was needed for classrooms; inadequately trained personnel are in charge of half of the libraries studied; and there was an average of seven to nine books per student in the schools.

144. Hopp, Ralph Harvey (Ph.D., University of Illinois, 1956). **A study of the problem of complete documentation in science and technology.** 129p. Order no. 18,152.

PURPOSE: The purpose of the study was to analyze the periodical literature of pure science to determine to what degree references in any given subject field are scattered in a large number of periodicals or concentrated in a small number.

PROCEDURE: The procedure was to analyze the references in comprehensive bibliographies of chemistry, mathematics, biology, and physics to determine the degree of scattering or concentration.

FINDINGS: A large number of periodicals were cited in the literature of the four subjects; the percentage of titles cited four times or less ranged from 53 percent in mathematics to 86 percent in physics. However, a considerable proportion of references in each bibliography was concentrated in a few periodicals. For example, 10 percent of the periodicals studied accounted for over half of the references cited. In chemistry, 3 percent of the periodicals accounted for 50 percent of the references cited.

CONCLUSIONS: The author concluded on the basis of the study that if a library selects its holdings carefully, it need not subscribe to a large number of periodicals in order to obtain relatively good coverage of the literature of the pure sciences.

145. Kaser, David Edwin (Ph.D., University of Michigan, 1956). **Messrs. Carey & Lea of Philadelphia, 1822-1838.** 286p. Order no. 21,189.

PURPOSE: The purpose of the study was to trace the development and outline the importance of the publishing firm of Carey & Lea, during a transitional period of American book publishing.

FINDINGS: It was during this period of time that American authors received their first patronage, and foreign authors received the first remuneration for American publication of their books. The firm of Carey & Lea was the largest American publishing firm during the period studied, and their innovations had a significant effect on American literary history and on the book trade.

146. Kronick, David (Ph.D., University of Chicago, 1956). **The origins and development of the scientific and technological press, 1665-1790.** 346p.

PURPOSE: The purpose of the study was to explore the backgrounds of the technological press, and the characteristics it assumed during the first century of its existence.

PROCEDURE: The study used the historical method and content analysis in gathering the data.

FINDINGS: The scientific periodical was created in response to the needs of scholars of the time, a demand for shorter communications based on the unity of each observation or experiment. Previously, the need had been for a highly organized, comprehensive, and self-consistent system of knowledge.

CONCLUSIONS: The author concluded that newspapers, almanacs, and scholarly correspondence created the pattern for the development of the format and the role of the scientific periodical. The audience served during this period, however, was considerably different from the audience it serves today.

147. LaoSunthara, Maria Eugenia (Ed.D., Indiana University, 1956). **Some bibliographical characteristics of serial literature in the field of geology.** 94p. Order no. 17,772.

PURPOSE: The purpose of the study was to determine the most important serials for geological reserach.

PROCEDURE: The procedure was to pick the most important serials by the "reference counting" method, and then to investigate such characteristics as time span, subject dispersion, language distribution, national origin, and title dispersion.

FINDINGS: The findings indicated that there was a high rate of subject and title dispersion; 51 percent of the titles cited were in fields other than geology. A high percentage of the literature cited by American geologists was in English. The dates of the material used indicated that researchers found useful information in journals dating back many years.

RECOMMENDATIONS: The author suggested the following changes: that priority should be given to the acquisition of journals found to be the most useful in this study; that university libraries in geology and other science fields work closely together in order to avoid unnecessary duplication of materials; and that the most frequently used serials be located in easily accessible places, while those rarely used should be kept in storage.

148. Lewis, Benjamin Morgan (Ph.D., University of Michigan, 1956). **A history and bibliography of American newspapers, 1800-1810.** 333p. Order no. 18,619.

PURPOSE: The purpose of the study was to delineate the extent of magazine development during the decade, and to define its significance.

PROCEDURE: The basic approach in this study was the historical method.

FINDINGS: The study included bibliographical information about 138 magazines published between 1800 and 1809. The most active year during the decade in terms of magazine activity was 1807, when 50 were being published.

CONCLUSIONS: The author has indicated the following conclusions from the study: that originality in the material published was lacking; that literary excellence was attained by very few of the publications; and that the chief value of the magazines was that they served as a vehicle for discussion for the many men who served as their editors and contributors.

149. McCoy, Ralph Edward (Ph.D., University of Illinois, 1956). **Banned in Boston: the development of literary censorship in Massachusetts.** Order no. 18,173.

PURPOSE: The purpose of the study was to trace the development of book-banning in Boston from the colonial period to the present.

PROCEDURE: The historical method was used, employing primary and secondary sources.

FINDINGS: The atmosphere surrounding the creation of the New England Watch and Ward Society in 1878 is described, along with its attempts to enforce a rigid concept of purity in written expression. The decisions made by the Society, supported by the Boston booksellers in 1909, were not challenged until shortly after H. L. Mencken defiantly sold a copy of the *American Mercury* on the Boston Common in 1926. Today there is a strong civil liberties movement in Boston, supported by lawyers and booksellers, and the experience with literary censorship should ultimately form a basis for an accommodation between the ideologies of puritanism and democracy.

150. MacWilliam, Mary Isabella (Ed.D., University of California, Berkeley, 1956).
A survey of the library resources in the California public high schools.
PURPOSE: The purpose of the study was to survey the library resources of the
California high schools in terms of the minimum standards of the California School
Library Association. Particular stress is placed on the changes that have occurred
since 1936, the date of a previous study of a similar nature.
PROCEDURE: The data were derived from a search of the literature, and from
questionnaires and checklists submitted by 560 (of 636) California secondary high
schools having central libraries.
FINDINGS: The study indicated that there has been some progress in the high
school libraries of California, particularly in the use of a wider diversity of materials and in providing better housing. However, progress has been uneven; a great
many of the high schools lack adequate professional and clerical assistance, and
many of the librarians are lacking in the professional education requisite to providing effective library service.
CONCLUSIONS: The author has concluded that the reason there are inadequate
expenditures by most schools for developing and maintaining effective library collections is that the librarians are deficient in professional preparation.

151. Penalosa, Fernando (Ph.D., University of Chicago, 1956). **The Mexican
book industry.** 417p.
PURPOSE: The purpose of the study was to examine the legal basis for, and the
structure of, the book industry in Mexico City and its suburbs.
PROCEDURE: The data were collected by a search of the literature and by the
survey technique.
FINDINGS: The study indicated that publishing is controlled by the booksellers,
whose profits are derived largely from the sale of foreign books. There is a lack of
clear distinction between the functions of the publisher and those of the whole-
salers and retailers. The publishing industry is dominated by people who have close
personal and business ties with foreign countries. The development and exploita-
tion of the domestic market is hampered by widespread illiteracy in Mexico, and
the limited opportunities there for education.

152. Smith, Susan Seabury (Ed.D., Columbia University, Teachers College, 1956).
The role of the school librarian in curriculum improvement.
PURPOSE: The purpose of the study was to analyze the school librarian's contribution to curriculum improvement in New York state schools having central libraries.
PROCEDURE: The data were gathered from a review of the literature of the field
and from questionnaires. The questionnaires were returned by 80 of 176 New York
schools employing a librarian who holds a state certificate for school librarianship and who is employed full-time in providing service and instruction in the
school library.
FINDINGS: The study indicated that librarians were most frequently concerned
with providing guidance materials and guidance fiction, as far as curriculum improvement was concerned. The least frequently reported activity was participating in
curriculum improvement meetings.

153. Zimmerman, Irene (Ph.D., University of Michigan, 1956). **Latin American periodicals of the mid-twentieth century as source material for research in the humanities and the social sciences.** 390p. Order no. 21,381.
PURPOSE: The purpose of the study was to develop a bibliography of outstanding Latin American periodicals useful for research in the humanities and the social sciences.
PROCEDURE: This study combined the bibliographical and historical methods of research.
FINDINGS: The author described the growing realization of the value of these periodicals in research, and the main reference tools that offer information about them. Criteria for objective selection is delineated, and information is provided about the most important titles to show their potentialities for research purposes.
CONCLUSIONS: The study showed that Latin American periodicals are an underused resource in research. More adequate indexing of the periodicals is needed in order to encourage fuller use of them.

1957

---

154. Abbott, John Cushman (Ph.D., University of Michigan, 1957). **Raymond Cazallis Davis and the University of Michigan General Library, 1877-1905.** 309p. Order no. 58-1,370.
PURPOSE: The purpose of the study was to trace the development of the General Library of the University of Michigan under the administration of Davis.
PROCEDURE: The historical method of research was used, employing both primary and secondary sources.
FINDINGS: The administration of Davis was a significant one for the Library of the University of Michigan. The major achievements of his regime were: the construction of the library building in 1883, the large increase in the book collection to meet the growing research and instruction needs of the University, improvements in the card catalogs, and innovations in classification.

155. Burke, John Emmett (Ed.D., Universityof Denver, 1957). **State department of education library services in states of the Southern Association of Colleges and Secondary Schools.**
PURPOSE: The purpose of the study was to investigate the role of state departments of education in provision of library service in 11 Southern states.
PROCEDURE: The data in the study were gathered from a literature search, from official records, and from interviews and correspondence with state library supervisors. The 11 states included were Alabama, Florida, Georgia, Kentucky, Louisiana, Mississippi, North Carolina, South Carolina, Tennessee, Texas, and Virginia.
FINDINGS: Among the findings mentioned in the study are: school library supervision by the state permits and encourages long-range planning; legislation fails to provide for contractual and cooperative service among school libraries and other library agencies in the state; state financial and other assistance not only

FINDINGS (cont'd): helps local libraries to meet established standards, but also stimulates local interest in school libraries; state supervision results in the improvement in the preparation requirement for librarians; centers for the preparation of librarians are encouraged and stimulated by the certification requirements of the state; and the greatest weakness in school library service in this area is in the lack of adequately prepared librarians.

156. Cyphert, Frederick R. (Ed.D., University of Pittsburgh, 1957). **Current practice in the use of the library in selected junior high schools in Pennsylvania.** 234p. Order no. 24,738.
PURPOSE: The purpose of the study was to determine the extent and value of instruction in library usage skills in junior high schools.
PROCEDURE: The basic research instrument was the questionnaire, surveying the pattern in 73 three-year junior high schools in Pennsylvania.
FINDINGS: The surveys showed that most junior high schools offer some type of pre-planned library instruction, and that school libraries are most often visited by students in English, social studies, and core areas. Most of the schools have full-time certified librarians who spend at least 75 percent of their time with professional duties, but have very little involvement in curriculum planning.
RECOMMENDATIONS: The author has recommended that service to junior high schools be recognized as a distinct specialty within librarianship. Other recommendations include: teacher-training institutions should devote more effort to library services and materials; teachers and administrators should be more aware of the library's role in support of superior instruction; and librarians should devote more time to curriculum study.

157. Daily, Jay Elwood (D.L.S., Columbia University, 1957). **The grammar of subject headings: a formulation of rules for subject headings based on a syntactical and morphological analysis of the Library of Congress list.** 234p. Order no. 21,780.
PURPOSE: The purpose of the study was to analyze the subject headings in the Library of Congress list in order to determine the function of each grammatical form in the structure of the list.
PROCEDURE: The investigation was based on the fifth edition, 1948 listing. The 21,451 main headings were grouped according to form, punctuation, and inflection of words.
FINDINGS: The study indicated that 47 percent of the main headings are composed of two or more words, and 32 percent consist of one word.
CONCLUSIONS: A comparison of grammatical forms used in seven special lists indicated that a single area of usage could be determined for each mark of punctuation. The problems of grouping and dispersal of headings suggested a need for a classified guide to supplement the alphabetical list of headings, and the use of a mark of punctuation instead of prepositions and conjunctions.

158. Douglass, Robert Raymond (Ph.D., University of Chicago, 1957). **The personality of the librarian.**
PURPOSE: The purpose of the study was to determine the extent to which the library profession "selects" members exhibiting a characteristic personality configuration and identifies, as traits generally ascribed to stereotype of the

PURPOSE (cont'd): librarian, extreme deference, submissiveness, and respect of authority.

PROCEDURE: A questionnaire and five structured personality inventories (furnishing a total of 27 measures) were distributed to several control groups and to an experimental group consisting of 125 men and 400 women enrolled during 1947-48 in 17 of the 36 A.L.A. accredited library schools. The levels of significance of differences among the groups was determined through use of the t-test and the chi-square measure.

CONCLUSIONS: The author concluded that, in terms of personality structure, the library profession does exercise selective influence in recruiting its members. The study enumerated 10 traits of the "modal" or "average" librarian. For example, they are generally orderly, conscientious, responsible, conservative, undominating, interested in people, and not neurotically anxious.

159. Dyke, James Parvin (Ph.D., University of Illinois, 1957). **Validation of the University of Illinois Library School placement examination.** 177p. Order no. 25,213.

PURPOSE: The purpose of the study was to investigate the validity of the placement examination administered by the University of Illinois Library School.

PROCEDURE: The study included background information on the history of library education, a survey of the use of tests and measurements in library education, suggestions for examination within the structure of library education, and a report on activities of the Library School faculty with respect to such examinations. The examinations were analyzed and tested for content validity, concurrent validity, and construct validity.

FINDINGS: The data established the validity of the placement examination, thus substantiating its use as a screening instrument.

CONCLUSIONS: The author concluded that the examination was a valid screening instrument for placement, and that this conclusion justified both library school policies on exemption from core courses and individual judgments resulting from these policies, showing them to be defensible, equitable, and objective. The author believes that the validation also supports the concept of a core curriculum for library schools, and the possibility of development of a national certification examination for the library profession.

160. Herald, Homer Wayne (Ed.D., Stanford University, 1957). **Planning library facilities for the secondary school.**

PURPOSE: The purpose of the study was to measure the facilities of 25 recently constructed secondary school libraries against the standards proposed by the American Library Association to determine which of the standards were the most difficult to meet. The study also proposed a procedure for the use of standards in planning library facilities.

PROCEDURE: The data were gathered from personal interviews and from field observations.

FINDINGS: The libraries were analyzed in detail, and revealed a number of basic weaknesses: insufficient flexibility in the planning of library facilities, a slighting of functional details, and a loss of efficiency because of poor spatial planning. Many of the libraries could have met the standards if planning operations had included the development of educational specifications for the library center,

65

FINDINGS (cont'd): with the librarian playing a leading part on the planning team.
CONCLUSIONS: The author concluded that library standards are most effective in planning libraries when the standards are used as a resource by librarians, administrators, and architects in a cooperative team effort.

161. Johnson, Robert Kellogg (Ph.D., University of Illinois, 1957). **Characteristics of libraries in selected higher military institutions in the United States.** 373p. Order no. 20,867.
PURPOSE: The purpose of the study was to ascertain the role which the library plays in the higher military educational institutions.
PROCEDURE: A number of different research tools were used in obtaining the data from 18 libraries in 16 armed service schools: manuscripts and published sources, questionnaires, and the author's observations.
FINDINGS: The study revealed that libraries receive a relatively low priority in military institutions, that financial support is inadequate and undependable, that controls are overly elaborate, and that military personnel are unsuited for "civilian-type" library jobs. It was also reported that the most important experiments and library developments have occurred in those areas of library practice that are least subject to military and governmental control.

162. Kennerly, Sarah Law (Ph.D., University of Michigan, 1957). **Confederate juvenile imprints: children's books and periodicals published in the Confederate States of America, 1861-1865.** 492p. Order no. 58-1,025.
PURPOSE: The purpose of the study was to describe and analyze the publishing of children's books and periodicals during the Civil War period in the South.
PROCEDURE: The historical method was used, with some content analysis.
FINDINGS: The study indicated that the publications of this period were mediocre in style and moralistic in tone. The literature was not of lasting value, but it did reflect the South's attitude toward the training of children. A classified, annotated bibliography giving the location of extant titles is included in the study.

163. Knapp, Patricia B. (Ph.D., University of Chicago, 1957). **The role of the library of a given college in implementing the course and non-course objectives of that college.** 298p.
PURPOSE: The purpose of the study was to investigate student use of the college library to determine the relationship between student borrowing and the instructional program that generated it.
PROCEDURE: Data were gathered by the author about the borrowing of materials, certain characteristics of the student borrowers, and characteristics about the courses which stimulated the borrowing.
FINDINGS: The study revealed that the student use of the library was almost entirely course-oriented, with reserve book use providing more than half of the circulation. The borrowing was concentrated in a small group of students. Factors that influenced use of the library for instructional purposes were the size of the class, level, kinds of material required, and subject.
CONCLUSIONS: The author concluded that the contribution of the library to the college program is limited, and that the library staff should emphasize its teaching role so as to promote a broader concept of what the library can contribute to instruction.

164. Knox, Margaret Enid (Ph.D., University of Illinois, 1957). **Professional development of reference librarians in a university library: a case study.** 412p. Order no. 23,345.

PURPOSE: The purpose of the study was to show that the fundamental principles and procedures of executive training programs in industry, as well as many techniques used in the development of managerial personnel, may be applied to professional growth of reference librarians in a university library. Such a program of instruction could be carried on even in the midst of a busy service schedule.

PROCEDURE: The reference department of a state university library was used as the subject for this case study. Training needs of each reference librarian in this department were employed for improvement of technical, human, and conceptual skills.

FINDINGS: The author reported that the ability and knowledge of every staff member increased to some degree during the training period, with the greatest progress made in the acquisition of technical knowledge. The program was more effective in developing conceptual skills than human ones.

CONCLUSIONS: The author concluded that the success of such a program depends upon the amount of professional interest in it, definition of a clearly understood purpose, careful preparation in advance, support from the library administration, and provision for periodic appraisals of its achievements.

165. Lowell, Mildred Hawksworth (Ph.D., University of Chicago, 1957). **Indiana University Libraries, 1829-1942.** 453p.

PURPOSE: The purpose of the study was to trace the development of the Indiana University Libraries during a significant period in the history of American higher education.

PROCEDURE: The historical method was used, utilizing primary and secondary sources.

FINDINGS: The study was divided into periods: dominance by the board of trustees, dominance by the university president, the Jenkins administration, and accelerated growth. The author indicated that although the library adopted a new role during the period covered, changes resulted chiefly from measures undertaken to meet the contingencies of the moment.

166. Mack, Edna Ballard (Ph.D., University of Michigan, 1957). **The school library's contribution to the total educational program of the school: a content analysis of selected periodicals in the field of education.** 378p. Order no. 58-1431.

PURPOSE: The purpose of the study was to ascertain the role of the library in the total school program, as seen in the educational literature.

PROCEDURE: The author surveyed the contents of 13 selected educational periodicals published between September 1, 1954, and August 31, 1955. While only 11 of the 1,561 articles considered were found to deal specifically with school librarianship, 255 others, as well as 38 other items in the periodicals, mentioned school libraries.

FINDINGS: The data revealed that considerable attention was paid in the journal articles to the library's contribution to language arts instruction, but much less was said about the library's participation in other areas such as science and social studies. There was almost no mention of the library as it might concern other

FINDINGS (cont'd): areas in the curriculum or in extracurricular activities. No information was given about the librarian as administrator, the recruitment or training of school librarians, or the provision of supervisory or consultant services.
CONCLUSIONS: On the basis of the information obtained in the study, the author concluded that few school librarians write for education periodicals, and that in these periodicals, information about administrative provisions for school library service is limited in amount and scope, and is inadequate for the needs of administrators.

167. Maizell, Robert Edward (D.L.S., Columbia University, 1957). **Information gathering patterns and creativity: a study of research chemists in an industrial research library.** 152p. Order no. 58-1,348.
PURPOSE: The purpose of the study was to determine the extent to which differences in information-gathering behavior and literature use are related to differences in creativity among industrial research chemists.
PROCEDURE: A sample of 94 industrial research chemists from one laboratory was selected; each chemist was rated by at least two of his supervisors and this information was validated by two independent creativity tests. The data on information-gathering patterns were collected from questionnaires and from records submitted by the chemists at the end of each 10-day working period.
FINDINGS: The study revealed that there was no statistical difference between years of professional experience or supervisory responsibility and the information-gathering habits of the most creative chemists. The information did indicate that the Ph.D. holder consulted the literature more extensively than did the individual not possessing the Ph.D.

168. Meyer, Floyd Raymond (Ed.D., University of Nebraska, Teachers College, 1957). **Library facilities and services in Nebraska secondary schools accredited by the North Central Association.** 220p. Order no. 28,922.
PURPOSE: The purpose of the study was to evaluate the library facilities and services in Nebraska secondary schools having superior programs according to the accepted standards, and to compare, describe, and analyze them critically.
PROCEDURE: The data were gathered from a literature search, interviews of librarians selected at random, and from questionnaires. The questionnaires were prepared from the A.L.A. *Planning Guide for High School Library Program* by paraphrasing and putting the statements in questionnaire form.
FINDINGS: The study included many items which should be incorporated into any school library program, such as activities and services for students, services performed by the librarian in connection with social guidance and use of the library, and teacher participation in the library program.
RECOMMENDATIONS: One of the author's recommendations was that the library responsibility should be considered part of the teaching load, not an extra activity apart from the instructional program.

169. Reagan, Agnes Lytton (Ph.D., University of Illinois, 1957). **A study of certain factors in institutions of higher education which influence students to become librarians.** 110p. Order no. 23,377.
PURPOSE: The purpose of the study was to identify the factors in institutions of higher education that influence students to become librarians.

PROCEDURE: The data were gathered from questionnaires sent to 1,479 graduates of accredited fifth-year library schools (1948-55). Usable replies were received from alumni of 23 liberal arts colleges, 16 teachers colleges, and 12 universities.
FINDINGS: The study indicated that the most important influence is that of librarians, who try to make students aware of librarianship. In a few schools, faculty members exerted more influence than did librarians, but the effects were usually indirect and somewhat delayed. Another influence was the presence of a library school on campus.

170. Schick, Frank Leopold (Ph.D., University of Michigan, 1957). **The paper-bound book in America: the history of paperbacks and their European antecedents.** 262p. Order no. 58-984.
PURPOSE: The purpose of the study was to explore the history of paperback publishing in America, including its European influences, and to explain the growth of the paperback industry.
PROCEDURE: The data for recent history were obtained from personal interviews and correspondence with executive personnel of 43 paperback publishers.
FINDINGS: The study presents a summary history of individual paperback firms, including their paperback production. Separate sections are devoted to censorship, literary output, problems of technical production, relationship between authors and publishers, and patterns of distribution.
CONCLUSIONS: The paperback industry, because it brings book ownership within the reach of all Americans, has a high cultural significance. It is also important abroad in the evaluation of our literary and cultural standards, because paperbacks are the only books that foreign countries can afford to import in large quantities. Since paperbacks have already changed the acquisitions policies of American libraries, the author suggests the possibility that they may also change the established patterns of publishing.

171. Stephenson, Harriet Shirley (Ph.D., Louisiana State University, 1957). **History of the Louisiana State Library, formerly Louisiana Library, formerly Louisiana Library Commission.** 492p. Order no. 24,729.
PURPOSE: The purpose of the study was to trace the development of the Louisiana State Library from 1920 to 1955, with an evaluation of the demonstration method of library development used by this agency.
FINDINGS: The study included information on the founding of the Library, its accomplishments, its programs for extending library services throughout the state, the enactment of library laws and the library's role in that enactment, and the establishment of the library school at Louisiana State University.

172. Tolman, Lorraine Enid (Ed.D., Boston, University, 1957). **Initiation of elementary school library service.** Order no. 58-1,069.
PURPOSE: The purpose of the study was to explore those activities and plans used in the promotion of elementary school library service which would be of interest to principals and teachers.
PROCEDURE: The data were gathered from a literature search and from the use of a questionnaire completed by 126 principals and 200 teachers. The questionnaire was in the form of a checklist with items dealing with teaching techniques, adequacy of materials, and aspects of organization.

FINDINGS: The data revealed two basic problems, in the opinion of the principals: teacher readiness for library service, and determination of the best type of service to be rendered.

173. Tsien, Tsuen-Hsuin (Ph.D., University of Chicago, 1957). **The pre-printing records of China: a study of the development of early Chinese inscriptions and books.** 302p.
PURPOSE: The purpose of the study was to present a general history of the development of Chinese written records from the 14th century B.C. to the introduction of printing about 700 A.D.
FINDINGS: A variety of materials was used to record the first writings; writings preserved on perishable materials are called books and those preserved on hard surfaces are called inscriptions. Texts of surviving records show an increase in the number of characters in the Chinese language from some 2,000 used in bone inscriptions to about 18,000 characters known in 700 A.D.

174. Walther, LaVern Arlene Doubt (Ed.D., Indiana University, 1957). **Legal and governmental aspects of public library development in Indiana, 1816-1853.** 113p. Order no. 24,840.
PURPOSE: The purpose of the study was to trace the development of library service in Indiana, including state library service and legislation dealing with libraries.
PROCEDURE: The basic approach used was the historical method, utilizing both primary and secondary sources.
FINDINGS: A comparision is made between public library development in Indiana and elsewhere in the United States. The factors, such as social, geographic, and educational, which brought about the development of library service in the state are described. The data indicated that statistically, Indiana libraries compare favorably with those of the other states. Library service in rural areas has been difficult to maintain because of the particular geographic makeup of the state and because of the shifts in population.

1958

175. Anders, Mary Edna (D.L.S., Columbia University, 1958). **The development of public library service in the Southeastern states, 1895-1950.** 270p. Order no. 58-2,670.
PURPOSE: The purpose of the study was to trace the development of public library service in the Southeast from the 1890's to 1950, including the factors that have affected the development.
FINDINGS: The study revealed that support for the library movement in this area originally came from women's clubs and spread to state and professional associations. Federal programs, such as the WPA and TVA, have stimulated library growth, as has the aid from philanthropic foundations. The Southeast has

FINDINGS (cont'd): adopted county and regional library organization more widely than has the rest of the nation, but it does not serve as great a proportion of the people. The rate of growth of library income and collections is not as great as the rest of the nation, but use of the libraries has increased while often declining elsewhere. The study also showed a positive relationship between improvement in social and economic conditions and library progress.

176. Autio, Andrew William (Ed.D., University of Nebraska, Teachers College, 1958). **A study of library practices and facilities provided in selected elementary schools of Nebraska.**
PURPOSE: The purpose of the study was to emphasize the importance of improving library practices and facilities in the elementary schools of Nebraska, and to evaluate the status of selected elementary school library programs.
PROCEDURE: The data were obtained from questionnaires sent to teachers, principals, and superintendents in 26 school systems in the large cities of the state.
FINDINGS: The findings showed the following composite opinion regarding elementary school libraries: that in schools that have classroom collections only, there should be some provision for adequate circulation of materials and to prevent unwanted duplication of materials; that adequately trained librarians are needed to supply a desirable quality of library service to students and faculty; that it is necessary for librarians to have professional training in library science as well as in classroom teaching; and that specific lessons on the use of the library should be taught by both teachers and librarians at all levels in the elementary school.

177. Erickson, Ernst Walfred (Ph.D., University of Illinois, 1958). **College and university library surveys, 1938-1952.** 449p. Order no. 58-5412.
PURPOSE: The purpose of the study was to determine the consequences of the 12 major surveys of college and university libraries conducted by outside experts between 1938 and 1952.
PROCEDURE: The data in the study were collected from questionnaires, correspondence, literature searches, annual reports of the libraries, special reports, and interviews. The university libraries included were Florida, Georgia, New Hampshire, Notre Dame, South Carolina, Indiana, Cornell, Montana State, Stanford, Texas A and M College, and Alabama and Virginia polytechnic institutes.
FINDINGS: The following findings resulted from the study: (1) of 775 recommendations resulting from the 12 surveys, 531 were carried out to some degree, 269 of them were completed; (2) 45 percent of the recommendations were carried out within two years of the completion of the survey; (3) in most cases, after termination of the survey, library organization improved, budgets increased, reader services were bettered, technical processes were made more efficient, and other improvements noted; (4) there were important by-products of the survey, such as better library-consciousness on the part of the academic community.
CONCLUSION: The author concluded that results conducive to the growth and betterment of the library are shown as a result of surveys done by outside experts.

178. Gribbin, John Hawkins (Ph.D., University of Chicago, 1958). **Relationships in the patterns of bibliographic devices.** 159p.
PURPOSE: The purpose of the study was to test the hypothesis that the growth

PURPOSE (cont'd): of bibliographic apparatus of a subject field is related to growth of other manifestations of development of that field.

PROCEDURE: The author traced the history of three kinds of bibliographic devices (libraries, abstracting journals, and indexes to serial literature) in chemistry, geology, and botany.

FINDINGS: Five manifestations of growth considered in relation to bibliographic devices were development of professional societies, increases in physical production, rising number of patents granted, expansion of literature in the field, and the development of an educational apparatus.

CONCLUSIONS: The author concluded that although patterns of bibliographic devices in these areas developed along similar lines, extensiveness of their bibliographic apparatus varied enormously from field to field. Predictions about the pattern of bibliographic activity in a given field can be based on study of the patterns of certain manifestations in that field.

179. Hertel, Robert Russell (Ph.D., University of Illinois, 1958). **The decline of the paperbound novel in America, 1890-1910.** 273p. Order no. 58-5432.

PURPOSE: The purpose of the study was to identify those factors that were significant in producing the decline of the paperbound novel between 1890 and 1910.

FINDINGS: Previous studies had indicated that the chief cause of the decline was the International Copyright Law of 1891. This study revealed that there were three additional factors in the decline of paperback publishing: the existence of a large number of firms issuing the novels singly and in series; the publication of large editions; and the existence of a large body of fiction that was not in copyright. The high cost of new material led to the piracy of literary works and to the publication of old and ephemeral material. Publishers became convinced that it would be more profitable to reprint clothbound editions of their bestselling copyrighted novels than to resort to the paperbound market.

180. Hewlett, LeRoy (Ph.D., University of Michigan, 1958). **James Rivington, Loyalist printer, publisher and bookseller of the American Revolution, 1724-1802; a biographical-bibliographical study.** 525p. Order no. 58-7,727.

PURPOSE: The purpose of the study was to develop a full-scale biography of Rivington as a printer, as well as a detailed bibliography of his American publications.

PROCEDURE: The historical method of research was used in this study.

FINDINGS: The bibliography indicates the present location of extant copies in various libraries in the United States, Canada, and Great Britain. The biographical material related Rivington's life to the times in which he lived, stressing his Loyalist publications. Additional material is supplied about freedom of the press, American publishing history, and bookselling practices during this period of time.

181. Jones, Robert Corwin (Ed.D., University of Denver, 1958). **The administrative relationships of the library and the junior college.**

PURPOSE: The purpose of the study was to examine the relationships that exist between the junior college library and its parent institution in terms of the principles of administration.

PROCEDURE: The data were gathered from a literature search and from interviews with the presidents and librarians of six junior colleges in Colorado. FINDINGS: The data indicated that the failure to establish statements of library policy, government, and control has left doubt as to what objectives are sought by the administration and how they may be achieved. None of the institutions studied had established a faculty-library committee. RECOMMENDATIONS: The author suggested the following recommendations: the college president should issue a statement clearly setting forth the librarian's duties, responsibilities, and administrative relationships; formal channels of communication between the librarian and the officer in charge of curriculum should be made mandatory; a faculty-library committee should be established; there should be more formal channels of communication between the college and the community in which it is located.

182. Krummel, Donald William (Ph.D., University of Michigan, 1958). **Philadelphia music engraving and publishing, 1800-1820.** 394p. Order no. 58-7,749.
PURPOSE: The purpose of the study was to identify the extent of engraved music during the two decades, to locate the publishers and their publications, and to relate the music to the cultural environment they served.
PROCEDURE: The historical method was used in this study.
FINDINGS: A total of 1,200 publications were located and dated for the study. This information served to indicate the extent of popularity of individual compositions and also suggested trends. The study also gives information on the dating of publications from printing information.

183. Kruse, Paul (Ph.D., University of Chicago, 1958). **The story of the Encyclopaedia Britannica, 1768-1943.** 435p.
PURPOSE: The purpose of the study was to trace the origins and development of the *Encyclopedia Britannica.*
FINDINGS: Information has been included about the development of encyclopedias and encyclopedia publishing prior to the origin of the *Encyclopaedia Britannica.* The various editions of the *Encyclopaedia* are covered, including information on the various owners. The problem of piracy of material, and court decisions on copyright are detailed.
CONCLUSIONS: The author has concluded that *Britannica* represented an anomalous union between business and scholarship. It has enjoyed the longest successful career of any encyclopedia published, and has contributed a great deal to the popularization of knowledge.

184. Lincoln, Sister Mary Edmund (Ph.D., University of Minnesota, 1958). **Cultural significance of the Minneapolis Public Library in its origins and development: a study in the relations of the public library and American society.** 388p. Order no. 60-974.
PURPOSE: The purpose of the study was to trace the development of the Minneapolis Public Library in the larger context of the public library movement during the nineteenth century.
PROCEDURE: The historical method was used in the study.

FINDINGS: The study centered on four factors that had a major influence on library origins during the nineteenth century: economic ability, a favorable attitude toward culture, civic pride, and popular support. Other factors of immediate significance in the establishment of the Minneapolis Public Library were: the traditional faith in education and reading, philanthropic contributions, the growth of industry, and the efforts of the local government to increase its services.

185. Linder, Leroy H. (Ph.D., University of Chicago, 1958). **Rise of current complete national bibliography in England, France, Germany, and the U.S., 1564 to 1939.** 290p.
PURPOSE: The purpose of the study was to survey the development of current complete national bibliographies in France, England, Germany, and the U.S. from their beginnings to the outbreak of World War II.
PROCEDURE: The basic methodology used in this study was the historical approach, utilizing both primary and secondary sources.
FINDINGS: The study indicated that almost 90 percent of the bibliographies studied owed their origin and support to booksellers. The scope of bibliographies has constantly enlarged with the passing years, and the number of bibliographical details supplied with an entry has increased. In arrangement, the United States has favored the alphabetical listing, while Germany, France, and Great Britain have all favored a classified listing; however, trends indicate that the alphabetical arrangement may eventually prevail in most national bibliographies. The author noted two major trends: an integrated group of lists or proliferation of lists seem to be replacing the single, all-inclusive list; there was also a consolidation in a single bibliography of entries formerly found in separate lists.

186. McGuire, Alice Brooks (Ph.D., University of Chicago, 1958). **Developmental values in children's literature.** 209p.
PURPOSE: The purpose of the study was to demonstrate and test three propositions about developmental values in books written for adolescents.
PROCEDURE: The authors' purposes and the values that they intended to communicate were identified and studied in relation to statements of developmental tasks; then teachers and librarians working with children were asked to assess the potential values and implications of the books in terms of nine specific developmental tasks. A sample of the boys and girls was surveyed immediately after reading the books and again one year later in order to determine whether the developmental tasks had been absorbed and applied.
FINDINGS: The study showed that the authors usually tried to communicate some combination of developmental values, and that the adult appraisers generally assessed these values correctly.
CONCLUSIONS: The author offered the conclusion that stories which provide enjoyable reading experiences for children are most effective in communicating developmental values.

187. MacVean, Donald Sidney (Ed.D., University of Michigan, 1958). **A study of curriculum laboratories in Midwestern teacher-training institutions.** 234p. Order no. 58-3706.
PURPOSE: The purpose of the study was to report on the current status of the curriculum laboratories in Midwestern teacher-training institutions, to identify

PURPOSE (cont'd): the characteristics that make them successful, and to describe the contribution that the curriculum laboratory makes to the teacher-education program.

PROCEDURE: Data were collected by questionnaires, correspondence, and personal visits. The curriculum laboratories were in Indiana, Iowa, Michigan, Wisconsin, and Minnesota.

FINDINGS: The study outlines the objectives of curriculum laboratories, and lists those services reported by 10 or more institutions. It also describes the laboratories in terms of relationship with the parent institution, training of staff members, nature of materials selected, and annual budgets.

CONCLUSIONS: The author made the following conclusions as a result of the study: that curriculum materials are most useful when organized into a separate collection; that most institutions consider the operation of a curriculum laboratory a library function; and that the person in charge should have experience in teaching and in library work.

188. Maddox, Lucy Jane (Ph.D., University of Michigan, 1958). **Trends and issues in American librarianship as reflected in the papers and proceedings of the American Library Association, 1876-1885.** 590p. Order no. 58-7,763.

PURPOSE: The purpose of the study was to trace the history of the modern American library movement, and to identify the issues that developed during the decade from 1876 to 1885.

PROCEDURE: The historical method was used in this study.

FINDINGS: Among the issues most widely discussed were the following: classification and cataloging, cooperative ventures, the development of public library service to adults, library cooperation with the public schools, planning of functional library buildings, training of librarians, government publications, bibliography as a science, and charging systems.

CONCLUSIONS: The author concluded that although librarians have expanded their area of service, the methods established during the first decade of existence of the American Library Association are still widely used. Many of the general patterns that emerged at that time have formed the basis for library achievements of later years.

189. Poste, Leslie I. (Ph.D., University of Chicago, 1958). **The development of U.S. protection of libraries and archives in Europe during World War II.** 427p.

PURPOSE: The purpose of the study was to identify the actions, and their backgrounds, taken by the U.S. government in the protection of libraries and archives in Europe during World War II.

PROCEDURE: The basic methodology in the study was the historical approach.

FINDINGS: The study indicated that international agreements protecting libraries were nineteenth century extensions of agreements protecting private property. Libraries in German-occupied areas suffered the most from plundering, and German libraries suffered the most from aerial bombardment. They were the first to take measures for the preservation of cultural resources, but the problems of libraries in war were of such magnitude that the measures were inadequate. The most effective protection proved to be the dispersion of materials away from densely populated areas.

190. Sharify, Nasser (D.L.S., Columbia University, 1958). **A code for the cataloging of Persian publications.** 146p. Order no. 58-2,714.

PURPOSE: The purpose of the study was to attempt to provide rules for entry, descriptive cataloging, and a transliteration scheme for cataloging Persian publications.

PROCEDURE: The study was divided into four areas: Persian transliteration for library purposes; cataloging rules for entry; cataloging rules for description; and aids to catalogers for the establishment of entries. Included in the work are a bibliographic survey of literature on Persian transliteration, and a critical analysis of 41 cataloging codes issued by 23 countries.

191. Tracy, Warren (Ph.D., University of Chicago, 1958). **The public library and the courts.**

PURPOSE: The purpose of the study was to review court decisions relating to the American public library, and to try to formulate a systematic presentation of the principles of law that affect the public library.

PROCEDURE: The author's procedure was to analyze court decisions applying to the American public library, and to investigate all cases containing references to the library as a public institution.

FINDINGS: Chapters are included on the following topics: the public library board; the public library and the state; trusts and the public library; public library money; public library contracts; the acquisition of property for and by libraries; and library status in general.

192. Whitten, Joseph Nathaniel (Ed.D., New York University, 1958). **Relationship of college instruction to libraries in seventy-two liberal arts colleges.** 290p. Order no. 58-5,658.

PURPOSE: The purpose of the study was to analyze the teaching responsibilities of college librarians in order to describe how the college library may become an integral and functional part of the academic program.

PROCEDURE: The data were derived from a questionnaire, which was completed by 28 librarians, and from personal interviews with 44 others. In addition, a "Board of Authority," made up of administrators, faculty members, and experts in fields of college teaching, college administration, and librarianship prepared statements against which were measured the replies received from the sample.

CONCLUSIONS: The author listed the following conclusions based on the study: instructional service is an essential part of the college library's function; the librarian is obligated to relate his work in a positive and definite manner to the instructional process of the college; the majority of those surveyed, as well as the "Board of Authority," acknowledged this obligation.

1959

193. Harmer, William R. (Ph.D., University of Minnesota, 1959). **The effect of a library training program on summer loss or gain in reading abilities.**
PURPOSE: The purpose of the study was to determine the influence of a public library training program during a summer vacation period on the reading ability of 4th grade children.
PROCEDURE: The procedure was to obtain information from a study of the literature, and test results from 470 pupils in eight experimental and eight control classes selected from the Minneapolis public schools. The experimental group underwent a ten-day training session by children's librarians of the Minneapolis Public Library, while the control group did not have such a session.

194. Lilley, Oliver Linton (D.L.S., Columbia University, 1959). **Terminology, form, specificity, and the syndetic structure of subject headings for English literature.** 491p. Order no. 59-3116.
PURPOSE: The purpose of the study was to investigate the inherent characteristics of the alphabetical subject headings system and to identify some practices which have led to variations on the Library of Congress system used in American libraries.
PROCEDURE: The study included an analysis of subject headings, scope notes, and references employed by 18 sources in the field of English literature.
FINDINGS: The information revealed a high degree of adaptability to variations of terminology, form, and specificity, and to different theories of needs. Inadequacies of subject headings in modern library catalogs are attributed to practices adopted in their construction rather than to limitations imposed by basic design. Terminology and form of subject headings for English literature are usually appropriate and while apparatus is the most important element, it is the least adequately provided for by modern subject heading practices.

195. Linderman, Winifred (Ph.D., Columbia University, 1959). **History of the Columbia University Library, 1876-1926.** 597p. Order no. 59-2,859.
PURPOSE: The purpose of the study was to trace the development of the Columbia University Library from the time it was a small undergraduate college to 1926, when it was a large metropolitan university.
PROCEDURE: The author used the historical method of research, utilizing primary and secondary sources.
FINDINGS: Two events within a four-year period had a marked effect on the development of the Columbia University Library: the arrival in 1876 of Professor John W. Burgess, who insisted on adequate and properly maintained library collections, and the establishment in 1880 of a graduate school with an emphasis on research.

196. Lowrie, Jean Elizabeth (Ph.D., Western Reserve, 1959). **Elementary school libraries: a study of the program in ten school systems in the areas of curriculum enrichment and reading guidance with emphasis on fourth, fifth, and sixth grades.** 305p.

PURPOSE: The purpose of the study was to determine the role of the library in the elementary school.

PROCEDURE: The study included 48 well-established and well-supported libraries in elementary schools of 10 school systems representing various types of communities in different sections of the country. The information was obtained through interviews with students, parents, teachers, librarians, and administrators, and through observation in libraries and classrooms.

FINDINGS: The study emphasized two major areas of library service: curriculum enrichment and reading guidance. Programs involving the presentation and use of library materials are described.

CONCLUSIONS: The author concluded that: greater emphasis should be placed on meeting the minimum standards of the American Library Association; professional teacher training should include backgrounds in children's literature and information on library competencies; the elementary school librarian should be taught to understand curriculum trends and child growth and development; and the correlation between library services and the reading abilities of children should be investigated further.

197. Stokes, Katharine Martin (Ph.D., University of Michigan, 1959). **Book resources for teacher education: a study toward the compilation of a core list.** 212p. Order no. 59-4996.

PURPOSE: The purpose of the study was to compile a basic list of books for use in building collections in teachers' colleges.

PROCEDURE: A card file was developed to show the materials used in preparation of M.A. theses and with graduate courses in education at Western Michigan University and the University of Michigan. This file was compared with a number of published lists and the resulting compilation of 1,019 entries was sent to 29 teacher-education institutions to be checked against their collections.

FINDINGS: Titles held by fewer than five libraries were dropped from the list, leaving a core of 1,000 titles. The 602 titles held by 21 or more libraries were judged to be the most important. Half of the books were published after 1950, and 40 percent in the preceding 10 years.

198. Vann, Sarah Katherine (Ph.D., University of Chicago, 1959). **Training for librarianship before 1923 or prior to the publication of Williamson's report on training for library service.**

PURPOSE: The purpose of the study was to examine the development of education for librarianship in the period of "Dewey to Williamson," the opening of the Columbia School of Library Economy to the report on *Training for Library Service*.

PROCEDURE: The historical method was used, employing both primary and secondary sources.

FINDINGS: The study included a survey of library training prior to 1923, and explored the antecedents of Williamson's recommendations in writings, speeches, and activities from 1887 to 1923.

CONCLUSIONS: The author concluded that many "revolutionary" ideas of 1923 and later were expressed, debated, and evaluated during the period covered. This was a time of cautious but positive progress toward library education. Conflicting ideas delayed progress, but prepared the profession for the Williamson report.

199. Villalon-Galdames, Alberto (Ph.D., University of Michigan, 1959). **An intro-**
duction to Latin American juridical bibliography. 521p. Order no. 59-3,965.
PURPOSE: The purpose of the study was to present in annotated bibliography
form the legal literature of Latin America.
FINDINGS: There are separate chapters on bibliographic techniques and international cooperation, bibliography, and Latin American juridical bibliography. A
bibliographic chapter is devoted to each Latin American country and Puerto Rico.
CONCLUSIONS: The author has concluded that there is no adequate bibliographical
apparatus for control of the juridical output of the world. Latin America, which has
an important body of juridical literature but no satisfactory control, should focus
efforts on the establishment of a continental, supra-national bibliographical service.

200. Williamson, William Landram (Ph.D., University of Chicago, 1959). **William**
Frederick Poole and the modern library movement. 2v.
PURPOSE: The purpose of the study was to show the influence William Frederick
Poole had on the development of modern librarianship.
PROCEDURE: The historical method of research was used.
FINDINGS: *Poole's Index*, an index to periodicals, was William Frederick Poole's
most important contribution to scholarship. In librarianship, he stood for flexibility and adaptability. Two of his ideas have been widely accepted by librarians:
the abandonment of the monument-type of library structure in favor of low-
ceilinged, flexible buildings, and subject departmentalization as a means of meeting the needs of the patron.

1960

---

201. Booth, Robert Emond, and Harrison Morton Wadsworth, Jr. (Ph.D., Western
Reserve University, 1960). **A stochastic theory of documentation systems.**

PURPOSE: The purpose of the study was to develop statistical and mathematical
models for various aspects of documentation, as guidelines for additional research.
PROCEDURE: The study was based on a literature search and on the authors'
background knowledge.
FINDINGS: The authors describe and discuss possible choices of action in various
documentation situations, taking into account recent developments in statistical
decision theory. The thesis is offered that documentation consists primarily of a
scientific attitude toward research librarianship.

202. Bundy, Mary Lee (Ph.D., University of Illinois, 1960). **The attitudes and**
opinions of farm families in Illinois towards matters related to rural library
development. 261p. Order no. 61-92.
PURPOSE: The purpose of the study was to survey Illinois farm families to determine what library materials and services they would like to have available through
a public library, and to gain an indication of their present attitude toward library
development in the state.

PROCEDURE: The basic research instrument was the questionnaire, surveying 800 Illinois farm families.
FINDINGS: The information showed that farmers were unaware of a need for improvement in library service, and were accustomed to paying a fee for the use of books.
CONCLUSIONS: The author noted that in order for library promotion to be effective, it must be based on an understanding of the farmer's way of life and the role of other agencies that serve the farmer's communications needs. Additionally, there must be a recognition of the changes that are taking place in the farm economy.
RECOMMENDATIONS: It was suggested by the author that common library practices, such as the use of bookmobiles in rural areas, should be reexamined.

203. Cantrell, Clyde Hull (Ph.D., University of Illinois, 1960). **The reading habits of ante-bellum Southerners.** 404p. Order no. 60-3886.
PURPOSE: The purpose of the study was to determine the reading habits of Southerners in the ante-bellum period from a small representative sample.
PROCEDURE: The procedure was to gather information on the reading habits of 13 persons, representing all classes in ante-bellum South except the slaves. The information was gathered from diaries, journals, autobiographies, and letters written by the individuals studied.
FINDINGS: There were 1,157 book titles mentioned in the study, divided as follows: 64 percent in the humanities, 26 percent in the social sciences, and 5.6 percent in the sciences.
CONCLUSIONS: The author indicated that the standard claims of critics who indicated that Southerners of this period read little besides Scott, the Bible, and newspapers, were refuted by the findings in this study.

204. Carrier, Esther Jane (Ph.D., University of Michigan, 1960). **Fiction in public libraries of the United States, 1876-1900.** 588p. Order no. 60-2,513.
PURPOSE: The purpose of the study was to survey the attitudes of librarians and the policies of libraries toward fiction. A comparison is also made of librarians' opinions of selected contemporary books, as opposed to the opinions of literary critics, as expressed in book reviews.
FINDINGS: During the period studied, there were two major types of fiction: in the earlier years it was the popular domestic and sensational novel, and later it was the realistic novel. While librarians supported a critical attitude toward fiction, study of popular literature of the day revealed that they were not overcritical. Two points were generally agreed on among librarians: there should be no immoral literature in the library, and librarians should endeavor to raise the level or reading. However, there was no agreement as to what was immoral, and what beginning level books should be provided. The study also showed that librarians demonstrated more leadership in demanding better books than did the literary critics.

205. Darling, Richard Lewis (Ph.D., University of Michigan, 1960). **Reviewing of children's books in American periodicals, 1865-1881.** 548p. Order no. 60-6857.
PURPOSE: The purpose of the study was to show the trends and significance of reviewing of children's books during the post-Civil War period.

FINDINGS: The study revealed that the publishing of children's books constituted an important part of publishing during this period, and that large numbers of such reviews appeared in nearly every type of contemporary magazine. The reviews, especially in *The Nation* and *Literary World*, were of high quality, evaluating both the literary quality and the interest to children.

206. Denum, Donald David (Ph.D., University of Texas, 1960). **A system of data banking and retrieval for educational research.** 172p. Order no. 60-6612.
PURPOSE: The purpose of the study was to attempt to develop a system for storage and retrieval of information for use by teachers and researchers.
PROCEDURE: The author investigated two types of systems based on concept of the bibliography of ideas: one provides for the storage of document characteristics according to a prearranged pattern fixed at the time of storage; the other, based on principles of coordinate indexing, combines flexibility of category manipulation with simplicity of classification, but contains some serious weaknesses. A modified system designed to minimize these weaknesses and to develop full potential of the coordinate indexing system is described. The study sets forth reasons for, and a description of, various operational techniques, using both a large-scale random-access (IBM Ramac 305) and a simple searching machine (the sorter).

207. Dorin, Alex (Ed.D., New York University, 1960). **Current practices in vocational high school libraries in New York City.** 212p. Order no. 60-1939.
PURPOSE: The purpose of the study was to examine the programs and practices in vocational high school libraries in New York City in terms of specific criteria, and to make recommendations for improvement.
PROCEDURE: The data were gathered from annual reports of the libraries, reports of the Director of School Library Services, from minutes and reports of the New York City School Librarians Association, from correspondence, and from interviews with approximately 100 principals, department chairmen, guidance counselors, remedial reading coordinators, and librarians.
FINDINGS: Among the findings of the study are the following: 42 percent of the high schools are staffed with two professional librarians; the library is a separate department in over 50 percent of the schools; organized programs of instruction are offered in most of the libraries; it is difficult to make use of student assistance in these schools because of their nature and organization; and libraries have difficulty in providing suitable materials, particularly in shop and technical subjects, which will meet the needs of the students.
RECOMMENDATIONS: The author recommended a systematic reappraisal of the library instruction program and adoption of a vigorous program of activities that will stimulate interest in the national cultural heritage.

208. Ducat, Sister Mary Peter Claver (D.L.S., Columbia University, 1960). **Student and faculty use of the library in three secondary schools.** 279p. Order no. 60-2,449.
PURPOSE: The purpose of the study was to determine the nature and extent of library use in three secondary schools. The study described such characteristics as sex, grade, I.Q., academic rank in class, and reading level of users and nonusers.
PROCEDURE: A number of research tools were used in the study. Questionnaires were sent out to determine the use of and attitudes toward libraries, and were

PROCEDURE (cont'd): answered by 2,266 students and 108 teachers in three coeducational parochial secondary schools in the Middle West. Records were also kept for one week to check the library use made in one school by the teachers and students. Finally, supplementary data were obtained from 932 students in one school for a depth study of characteristics of these students in relation to their use of school and public library facilities.

FINDINGS: Among the findings of the study are the following: there is a wide variance in estimates of importance of library materials among teachers within the same subject areas; only a small proportion of the students make regular and frequent visits to the school library; more good students than poor students make use of the school library; and most students use the public library to complement the school library.

CONCLUSIONS: The author found little evidence to indicate that the school library plays a vital role in the total school program. Some of the blame is placed on administrators, who do not encourage their teachers to use the school libraries as sources of materials in the teaching programs.

209. El-Sheniti, El-Sayed Mahmoud (Ph.D., University of Chicago, 1960). **The university library and the scholar: a study of the recorded faculty use of a large university library.**

210. Garrison, Guy Grady (Ph.D., University of Illinois, 1960). **Voting behavior on public library bond issues: an analysis of three elections in Seattle, Washington, 1950-1956.** 193p. Order no. 60-3919.

PURPOSE: The purpose of the study was to consider the relationships between socioeconomic characteristics of population groups and their rate of voting favorably on bond issues for the construction of a new central library building.

PROCEDURE: Socioeconomic indexes were developed, based on 1950 census data. Scores for 94 census tracts of the city given according to educational level, occupational status, social rank, urbanization, median income, home ownership, women in the labor force, and single-family dwellings. These variables were then correlated with the indexes to voting behavior to provide a basis for analysis of elections in 1950, 1952, and 1956.

RESULTS: The following results were indicated from the data: the favorable vote increased in each election; areas that increased most were those most favorable in the first election; there was a strong positive correlation between educational level and rate of favorable vote, and definite correlation between occupational status and favorable vote; there was negative correlation between median income and favorable vote and between home ownership and favorable vote; and there was a general resistance in areas where single-family, owner-occupied residences was the pattern, and where laborers formed the main occupational group.

211. Gelfand, Morris Arthur (Ph.D., New York University, 1960). **A historical study of the evaluation of libraries in higher institutions by the Middle States Association of Colleges and Secondary Schools.** 449p. Order no. 61-324.

PURPOSE: To investigate the historical background and to trace the development of policies regarding the evaluation of libraries of academic institutions by the Middle States Association of Colleges and Secondary Schools. The origin, development, and present state of accreditation by the Association is described.

PROCEDURE: The historical method was used to develop the background of the evaluation procedures. A questionnaire was then sent to librarians of all institutional members of the Association.

FINDINGS: The Association emerged as a leader in the accrediting movement in 1946 when it published new accrediting procedures. The new policies resulted in the following significant changes: the use of visiting teams of experts to conduct institutional evaluations; periodic re-evaluation of member institutions; and the use of a large number of brief statements on good educational policy and philosophy. The questionnaire revealed that the Association has been increasingly effective in encouraging the improvement of libraries.

RECOMMENDATIONS: The basic library document of the Association should be revised to make it more helpful to librarians. The Association should make future use of its basic questionnaire optional with members, but required of candidates for membership.

212. Harlan, Robert Dale (Ph.D., University of Michigan, 1960). **William Strahan: eighteenth-century London Printer and publisher.** 306p. Order no. 60-6877.

PURPOSE: The purpose of the study was to trace the development of William Strahan's publishing career between 1736 and 1785.

PROCEDURE: The information was drawn from the business records of Strahan, the books printed by his firm, and his correspondence with David Hall.

FINDINGS: Strahan was denied the right to publish by a powerful group of London publishers, so he purchased shares in authors' books. The financial success of this arrangement was such that the publishers were forced to accept Strahan as their peer. His ability to recognize bestselling potential, and his generosity to authors contributed to his eminence as a publisher.

213. Jahoda, Gerald (D.L.S., Columbia University, 1960). **Correlative indexing systems for the control of research records.** 211p. Order no. 60-3082.

PURPOSE: The purpose of the study was to investigate installations making use of correlative indexes in the physical and biological sciences to determine whether another sort of index might have been employed with equal success in these situations.

PROCEDURE: The data were gathered from a search of the literature in the field published since 1948, questionnaires, and follow-up interviews with users of correlative indexes.

CONCLUSIONS: The author concluded that the traditional indexes can be used as efficiently as correlative indexes, except in areas of chemical structure, and that, in general, different types of correlative indexes can be used with the same degree of efficiency.

214. Kephart, John Edgar (Ph.D., University of Michigan, 1960). **A voice for freedom: The Signal of Liberty, 1841-1848.** 235p. Order no. 60-2,543.

PURPOSE: The purpose of the study was to analyze and evaluate the *Signal of Liberty*, which was the official newspaper of the Michigan Anti-Slavery Society and the Michigan Liberty Party.

PROCEDURE: The author used the historical method and content analysis in the study. Among the factors considered were format, content, financial operation, and opinions and atittudes of the editors.

FINDINGS: Both the editor and his associate were active in politics and advocated reform in many areas of politics and government. The newspaper reflected the changes that were taking place within the Liberty Party leading to its collapse. CONCLUSIONS: The author has concluded that the newspaper aided the development of radical thinking which led to the formation of the Republican Party. Both the editor, Theodore Foster, and his associate, Beckley, deserve recognition for their part in the growth of Liberty Party doctrines in Michigan.

215. Kidder, Robert Wilson (Ph.D., University of Illinois, 1960). **The contribution of Daniel Fowle to New Hampshire printing, 1756-1787.** 520p. Order no. 60-1655.
PURPOSE: The purpose of the study was to trace the development and to point out the significance of the career of Daniel Fowle, printer.
PROCEDURE: The historical method of research was used, employing both primary and secondary sources.
FINDINGS: The study revealed that 50 percent of Fowle's printing was for the government. In the other categories of his printing, 56 percent was in theological works, and the next largest percentage was in the publishing of almanacs.
CONCLUSIONS: The author concluded that in general, the practices of Fowle's printing firm conformed to the accepted practices of the other colonial printers. Through his training of apprentices and his employment of junior partners, Fowle had an important effect on other printing firms in Portsmouth and Exeter.

216. Kraus, Joe Walker (Ph.D., University of Illinois, 1960). **Book collections of five colonial college libraries: a subject analysis.** 312p. Order no. 60-1,661.
PURPOSE: The purpose of the study was to consider the availability of books and the nature and use of the book collections at five colleges established during the colonial period.
PROCEDURE: The historical method was used, investigating ten printed catalogs and published lists citing principal book donations to Harvard, College of William and Mary, Yale, the College of New Jersey (Princeton), and the College of Rhode Island (Brown).
FINDINGS: The study includes a chronological account of the development of the collections, a description of the courses taught in the schools, methods used in teaching, and the academic preparation of students and teachers. The paper compares the five collections and shows the number of titles in each subject in each school. The data indicated the collections were well supplied with theological works, but not to the exclusion of important titles in history, literature, and science. Teachers and college presidents urged the students to use the libraries.

217. Kruzas, Anthony Thomas (Ph.D., University of Michigan, 1960). **The development of special libraries for American business and industry.** 361p. Order no. 60-6896.
PURPOSE: The purpose of the study was to trace the origins and development of special libraries.
PROCEDURE: The author analyzed the data from 1,000 company libraries established before 1941, and shows the distribution of libraries by type of company or business, dates of establishment, geographical distribution by state and metropolitan center, and distribution of libraries according to their functional character.

FINDINGS: The study traces company libraries from their beginnings in company offices and laboratories during the nineteenth century. Activities of company librarians, who transformed static collections into true special libraries around the turn of the century, are described.

218. Niemi, Taisto John (Ph.D., University of Michigan, 1960). **The Finnish Lutheran Book Concern, 1900-1960: a historical and developmental study.** 324p. Order no. 60-6914.
PURPOSE: The purpose of the study was to trace the historical development of a religious, Finnish-language press, as representative of the foreign language press in the United States.
PROCEDURE: The historical method of research was used, utilizing both primary and secondary sources.
FINDINGS: The study included all aspects of the historical development of the company, including the financial organization, printing activities, and its impact on Finnish immigrants. Information is also given on Finnish immigration and settlement in the United States.
CONCLUSIONS: The author concluded that the publishing house furnished excellent service to the members of the synod, as well as to other Finnish population in the area. The Concern has also furnished financial aid to the synod.

219. Parker, John (Ph.D., University of Michigan, 1960). **Books to build an empire: a bibliographical history of English overseas interests to 1620.** 419p. Order no. 60-6918.
PURPOSE: The purpose of the study was to present a survey of the literature reflective of English interest in overseas regions up to the end of 1620. An attempt was made to establish the extent of popular interest in such literature, based on the frequency with which the titles appeared.
PROCEDURE: The basic procedure was the historical method, utilizing primary and secondary sources. The author noted appeals made by authors, translators, and publishers, as well as their comments on the public attitude.
FINDINGS: Until the middle of the sixteenth century few books were published with the intent to interest English readers in acquiring overseas territories or extending commerce or religion to newly discovered lands. The travel and exploration literature published in England from 1552 to 1603 showed a gradual development of interest in discoveries of the explorers. There was also a deep concern for finding new markets and establishing colonies in the new world in order to solve England's export and population problems.

220. Penland, Patrick Robert (Ph.D., University of Michigan, 1960). **The image of public library adult education as reflected in the opinions of public library supervisory staff members in the public libraries of Michigan serving populations over 25,000.** 251p. Order no. 60-6921.
PURPOSE: The purpose of the study was to determine the image that public librarians in Michigan have of the educational function of the public library, and to decide whether the attitudes of practicing supervisory librarians are strong enough to implement the educational objectives of the library.
PROCEDURE: A sample of 260 supervisory librarians serving populations of over 25,000 completed questionnaires based on the current image of the ideal library-

PROCEDURE (cont'd): educator, and on a rating scale derived from four concepts of the mature personality according to a professional consensus on attitudes: (1) conviction that the librarian is an educator; (2) belief in the library's responsibility for adult education; (3) conviction that librarians should work with other adult education agencies; (4) the desire to serve as a resource in community improvement.

CONCLUSIONS: The author arrived at the following conclusions as a result of the study: (1) there is confusion in the minds of librarians as to what they are to do in educating adults; (2) attitudes of librarians do not keep pace with professional theory; (3) librarians are reluctant to assume educational leadership and work with consultants for community-wide adult education programs.

221. Ranz, James (Ph.D., University of Illinois, 1960). **The history of the printed book catalogue in the United States.** 326p. Order no. 60-3980.

PURPOSE: The purpose of the study was to present the historical evolution of the book catalogue from colonial times to the late nineteenth century.

PROCEDURE: The data were obtained from about 1,000 printed book catalogues, and from annual reports and histories of individual libraries.

FINDINGS: The study includes information on the development of cataloging practices, the form and rules of entry, and various efforts to develop a scheme of centralized or cooperative cataloging. The author explains why this form of catalogue. was so long regarded as ideal, and why librarians were finally forced to abandon it in favor of the card catalogue.

222. Rockwood, Ruth Humiston (Ed.D., Indiana University, 1960). **The relationship between the professional preparation and subsequent types of library positions held by a selected group of library school graduates.** 174p. Order no. 60-6,064.

PURPOSE: The purpose of the study was to examine the relationship between the professional preparation of the alumni of Florida State University Library School and positions they held after graduation.

PROCEDURE: The data were obtained from official bulletins, from records showing the courses selected, and from questionnaires covering employment and other activities since graduation.

FINDINGS: Of the 251 librarians who responded to the questionnaire, the majority had majored as undergraduates in English, education, library science, or history, and had specialized in college library service or reference work in the Library School. A close relationship was shown between the electives chosen in the area of specialization and subsequent positions. There was little relationship between the undergraduate majors and the ensuing employment.

CONCLUSIONS: The author concluded on the basis of the study that the specialized approach to library education at Florida State University should continue.

RECOMMENDATIONS: Among the recommendations offered by the author is one that library schools should consider offering a two-year sequence of highly specialized courses.

223. Scherer, Henry Howard (Ed.D., University of Southern California, 1960). **Faculty-librarian relationships in selected liberal arts colleges.** 194p. Order no. 60-4,470.

PURPOSE: The purpose of the study was to determine the nature of the relationship between faculty and librarians in liberal arts colleges.
PROCEDURE: The data were gathered from a literature search, from interviews
with faculty members and librarians, and from questionnaires completed by 1,197
individuals in 275 schools.
FINDINGS: Among the findings of the report are the following: librarians are, in
general, well-trained and accepted as full members of the faculty; the chief functions of the college library committee are to provide faculty-library liaison, develop
library resources, and integrate educational activities; faculty members and librarians cooperate to the fullest extent in acquiring and using library materials; and
faculty members and librarians regard each other as working partners in carrying
out the educational aims of the liberal arts college.
RECOMMENDATIONS: The author made the following recommendations: that
faculty members should be avid library users, expect students to use the library,
and plan assignments to make library use essential; that members of the faculty
library committee be chosen with great care; that faculty members and librarians
keep each other informed of their publications; and that the librarian should be a
member of the president's cabinet and the curriculum committee.

224. Simonton, Wesley Clark (Ph.D., University of Illinois, 1960). **Characteristics
of the research literature of the fine arts during the period 1948-1957.** 83p.
Order no. 60-1,689.
PURPOSE: The purpose of the work was to determine the characteristics of
research in the fine arts by analyzing the literature references during the 10-year
period covered.
PROCEDURE: The procedure was to analyze the footnote citations in six scholarly
journals in the field of fine arts published during the 10-year period. The journals,
chosen to represent the work of scholars of different nationalities, were *Archivo
Español de Arte, Art Bulletin, Bollettino d'Arte, Burlington Magazine, Gazette
des Beaux-Arts*, and *Zeitschrift für Kunstgeschichte*.
FINDINGS: Relatively few of the titles (18 percent) were cited more than once,
and 71 percent of all those cited were nonserial titles. Although 75 percent of the
works cited were published after 1900, less than 25 percent were published after
1940. The language and subject dispersion figures varied considerably.
CONCLUSIONS: The findings indicated that fine arts scholars are more dependent
on nonserial titles, foreign language works, and older materials than are either
scientists or social scientists.

225. Skipper, James Everett (Ph.D., University of Michigan, 1960). **The Ohio
State University Library, 1873-1913.** 321p. Order no. 60-6,937.
PURPOSE: The purpose of the study was to trace the origin and development of
the Library of Ohio State University.
PROCEDURE: The data were gathered from annual reports, committee reports,
correspondence files, newspapers, accession books, and archival material.
FINDINGS: The University was one of the many institutions of higher education
established as a result of the Morrill Act. Its library reflected the evolving educational philosophy that attempted to provide educational opportunities for the industrial and agricultural classes while attempting to maintain intellectual standards
equal to those in liberal arts schools. The study included the physical facilities,

FINDINGS (cont'd): the administrative structure, the collections, and problems concerned with the integration of departmental collections.

1961

---

226. Baillie, Gordon Stuart (Ed.D., Washington University, 1961). **Objective admission variables as they relate to academic and job success in one graduate library education program.** 228p. Order no. 61-5239.
PURPOSE: The purpose was to predict the success in graduate library school, using a group of predictor variables. A second aspect was to predict job success, using a "Job Success" rating scale. A third aspect concerned a description of the "normal" or "modal" librarian from the point of view of personality.
PROCEDURE: A group of 94 graduates of the University of Denver School of Librarianship, on the job for two years, were sent copies of the California Psychological Inventory and the "Job Success" rating scale, with directions for their use. Personal records, showing such admission variables as undergraduate grade point averages and the Graduate Record Examination scores, were also used.
FINDINGS: The following correlations with graduate grade point average were significant: undergraduate grade point average (.42); Graduate Record Examination Verbal (.34); Graduate Record Examination Quantitative (.39); California Psychological Inventory, intellectual efficiency (.22); California Psychological Inventory, psychological-mindedness (.29). The independent variables of graduate grade point average and the California Psychological Inventory scales of dominance and self-acceptance, correlated with the library "Job Success" rating scale, produced a multiple R of .33, significant at the .15 level of confidence.
CONCLUSIONS: The magnitude of the correlations between predictor variables and success in library school was large enough to warrant reliance on them for improved admissions. The conclusion that the successful graduate student in library school is, *per se*, the successful librarian on the job was positive. Correlations in this case were not strong.

227. Bedsole, Danny Travis (Ph.D., University of Michigan, 1961). **Library systems in large industrial corporations.** 540p. Order no. 61-6318.
PURPOSE: The purpose of the study was to furnish a body of knowledge and theoretical conclusions upon which the industrial corporation could base its future decision as to the organization of its library.
PROCEDURE: The procedure was to examine the organizational structures found in the following types of industrial libraries: autonomous libraries, main libraries, and branch libraries. A four-page questionnaire was mailed to 117 large industrial libraries, a case history study of one large industrial concern was made, and a personal interview survey of 21 large libraries was conducted.

228. Boll, John Jorg (Ph.D., University of Illinois, 1961). **Library architecture 1800-1875: a comparison of theory and buildings, with emphasis on New England college libraries.** 461p. Order no. 61-4263.

PURPOSE: The purpose of the study was to examine ideas on library architecture as presented in nineteenth century works on library science, and to compare these ideas with New England college libraries built prior to 1875. An examination was also made of the librarian's role in the planning of these buildings.

PROCEDURE: The historical method was used to trace the development of library architecture.

FINDINGS: The buildings constructed during this period actually conformed in many details to the theoretical ideas advocated during the nineteenth century. However, most of the structures were not in the forefront of library architecture. New ideas were largely introduced by the major libraries on both sides of the Atlantic. But the New England college libraries were functional in design; they also introduced the concept of an exit control point and were administered in a way that permitted an increasing degree of public access. The literature generally insisted that the librarian be consulted in planning the building, but this was almost never the case in practice.

229. Coburn, Louis (Ed.D., New York University, 1961). **A plan for centralized cataloging in the elementary school libraries of New York City.** 148p. Order no. 62-1439.

PURPOSE: The purpose of the study was to propose a plan for centralized cataloging in New York City's elementary school libraries.

PROCEDURE: The procedure was to gather data by means of conferences with the director of School Library Service in New York, personal visits to selected elementary school libraries, and reports submitted by principals to the Bureau of Libraries. In order to gather information on the procedures related to centralized cataloging, personal interviews were conducted with individuals at the Library of Congress, the Veterans Administration, the H. W. Wilson Company, the Brooklyn Public Library, the New York Public Library, the Queens Borough Public Library, and with companies manufacturing or distributing duplicating equipment in the metropolitan area. The proposed plan was submitted to a panel of experts for their critical evaluation, and their comments were incorporated into the final version.

RECOMMENDATIONS: Recommendations are made relative to the following items: the maintenance of a ratio of professional to clerical staff; the size and composition of supervisory, cataloging, and clerical personnel; the most desirable type of machinery to be obtained; the different kinds of records to be maintained; the content of cataloging for elementary schools; and standards for work space in the central unit. It is also suggested that the category "librarian-in-training" should be added to the central staff, and that there should be increased emphasis in library schools on centralized operation of cataloging.

230. El-Hagrasy, Saad Mohammed (Ph.D., Rutgers University, 1961). **The teacher's role in library service; an investigation and its devices.** 275p. Order no. 61-4185.

PURPOSE: The purpose of the study was to examine the validity of the hypothesis that there should be a measurable relationship between (1) teachers' reading habits and library backgrounds, as predictors and (2) pupils' reading and library skills, as criteria.

PROCEDURE: The research field consisted of 18 teachers and 161 sixth-grade children in two schools.

CONCLUSIONS: The hypothesis that there is a measurable relationship between teachers' reading habits and library backgrounds, and pupils' reading and library skills is substantiated for this sample: (1) when a teacher's reading habits and library backgrounds are significantly low, then his class's reading and library skills are significantly low; and (2) when a class's reading and library skills are significantly high, then the teacher's reading habits and library backgrounds must have been at least relatively high.

231. Ennen, Robert Campion (Ph.D., University of Michigan, 1961). **The Gradus Ad Parnassum.** 226p. Order no. 61-6348.
PURPOSE: The purpose of the study was to describe the history of the *Gradus Ad Parnassum* and its sources.
PROCEDURE: The historical method was used to trace the origin of the work in the seventeenth century and its development in the eighteenth century in France, Germany, and England.

232. Forrest, Earl Arwin, Jr. (Ph.D., University of Illinois, 1961). **A history and evaluation of English historical annuals for 1701-1720 and 1739-1743.** 646p. Order no. 61-1612.
PURPOSE: The study purposed to trace the origin, development and influence of English historical annuals through 1743, and to evaluate their accuracy and usefulness as historical and reference sources.
PROCEDURE: The dissertation was primarily concerned with four anonymously published accounts of the events of a single year published once a year: *A Compleat History of Europe* by David Jones, January 1701—August, 1714; *The History of the Reign of Queen Anne, Digested into Annals*, by Abel Boyer, March 9, 1702—April, 1713 (commonly known as *Annals of Queen Anne*); *Annals of King George*, August 1714—August 1720; *Annals of Europe*, by George Gordon, 1739-1743. The contents of the annuals were compared.
FINDINGS: The *Annals* were better in parliamentary reporting; the *Compleat History* was better for obituaries and civil and military lists. The annuals were remarkably similar in selecting and reporting of events; this is due both to copying from one another and to use of the same sources (e.g., Boyer's *Political State of Great Britain*). In checking historical and biographical works it was found that the annuals were rarely used. The annuals contain a considerable amount of raw materials: documents, letters and other papers. They are most useful today for reports of obscure events, civil and military lists, biographies, observations on personalities and events, and as a general review of the times. They influenced the content and form of such periodicals as *Political State*, the *Gentlemen's London*, and *Scots*. The annuals and the magazines were precursors of the annual register type. Bibliographies of English and American publications of this type through 1835 are appended in the dissertation.

233. Hagler, Ronald Albert (Ph.D., University of Michigan, 1961). **The selection and acquisition of books in six Ontario public libraries in relation to the Canadian publishing system.** 255p. Order no. 61-1392.
PURPOSE: The purpose of the study was to investigate the selection and purchase of English language books by medium-sized public libraries in English speaking Canada.

PROCEDURE: The study involved an eight-month period, during which time a record was kept of purchases of adult titles. The record included such items of information as subject, time of publication, country of origin, etc. A sample of 4,000 titles actually selected by the six libraries was gathered.

FINDINGS: There are relatively few Canadian selection guides available to the Canadian librarian. This means that the librarian is forced to use the British and American reviews and bibliographies. As a result, there is a broader range of acquisitions in Canadian libraries than in comparable libraries elsewhere. Since there are fewer British selection tools than American, there is an observed tendency toward ignoring British publications. The Canadian publishing system helps to maintain a balance between British and American acquisitions.

234. Hines, Theodore Christian (Ph.D., Rutgers University, 1961). **The collectanea as a bibliographic tool.** 233p. Order no. 61-4194.

PURPOSE: The purpose of the study was to determine the usefulness of the collectanea as a bibliographical tool.

PROCEDURE: The procedure was to examine in some detail a number of existing information retrieval systems that are collectanea.

FINDINGS: As a mechanical information retrieval device, the collectanea has higher costs than other tools that provide the same service except in unusual circumstances, in which the use level is high and special conditions can markedly reduce input costs.

CONCLUSIONS: The collectanea concept is a useful one. Alternatives to the collectanea include state-of-the-art studies and encyclopedic summaries as well as other bibliographic studies.

235. Hoage, Alethia Annette Lewis (D.L.S., Columbia University, 1961). **The Library of Congress Classification in the United States: a survey of opinions and practices, with attention to problems of structure and application.** 245p. Order No. 61-3434.

PURPOSE: The purposes were to (1) study the development and structure of the Library of Congress Classification in relation to its use; (2) survey librarians' views and determine the extent of their direct and modified use of it as a classification aid; and (3) analyze and make suggestions for use of the classification by patrons.

PROCEDURE: Questionnaires, interviews, and related literature were used in the study; a sample of 117 libraries was selected for the research. Patrons in nine libraries also completed questionnaires.

FINDINGS: The classification was rated highest for comprehensiveness, practicality, and up-to-dateness. Catalogers estimated that they accept 90 to 99 percent of the numbers in the schedules and on the cards and proof-sheets. A majority of the classifiers reported that a comprehensive index and more assistance in interpreting the schedules are needed.

RECOMMENDATIONS: Suggestions for further research include studies of the acceptance of centralized classification, use of the classification as an aid in reference service, patron behavior, and the classification process.

236. Holley, Edward Gailon (Ph.D., University of Illinois, 1961). **Charles Evans: American bibliographer.** 593p. Order no. 61-4311.

PURPOSE: The purpose of this work was to point out the importance of Charles Evans as a pioneer in American bibliography and librarianship.
PROCEDURE: The historical method was used.
FINDINGS: Evans' greatest contribution was his *American Bibliography*, recording American printing from 1639 to 1799.

237. Kilpela, Raymond Earl Oliver (Ph.D., University of Michigan, 1961). **A comparative study of library legislation in Indiana, Michigan, and Ohio.** 397p. Order no. 61-6376.
PURPOSE: The purpose of the study was to describe, analyze, and compare the legal basis, structure, powers, and sources of support of the public library in Indiana, Michigan, and Ohio.
PROCEDURE: Materials used for this comparative study were the statutes, court decisions, attorneys'-general opinions, and municipal charters.
FINDINGS: Two major differences exist between the Michigan library legislation and the Indiana and Ohio library laws. Library boards in Michigan represent the "weak" type of boards, and the boards of Indiana and Ohio represent the "strong" type.

238. Kittle, Arthur Thomas (D.L.S., Columbia University, 1961). **Management theories in public library administration in the United States, 1925-1955.** 289p. Order no. 61-3446.
PURPOSE: The purpose was to show the extent to which concepts of administration-staff relationships in public libraries have paralleled developments in comparable aspects of administrative theory in the field of management.
PROCEDURE: The subject was approached through the literatures of management and librarianship, and through a case study of a public library system. The Enoch Pratt Free Library in Baltimore was selected for the case study. Three aspects of its development were reported: (1) growth and extension of services; (2) growth of personnel; and (3) administration-staff relationships.
FINDINGS: The beginning of management theory occurred in the nineteenth century. Several librarians during that early period expressed an interest in a business-like approach to library management, but the ideas of scientific management were not treated prominently in library literature until after World War II.

239. Morrison, Perry (D.L.S., University of California, Berkeley, 1961). **The career of the academic librarian.**
PURPOSE: The purpose of the study was to present a picture of the people employed as academic librarians, in terms of their personal characteristics, family background, education, interests, attitudes, and motivations.
PROCEDURE: The questionnaire was the basic research instrument in the study. The primary group studied was composed of 231 head librarians who earned more than $6,000 in 1956-57. The control group consisted of 476 "ordinary" librarians chosen from the 1955 edition of *Who's Who in Library Service*.
FINDINGS: Among the findings of the group are the following: (1) people entering academic librarianship during the period tended to come from families of rather high social and educational, but not economic, status; (2) the Midwest tends to export library talent to other parts of the country; (3) the second-year master's degree in library science was an influential degree, particularly for women; (4) the

FINDINGS (cont'd): practice of appointing doctorates in library science seems to be supplanting the older tendency to recruit executives from among members of the faculty who do not have library science training; (5) among academic librarians, early consideration of, and commitment to, librarianship as a career is associated with high future status and salary; (6) academic librarians can be described as cultured and intelligent, but lacking in traits associated with forceful leadership.

240. Rouse, Roscoe (Ph.D., University of Michigan, 1961). **A history of the Baylor University library, 1845-1919.** 390p. Order no. 62-3257.
PURPOSE: The purpose of the dissertation was to trace the history of the library of Baylor University from its earliest recorded existence to 1919.
PROCEDURE: The historical method was used, from private papers, association and board minutes, correspondence, and other archival material.
FINDINGS: Evidence indicates that a library existed within the institution early in its history. By the close of the study in 1919, the library was an established, functioning, and effective service department of the University.

241. Sisson, Silvanus Hull (Ed.D., The University of Nebraska Teachers College, 1961). **Planning the junior high school library program.** 142p. Order no. 61-1,473.
PURPOSE: The objective of this study was to describe an adequate program of library service for the junior high school. It was proposed to identify those elements of superior libraries that inadequate library programs lack and to determine their importance to the junior high school program.
PROCEDURE: Questionnaires were sent to 50 state departments of education. A checklist of 40 "Significant Elements Making for Adequate Library Service in Junior High Schools" was given to 29 selected librarians and others writing and working on school library problems.
FINDINGS: There was no evidence of any planning for the "unique needs" of the junior high school library by the state departments of education. The quantitative standards provided in state regulations for any level of school library service were far below those recommended nationally by the American Association of School Librarians. Many of the states had one minimum professional level for all school librarians, but the majority still set or permitted lesser standards for those librarians serving in the elementary or junior high schools. Many library programs in junior high schools lacked those features declared essential by the panel of expert opinion utilized in this study.

242. Stevens, Norman Dennison (Ph.D., Rutgers University, 1961). **A comparative study of three systems of information retrieval.** 143p. Order no. 61-4217.
PURPOSE: The purpose of the study was to compare three systems of information retrieval: a punched card file, a handbook reproduced from that file, and the more conventional library reference approach.
PROCEDURE: The three systems were examined in terms of input, use, and output factors to determine elements affecting conditions of use.
FINDINGS: It was found that for most questions the handbook was a more efficient retrieval tool than the card file. Input costs, as well as cost per usage, were much higher for the mechanized data-extracting approach than for library

FINDINGS (cont'd): techniques. On almost every basis the conventional library approach compared favorably with the other two systems.

243. Van Note, Roy Nelson. (Ph.D., University of Illinois, 1961). **Brush and Pencil: tastemaker of American art.** 446p. Order no. 62-690.
PURPOSE: The purpose of the study was to describe the development and importance of the periodical *Brush and Pencil* from 1897 to 1907.
FINDINGS: The periodical maintained a fairly conservative attitude toward painting. It displayed a strong interest in the American interpretation of the arts and craft movement. It encouraged sculpture, but frowned on bold innovation. It also encouraged art education at all levels, and even suggested aids for teaching art in the grade schools.

244. Wasserman, Paul (Ph.D., The University of Michigan, 1961). **Toward a methodology for the formulation of objectives in public libraries: an empirical analysis.** 207p. Order no. 61-1804.
PURPOSE: The purpose of the study was to design and to test a method for eliciting attitudes from the various groups concerned, which public libraries in cities of medium size—30,000 to 50,000 population—can make use of in the formulation of their goals and objectives.
PROCEDURE: Questionnaires and field analyses were used to test objective formulation in three different public libraries of varying size, composition and levels of financial support.
FINDINGS: The impetus for specification of goals in any given institution must come from the professional librarians; serious and sustained attention to problems of objective formulation is highly unlikely in an underfinanced or understaffed library; and, a complete inventory of complementary programs in the community is essential to an institutional formulation.

1962

245. Bishop, Olga Bernice (Ph.D., University of Michigan, 1962). **Publications of the government of the Province of Canada, 1841-1867.** 407p. Order no. 63-314.
PURPOSE: The purpose of the study was to investigate the type of documents published and to prepare a bibliography of the publications issued by the government of the province of Canada, 1841 to June, 1867.
PROCEDURE: Three libraries rich in Canadiana and government publications were selected for the study, and their catalogs checked for any publications on Canada issued between 1841 and 1867. The journals of the Legislative Council and Legislative Assembly of Canada were checked for reports printed by these two bodies.
FINDINGS: The study showed that over 1,400 titles were published by the government of the Province of Canada. The documents can be classified under seven services: Governor-General, Legislative, Executive, Educational and Scientific

FINDINGS (cont'd): Institutions, Administration of Justice, and Miscellaneous Boards and Trusts. Within each service the documents can be classified under the several branches or departments that make up any given service.

CONCLUSIONS: The following conclusions have been drawn from the study: (1) the documents constitute one of the excellent primary sources of information on Canada between the years 1841 and 1867; (2) the documents need to be examined for an understanding of twentieth century political, economic, and social institutions in Canada; and (3) the documents produce little of value in the scientific field, since the founding of scientific institutions in Canada belongs largely to the twentieth century.

246. Harrar, Helen Joanne (Ph.D., Rutgers University, 1962). **Cooperative storage warehouses.** 209p. Order no. 62-5297.

PURPOSE: The purpose of the study was to examine and evaluate the philosophy, programs and operations of each warehouse, and to recommend optimum measures for achieving their objectives.

PROCEDURE: Each warehouse was visited, its operations observed, desk audits made, and records of materials input and use studied.

CONCLUSIONS: There were four major conclusions: (1) the cost of operating cooperative warehouses is higher than the literature indicates; (2) the cost of cataloging is lower due to the use of simplified cataloging; (3) there is a growing trend away from the demand for off-campus cooperative storage, even among the participants in these centers; (4) gains actually achieved by cooperative storage warehouses could be obtained at lower cost and with greater convenience of access through identical storage and processing of materials by the individual libraries.

247. Maciuszko, Jerzy Janusz (Ph.D., Case Western Reserve University, 1962). **The Polish short story in English translation: a critical bibliography.**

248. Marino, Samuel Joseph (Ph.D., University of Michigan, 1962). **The French-refugee newspapers and periodicals in the United States, 1789-1825.** 394p. Order no. 63-400.

PURPOSE: The purpose of the study was to examine the newspaper and periodical publications of the French refugees in the United States between 1789 and 1825.

PROCEDURE: The historical method was used in describing the French-language newspapers and periodicals of this period.

FINDINGS: One chapter deals with the historical summary of the emigrations to the United States, and includes a general profile of the editors of the publications. The second chapter is a history of French-language printing in this country to 1825. The third chapter is a study of the general characteristics of the newspapers and periodicals.

CONCLUSIONS: Much of the content of the publications is valueless; the bulk simply reprints of the mediocre literary talent of the pre-Romantic period, newspaper borrowings of current events, and documents.

249. Melvin, Sister M. Constance (Ph.D., University of Chicago, 1962). **History of public school libraries in Pennsylvania.** 600p.

250. Monroe, Margaret Ellen (D.L.S., Columbia University, 1962). **The evolving conception of adult education in three public libraries: 1920-1955.** 551p. Order no. 65-7384.

PURPOSE: The purpose of the study was to trace the evolution of library adult education to see what extent the concept changed in basic direction, to what extent the changes were in fulfillment of a consistent purpose, and to what extent the library's materials were a dominant factor in the determination of the adult education services.

PROCEDURE: Reports of the three libraries, plus books and articles written by members of the staffs, were subjected to textual analysis. The content analysis was supplemented by interviews.

FINDINGS: There have been two major achievements of library adult education. It has been the means by which services to adults have been professionalized. It has also provided leadership to the library profession.

251. Montgomery, John Warwick (Ph.D., University of Chicago, 1962). **The libraries of France at the ascendancy of Mazarin: Louis Jacob's Traicte des plus belles bibliothèques.**

252. Munn, Robert Ferguson (Ph.D., University of Michigan, 1962). **West Virginia University library, 1867-1917.** 260p. Order no. 62-2770.

PROCEDURE: The historical method was used. In addition, one chapter presents a comparison with five other state university libraries.

FINDINGS: The pattern of reasonably adequate library service was established in a brief "golden period" from 1897 to 1901. The period between 1897 and 1912 was a great era of reform in the five other state university libraries, as well as at West Virginia University. New buildings were erected, professional librarians employed, and financial support increased. West Virginia was a leader in this reform. It was the first of the six schools to employ a trained head librarian, the first to build an adequate library building, the first to offer instruction to school librarians, and among the first to carry through a complete recataloging program.

253. Parker, Johnny Robert (Ed.D., The University of North Carolina, 1962). **An analysis of library services in elementary grades of selected classified schools in North Carolina.** 166p. Order no. 63-3510.

PURPOSE: The purposes of this study were (1) to determine the status of library services provided for elementary school children in North Carolina, (2) to analyze these library services in terms of state and national standards, and (3) to develop a plan for improving elementary school library services in North Carolina.

PROCEDURE: Data for this study were taken from the 1960-1961 annual report on "Instructional Materials: Library and Audio-Visual" submitted by 191 school principals to the North Carolina Department of Public Instruction and from a questionnaire sent to the principal of each school included in the project.

FINDINGS: While two-thirds of the schools met the North Carolina requirement for having a "teacher-librarian," little more than one-fourth of them allotted the librarian as much as two hours per day for library work with elementary school children. No schools met the national standard for library personnel. The average per student expenditure for library books and magazines was found to be $1.39. A clear picture of the expenditure for audio-visual aids could not be secured. State funds

FINDINGS (cont'd): constituted the chief source of funds for the purchase of library materials. Book collections averaged between six and seven books per student. Only four schools failed to meet the state standard of three books per student; 24 schools met the national standard of 10 books per student. Organization for easy access to materials was lacking in most schools. Most schools provided a fairly adequate central library room, but not facilities for conferences or work-storage. A good program of library instruction and reading guidance was found in few schools.

CONCLUSIONS: The findings indicate the need for a revision of North Carolina standards for the elementary school library. The budget for printed materials should average $4.00 per student. The book collection should average 10 books per student. Seating space for 10 percent of the student body should be provided in a central library with space requirements based upon 30 square feet per reader.

254. Slamecka, Vladimir (D.L.S., Columbia University 1962). **The semi-centralized system of technical documentation and information of the Czechoslovak Socialist Republic and East Germany.** 216p. Order no. 62-4249.

PURPOSE: The objectives of the study are as follows: (1) to describe two variants of the "semi-centralized" national system of technical documentation and information; and (2) to analyze and discuss effects of the objectives, organization, and operation of the two variants of the semi-centralized system on five parameters of performance of this system type.

PROCEDURE: The method of documentary analysis was used by the author in this study.

FINDINGS: The study describes the organization and operation of the Czechoslovak and East German national systems, and identifies the political, economic, and administrative factors associated with their choice and development.

255. Vance, Kenneth E. (Ed.D., University of Michigan, 1962). **The professional status of school librarians in Michigan elementary schools enrolling 500 or more students.** 232p. Order no. 63-463.

PURPOSE: The purpose of the study was to determine the professional status of librarians in Michigan.

PROCEDURE: The study was limited to librarians employed in public elementary schools enrolling 500 or more students during the 1959-60 school year. Data were gathered by questionnaires sent to 285 school librarians in 224 accredited schools. The returns of the 252 respondents were grouped according to the accreditation status of the school in which they were employed, and the amount of time devoted to the library.

FINDINGS: The study showed that considerable progress had been made during the past 30 years in regard to the professional status of librarians. The respondents meet the criteria of the North Central Association of Colleges and Secondary Schools in regard to academic and professional training and certification. The schools, however, do not meet entirely the specifications in terms of numbers of personnel. In general, the librarians hold the status of teacher. Most of the respondents indicated satisfaction with school librarianship as a profession.

RECOMMENDATIONS: The following recommendations are made for more effective school library programs: (1) more knowledge about the availability and use of non-book materials; (2) greater competency in the production of instructional

RECOMMENDATIONS (cont'd): materials; (3) closer working relationships with administrators in planning new programs and facilities; (4) closer relationships with audiovisual departments; (5) added services to teachers; (6) planned programs of library instruction for all students; (7) closer cooperation with the public library; (8) greater participation in in-service programs; (9) more clerical assistance in libraries; (10) more supervision of school libraries by trained library personnel.

1963

---

256. Artandi, Susan Szerdahelyi (Ph.D., Rutgers University, 1963). **Book indexing by computer.** 211p. Order no. 63-8074.
PURPOSE: The purpose of the study was the development and evaluation of a method of deriving suitable index entries automatically from natural language text.
PROCEDURE: The experimental procedure produced an index, which was then evaluated by using a measure of indexing developed for this purpose. Evaluation was based on a comparison of the experimental index with actual published indexes.
FINDINGS: The dictionary, a selective list of terms that can be anticipated for a subject area, can be an effective tool for the selection of indexable matter from natural language text. The index produced by the experimental procedure compares favorably with the average published index. The cost can be reduced by eliminating some of the procedures used in this study, and by using more suitable equipment. The dictionary method is limited to indexing of secondary publications. Machine indexing of proper nouns is more expensive than manual indexing of proper nouns.

257. Badr, Ahmad Aly (Ph.D., Case Western Reserve University, 1963). **International cooperation in scientific documentation and its implications within the functionalist approach to international relations with special reference to Indian, U.S.S.R., U.A.R., and U.S.A.**

258. Bishop, Martha Dell (Ed.D., George Peabody College for Teachers, 1963). **Identification of valuable learning experiences in centralized elementary school libraries.** 147p. Order no. 64-4000.
PURPOSE: The purpose of the study was to identify experiences that children have in good centralized libraries in elementary schools, and to determine which experiences facilitated and which retarded learning.
PROCEDURE: A group of 397 fifth and sixth grade students from six schools in Oak Park, Illinois, and Arlington, Virginia, was used. The "critical incident" technique was used to gather the data. This consisted essentially of obtaining descriptions of specific incidents during personal interviews. The behaviors involved determined whether the children's experiences were good or bad.
FINDINGS: The seven critical elements that influenced the outcome of the incidents were the librarian, materials and equipment, activities and privileges, conduct of the persons in the library, atmosphere in the library, the other pupils, and the library as a separate entity. Conduct was a vital concern, with misbehavior mentioned most frequently.

259. Clarke, Robert Flanders (Ph.D., Rutgers University, 1963). **The impact of photocopying on scholarly publishing.** 88p. Order no. 63-8071.

PURPOSE: The study was undertaken to determine the impact of photocopying on publishing.

PROCEDURE: The procedure was first to examine records of photocopying of dissertations for separate bibliographic units. Next, records of journal photocopying were examined at three major library photocopy services.

FINDINGS: For dissertations, neither the mean nor the median number of photocopies produced reached a level of three copies. Most dissertations were never copied and approximately 90 percent of them were copied five times or less. Less than one percent of them were copied more than 20 times. For journal photocopying, over 50 percent of the articles copied came from foreign periodicals. On a projected nationwide basis, the amount of journal photocopying amounted to less than one percent of the volume of articles originally published.

CONCLUSIONS: The volume of photocopying of dissertations does not approach that of conventional publishing, and there is no indication that it is likely to do so. The volume of photocopying of journals is so small, in relation to the total subscriptions, that it could not make any appreciable difference in sales. Over a period of 20 years, if one or two articles are needed per year from any one-year volume, it is almost always cheaper to own the periodical than to buy photocopies.

260. Dougherty, Richard Martin (Ph.D., Rutgers University, 1963). **The scope and operating efficiency of information centers as illustrated by the Chemical-Biological Coordination Center of the National Research Council.** 249p. Order no. 63-8103.

FINDINGS: A comparison with other agencies showed that the Center's functions were similar to those of other information centers. Although lack of cost data prevented precise measurement of input and retrieval costs, it was found that input costs per request successfully answered from the files amounted to $1,873.

CONCLUSIONS: An information center's objectives and scope must be clearly defined in order to achieve optimum usefulness. The study also concluded that a successful center must have the following skills represented: specialized subject knowledge; bibliographic technique; knowledge of alternative devices for handling information; and administrative ability to identify, direct, and coordinate the first three functions.

261. Gambee, Budd Leslie, Jr. (Ph.D., University of Michigan, 1963). **Frank Leslie's Illustrated Newspaper, 1855-1860: artistic and technical operations of a pioneer pictorial news weekly in America.** 447p. Order no. 63-6897.

PURPOSE: The purpose of the study was to describe the first successful attempt to establish pictorial journalism on a highly developed scale.

PROCEDURE: The historical method was used, in examining the first five years of the newspaper. Biographical material was provided for Leslie (Henry Carter) and for the seven artist-reporters who created most of the news illustrations for the paper during the period.

262. Heinritz, Fred John (Ph.D., Rutgers University, 1963). **Book versus card catalog costs.** 168p. Order no. 64-543.

PURPOSE: The purpose of the study was to determine from an existing situation whether it was cheaper to produce, distribute, and use a book catalog or a card catalog.

PROCEDURE: Consultation times for book and card were determined by looking up sample entries in the card catalogs of a small college library and a large public library. The same entries were then looked up in the *National Union Catalog*. Production and distribution costs were studied at *Engineering Index* offices, because it produces a file in both card and book form.

CONCLUSIONS: The basic conclusion was that the book form of the catalog was cheaper than the card form. A secondary conclusion was that the book form of the catalog was cheaper than a combination card-book form. It was found that using the book catalog took more time. This user cost was more than offset by the book catalog savings in the matter of production, distribution, filing, equipment, and space.

263. Hiatt, Peter (Ph.D., Rutgers University, 1963). **Public library branch service for adults of low education.** 253p. Order no. 63-5886.

PURPOSE: The purpose of the study was to investigate the effectiveness of specially adapted branch library services in encouraging interest in library use among adults of low education.

PROCEDURE: The case study approach was used, involving two branch libraries which have high adult registration percentages and programs of special services. A community profile and a study of the program of adult services for each branch was included. Adults of eighth grade education were interviewed in each branch, and an analysis of the interviews made.

FINDINGS: The following adapted adult services were shown to have a direct relationship to interest in library use by adults: location of a high-quality branch library in a low education neighborhood; easy accessibility to professional librarians; special attempt to build rapport and make the adults feel comfortable in the library; easy reading materials for adults; film programs and other group programs.

264. Kortendick, James J. (Ph.D., Catholic University, 1963). **The library in the Catholic theological seminary in the United States.** 365p. Order no. 63-7565.

PURPOSE: The author had three purposes in mind in undertaking this study: to investigate the role of the library in the training of students for the Catholic priesthood; to interpet the objectives of the library in light of the objectives of the seminary; and to survey the administrative and organizational structure of the seminary library.

PROCEDURE: A group of 104 theological seminaries were surveyed by questionnaire.

FINDINGS: Seminary libraries have not shared in the rapid development of college and university libraries during the previous 25 years. Reasons given for this retarded growth are: shortage of personnel, limited funds, fewer curriculum changes, and a lack of conviction on the part of the administration concerning the importance of the library.

265. Laugher, Charles Theodore (Ph.D., Case Western Reserve University, 1963). **The beginnings of the library in colonial America: Dr. Thomas Bray and the religious societies, 1695-1795.**

266. Lesser, Daniel (Ed.D., Syracuse University, 1963). **A study to determine the nature and status of children's film programs in public libraries of the Northeastern United States.** 153p. Order no. 64-5671.

PURPOSE: The purpose was to determine the extent to which children's film programs have been provided in public libraries of the Northeast, and to describe the principal characteristics of these programs.

PROCEDURE: A questionnaire instrument was formulated and administered to 384 libraries representing a 20 percent random sampling of this 11-state region.

FINDINGS: The author reported the following findings: (1) 16 percent of the respondents reported making regular use of children's films; (2) film cooperatives were used predominantly by the larger institutions, while the smaller organizations tended to rely on lending agencies; (3) the largest proportion of showings were for children in the primary and intermediate grade levels; (4) newspapers and school announcements were considered the best publicity media for attracting audiences; (5) inadequate financing appeared as the primary cause for omission of the film programs.

RECOMMENDATIONS: The findings led to the following recommendations: (1) practicing librarians should acquire knowledge and experience in film utilization through in-service education activities; (2) information of successful film programs should be publicized through the professional literature; (3) cooperatives should be established for the acquisition and distribution of films; (4) librarians should cooperate with filmmakers in order to insure the availability of films for juvenile audiences; (5) comprehensive survey studies should be conducted on various aspects of children's film programs in public libraries throughout the country.

267. McCreedy, Sister Mary Lucille (D.L.S., Columbia University, 1963). **The selection of school librarianship as a career.** 356p. Order no. 64-5420.

PURPOSE: The major purpose of the study was to determine the factors which influenced school librarians to select their profession. Another purpose was to determine the reasons why students select other areas of librarianship instead of the school field.

PROCEDURE: The basic research instrument was the questionnaire, with responses from 560 secondary school librarians and school library supervisors in four states; 1,297 students in accredited library schools; and 297 students in selected undergraduate library science departments.

FINDINGS: The following finds resulted from the survey: (1) a wide range of reasons were given for the selection of school librarianship, including enjoyment of books, liking for young people, and a desire for intellectually stimulating work; (2) many school librarians were influenced to enter school librarianship while engaged in another profession, especially teaching; (3) working as a student assistant in a school library was often mentioned as a contributing factor in the decision to become a school librarian; (4) good school libraries with active programs of service attracted many people into the profession.

268. McCusker, Sister Mary Girolama (D.L.S., Columbia University, 1963). **The accessibility of books in elementary schools without libraries.** 331p. Order no. 64-2773.

PURPOSE: The purpose of the study was to test the hypothesis that Iowa elementary schools without school libraries do not have well-rounded and well-selected

PURPOSE (cont'd): book collections that meet the needs of the modern elementary school's teaching program and its pupils.

PROCEDURE: Questionnaires were sent to 432 teachers, 272 school district superintendents, 49 county superintendents, 415 parents, and 192 children. Case studies were made by visiting all schools and public libraries in one representative county, two schools and public libraries in a city, and one school and public library in a town.

FINDINGS: The major findings were as follows: (1) the median per pupil expenditure for books was $1.31; (2) book selection was often done from book clubs, book company salesmen, and education periodicals; (3) none of the case schools had aggregate collections that met state or national standards for size of collection; (4) classroom collections were inadequate to satisfy the reading needs of the students; (5) there were almost no other sources of books in the county.

RECOMMENDATIONS: Since collections assembled by personnel not trained in book selection were inadequate, the answer to providing well-selected book collections lies in the provision for school libraries staffed by qualified librarians. A state school library supervisor should be appointed to provide leadership in the development of adequate library programs. Educational institutions should cooperate in preparing teachers and administrators for their responsibility with regard to the role of the school library.

269. Oller, Anna Kathryn (Ph.D., University of Michigan, 1963). **Christopher Saur, colonial printer. A study of the publications of the press, 1738-1758.** 340p. Order no. 64-865.

PURPOSE: The purpose of this study was to investigate the output of the press of Christopher Saur in order to substantiate his contribution to colonial printing and to show the kinds of material available from a German language press.

PROCEDURE: The author analyzed the content of the extant publications of the press, including the almanac, the newspaper, and 150 books, pamphlets, and broadsides issued.

CONCLUSIONS: The following conclusions are offered as a result of the study: (1) the reading material provided by this press was a contributing factor in molding the political and religious opinions among the German colonists and, to a lesser extent, among other colonists; (2) the press attempted to be an educational agency for the German immigrants; (3) and the press set a standard of typographical excellence not usually met during this period.

270. Painter, Ann Forbes (Ph.D., Rutgers University, 1963). **An analysis of duplication and consistency of subject indexing involved in report handling at the Office of Technical Services, U.S. Department of Commerce.** 141p. Order no. 64-1166.

PURPOSE: The purpose of the study was to determine the amount of duplication and the consistency of the subject indexing done at the Office of Technical Services, with a view toward machine application.

FINDINGS: Machine search was considered to be feasible at the simplest level of processing. A study of three indexing systems indicated that there was 60 to 70 percent consistency in indexing. The relatively low level of consistency showed that a table of equivalents is at present of little value in either a manual or a machine system.

271. Searcy, Herbert Lyman (Ph.D., University of Illinois, 1963). **Parochial libraries in the American colonies.** 234p. Order no. 64-6,146.

PURPOSE: The purpose of the study was to trace the development of parochial libraries in the colonies, and particularly the role of Dr. Thomas Bray in that development.

FINDINGS: Thomas Bray was responsible for the establishment of at least 39 key parochial libraries, and for sending 34,000 books, tracts, and pamphlets to the American colonies.

272. Tate, Elizabeth Lamb (Ph.D., University of Chicago, 1963). **Effective main entries: a comparison of the A.L.A. Cataloging Code with Seymour Lubetzky's draft revision in relation to bibliographic citations.**

PURPOSE: The purpose of the study was to determine if the main entries stipulated by the revised rules will locate items more directly than the main entries prepared according to the second edition of the A.L.A. Code.

PROCEDURE: A random sample of 606 bibliographic citations was collected. The authorship of each citation was determined. An attempt was made to locate each citation in the appropriate catalog of the Library of Congress. Headings of the Library of Congress cards that conformed to the second edition of the A.L.A. Code were accepted verbatim; the others were revised. The two main entries were then compared with the authorship element of the citation. For each of the 606 works, the choice of main entry and, when necessary, the form of the main entry were determined first, according to the provisions of the 1949 edition of the A.L.A. Code and second in accordance with the "Code of Cataloging Rules" as of September 1961 (Lubetzky).

FINDINGS: The main entries constructed according to the rules of the September, 1961, version of the revised code will link the citations with the work more directly than the main entries produced by the rules of the 1949 edition of the A.L.A. Code. The rules in the revised code that proved most efficacious in effecting this improvement are the rules that provide for entry under the form of name as used by an author, and especially the rule that permits entry of a serial under its successive titles. Corporate authorship, and especially governmental headings, will probably remain the major problem in finding materials. A.L.A. rules proved no more effective in locating legal materials than did the rules in the "Code of Cataloging Rules." With regard to secondary entries, reasonably close correspondence between the title reported in the citation and the title in the work was observed. The data suggested that the title added entry has very considerable potential in locating material. The added entry for a joint author is the most useful of the other secondary entries for locating material.

273. Walker, Richard Dean (Ph.D., University of Illinois, 1963). **The influence of antecedent library service upon academic achievement of University of Illinois freshmen.** 120p. Order no. 64-2983.

PURPOSE: The purpose of the study was to test whether or not the availability of high school and public library service makes a significant contribution to the formal education of students.

PROCEDURE: In order to test the hypothesis, multiple regression analysis was used. There were three samples: a primary sample consisted of 552 students from the state of Illinois, a subsample consisted of 86 students from Chicago, and a

PROCEDURE (cont'd): second subsample consisted of 466 non-Chicago residents.

FINDINGS: The study showed no significant difference in grades for students originating from communities with high level library service available and students from communitites with poor or no library service available. There seemed to be a difference in the contribution made by the availability of library service to academic achievement of students in the various colleges of the University of Illinois.

274. Warner, John Ellsworth (Ed.D., Columbia University, 1963). **The role of the librarian as a co-worker in guidance from the viewpoint of the guidance worker.** 236p. Order no. 63-5867.

PURPOSE: The purpose of the study was to determine the contribution of librarians to educational, vocational, social, and personal guidance, as viewed by guidance workers.

PROCEDURE: The basic information was elicited from a questionnaire completed by guidance workers in selected schools representing each region of continental United States.

CONCLUSIONS: Much work remains if the librarian is to be effective as a co-worker in guidance. School librarians will need to acquire specialized training in guidance. Guidance workers will need to re-examine their attitudes toward the potential contributions of other faculty members in guidance, and be responsible for in-service training of other faculty members in guidance work.

275. Webb, David Allen (Ph.D., University of Chicago, 1963). **Local efforts to prepare library assistants and librarians in Texas from 1900 to 1942.** 357p.

1964

276. De Hart, Florence Elizabeth (Ph.D., Rutgers University, 1964). **The application of special library services and techniques to the college library.** 223p. Order no. 64-10,908.

PURPOSE: The purpose of the study was to test the hypothesis that the provision of special library services and techniques by a college library for a current, on-going course will result in more and better service to users than when they were not provided.

PROCEDURE: In two phases there were additional services made available to a selected group of English professors. In order to measure usage of library materials promoted in the two phases, a recording device was established. Questionnaires were also sent to the professors and to students in one class.

FINDINGS: The data disproved the hypothesis of the study. There was some agreement that the information and services provided were of some value, although there was no immediate effect on the courses being taught.

277. De Koster, Lester Ronald (Ph.D., University of Michigan, 1964). **Living themes in the thought of John Calvin. A bibliographical study.** 572p. Order no. 64-12,584.

PURPOSE: The author had three purposes in mind in undertaking this study: (1) to investigate which facets of thought of John Calvin elicit modern scholarly attention; (2) to investigate what Calvin himself had to say about these matters; and (3) to furnish a guide to the literature written about each of these facets since 1900.

PROCEDURE: A bibliography of 1,730 books and periodical articles was compiled. These studies of Calvin and Calvinism were then divided into "themes" to ascertain which facets of Calvin's system are still alive in modern scholarly discussion. The second phase was the compilation of representative quotations that would adequately exhibit Calvin's own views on the "themes." The third aspect of the study was to develop a separate introduction to each thematic bibliography.

278. Dickinson, Donald Charles (Ph.D., University of Michigan, 1964). **A bio-bibliography of Langston Hughes, 1920-1960.** 303p. Order no. 65-5891.

PURPOSE: The purpose of the study was to describe and analyze the literary output of Langston Hughes between 1920 and 1960.

PROCEDURE: Langston Hughes' works were analyzed from both the biographical and the bibliographical points of view.

FINDINGS: Langston Hughes was a leader in the Harlem Renaissance, a group of young Negro writers who believed in a realistic portrayal of their own people. Hughes was popular, yet he never received the critical acclaim due him.

279. El-Benhawy, Mohamed Amin (Ph.D., University of Michigan, 1964). **The Suez Canal. A descriptive bibliography.** 316p. Order no. 64-12,588.

PURPOSE: The purpose of the study was to present a selective bibliography of materials relating to the Suez Canal, from the beginning of the nineteenth century to the end of 1962.

PROCEDURE: The study is divided into three parts. Part I presents an historical overview analyzing the printed output on the Suez Canal. Part II deals with library catalogs, bibliographies, abstracts, indexes, and periodicals. Part III is the subject bibliography of 1,241 entries.

280. El-Hadi, Mohamed Mohamed (Ph.D., University of Illinois, 1964). **Arabic library resources in the United States: an investigation of their evolution, status and technical problems.** 306p. Order no. 65-808.

PURPOSE: The author's purpose in undertaking this study was to show whether or not American library resources in the Arabic language are adequate for the needs of American scholarship.

PROCEDURE: Data were gathered by the following methods: literature search, questionnaire, checklist procedure, interviews, and observations.

FINDINGS: There is a great concentration of Arabic materials in university libraries, primarily in the northeast region of the United States. The present inventory of Arabic printed books and periodicals is inadequate to meet present demands. Because of inadequate organization and a lack of guides, what is held by libraries is often unknown and inaccessible.

RECOMMENDATIONS: An administrative device of establishing a Near Eastern

RECOMMENDATIONS (cont'd): section or unit with broad responsibilities in a library is recommended. To standardize cataloging practices, a rule for entry under the well-known part of the classical Arabic name is recommended, and a rule for entering modern Arabic names by the last part of the name is widely favored. Maintaining a separate card catalog devoted wholly to Arabic materials and grouping Arabic library resources together is also recommended.

281. Farley, John J. (Ph.D., New York University, 1964). **Book censorship in the senior high school libraries of Nassau County, New York.** 386p. Order no. 65-969.

PURPOSE: The author's purpose was to discover what book censorship was performed in the high schools of Nassau County, to identify the sources of this censorship, and to ascertain its rationale.

PROCEDURE: The basic method was a detailed structured interview with the head librarian in each of the 54 Nassau County high school libraries.

FINDINGS: A majority of the librarians had had experience with censorship attempts, most often by parents. Most attempts were unsuccessful, and came from individuals rather than from groups. All of the librarians performed some censorship, but fewer than 10 percent habitually censored books. The types of books most often censored were: the novel which treated sex too lightly, books presenting a one-sided treatment of communism or race, and art books containing pictures of nudes. The reasons most commonly cited by the librarians for the censorship that they performed were the youth and immaturity of high school students, and the belief that some kinds of reading can have ill effects upon character and conduct.

CONCLUSIONS: Voluntary censorship performed because of the librarians' own convictions was more prevalent than was involuntary censorship. Except in the cases of some books seen as extremely controversial, there was no unanimity among the librarians concerning what books should properly be censored.

282. Greer, Roger C. (Ph.D., Rutgers University, 1964). **The current United States national book bibliography: an analysis of coverage with recommendations for improvement.** 104p. Order no. 64-8537.

PURPOSE: The purpose of this study is twofold: (1) to find out what the state of current U.S. national book bibliography is, and (2) to suggest improvements based on objective data from this study.

PROCEDURE: *Publishers' Weekly* (PW), *American Book Publishing Record* (BPR), *Cumulative Book Index* (CBI), *National Union Catalog* (NUC), and *Library of Congress Catalog—Books: Subjects* were judged basic components of the current national book bibliography and were studied by means of quantitative comparisons of the following characteristics: completeness, duplication, promptness, accessibility of information, and information presented in entries. A random sample of five percent of the reported 18,060 books published in 1961 was taken from NUC. Comparisons were made between 1961 issues of PW-BPR and NUC, CBI and NUC, and CBI and PW-BPR. A one percent sample was taken from CBI to test the completeness of NUC.

FINDINGS: All bibliographies analyzed were incomplete, singly and in combinations of any two; the NUC was most complete (93 percent). All combined were necessary for the most complete coverage. Accessibility is best by author and weakest through classified subject. CBI provides the most access at the most intervals.

FINDINGS (cont'd): Duplication of access is necessary at present in order to have complete access to information about current imprints. BPR was faster than CBI in listing new books. Compared to other monthlies, NUC was faster. PW-BPR listed new books first most of the time. Information presented in entries was generally uniform.

RECOMMENDATIONS: It is recommended that current American imprints in NUC (plus other items currently omitted) provide the contents of a monthly classified (by Dewey) bibliography with author, title, and alphabetical subject indexes cumulating quarterly, semi-annually, annually, and quinquennially.

283. Grotzinger, Laurel Ann (Ph.D., University of Illinois, 1964). **The power and the dignity: librarianship and Katharine Sharp.** 375p. Order no. 65-821.

PURPOSE: The purpose was to describe the life and contributions of Katharine Sharp, pioneer in American education for librarianship.

FINDINGS: Katharine Sharp was a pupil of Melvil Dewey, and she carried his philosophy of library organization to the midwestern states. She stressed knowledge of library economy and service to the people. As Director of the Library School at the University of Illinois, she personally made the school second only to the New York State Library School in admission requirements, professional staff, and renowned graduates.

CONCLUSIONS: Katharine Sharp's enthusiasm and capability had a positive effect on the acceptance of formal education for librarianship. She stands as a representative of the uniquely dedicated pioneers who characterized the nineteenth century world of librarianship.

284. Jones, Milbrey Lunceford (Ph.D., Rutgers University, 1964). **Socio-economic factors and library service to students.** 227p. Order no. 64-8540.

PURPOSE: The author tested the hypothesis that provision for library service to senior high school students varies according to the socio-economic level of the neighborhood.

PROCEDURE: The public libraries selected were the main public library and four branch libraries in each of two large cities, and four suburban or small town libraries. Eight high schools were selected as follows: two urban high schools in low socio-economic areas; two urban high schools in higher socio-economic areas; and four suburban or small town high schools. Data were collected on the socio-economic characteristics of the six communities and on a 10 percent sample of the twelfth grade pupils from each of the eight schools.

FINDINGS: The hypothesis was substantiated by data on hours of service, number of professional personnel, size of library collections, and quality of collections.

285. Kim, Shoong Han (Ph.D., Rutgers University, 1964). **A study of public library film services.** 223p. Order no. 65-5498.

PURPOSE: The purposes of this study are as follows: (1) to determine the effectiveness of public library film circuits; (2) to identify the characteristics of library film borrowers, communities, and library film services that are significantly related to the amount of library film circulation; and (3) to recommend optimum measures for the acquisition and circulation of films by a public library.

PROCEDURE: The operations of the New Jersey Library Film Circuit and the

PROCEDURE (cont'd): Connecticut Public Library Cooperative Film Circuit were studied; a questionnaire study was made of library film borrowers from six libraries; and nine member libraries of the New Jersey film circuit were studied. FINDINGS: The following findings were observed by the author: (1) it was more economical for a library to own and wear out in six years films having a potential circulation of 24 or more per year, than to share such films through the circuit; (2) it was advantageous to use the circuit for films circulating less than five times per year; (3) films needed no more than three times in five years could be obtained more economically from a university rental source; (4) public library film borrowers were predominantly professional or white-collar workers; (5) frequency of film borrowing was related to skill in projector operation or ownership of equipment; (6) film circulation to community groups was directly related to the amount of time spent on film service by library personnel.

286. Meder, Marylouise Dunham (Ph.D., University of Michigan, 1964). **Timothy Green III, Connecticut printer, 1737-1796. His life and times.** 417p. Order no. 64-12,646.

PURPOSE: The purpose of this study was to assess the contribution of Timothy Green III, one of the famous family of colonial printers, to the history of publishing in America.

PROCEDURE: A biographical portrait followed by a bibliography of Timothy Green's publications form the two divisions of this study.

FINDINGS: A check of printer's bills revealed that many of the publications of Connecticut that bibliographers had attributed to Green were actually the work of other printers. Though not the best known printer of the Green family, Timothy III was influential in spreading the craft of his forefathers to towns without presses in Connecticut and in other states. His press was important because it disseminated ideas of national as well as local figures during the American Revolution and the early years of the new nation. Green's most significant contribution was his newspaper, which he established in 1763 and continued to publish until 1793.

287. Moid, Abdul (Ph.D., University of Illinois, 1964). **Urdu language collections in American libraries.** 295p. Order no. 65-3643.

PURPOSE: The purpose of this study was to determine the status of Urdu language collections in American libraries prior to the inauguration of Public Law 480, and to determine their relative importance.

PROCEDURE: The data were collected through questionnaires and visits to 21 libraries in the United States and Canada.

FINDINGS: The data indicated the following findings: (1) the major technical problems encountered by libraries were inadequacy of bibliographical tools, lack of information about publishers and booksellers of Urdu materials, a lack of uniformity in transliteration, and inconsistency in the choice of form of author's name; (2) six libraries were found to have significant Urdu collections; (3) Urdu materials in linguistics and literature received more attention in libraries because of South Asian studies programs.

288. Nash, William Verlin (Ph.D., University of Illinois, 1964). **Characteristics of administrative heads of public libraries in various communications categories.** 236p. Order no. 65-3446.

PURPOSE: The purpose of the study was to determine the characteristics of administrative heads of public libraries in various communications categories: isolate, localite, library localite, cosmopolite, and library cosmopolite.
PROCEDURE: The instrument of research was the questionnaire. One questionnaire was completed by 175 administrative heads of Illinois public libraries. A second questionnaire was completed by 78 percent of the respondents of the first questionnaire.
FINDINGS: The study tested 29 factors for each of the communications categories. Of the 29, 11 were significant at the .01 or .05 percent level of confidence. Two more were significant at the 10 percent level. At the 20 percent level of confidence, three more were significant.

289. Reynolds, Michael M. (Ph.D., University of Michigan, 1964). **A bibliographic center in the West Virginia region: an analysis of present needs and future directions.** 319p. Order no. 64-12,664.
PURPOSE: The purpose of the investigation was to find ways to make the most effective use of the total library resources in the West Virginia region through providing the academic and special libraries with access to the region's primary research collection.
PROCEDURE: The basic method of data collection was the questionnaire.
FINDINGS: The academic libraries in the region do not have the resources or the staff necessary to provide their patrons with adequate service, yet they do not make any special effort to utilize the resources of other libraries. Special libraries are far more disposed to ask other libraries for assistance. Most academic libraries in the region use the West Virginia University Libraries for the largest part of their borrowing.
CONCLUSIONS: The study indicated that the role of the West Virginia University Libraries cannot be merely a passive one, but must be one in which there is active work to develop library service within the region.

290. Rogers, Amos Robert (Ph.D., University of Michigan, 1964). **American recognition of Canadian authors writing in English 1890-1960.** 818p. Order no. 64-12,669.
PURPOSE: The purpose of this study was to determine the extent to which English-Canadian writers have received recognition in the United States and to identify those factors that contribute to American recognition. The study was confined to works of *belles lettres.*
PROCEDURE: The following areas were investigated: the teaching of Canadian literature in American universities; the collection of Canadian literature in American universities; American publication of books by Canadian writers; inclusion of Canadian poetry in American anthologies; publications of works of *belles lettres* by Canadian authors in American magazines; American literary awards won by Canadians; inclusion of books by Canadian writers on American best seller lists; and American reviews of books by Canadian authors.
FINDINGS: Canadian literature is generally not taught as a separate subject in American universities. A very large percentage of Canada's literary output is in American libraries. Canadian authors are included often in anthologies and American magazines; Canadian poetry, however, has not received much American recognition. Canadians have won a number of significant American literary awards. A

FINDINGS (cont'd): few Canadian books have been American best sellers. Over half of the books written by the 278 authors studied were published in the United States and many of these were widely reviewed in American periodicals.

291. Slack, Kenneth Thurston (Ed.D., University of Utah, 1964). **A survey of centralized and cooperative library activities looking to the development of a centralized or cooperative library program for the unified school system of the Church of Jesus Christ of Latter-Day Saints.** 241p. Order no. 65-1784.
PURPOSE: The purpose of the study was to examine various centralized and co-operative library systems in order to develop a body of knowledge and administrative theory upon which a similar system could be built for the Church of Jesus Christ of Latter-Day Saint schools.
PROCEDURE: A survey was made of the existing libraries in the L.D.S. Church schools, and profiles of each library were constructed. Survey trips were made to the outstanding centralized or cooperative library activities in California. An intensive study was made of the Oregon State System of Higher Education Library System, the only example of a completely consolidated state system.
FINDINGS: The libraries of each school in the L.D.S. Church system have developed autonomously and unevenly. In every library, all or the major part of their service was below the American Library Association standards. Other findings were: (1) centralized processing would be feasible when a substantial proportion of the material was acquired in common by a number of libraries in the system; (2) centralized processing of the basic collection for new libraries was effective; (3) the book catalog produced by the Los Angeles County Public Library for its 200 branches was far more economical than providing a union catalog at each outlet; (4) the Oregon experience demonstrated the futility of attempting strong centralization of activities that are decentralized geographically; (5) the survey of automation activities indicated that automation in the small library was uneconomical.

292. Smith, Jessie Carney (Ph.D., University of Illinois, 1964). **Patterns of growth in library resources in certain land-grant universities.** 227p. Order no. 65-917.
PURPOSE: The purpose of the study was to investigate the patterns of growth in library resources in certain land-grant universities, and to determine what effect certain major factors had on the growth of library collections in these institutions. The author also attempted to discover what progress had been made in the growth and development of library resources in these institutions between 1930 and 1960.
PROCEDURE: Data were gathered at 10-year intervals from 1870 to 1930, and at five-year intervals from 1930 to 1960 from such sources as college catalogs, reports of boards of trustees, annual reports of presidents of the universities, financial reports, and annual reports of librarians.
FINDINGS: Various patterns of development existed in the curricula of land-grant and major state universities between 1910 and 1960. From 1870 to 1960, the state university libraries acquired significantly more volumes than the land-grant university libraries, and similarly spent significantly more money on books than did the land-grant institutions. Curricular expansion did not determine growth of library resources. The maintenance of departmental library collections does not insure the maintenance of adequate library collections in these areas.
CONCLUSIONS: There is no significant relation between curricular development and growth in library resources in the areas of science and technology in institutions included in this study.

293. Trueswell, Richard William (Ph.D., Northwestern Universtiy, 1964). **User behavioral patterns and requirements and their effect on the possible applications and computer techniques in a university library.** 263p. Order no. 64-12,347.

PURPOSE: Behavioral patterns and requirements of users of a large university library system were studied in an effort to determine their relationship to the possible applications of data processing and computer techniques in such a library system.

PROCEDURE: Questionnaires were sent to a 50 percent sample of the faculty, a seven percent sample of the student body, a 50 percent sample of the faculty in the University's Technological Institute and were distributed within the library for completion and return during the user's visit. In addition, photoelectric counters were installed in key areas of the libraries, samples of current circulation were made and some observations of card catalog use occurred.

FINDINGS: A method for predicting implementation times and work loads for a punched card circulation control system using punched book cards for a much smaller portion of the library's holdings than other proposed systems was developed. A quantitative approach to stack thinning (for the libraries studied) was proposed such that the thinned collection should satisfy well over 99 percent of user circulation requirements with less than half the present holdings. A low volume and a high volume version of a proposed punched card circulation control system were presented. A service for notifying users about the receipt by the library of journals of specific interest to the user was also described. Analysis of the data revealed that in some areas several user benefits could be obtained from the use of data processing techniques while in other areas its use would be unwarranted.

294. Williams, Wiley Julian (Ph.D., University of Michigan, 1964). **Evolving a policy for state printing: the Michigan experience, 1835-1861.** 355p. Order no. 65-5959.

PURPOSE: The purpose of the study was to describe the printing problems of one Midwestern state during its first quarter century.

PROCEDURE: The basic material for the thesis was taken from the journals, documents, and laws of the Michigan legislature; the state constitutions, opinions of the state courts and the attorneys general, contemporary newspapers, and various manuscript collections.

FINDINGS: The selection of the state printer was a sensitive barometer of the political climate. Three different methods of selecting the state printer were tried: by legislative appointment, by award to the lowest responsible bidder, and by popular election. State printing costs were very often considered to be excessive. Printing was administered in a haphazard manner, with each department apparently desiring printing autonomy.

295. Barrilleaux, Louis E. (Ph.D., University of Iowa, 1965). **An experimental investigation of the effects of multiple library sources as compared to the use of a basic textbook on student achievement and learning activity in junior high school science.** 281p. Order no. 66-3406.

PURPOSE: This study compared the effects of instruction on achievement and learning activities of students in eighth and ninth grade science classes with and without the use of an issued basic textbook, but with the use of a school library.
PROCEDURE: Fifty-six eighth grade students in 1962-63 at Malcolm Price Laboratory School, State College of Iowa, constituted the sample; of these students, 42 were studied an additional year (1963-64), while enrolled in ninth grade. Two instructional groups were "matched" with reference to mental ability and preference for science. The variation in treatments resulted from the use of different reading and reference materials; both sections were encouraged to use library materials, but only the control group was issued a textbook. Hypotheses concerning differences were tested by the methods of analysis of variance and the F-test at the .05 level of significance.
FINDINGS: Achievement in the class using school library materials without a text was, on the average, about the same as in the class using a textbook. The library materials approach resulted in significantly higher mean scores, after two years, over the use of an issued text. The library-nontext approach resulted in superior student achievement to the use of a textbook, but not to a statistically significant degree. The class using school library materials without a text, after one and after two years, achieved significantly higher scores than the class using a text. Mean scores for students without a text and who used library materials were, on the average, significantly higher than mean scores for the students who used an issued text. Students of average ability profited significantly more from the library materials procedure. The experimental (library-nontext) group scored significantly higher mean ratings than the control (textbook) group in total number of library visits, time devoted to library activities related to science classes, and time devoted to total library activities.

296. Bartel, Elaine Vetter (Ph.D., University of Wisconsin, 1965). **A study of the feasibility of an individualized instructional program in elementary school mathematics.** 256p. Order no. 65-14,846.

PURPOSE: This study was concerned with determining the feasibility of building a mathematics curriculum to include both the new mathematics and a program of individualized instruction at the intermediate grade level.
PROCEDURE: The individualized mathematics program was implemented in two fourth-grade classrooms at Brodhead, Wisconsin, during the second semester of the 1964-1965 school year. Weekly visits were made and data were collected for use in determining adequacy of materials as well as attitudes of the participating teachers and pupils. A fourth-grade control group was identified at the same school and pre- and post-tests (using standardized arithmetic achievement tests and

PROCEDURE (cont'd): a specifically prepared Concept Test) were administered. Analysis of covariance was applied to these data.

FINDINGS: The library of multiple texts and enrichment materials enabled the students to self-select materials in a logical and meaningful way. The children were able to adequately select materials as well as topics for study. Participating teachers and pupils were quite positive in their statements of attitudes toward the program. The analysis of covariance indicated no difference in achievement between pupils in the two programs. When the Concept Test was used, however, pupils in the individualized program scored consistenly and significantly (at the .01 level) higher.

297. Beard, John Robert (D.L.S., Columbia University, 1965). **Canadian provincial libraries.** Order no. 68-8539. (Specific instructions: "To obtain a copy, please order directly from the Canadian Library Association, Ottawa, Ontario, Canada.")

PURPOSE: The purpose of the study was to ascertain the present status of the 20 Canadian provincial libraries as a basis for discussion of their potential role and of plans for future development.

PROCEDURE: Data on the history of the libraries were obtained through examination of manuscripts and publications in the fields of the libraries and elsewhere. Data on present structure and operation of the libraries were gathered from questionnaires sent to and interviews held with the chief executive officers, published sources and observations during visits to the libraries. Opinions on the potential role of the libraries were obtained through interviews with provincial librarians and questionnaires sent to sampled Canadian library leaders.

FINDINGS: There is no single pattern of organization that applies to all the libraries, but a common characteristic is that none provides complete integration of all library services of the provincial government. Present personnel of provincial libraries is inadequate. Only half of the librarians have professional qualifications. The legislative libraries tend to be research oriented, while the extension agencies tend to collect more popular materials. Provincial librarians and other library leaders were generally in accord on the organization, services, functions, and resources desirable for provincial libraries. Most of the libraries fell short of their potential.

RECOMMENDATIONS: A legal basis is needed for some of the libraries. Additional personnel or modification of organizational structure should take place. The libraries should be program planning, budgeting and reporting on activities. Detailed written acquisitions policies are needed. Government aid should be sought. Minimal standards for provincial libraries should be established.

298. Bendix, Dorothy (D.L.S., Columbia University, 1965). **Labor unions and public library service.** 300p. Order no. 66-6,922.

PURPOSE: The purpose of the study was to explore the use that labor unions made of educational and information resources with emphasis on public library group and reference services.

PROCEDURE: The investigation was conducted in the six New Jersey cities with a population of 100,000 or over. The labor union sample included 114 organizations and 119 individual respondents, all officers and staff members. The union data were gathered mainly by interviews and questionnaires; the library data mainly by interviews. The *Guide for Developing a Public Library Service to Labor Groups*, published by the American Library Association, was used as a checklist of holdings of six libraries in the labor field.

FINDINGS: Labor unions were generally less articulate in requesting public library services than were other community groups. The anonymous use of public library information and reference service by the labor respondents was found to be substantially larger than that estimated by library staff members. Adequacy of library resources—measured by per capita financial support, book stock, volumes added per year, and holdings of labor material—was only one of the factors influencing the use of the libraries as a source of information for union purposes. Other factors were special communication with labor groups and general library publicity, and the motivation of the labor respondents. Almost one-half of the labor respondents used educational films and 88 percent of the film users expressed an interest in public library film services. There was a need for improved communication between public libraries and labor unions.

299. Cazden, Robert Edgar (Ph.D., University of Chicago, 1965). **Free German and Free Austrian press and book trade in the United States (1933-1950) in the context of German American history.** 350p.
PURPOSE: The study investigates the publication and distribution of German books by anti-Nazi Germans (or sympathetic publishers of other nations) outside of Germany during the years of the Hitler regime through 1950.
FINDINGS: The Free German book trade was a composite of three fairly distinct networks of production and distribution whose origins may be traced to the ideological antagonisms of Weimar politics: the German Communists, the Social Democrats, and the independent publishers. It was largely due to efforts of emigre bookdealers from Germany and Austria that this literature was distributed in the United States. It was found, however, that no dealer could subsist by (1) trading in Free German publications alone, or (2) by serving only the needs of the immigrant group. With the total collapse of Hitler's regime in 1945, it took another five years for the reorganized German publishing industry to get on its feet. That made further continuance of Free German printing superfluous.

300. Clayton, Howard (Ph.D., University of Oklahoma, 1965). **Investigation of various social and economic factors influencing current use of one college library.** 140p. Order no. 65-12,993.
PURPOSE: The purpose of the study was to determine whether socio-economic factors in the background of students at a small Midwestern college were connected to the fact that some students make extensive use of the campus library's lending facilities while others generate little or no use of these services.
PROCEDURE: The socio-economic variables under consideration were: occupation of students' parents; level of education attained by parents; and size of high school from which the students graduated. In studying the occupational variable, students were categorized according to farmers, professional, business owners, salary, and hourly wage earners.
FINDINGS: When students were categorized according to occupation, the differences in mean number of loans per students were slight and statistically insignificant. When students were categorized by the level of parental education, it was found that differences in library use among these groups were not significant. The size of the high school from which the students graduate was of no significant importance, with one exception. Students from schools with enrollments under 125 borrowed so many more reserve books than did students from schools with

FINDINGS (cont'd): over 850 enrollment that the statistical probability of this difference happening by chance was less than five percent. Chi-square contingency tables were used to see if the socio-economic variables were associated with negligible use of the library. Income and education of parents were most highly associated with negligible use, while income and occupation were also related particularly with reserve books. Occupation and education were associated, but not to the same statistical degree.

301. de los Santos, Alfredo Guadalupe, Jr. (Ph.D., University of Texas, 1965).**Book selection factors and the nature of the junior college library.** 125p. Order no. 65-10,722.
PURPOSE: The purpose of the study was to determine the effect of certain factors on the nature of the library book collections in six Texas public junior colleges.
PROCEDURE: Data were gathered from college catalogs, personal visits to each junior college, and from the files of the Junior College Division of the Texas Education Agency. From the literature four factors were identified as affecting the size of the collection: student enrollment, curricular offerings, funds available for the library, and the per-student institutional expenditure.
FINDINGS: A .819 correlation coefficient, significant at the .05 level, was found between the number of volumes and the size of the college. A .948 correlation coefficient, significant at the .01 level, was found between the funds available to the library and the number of volumes. A .898 correlation coefficient, significant at the .01 level, was found between the funds available to the library and the number of volumes. The .393 correlation coefficient between the per-student institutional expenditure and the number of volumes was smaller than the .811 value needed for significance at the .05 level.

302. Drumm, Sister Robert Mary, O.P. (Ph.D., Western Reserve University, 1965). **Johnson, Arnold and Eliot as literary humanists.** 233p. Order no. 66-5187.
PURPOSE: In order to determine some of the directions that literary humanism has been taking, the author examined the views of Samuel Johnson, Matthew Arnold, and T. S. Eliot as they relate to the topic. Much of the study is devoted to an examination of aspects of these critics' attitudes toward reality, their concepts of the processes of knowing and views of the mind of the poet and the ways in which they saw poetry relating to the circle of knowledge.
FINDINGS: Literature for Johnson was cognitive, and he retained much of a traditional view of the whole mind at work in the poetic process. For Arnold, the "idea" in poetry is the result of the process that he called criticism and is characteristically a relating, rather than an intuition in the Romantic sense. For Eliot, poetry is close to an objectification of feeling, in the Bradleyan sense and it has autonomy and uniqueness, and it has meaning, but the meaning is not identified with philosophical statements, although the two may be related at times. Literary humanism as seen in Johnson, Arnold and Eliot involves perceiving ways in which art transforms reality, and is thus apart from it; but it also means a willingness to see relationships to the rest of life.
CONCLUSIONS: The question of function, both in its narrow formulations and from the view of literary humanism, has repercussions in many facets of our culture. In the public library, narrow views of function may be reflected in concrete form ranging from problems of cataloging to book selection. The centrality of

CONCLUSIONS (cont'd): the humanistic position affords a perspective from which to assess marginal views, whereas its breadth permits consideration of the ways in which literature is related to other disciplines.

303. Edgar, Neal Lowndes (Ph.D., University of Michigan, 1965). **A history and bibliography of American magazines, 1810-1820.** 517p. Order no. 65-10,949.
PURPOSE: The purpose of the study was to provide a list of magazines published in the United States at any time between 1810 and 1820.
PROCEDURE: The author's procedure was to determine titles from available bibliographies, collections of large libraries, and references in historic and literary sources.
FINDINGS: A total of 223 magazines are annotated, giving titles and variants, editors, printers, publishers, place and span of publication, frequency, price, length, and size. A brief bibliography of books and articles about the magazines is appended.
CONCLUSIONS: The author saw three trends develop during this period: the appearance of the special subject magazine, the desire to produce an indigenous American literature, and the creation of a potential magazine audience for the future.

304. Galloway, Noel Louise (Ed.D., Columbia University, 1965). **An analytical study of the extent and nature of the reviewing of juvenile books in eight journals and newspapers with special regard to their usefulness as selection aids for school libraries.** 148p. Order no. 65-10,032.
PURPOSE: The purposes of the study were to determine the extent to which juvenile trade books were reviewed in the journals and newspapers that regularly review new juvenile books, and to assess the usefulness of these media in selecting books for school libraries.
PROCEDURE: The eight reviewing media were *The Booklist and Subscription Books Bulletin, Bulletin of the Center for Children's Books, Elementary English, Horn Book Magazine, Junior Libraries, New York Herald Tribune Books, New York Times Book Review,* and *Saturday Review.* The project focused on juvenile trade books published in 1959 and reported in *Publishers' Weekly* "Weekly Record," a total of 1,617 books. Reviews were then checked in the reviewing media for the period January 1959 through March 1960.
FINDINGS: Only 14 of the 1,617 books listed were reviewed in all eight media. Only two, *Booklist* and *Junior Libraries,* reviewed more than 50 percent of the books published.
CONCLUSIONS: The reviews commonly included statements of theme, comments on illustrations, and evaluations of quality and style of writing; the general tenor of the reviews was favorable; reviews failed to make adequate comparisons with other books by the same authors or on the same subjects.
RECOMMENDATIONS: More descriptive and critical reviews of juvenile books are needed; more space is needed for reviews of juvenile books; other media should be studied for the usefulness of their reviews of juvenile books; reviewers need to be more aware of the diverse audience that makes use of the reviews; and there needs to be a periodic assessment of reviews of juvenile books.

305. Goudeau, John Milford (Ph.D., Western Reserve University, 1965). **Early libraries in Louisiana: a study of the Creole influence.** 711p. Order no. 66-8005.

PROCEDURE: The historical method was used in this study. Inventories of important libraries were examined, and information about early private libraries was found in wills and in newspapers.

FINDINGS: The Creole population was very literate and did cooperate with the Americans in the administration of public libraries and public schools. Both New Orleans and Louisiana had library facilities comparable to other areas. The most substantial and singular contribution of the Creoles is the Napoleonic Code, still the basis of Louisiana law.

306. Grunau, Allen R. (Ed.D., University of Kansas, 1965). **An investigation of existing approaches to the problem of providing library service in the rural Kansas community: a study of the interrelationships of the public library and the public school library in selected rural communities of Kansas.** 212p. Order no. 66-6026.

PURPOSE: The purpose of the investigation was to provide a description of a variety of attacks on the problem of providing effective library service for rural Kansas communities.

FINDINGS: When resources were very limited, it was common for communities to open school libraries to the public. More often, however, the public and public school libraries operate separately. The two library units may work together on their common problems, or they may each do what they regard essential to their own service without real notice of the program of the other.

CONCLUSIONS: The investigation revealed that the rural Kansas community can obtain library service of a type if it desires it. However, it was evident that if this is to be effective library service, then sharing with the resources of a larger library or of a cooperative library system will be necessary.

307. Grundt, Leonard (Ph.D., Rutgers University, 1965). **An investigation to determine the most efficient patterns for providing adequate public library service to all residents of a typical large city.** 356p. Order no. 65-6554.

PURPOSE: The purpose of the author was to determine the most efficient patterns for providing adequate public library service to all residents of a typical city with more than 500,000 inhabitants (Boston).

FINDINGS: Public library service outlets were found to be not equally accessible to all residents of the city. Adequate public library service was found to be unavailable to some residents, even if outlets were equally accessible.

CONCLUSIONS: A regional library system would provide more adequate library service to all age groups than the traditional branch system. The level of service provided by branch libraries is lower than the level of service available at the main branches of independent municipalities serving equivalent population groups. It is possible to provide superior service at the same or lower cost by a better distribution of branches.

308. Hamadeh, Muhammad Maher (Ph.D., University of Michigan, 1965). **Muhammad the Prophet: a selected bibliography.** 321p. Order no. 65-10,968.

PURPOSE: The purpose of the study was to compile a bibliography of works on Muhammad.
FINDINGS: Part I of the study was concerned with an introduction to the writings on Muhammad, beginning with the seventh century. The second part concentrates on biographical publications about Muhammad's life and activities.

309. Jones, Norma Louise (Ph.D., University of Michigan, 1965). **A study of the library book collections in the biological sciences in fifty-four Michigan high schools accredited by the North Central Association of Colleges and Secondary Schools.** 660p. Order no. 66-6,751.
PURPOSE: The objectives of the study were to evalute, both quantitatively and qualitatively, the library book collections in the biological sicences, to determine the extent to which federal funds (designated in Title III of the National Defense Education Act) were used to purchase books in the biological sciences, to identify an average library biology collection and to compile a core list of biology titles that appeared most frequently in the collections.
PROCEDURE: Schools were selected randomly. A master list of titles in the biological sciences was compiled from five standard book selection bibliographies. Libraries were visited and questionnaires were sent to librarians and teachers.
FINDINGS: There was a smaller percentage of the average book collection devoted to the biological sciences (5.7 percent) than that recommended in two of the standard bibliographies used in the study. A large proportion of the average collection was old. Although some biology teachers were using a few of the methods of teaching which require pupils to use library materials, there were others who did not use them to any great extent. There was some evidence that N.D.E.A. was beginning to help build school library book collections in the biological sciences.

310. Katz, William Armstrong (Ph.D., University of Chicago, 1965). **Public printer: Washington territory, 1825-1889.** 155p.

311. Krzys, Richard Andrew (Ph.D., Western Reserve University, 1965). **Education for librarianship in Colombia.** 261p. Order no. 66-8,012.
PURPOSE: The purpose of the study was to trace the development of education for librarianship in Colombia.
FINDINGS: Colombian librarianship of the sixteenth century, similar to other activities of that time, had a religious orientation. The country's first libraries were in monasteries or seminaries; a member of a religious order was assigned by his superior to assume responsibility for the library. Formal training in librarianship did not begin until 1936. Between 1936 and 1942 short courses were the only form of training offered. In 1942 Rudolph Gjelsness of the United States introduced a broad program of training at the Bogota Library School patterned after American undergraduate library schools. Colombia has had four library schools. The most recently formed institution, the Escuela Interamericana de Bibliotecología (1956) offers high quality instruction, on a university level, and is well suited to the country's needs. Since its inception in 1936, education for librarianship in Colombia has been influenced by America, by professional associations, by international cooperation, by the establishment of the Biblioteca Pública Piloto, and by the founding of the Escuela Interamericana de Bibliotecología. Influences that blocked progress have been, among others, scarcity of well-prepared library science teachers,

FINDINGS (cont'd): indifference to library matters, and inadequate library legislation.

CONCLUSIONS: In the past North American influences have shaped Colombian library education, but its progress will be increasingly dependent upon leadership provided from within its own country. This leadership hinges entirely on the continuance of the Escuela Interamericana de Bibliotecología.

312. Matta, Seoud Makram (D.L.S., Columbia University, 1965). **Card catalog in a large research library: present conditions and future possibilities in the New York Public Library.** 248p.

313. Mehit, George (Ed.D., Western Reserve University, 1965). **The effects of type of library service upon utilization of books by sixth grade pupils in selected county elementary pupils of northeastern Ohio.** 206p. Order no. 66-8018.

PURPOSE: The purposes of the study were (1) to survey the library services offered in the elementary schools of northeastern Ohio; (2) to describe the three types of library service available to the children of this area; (3) to determine whether there is a significant difference among sixth grade pupils in the utilization of books within the three types of library service; (4) to determine whether a significant difference exists among the means of utilization of school library and outside reading source books by sixth grade pupils in each of the three types of library service; and (5) to determine whether proximity to a city of 10,000 population has an effect on results of utilization of school library and outside reading source books by sixth grade pupils.

PROCEDURE: A sample of 18 schools were selected for the study. Data were gathered by personal visit and through questionnaires, observation, and printed materials.

FINDINGS: The schools in this area studied appear to be in better financial condition than county schools in other parts of the state. Average library expenditures surpass the state minimum standards, but the facilities tend to be inadequate and professional personnel is lacking. There was no significant difference among the means of the number of school library books utilized by the sixth grade pupils of each category (classroom, central, combination). There was no significant difference between the means of the number of school library and outside reading source books utilized by sixth grade pupils within five miles of a city of 10,000, and those pupils not within five miles of a city of 10,000.

RECOMMENDATIONS: Educators should not simply collect books into a central place if adequate funds and personnel are not available. In-service programs should be conducted to make all teachers aware of ways to use existing facilities to the optimum advantage. University library science departments should conduct workshops for teachers. Educators should influence state legislators to make school library laws mandatory, and to assign authority to state library departments to act so that adequate library facilities are available to all students.

314. Murphy, Layton Barnes (Ph.D., University of Michigan, 1965). **John Holt, patriot, printer and publisher.** 449p. Order no. 65-11,004.

PURPOSE: The purpose of this bio-bibliographical study was to help fill a void in American publishing history.

FINDINGS: Part I is a biographical sketch of Holt, based on Holt's newspapers and his personal letters. Part II is an annotated bibliography of 348 imprints traced to Holt from 1762 to 1776. Current library locations, when known, are given for the entries.
CONCLUSIONS: The large amount of political publications, with their obvious importance to the Whig cause, are evidence of Holt's impact on his contemporaries.

315. O'Connor, Joel Sturges (Ph.D., University of Rhode Island, 1965). **The development of an information retrieval center for the aquatic sciences.** 119p. Order no. 65-11,251.
PURPOSE: This thesis discusses the development and evaluation of a mechanized literature storage and retrieval system for the aquatic sciences.
FINDINGS: A system was developed to augment conventional documentation services by marketing comprehensive bibliographies and regularly issued lists of references to current literature on topics requested by users. Holdings of annotated references to the world's aquatic science literature are regularly augmented by punch paper tape manuscript of the most comprehensive serial bibliography for the aquatic sciences. This bibliographic information is indexed by manually assigning descriptors to each entry. The entries may then be searched routinely to prepare bibliographies on specific topics.

316. Sheil, Marion Dorinda (Ph.D., Western Reserve University, 1965). **Library services in public secondary schools of Ohio, 1955-1963.** 304p. Order no. 66-3044.
PURPOSE: The purpose of the study was to judge Ohio's public secondary schools in 1963 in terms of the conditions that had existed at the time of an earlier comprehensive survey in 1956.
FINDINGS: In 1963, the high school libraries were judged inadequate by one-third of the principals in terms of one or more of the following characteristics: equipment, books and related materials, personnel, and funding. There were many changes noted from 1956, attributed to the wide acceptance of the A.L.A. standards and to the increasing demands on library resources. Four major improvements were noted over the 1956 survey: quarters and equipment tended to be more nearly adequate; professional personnel had been increased by 60 percent; through community action, interest in the library had been increased; and library budgets tripled. The improvements were noteworthy, but greater needs were indicated than in 1956. In 1963, only 22 percent of the school libraries met the new standards, and 50 percent of the libraries lacked the periodicals recommended.

317. Slavens, Thomas Paul (Ph.D., University of Michigan, 1965). **The library of Union Theological Seminary of the city of New York, 1836 to the present.** 368p. Order no. 66-6705.
PURPOSE: The author's purpose was to investigate the materials concerning the history of the Library of the Union Theological Seminary with a view to determining the means by which the collection was developed. A secondary purpose was to show how other theological libraries might benefit from the experience of the Union.
FINDINGS: The long ecumenical tradition of the school partially accounts for the development of the Library. The collection has long included works representing

FINDINGS (cont'd): other points of view. Another characteristic has been the influence of laymen in the development of the Library, for they have contributed the funds and supervised the expenditures. This has prevented the Library from becoming theologically introverted.

CONCLUSIONS: The history of the Seminary illustrates the importance of representing many points of view in a theological collection, of building a climate of free inquiry, of securing the support of wealthy laymen to contribute toward library strength, and of locating in a large city with its many resources.

318. Snider, Felix Eugene (Ph.D., Unversity of Illinois, 1965). **The relationship of library ability to performance in college.** 215p. Order no. 66-4297.

PURPOSE: The purpose of the study was to determine the relationships between a student's ability to use books and libraries (LAR) and his or her performance in college, particularly grade point average (GPA).

PROCEDURE: The author studied 1,490 freshmen at Southeast Missouri State College from spring 1957 through spring 1959.

FINDINGS: General findings regarding LAR median scores were: women were considerably higher than men; upper classmen were slightly higher than freshmen; stay-ins were higher than drop-outs; and degree earners were higher than those not earning a degree. The 100-item, objective-type test used to determine LAR gave evidence to being a reliable instrument, with an internal reliability coefficient of at least .83.

319. Voos, Henry (Ph.D., Rutgers University, 1965). **Standard times for certain clerical activities in technical processing.** 141p. Order no. 65-6553.

PURPOSE: The author's purpose in undertaking the study was to determine standard times for certain tasks common to a majority of libraries.

PROCEDURE: Micro-times for the various tasks were determined, using a stop watch. The mean was then used as the measure of central tendency.

FINDINGS: A formula for comparison of operations was derived, as well as a means for using the incremental data determined to derive operational times.

320. Whalen, Sister Mary Lucille (D.L.S., Columbia University, 1965). **The literature used in Catholic and protestant research in theology.** 178p. Order no. 66-6965.

PURPOSE: The purpose of the study was to determine characteristics of literature used in doctoral research in theology as some basis for selecting, servicing, and housing of theological library collections.

PROCEDURE: Eight thousand bibliographic references were compiled from 100 doctoral research studies in six areas of theology, selected on the basis of a stratified random sampling of all dissertations completed between 1952 and 1961.

FINDINGS: It was found that 72 percent of the materials were monographic, 22 percent in serial form, and six percent in other forms. The highest percentage of books and periodicals were United States publications. Approximately two-thirds of the materials were in theology, and almost 80 percent of the materials were in the English language. Greatest use was made of materials published between 1946 and 1955.

321. Barker, Dale Lockard (Ph.D., University of Illinois, 1966). **Characteristics of the scientific literature cited by chemists of the Soviet Union.** 316p. Order no. 66-7706.

PURPOSE: The purpose of the study was to identify and describe statistically the literature of chemistry in terms of the following selected set of characteristics: form, serial title, elapsed time between publication and citation, geographic origin, language, and publishing source.

PROCEDURE: The characteristics mentioned above were examined through the medium of literature citations made by scientists of the Soviet Union. For this purpose, a sample of 10,000 citations was taken from the 1960 volumes of four major Russian chemical research journals, using a random sample. The time, title, and some other properties of the literature were analyzed by comparison of the citation distributions in mathematical models either previously proposed or especially developed for the purpose.

FINDINGS: All national literature had an apparent trend toward greater production. Changes in the roles of countries as literature producers were noted, and also the growing diffusion of chemical activity among more countries, cities, and serial titles. The time distribution of Soviet literature confirmed its image as a fast-growing literature. This growth was more than matched by a growing reliance of Soviet chemists on Soviet publications. Soviet research and publication appeared heavily concentrated geographically in Moscow and Leningrad, and institutionally in the Akademiia Nauk SSSR.

322. Bobinski, George Sylvan (Ph.D., University of Michigan, 1966). **Andrew Carnegie's role in American public library development.** 360p. Order no. 66-14,492.

PURPOSE: This study presents a history of Carnegie public library philanthropy and evaluates its effect on the development of public libraries in the United States.

PROCEDURE: The original correspondence of the 1,637 towns that requested Carnegie grants, special reports of the Carnegie Corporation, published contemporary and current reaction to these gifts, questionnaires sent to Carnegie libraries, and correspondence from prominent librarians and Carnegie Corporation officials who were active during or shortly after the period of Carnegie philanthropy constituted the major sources for the work.

FINDINGS: Over $40 million for 1,679 buildings was donated to 1,412 communities in 46 states between 1886 and 1917. Difficulties frequently encountered by the towns receiving grants as well as the 225 communities that allowed offers to lapse were: finding a suitable site for the library, fulfilling the annual maintenance pledge, and meeting architectural requirements. By 1898, when Andrew Carnegie began his public library philanthropy on a grand scale, the public library was already established. Almost two-thirds of the communities receiving a building grant from Carnegie already had or were in the process of organizing a public library. Carnegie proved to be a great stimulant to library development. His philanthropy made more

FINDINGS (cont'd): libraries and more books available to more people. Furthermore, Carnegie widened the acceptance of the principle of local responsibility for the public library. In 1917 the Carnegie Corporation ended gifts for public library buildings, but supported the libraries through donations to library education and the American Library Association and by grants for centralized library services, projects, and special studies.

CONCLUSIONS: Public library development in the United States has had four important phases of growth: the public library enabling laws (1850's); Carnegie's gifts; library activities of the Carnegie Corporation; and federal support.

323. Carroll, Dewey Eugene (Ph.D., University of Illinois, 1966). **Newspaper and periodical production in countries of Europe, 1600-1950: a quantitative historical analysis of patterns of growth.** 921p. Order no. 67-6581.

PURPOSE: The purpose of the investigation was to undertake a summary analysis of two of the principal kinds of modern serial publications, newspapers and periodicals, with the specific attempt to determine the patterns of growth in their production in Europe since their introduction in the seventeenth century.

PROCEDURE: The historical method of research was used in the study.

FINDINGS: The growth of serial literature has been of an exponential nature that has seen the doubling of the gross annual levels of production at average intervals of 26 years. With regard to qualitative considerations, short-range fluctuations in the patterns of growth are seen to be related to episodic historical forces. Secular trends are viewed as being possibly reflective of the communication needs stemming from increasing specialization.

324. Churchwell, Charles Darrett (Ph.D., University of Illinois, 1966). **Education for librarianship in the United States: some factors which influenced its development between 1919 and 1939.** 220p. Order no. 66-12,304.

PURPOSE: The purpose of this study was to analyze and explain some movements, events, and influences that made distinctive contributions to the development of education for librarianship in the United States between 1919 and 1939.

FINDINGS: Through critical examination, the American Library Association discovered that its training agencies were not preparing the highly educated and skilled librarians that were needed. Recognition of this inadequacy led to the creation of the Board of Education for Librarianship. There were significant external forces at work outside of the Association improving the quality of library education: the fragmenting effects of specialization, the growing importance of research to business, the pedagogical revolution, the influence of regional accrediting associations, and, most importantly, the financial support of the Carnegie Corporation. The Carnegie Ten-year Program in Library Service provided for the new Graduate Library School at the University of Chicago, which emerged by 1939 as the dominant force giving new direction to the course of development of library education.

325. Coughlin, Violet Louise (D.L.S., Columbia University, 1966). **Factors in the development of larger units of public library service in Canada, with particular reference to the Provinces of Prince Edward Island, Nova Scotia and New Brunswick.** 423p. Order no. 70-6695.

PURPOSE: The purpose of this study was to examine the influence of lay interest, professional leadership, satisfactory provincial legislation, provincial interest in

PURPOSE (cont'd): implementing legislation and local government commitment in establishing regional libraries.

PROCEDURE: The statutes of Prince Edward Island, Nova Scotia and New Brunswick, the annual reports of Departments of Education, and contemporary newspapers were examined. Interviews with librarians, government officials, library board members, and others were conducted during two field trips.

FINDINGS: No effective larger unit has been formed without the presence of the factors set forth in the hypothesis. Evidence was also found that other elements such as economic conditions, population density, and education have an influence on the presence or absence of the factors under consideration, especially those of lay interest and local government commitment and support.

326. Dain, Phyllis (D.L.S., Columbia University, 1966). **The New York Public Library: a history of its founding and early years.** 872p. Order no. 67-789.

PURPOSE: The purpose of the study was to describe and analyze the founding and development of the New York Public Library.

PROCEDURE: The historical method was used to cover the period of time from the early 1890's to 1913, the death of John Shaw Billings, the Library's first Director.

FINDINGS: The administration of Dr. Billings was extremely important, for it was during this time that the lines of broad policy and physical and bibliographical development were established.

327. Harris, Ira Whitney (Ph.D., Rutgers University, 1966). **The influence of accessibility on academic library use.** 172p. Order no. 67-5262.

PURPOSE: The purpose of the study was to determine whether course-related use of academic libraries can be increased by improving access to the library's materials and services. The main hypothesis was: improved exposure to library materials and services results in increased use.

PROCEDURE: The improvement of exposure to materials and services was tested in four library activities at the University of Hawaii: reference service, reserve book service, a browsing exhibit, and a scholar-in-residence program. Reference service was subsequently re-tested at a California State College. The reference service experiments were evaluated by analysis of statistics of reference questions received by type of question, in periods before and during the tests. The other activities were evaluated by use of the questionnaire technique. Circulation statistics were used to cross-check the responses on questionnaires in the case of reserve book service and the browsing exhibit.

FINDINGS: The hypothesis was substantiated by the results of both reference service experiments and the reserve book service experiment. The browsing exhibit provided both improved exposure and increased use, but because other influences were involved at the same time, improvements in access could be claimed to be only one of several factors leading to heavier use. Even more pronounced and similar limitations characterized the scholar-in-residence program.

CONCLUSIONS: There are opportunities available to college librarians for independently increasing student use of their libraries.

328. Hendricks, Donald Duane (Ph.D., University of Illinois, 1966). **Comparative costs of book processing in a processing center and in five individual libraries.** 284p. Order no. 66-12,348.

PURPOSE: The author's purpose in undertaking the study was to test the hypothesis that centralized processing is less expensive than individual library processing.
PROCEDURE: The procedure was to compare the costs in a processing center with those costs for the same tasks in five independent libraries. The cost per volume in the center was determined by a gross cost accounting method. For the five libraries, costs were determined by keeping time records on each of a list of 21 activities in cataloging and preparations.
FINDINGS: The cost per volume in the processing center was $3.30 per volume. The mean cost in the non-participating libraries was $0.95. However, there were factors which lessen the difference between the two: the cost at the center was inordinately high because of first-year set-up and administrative costs; the quality or depth of cataloging done at the center was greater than that done at the individual libraries; the overhead charges for non-participating libraries were not computed, while all costs for the center were figured in; and professional salaries for the non-participating libraries were lower than for the processing center.
CONCLUSIONS: Centralized processing of books was questioned, since it appeared to have few advantages. Its greatest savings would seem to derive from the elimination or reduction in duplication of cataloging. If costs can be kept down, centralized processing is a useful technique for relieving professional shortages.

329. Hostrop, Richard Winfred (Ed.D., University of California, Los Angeles, 1966). **The relationship of academic success and selected other factors to student use of library materials at College of the Desert.** 317p. Order no. 67-537.
PURPOSE: The purpose of the study was to determine if certain student characteristics were associated with the use of library materials in one California junior college, College of the Desert.
FINDINGS: It was found that although there were some personal characteristics of students associated with library use, these were of minor importance in impelling use of the library. Instructors were the chief impellers of library use, and the assignment of term papers was the primary motivating factor. Less than five percent of the courses offered were responsible for more than 50 percent of the circulation. English/Speech courses made the greatest demand on the library collection. Nearly 20 percent of the students enrolled at the college did not check out any books during the period covered.
CONCLUSIONS: The author concluded that there was less use of library materials at this junior college than would be the case at a senior institution.
RECOMMENDATIONS: It was suggested that this same type of study be done at other junior colleges to determine library-course indexes as one means of evaluation. Circulation statistics should also be published in order to make cost analyses.

330. Jordan, Alma Theodora (D.L.S., Columbia University, 1966). **The development of library service in the West Indies through inter-library cooperation.** 476p. Order no. 66-9359.
PURPOSE: This study was designed to investigate the status of West Indian library services and assess the feasibility and potential contribution of all forms of inter-library cooperation to their development.
PROCEDURE: Questionnaires were distributed to 243 institutions comprising all public and special libraries, the university, secondary schools, and teacher-training

PROCEDURE (cont'd): colleges; 50 percent of these responded. Public librarians were interviewed. A representative group of libraries in each island was visited. FINDINGS: School and special libraries were less developed than public libraries. The larger the public library, the better its service and collection. Services to children and to rural areas were especially deficient in the smaller groups. The main public library service problems were: undersized units, inadequate funds, and a lack of professional staff. Several cooperative devices had been applied in the area, but few were fully developed or consistently used.
CONCLUSIONS: Inter-library cooperation would afford an economical and efficient means of promoting future library development although the scattered island pattern and future governmental structure would necessitate adaptations of the forms practiced elsewhere.

331. Koepp, Donald William (D.L.S., University of California, Berkeley, 1966).
Decision making for the public library function of municipal government.
258p. Order no. 66-15,822.
PURPOSE: The purpose was to investigate the extent to which the legal independence of library boards is exercised in seven cities, all with populations of between 50,000 and 100,000, and all having city managers and civil service systems.
PROCEDURE: The data were gathered by interviewing, insofar as possible, all of the councilmen, library board members, managers, and librarians about the processes through which decisions were made on a range of questions that an investigation of documentary material with regard to each library had previously indicated had been important in each city during the five-year period immediately preceding the study. The material was presented as a series of seven case studies.
FINDINGS: The data indicate that the legal status of library boards is largely irrelevant to the powers they actually exercise, and that major responsibility for making decisions about the library rests with the city manager. None of the decision-makers operates in the context of any overall consensus as to the functions of the public library, and the decisions are made through very minor changes in existing budgetary allotments, rather than through conscious and deliberate changes in existing programs.

332. Lane, Margaret Elizabeth Bergman (Ph.D., University of Washington, 1966).
A study of school library resources in Oregon as compared to state and national standards. 280p. Order no. 67-2175.
PURPOSE: The purpose of the study was to determine the adequacy of the school library resources according to state and national standards, and to utilize the findings to provide a base for establishing goals for improvement of school library programs in Oregon.
PROCEDURE: A questionnaire of 120 items was sent to 1,265 Oregon public schools. A second instrument was sent to districts in which there was some form of centralized organization or supervision of librarians on the district level. The analysis of data included univariate tabulations, bivariate tabulations, and chi-square analyses carried out to study the relation between responses to the items and the following variants: wealth of district, type of district, class of district, geographic location, enrollment, population of the community, and instructional levels.
FINDINGS: Relatively few school libraries were identified as having modern equipment, functional facilities, liberal budgets, adequate personnel, or as providing

FINDINGS (cont'd): optimum services for students and teachers. A large number of the schools reported that numerous facets of the library program needed strengthening or developing if national standards were to be met.

333. McCrossan, John Anthony (Ph.D., University of Illinois, 1966). **Library science education and its relationship to competence in adult book selection in public libraries.** 279p. Order no. 67-6675.
PURPOSE: The purpose of the study was to test the hypothesis that library school graduates are better book selectors for public libraries than untrained librarians.
PROCEDURE: Two groups of 10 librarians each were studied, one group composed of library school graduates and the other of untrained librarians. The two groups were matched on various relevant factors. All librarians were employed in small public libraries and were responsible for selecting all books added to the adult collections. The investigator visited each library, interviewed each librarian, and drew a five percent sample of 1965 adult book purchases.
FINDINGS: The library school graduates did somewhat better than the untrained librarians on most of the measurements used. The graduates used a significantly greater number of book selection aids. Books selected by the graduates were of higher quality than those selected by the untrained librarians. The untrained librarians made greater use of book salesmen, book clubs, and commercial lending agencies. Little difference was found between the two groups on various measures of attitudes and behavior toward controversial books.
CONCLUSIONS: In general, the study supported the belief that there is a real, but not large, difference between library school graduates and untrained librarians in book selection competence.

334. McGrath, Daniel Francis (Ph.D., University of Michigan, 1966). **American colorplate books 1800-1900.** 237p. Order no. 66-14,555.
PURPOSE: This dissertation is an attempt to trace the patterns of artists, engravers, printers, subjects, and (especially) techniques of American colorplate books of the last century. The narrative is supplemented by a bibliography of some 700 colorplate books which is based on Whitman Bennett's *A Practical Guide to American Nineteenth Century Color Plate Books.*
FINDINGS: The earliest American colorplate books were illustrated with hand-colored copperplate engravings. William Russell Birch and John Hill stand out above the other artists and engravers of the early years. About 1830, the hand-colored lithograph displaced the hand-colored copperplate. John James Audubon was a genius of this generation. Color printing, in the form of tinted lithography, which was a style of decoration rather than an attempt at chromatic representation, developed in the 1840's and was popular in the following decade. The best of the tinted illustrations appeared in the government reports of surveys and explorations. Also in the 1840's, full color lithographic printing, called chromolithography, began to compete with hand-coloring. By the end of the Civil War, chromolithography had eclipsed all other methods of color reproduction. The 1890's saw the emergence of the trichromatic halftone, growing out of such experiments as photolithography, hand-coloring photogravures, and trichromatic chromolithography.

335. Mason, Harold Jesse (D.L.S., Columbia University, 1966). **Industrial re-search and the academic library in the United States.** 438p. Order no. 66-9364.
PURPOSE: The purpose of this study was to examine the present relationship between academic libraries and industrial research organizations in the United States. PROCEDURE: Visits were made to dozens of industrial and academic libraries. Questionnaires were sent to a sample composed of the 62 American academic members of the Association of Research Libraries (95.2 percent return) and 449 selected industrial libraries (70.4 percent return). Close analysis was made of a private university library, a state-supported university library, and an industrial library.
FINDINGS: There was a significant amount of use of academic libraries by indus-try. This use had been continuously expanding; the staffs at academic libraries were devoting increasing time to making the resources and services of the library available to industry. The degree of involvement of these two types of libraries was determined by such factors as size, geographical location, and physical proxi-mity. Neither the participating academic nor the industrial librarians expressed dissatisfaction with the present arrangement.

336. Olson, Lowell Ellis (Ph.D., University of Minnesota, 1966). **Teachers', principals', and librarians' perceptions of the school librarian's role.** 208p. Order no. 66-12,230.
PURPOSE: The purpose of this study was to determine the role of the librarian in the school, as perceived by teachers, principals, and librarians.
PROCEDURE: The sample was taken from the 107 secondary schools in the Minneapolis-St. Paul area with full-time librarians. A printed questionnaire was sent to a random sampling of the teachers and to all principals and librarians in these schools. The items covered were librarian's status, objectives of library ser-vice, levels of preparation for librarians, activities of librarians, and background information about participants. Percentages were computed to describe partici-pants' perceptions of the role. Significance of differences in the general patterning of responses was tested by the t-test, analysis of variance, and chi-square techniques.
FINDINGS: There are significant differences in the perceptions that teachers, principals and librarians have of the librarians' status. Approximately half of the respondents likened the librarian's position to that of the classroom teacher. All groups agreed that in existing library programs technical processes receive the most attention, but felt that administration should be emphasized. The three groups differed in the stress they thought should be placed on reading guidance, teaching, administration, and technical processing in an expanded school library program.
CONCLUSIONS: The author concluded that there was a need for the librarian to inform teachers and principals of all aspects of their role, and for library associa-tions to educate the public to the requirements for school librarians. It is also important to involve teachers and principals in planning library services.

337. Shank, Russell (D.L.S., Columbia University, 1966). **Physical science and engineering societies in the United States as publishers, 1939-1964.** 447p. Order no. 67-5836.
PURPOSE: The purpose of the study was threefold: (1) to identify and delineate the factors that influenced engineering and physical society publishing programs in the U.S. between 1939 and 1964; (2) to describe the effects of these influences on

PURPOSE (cont'd): the publishing activities and the publications of societies; and (3) to assess the role of the society as an agent in the communication and control of scientific and technical information.

PROCEDURE: The administration of publishing programs and the output of publications of the following societies were examined: American Chemical Society, American Society of Chemical Engineers, American Nuclear Society, American Society of Lubrication Engineers, Mineralogical Society of America, and Optical Society of America. Data were gathered through content analysis of the published reports of the societies' committees, boards, and councils, from published comments and discussions by society and government officials and scientists, from interviews with society officials, and from an examination of the types of publications issued by the societies.

FINDINGS: The societies were responsive in molding publishing programs to meet the pressures of environmental influences, but were conservative in their decisions. The distribution of scientific and technical papers in journals remained the chief publishing activity of societies, and the only one common to them all. Societies generally have not been inventive of new methods and systems of communicating and storing information.

338. Stillman, Mary Elizabeth (Ph.D., University of Illinois, 1966). **The United States Air Force Library Service: its history, organization, and administration.** 292p. Order no. 67-6743.

PURPOSE: The purpose of the study was to examine the establishment, growth, organization, mission, and history of the United States Air Force Library Service.

PROCEDURE: The historical method was used in this study.

FINDINGS: The earliest libraries of the Air Force's predecessors began in 1918, and until 1945 all library service was provided by the Army Library Service. It is in the field of general library service that Air Force librarians have met their greatest challenge and achieved remarkable success. The Korean War was the first war in which the Air Force operated libraries in a combat area. Korea provided valuable experience in operating libraries under combat conditions, and this experience has proven useful in the Vietnamese conflict.

CONCLUSIONS: The basic conclusion of this study was that the Air Force Library Service emerged from World War II as a comprehensive permanent program, survived, flourished, and became an integral part of the Air Force because the Air Force needed a professionally administered library service and the civilian professional librarians of the Air Force were able to identify accurately specific needs and to fill satisfactorily these needs within the normal framework of Air Force policy, while still maintaining professional library standards.

339. Swarthout, Charlene R. (Ed.D., Wayne State University, 1966). **An approach to an in-service program to develop the concept of the school library as part of the instructional system.** 327p. Order no. 67-679.

PURPOSE: The dissertation seeks (1) to specify the theoretical educational base of the school library and its "selection policy," (2) to establish an educational base for cooperative planning, (3) to consider the professional competencies involved in planning and their interaction with materials, and (4) to consider applications of planning that support the educational positions delineated and emphasize the instructional role of the school librarian.

FINDINGS: A "selection policy" is established on the basis of the needs of symbolization and conceptualization. From a base of educational theory are derived implications for the autonomous process of inquiry and the instructional necessity for a responsive environment (the school library) that provides wide opportunity for data gathering to meet students' cognitive and conative needs. The professional competence of each staff member should include an understanding of the relationships of educational concerns, curriculum decisions, and the rationale of curriculum patterns. To insure the full operational benefits of the library, each staff member should participate in a continuing activity of selection, utilization, and production of library materials. The instructional role of the school librarian is developed through the support given to the instructional objectives of the classroom teacher that encourage student reliance on library resources.

340. Tague, Jean Mary (Ph.D., Western Reserve University, 1966). **Statistical measures of term association in information retrieval.** 659p. Order no. 67-4625.
PURPOSE: A review was made of previously proposed association measures and three of them, those used by Salton, Doyle, and Dennis (among others), were selected for an experimental comparison with two other methods of search strategy construction: the Western Reserve University semantic code and the original request terms alone.
PROCEDURE: The file for the experimental investigation consisted of the significant words in the titles of 210 documents representing all citations made in 10 papers from the journal *Diabetes*. The titles of the 10 papers served as requests and the citations set for each paper as the relevant set for its request-title. Results from the five searchers were compared on the basis of sensitivity, specificity, and effectiveness. Analysis of variance and the Newman-Keuls method were used to determine significant effects at the .01 level.
FINDINGS: Results, in general, indicated no real superiority of either the statistical association measures or the semantic code over the original request as bases for search strategy construction. No significant difference was found in the effectiveness of the five methods, averaged over all four numbers of matching terms.
CONCLUSIONS: Results might have been different had another measure of effectiveness, weighting sensitivity at the expense of specificity, been used and had a larger sample of requests been taken.

341. Totten, Herman Lavon (Ph.D., University of Oklahoma, 1966). **An analysis and evaluation of the use of educational media in the teaching of library science in accredited American graduate library schools.** 190p. Order no. 66-11,793.
PURPOSE: The problem of this study was to determine the extent to which educational media are used in the teaching of library science in accredited American library schools, and to analyze the judgments of library science teachers relative to how well they are using them in terms of established criteria.
PROCEDURE: The procedure involved four major steps: (1) the developing and validating of evaluative criteria relating to the use of educational media, based on professional literature and a jury of highly competent authorities in the educational media field; (2) the developing of an evaluation checklist and an inventory check sheet; (3) ascertaining the status of educational media used in the teaching

PROCEDURE (cont'd): of library science in the accredited library schools; and
(4) evaluating educational media used in teaching library science in accredited library
schools in relation to established criteria. The survey method and appraisal
technique were used in treating the data, formulating opinions, and ascertaining
facts. The participants in this study consisted of the 33 directors and the 215
full-time teachers in the accredited library schools.

FINDINGS: The findings indicated that the basic educational media equipment are
available to teachers. Further findings were that there was weak provision for in-
service instruction in educational media, that there was weak use of educational
television, teaching machines, records, opaque materials, slides, and filmstrips,
and that the use of educational media was generally the same in all institutions
regardless of their size.

RECOMMENDATIONS: The following recommendations were made: (1) provision of programs to cope with the evident existence of teacher inertia relative
to the use of educational media; (2) provision for programs to orient the teacher
to the unique contributions and role of educational media in instruction; and
(3) provision of programs of in-service education in the use of educational media.

342. Wilkinson, John Provost (Ph.D., University of Chicago, 1966). **History of
the Dalhousie University main library, 1867-1931.** 280p.

1967

---

343. Andrews, Charles Rolland (Ph.D., Case Western Reserve University, 1967).
A thematic guide to selected American poetry about the Second World War.
428p. Order no. 68-3298.

PURPOSE: Designed to serve as a guide and index to selected poetry about
America's involvement in the Second World War, this dissertation classifies into
17 theme-areas summaries and commentaries of 583 poems written between 1939
and 1965.

PROCEDURE: The 17 theme-areas are arranged roughly in chronological order.

FINDINGS: There was a variety of verse forms and techniques ranging from the
sonnet and the ballade to the long dramatic narrative. A poetry of considerable
frankness and honesty of expression, it was marked by a casualness and flippancy
unknown to the poetry of the First World War.

344. Axeen, Marina Esther (Ph.D., University of Illinois, 1967). **Teaching the use
of the library to undergraduates: an experimental comparison of computer-
based instruction and the conventional lecture method.** 208p. Order no.
68-1705. (Page 196, "Illinois Course Evaluation Questionnaire," not microfilmed at request of author. Available for consultation at the University of
Illinois Library.)

PURPOSE: The purpose of this research was to provide specific information concerning the effectiveness of computer-based instruction in teaching the use of the

PURPOSE (cont'd): library and to compare the amount of knowledge obtained, the instructor's time spent in preparing and teaching, and the students' time spent in completing the course in the two types of instruction.
PROCEDURE: The undergraduate students enrolled in L.S. 195 (Instruction to the Use of the Library) were assigned for three semesters either to the traditional lecture section or to the section using PLATO (Programmed Logic for Automatic Teaching Operations).
FINDINGS: The two groups did not differ significantly in the amount of knowledge gained as a result of their respective treatments. The experimental group covered the same amount of material in less time. No significant linear relationships were seen between the amount of time spent in class and gain in knowledge or between G.P.A. and gain in knowledge. More time was required for the initial preparation for PLATO Lessons, but subsequent preparations required less time than conventional lecture preparation. PLATO required less teaching assistance and instructor's time during the transmission of information.

345. Braden, Irene Andrea (Ph.D., University of Michigan, 1967). **The undergraduate library on the university campus.** 375p. Order no. 67-17,731.
PURPOSE: The purpose of the study was to demonstrate that the undergraduate library is one of the important concepts in library service to be developed in the last two decades by investigating its background, development, financing, physical plant, book collection, and staff.
PROCEDURE: Each of six separately housed undergraduate libraries in the United States (at Harvard, University of Michigan, University of South Carolina, Indiana University, Cornell, and the University of Texas) were studied. The materials for the research came from personal interviews and office files.
FINDINGS: The undergraduate library represents a whole new idea in library service. The specially assembled collection of books relates to the undergraduate curriculum. The librarians are service oriented. The basis of the library is to encourage reading and study; it functions as a means of self-education. The undergraduate library is expensive in terms of staff and collection costs but cheap in terms of operation.

346. Bunge, Charles Albert (Ph.D., University of Illinois, 1967). **Professional education and reference efficiency.** 213p. Order no. 68-8037.
PURPOSE: The purpose of this study was to gather and examine data on the relationship between certain variables, particularly formal library education, and effectiveness in answering reference questions.
PROCEDURE: Nine pairs of reference staff members working in medium-sized public libraries were chosen. The members of each pair were matched for undergraduate education and years of reference experience. However, one member of each pair had a fifth-year library degree; the other member had little or no formal library education. A test set of factual-type reference questions was developed. Efficiency in answering these questions was measured by the ratio between the number of questions answered and the total attempted plus the amount of time spent on each question attempted.
FINDINGS: There was no significant difference in accuracy between trained and untrained members of the pairs. Trained participants took significantly less time per question attempted and performed significantly more efficiently than did the

FINDINGS (cont'd): untrained. Lesser amounts of advantage for the trained members were found in pairs where the untrained members ranked high in amount of in-service training, where the difference between the trained and untrained members with regard to the amount of responsibility for the selection and handling of reference materials was small and where the library collection sizes were large. The general procedures used by the trained and untrained participants to seek answers to questions were quite similar. The most important procedural differences associated with differential efficiency were differences in classification by subject, in classification by type of material to be consulted, and in source use skills. Fewer than half of those reference sources in which the trained participants found answers to test questions were reported to have been studied in library school.

347. Farley, Richard Alan (Ph.D., University of Illinois, 1967). **The American library executive: an inquiry into his concepts of the function of his office.** 198p. Order no. 67-11,851.

PURPOSE: The purpose of this dissertation was to describe the executives as individuals, to identify certain patterns in the ways they responded to administrative problems, and to determine the ideas these library executives had on the expected activity of their positions.

PROCEDURE: In October 1961, 372 library executives in public, college, university and special libraries with library budgets in excess of $300,000 were surveyed; usable responses were received from 272 executives. Chi-square analysis of the data was employed.

FINDINGS: Library executives tended to be scientific in their approach to administrative problems. Female library executives did not appear less effective than male library administrators. Executives who held a Ph.D. in library science were more scientific than their colleagues. There were marked differences between the administrative patterns of directors of public and academic libraries. The directors of public libraries were the most scientific administrators. The executives in general tended to be somewhat ingrown, giving more attention to individual staff members and neglecting general planning and public relations. A large number of them admitted they were timid about dismissing incompetents.

348. Huang, Theodore Shih-shu (Ph.D., Rutgers University, 1967). **Efficacy of citation indexing.** 279p. Order no. 67-14,718.

PURPOSE: Three search methods (checking documents, using a citation index, using a subject index) were checked for efficacy, relative recall ratio, relative rejection ratio, noise ratio, redundancy ratio, unit search decision and unit search time, and pertinence ratio.

PROCEDURE: Three topics of current research interest were submitted by three geneticists, one each. A backward search by checking documents was done for one topic. A forward search in a citation index and a search in subject indexes were done for all three topics.

FINDINGS: A backward search, without elimination of noise at each step, retrieved an overwhelming number of references, most of them being noise, with the noise increasing at each step. The subject index searches for all three topics had a pertinence ratio of 68 percent, whereas the citation index search had a pertinence ratio of 37.5 percent. Subject index searches had greater efficacy than citation index searches. A backward search led to an immense number of references

FINDINGS (cont'd): whereas a forward search led to a relatively small number of references. The pertinence ratio decreased while the noise ratio increased with each step of a forward or backward search.

CONCLUSIONS: Citation index searching can be a supplementary aid to subject index searching when additional pertinent references are needed. Cycling does not appear to be a very promising reference retrieval aid. It would be useless to do machine searches without the elimination of noise at each step by human intervention.

349. Inada, Hide Ikehara (Ph.D., University of Michigan, 1967). **Translations from the Japanese into Western languages from the sixteenth century to 1912.** 298p. Order no. 67-15,638.

PURPOSE: The purpose of this study was to examine the achievements of early European and American Japanologists in the field of translation of Japanese works and to discern how early the Westerners began to study the Japanese language and to make translations.

PROCEDURE: The dissertation consists of two parts: a general survey and the bibliography. The general survey presents a brief account of Japanese-Western relations, a historical study of Japanese translations based on titles listed in the bibliography and concludes that the period covered is to be defined as the years of the first faltering attempts in translation. In the bibliography, the translations are listed chronologically and annotated. Indexes of original authors, original titles, translators and subjects follow the bibliography section.

350. Jasenas, Michael (D.L.S., Columbia University, 1967). **History of the development of the bibliography of philosophy.** 326p. Order no. 67-15,494.

PURPOSE: The purpose of the study was to trace all bibliographies of philosophy separately printed between 1592 and 1960 covering the whole subject field rather than aspects of the subject.

PROCEDURE: Twenty-seven bibliographies of philosophy were analyzed to reveal the themes emphasized by philosophers in various periods.

FINDINGS: Several factors influenced the development of the bibliography of philosophy: the state of philosophy at the time of the compilation of the bibliography, the compiler's background, and the patterns set by earlier bibliographers. During the early centuries, philosophy included all knowledge except law, medicine, and theology. Later the scope narrowed to cover only those subjects that represented the traditional branches of philosophy (logic, metaphysics, ethics). In the twentieth century, philosophy expanded to include publications dealing with speculative aspects of all areas of human knowledge. Changes both in coverage and in scope of philosophy bibliographies paralleled historical changes in the field. The nationality, education, and profession of the compilers and their association with certain philosophical schools influenced the bibliographies. Tradition also affected the coverage of major philosophers, the treatment of titles and the arrangement of the bibliographies.

351. Johnson, Robert Neil (Ed.D., University of Nebraska Teachers College, 1967). **State film library service at the University of Nebraska Extension Division: its present and future development.** 163p. Order no. 68-3789.

PURPOSE: The purpose of this study was to investigate how various selected

PURPOSE (cont'd): factors might affect the present and future development of the University of Nebraska Extension Division Film Library's service to the state of Nebraska.

PROCEDURE: Questionnaires were sent to 10 film libraries similar to the University of Nebraska Extension Division Film Library. Based on these findings, questionnaires were developed and sent to Nebraska public school administrators and teachers. Interviews were conducted with 14 of the respondents to supplement the data.

FINDINGS: The respondents relied heavily on instructional film catalogs as their major source of information about a particular film; they relied least on the audiovisual coordinator. The greatest hindrances in the use of 16mm instructional film were the lack of adequate budgets for its purchase and not being able to obtain the film for use at the time it was needed. Sponsored films were used by most of the public schools in Nebraska. The respondents felt that the University of Nebraska Film Library had not provided adequate information to Nebraska classroom teachers about available instructional films. A large majority considered the establishment of regional film libraries desirable. The majority of respondents were in favor of financial aid for the purchase and rental of films from federal, state, and local sources. Over one-half the respondents did not know or had not formed opinions about the Nebraska Legislative Bill No. 301.

352. Kaldor, Ivan L. (Ph.D., University of Chicago, 1967). **Slavic paleography and early Russian printing: the genesis of the Russian book.** 498p.

353. Kemper, Robert Eugene (D.B.A., University of Washington, 1967). **Strategic planning for library systems.** 311p. Order no. 68-3858.

PURPOSE: The purpose of the study was to determine if a common pattern for strategic planning exists within library administration, business administration and management in general.

PROCEDURE: A review of the literature and four libraries (University of Colorado, Oregon State Library, Denver Public Library, and Bellevue (Washington) Public School Libraries) was made to develop a strategic planning model and test instrument. Questionnaires were sent to a judgment sample of 303 leading libraries; a total of 153 college, public, school, state and federal libraries were analyzed.

FINDINGS: In the libraries studied, people involved in specifying the image of the organization needed to be directed to what was in the best interest of the organization. Strategic decisions were made at the library, institutional or outside level. Strategic, operational, and task planning were employed; strategic planning was not a highly developed process.

354. Klempner, Irving Max (Ph.D., Columbia University, 1967). **National Documentation Center abstracting and indexing services and the diffusion of results from government-sponsored research.** 410p. Order no. 70-17,023.

PURPOSE: This study established geographic, industrial, subject discipline and related distribution and use patterns for the federally produced abstracting and indexing services of *Nuclear Science Abstracts, Scientific and Technical Aerospace Reports, Technical Abstract Bulletin,* and *U.S. Government Research and Development Reports.* Although confined primarily to the U.S., the study also looked at the role played by the abstracting and indexing services in a number of Soviet bloc countries.

PROCEDURE: Data on 16,000 recipients and questionnaire responses from 836 recipients were analyzed.

RECOMMENDATIONS: Recommendations were made regarding national information dissemination policies affecting the distribution of the abstracting and indexing services under study.

355. Krause, Carrol Francis (Ed.D., University of Nebraska Teachers College, 1967). **Elementary school libraries.** 113p. Order no. 67-15,990.

PURPOSE: The purpose of this study was to develop guidelines for writing educational specifications for the centralized elementary school library in new school building construction and to determine how existing space in school plants might be used to establish a central library facility.

PROCEDURE: An investigation of 70 selected elementary schools of Nebraska which were part of K-12 accredited school districts was made.

FINDINGS: Centralized library facilities were not common in the elementary schools of Nebraska. Elementary schools without centralized libraries did not have their books in the classroom collections cataloged. Unused classrooms or other suitable space in an elementary school plant can be used to begin a centralized library. Most of the elementary schools with centralized libraries provided only for reading room activities. None of the 20 schools had provided the facilities necessary for a complete materials center. A high level of accreditation for a school district was no assurance that centralized elementary libraries would be available. Centralized libraries were found in school systems having more than one elementary attendance unit.

CONCLUSIONS: There were no elementary libraries that had been fully developed as instructional materials centers. Space was not available in existing school buildings to house the elementary library as a complete materials center. The book collections in elementary schools not having any type of centralized library facilities seemed to be limited in use to the classrooms in which they were located. It appeared that greater effort had been made to establish a centralized library in elementary schools that were housed in buildings separate from the high school grades. It appeared that a library materials center would be established only if plans for that purpose were included in school building projects.

356. Krikelas, James (Ph.D., University of Illinois, 1967). **The effect of arrangement on the successful use of library catalogs.** 162p. Order no. 68-8,139.

PURPOSE: The purpose of this study was to determine if dividing a traditional dictionary catalog to create a separate file for subject entries would result in an increase in the effective use of library catalogs.

PROCEDURE: A set of search-questions was developed as the data collection instrument. Two catalogs—one in dictionary arrangement (University of Illinois), the other divided into subject and non-subject entries (University of Wisconsin)— were selected and the appropriate sections verified in regard to similarity in size and complexity. Undergraduate participants were selected randomly at the two universities. Students were paired by matching on a number of criteria which measured familiarity and exposure to the catalog. Effective use of the catalog was measured in terms of a mean success score for subject searches. The scores achieved by the participants were compared for statistical significance using a t-test for difference between means.

FINDINGS: The means were not found to be different and it was determined that dividing the catalog was not a satisfactory device for making subject searches more effective. For any potential benefits attributable to the divided catalog (i.e., a larger percent of successful searches for one or more questions) there were corresponding disadvantages (i.e., lower rates of success for other questions). The rate of success or failure in obtaining the call number for two documents known to be in the collection was not related to the differences in the arrangement of the two catalogs.

357. Larsen, John Christian (Ph.D., University of Michigan, 1967). **A study in service: the historical development of the Michigan State Library and its territorial predecessor, the Legislative Council Library, 1828-1941.** 381p. Order no. 67-17,804.

PURPOSE: The study records the history of the Michigan State Library and investigates the extension of its services to all Michigan residents. Its development is shown against the changing background of the state's political and economic conditions. Consideration is also given to identifying the officials placed in charge of the expanding library.

FINDINGS: The Legislative Council Library, the territorial predecessor of the Michigan State Library, began as early as 1830 to authorize purchase of other materials in addition to law books and government publications. The Library was administered by temporarily appointed "assistant librarians" until the appointment of J. Eugene Tenney in 1858. In 1869, Tenney was succeeded by his wife, who became one of the first female state librarians in the country. Her appointment set a precedent in Michigan which has been followed to the present day. The Library's collection remained typical in its restriction to state officials until Mrs. Spencer, appointed in 1893, brought the concept of state library service to Michigan; almost at once the State Library opened to all residents and provided "traveling" libraries for residents without library service. Other innovations followed, including a legislative reference department, publication of library news bulletins, etc. During the 1930's a state board for libraries was established which replaced the governor in appointing the State Librarian. In 1941 the first professionally trained State Librarian was named and partisan disturbance in the Library ended permanently.

358. Liesener, James Will (Ph.D., University of Michigan, 1967). **An empirical test of the validity of the core concept in the preparation of university librarians.** 125p. Order no. 68-7660.

PURPOSE: This dissertation is an attempt at providing an exploratory test of the validity of the core concept in the preparation of university librarians.

PROCEDURE: The University of Michigan Library System was selected as the sample for the study. A job analysis was conducted of each of the professional positions (105) except for 17 positions that were primarily or totally administrative in character from September 1963 to February 1965. Job descriptions were written for each of the 105 positions. A classification scheme defining the kind of knowledge needed was developed and applied to each of these positions in most aspects of the core. The need or lack of need for knowledge of the various aspects of the core in the 17 unanalyzed positions was inferred from the job analysis data. A comparison, using chi-square single sample tests, was made between the knowledge assumed to be necessary in the core concept and the actual knowledge

PROCEDURE (cont'd): requirements of the positions studied. Five core areas were analyzed: Materials, Services, Administration, Communications, and Research. FINDINGS: The hypothesis that the core content is necessary for all university librarians was rejected. It was observed that knowledge of the various aspects of the core was generally greater in positions in departments organized primarily by subject and/or clientele (e.g., divisional or departmental libraries) rather than in departments organized primarily by function (e.g., cataloging, acquisitions, reference, etc.).

359. Lister, Winston Charles (Ph.D., Purdue, 1967). **Least cost decision rules for the selection of library materials for compact storage.** 281p. Order no. 67-10,225.
PURPOSE: The purpose of the study was to demonstrate that for a given selection criterion, least-cost storage quantities can be assessed by balancing the large circulation costs and the small shelving costs associated with stored materials.
PROCEDURE: An empirical evaluation of the storage models was made using data collected from three libraries at Purdue and estimates of cost parameters extracted from the literature.
FINDINGS: Significant savings can be realized from storage of materials, but the calculations indicated that a large portion of the collection must be stored. Usage rate policy was preferred over age policy. Choice for the length of the planning horizon had a relatively insignificant effect on the decision rules. Changes in the capacity related cost parameters will cause significant changes in the results.

360. Mathies, Mary Louise (Ed.D., University of California, Los Angeles, 1967). **A study of the information needs of junior college educators.** 230p. Order no. 68-230.
PURPOSE: An attempt was made to obtain specific data about the information requirements of junior college educators and to ascertain the ways in which an information storage and retrieval system might satisfy such needs.
PROCEDURE: Questionnaires were sent to two sample groups: individuals who had shown interest in the Clearinghouse for Junior College Information (an ERIC center) and individuals who were on the mailing list of the Clearinghouse. Responses were received from 1,062 educators.
FINDINGS: The interests of the junior college educators were centered on curriculum, instruction, and practices in other institutions.
RECOMMENDATIONS: New ways of reporting innovative practices to the field, expansion of services through increased cooperation with the American Association of Junior Colleges, and the development of programs to stimulate the progress of institutional research in junior colleges were recommended.

361. Musser, Necia Ann (Ph.D., University of Michigan, 1967). **Home missionaries on the Michigan frontier. A calendar of the Michigan letters of the American Home Missionary Society, 1825-1846.** 836p. Order no. 68-7679.
PURPOSE: This study consists of abstracts of 2,325 reports written by the Michigan missionaries of the American Home Missionary Society to the Society's offices in New York from 1825 to 1846. In addition to this calendar, the study includes an historical introduction, 180 biographical sketches of the Michigan missionaries, and a comprehensive index to the calendar.

138

FINDINGS: The American Home Missionary Society, founded in 1826, was supported chiefly by the Congregational and Presbyterian denominations. The cooperation of these two denominations in establishing churches on the frontier under the Plan of Union of 1801 is explored. Events leading to the Schism of 1837 in the Presbyterian Church and to the abrogation of the Plan of Union are outlined. In addition, information is given on the missionaries, the effect of the Panic of 1837 and the operation of the Society in Michigan. Biographies of the missionaries and agents who wrote the letters which comprise the calendar are presented; many references are given to further biographical information for the missionaries.

362. Qasimi, Abdus Subbuh (D.L.S., Columbia University, 1967). **A code for cataloging materials published in Urdu, Pushto and Panjabi.** 223p. Order no. 67-14,081.
PURPOSE: The difficulties in cataloging publications written in Urdu, Pushto and Panjabi were discussed and analyzed with a view to providing the cataloger with the information needed to make appropriate decisions. A code was designed not to replace but to supplement the rules of the American Library Association.
PROCEDURE: The work presents tables of transliteration with detailed rules of application and examples. There are extensive lists of authors' names divided into categories based on structure and meaning.

363. Schmitz, Eugenia Evangeline (Ph.D., University of Michigan, 1967). **A study of the library book collections in mathematics and the physical sciences in fifty-four Michigan high schools accredited by the North Central Association of Colleges and Secondary Schools.** 1182p. Order no. 67-8340.
PURPOSE: The study investigated the size, recency, and quality of the book collections in mathematics and the physical sciences in 54 Michigan high schools accredited by the North Central Association of Colleges and Secondary Schools. The study also attempted to identify average mathematics and physical science collections and to compile core lists of titles.
PROCEDURE: The master mathematics checklist was compiled from seven major book selection bibliographies; the master physical science checklist from five bibliographies. The investigator visited the 54 libraries to check the catalogs and shelf lists.
FINDINGS: The mathematics collections were rated "fair-poor" by 65 percent of the librarians. However, the majority rarely used the collection and did not use any teaching method (beyond encouraging student use) involving library materials. The majority of the respondents rated the physical science collections "excellent-good." Many of the librarians used them extensively. On the average, libraries had only 21 percent of the master checklist materials in their collections.
CONCLUSIONS: There is a need for quantitative and qualitative improvement in the mathematics and physical science collection and for their more efficacious use.

364. Sparks, Claud Glenn (Ph.D., University of Michigan, 1967). **William Warner Bishop, a biography.** 677p. Order no. 68-7732.
PURPOSE: The purpose of this biography was to present a study of William Warner Bishop's career and contributions in all areas of his endeavors, together with an account of Bishop the man.
PROCEDURE: The study was based upon the printed and manuscript materials

PROCEDURE (cont'd): relating to Bishop (primarily from the Bishop Papers in the University of Michigan General Library Archives) and interviews with persons who knew Bishop.

FINDINGS: Chronological in arrangement, the study begins in 1871 with Bishop's youth and his college days (1889-1893) at the University of Michigan. Then follows an account of his employment as a teacher and librarian from 1893 to 1915. It was as Librarian of the University of Michigan (1915-1941) that Bishop attained prominence as a library director. As founder of the Department of Library Science at Michigan, and as its Chairman (1926-1940), he made his reputation as a library educator. Bishop served as President of the American Library Association (1918-1919) and worked with the Carnegie Corporation and the Rockefeller Foundation as an advisor. He was active in the area of international intellectual cooperation. He worked as chief American advisor in the reorganization of the Vatican Library (beginning in 1927). He also had a leading role in the birth and development of the International Federation of Library Associations and its executive body, the International Library Committee. His prolific writing is treated non-critically in the dissertation.

CONCLUSIONS: Considering the catholicity of his activities, the record of his significant accomplishments, and his internationally recognized qualities of leadership, Bishop was pre-eminent among librarians of the United States at the time of his retirement from active work in 1941.

365. Subramaniam, Jonnalagadda Bala (Ph.D., Western Reserve University, 1967). **Magnetic resonance: specificity and exhaustivity of coverage of abstracting and indexing.** 285p. Order no. 67-15,555.

PURPOSE: An analysis was made of the extent to which four abstracting journals (*Chemical Abstracts, Chemisches Zentralblatt, Physics Abstracts,* and *Nuclear Science Abstracts*) cover and duplicate a small segment of an interdisciplinary area of special interest to physicists and chemists.

PROCEDURE: An authoritative, state-of-the-art annual review on "nuclear and electron spin resonance" was taken as a standard list against which the utility of the individual abstracting services or combinations thereof was assessed. The evaluation procedure took into account only the relevant material retrieved.

FINDINGS: *Chemical Abstracts* had the greatest coverage. *Physics Abstracts* presented the references sooner. *Chemical Abstracts* had the most unique references. The number of references common to all four abstracting journals was less than 10 percent. The validity of Bradford's Law of Scattering was shown in that 75 percent of citations came from three journals and 90 percent from nine journals. The categories of division of the subject field show a wide variation in all the four journals. Using the subject index, a user can retrieve best from *Chemical Abstracts* and least from *Nuclear Science Abstracts*.

CONCLUSIONS: The processing of a given journal or a given article by more than one service does not necessarily constitute wasteful duplication since services have different users and may be designed for different functions.

366. Thomson, Sara Katharine (D.L.S., Columbia University, 1967). **General interlibrary loan services in major academic libraries in the United States.** 279p. Order no. 68-8558.

PURPOSE: The general interlibrary lending services of major academic libraries in the United States, the characteristics of interlibrary loan requests and factors that

PURPOSE (cont'd): contribute to the success or failure of these requests were studied.

PROCEDURE: Data were gathered through (1) a sample of 5,895 interlibrary loan requests sent during a year to eight randomly selected university libraries: California at Berkeley, Colorado, Columbia, Florida, Harvard, Illinois, Johns Hopkins, and Ohio State; and (2) two questionnaires sent to all 63 academic libraries that reported lending 2,000 volumes or more in 1963-64 (59 libraries responded) and to 321 randomly selected other libraries represented in the sample of 5,895 requests (291 libraries responded).

FINDINGS: Most academic libraries did little or no interlibrary borrowing or lending. For those libraries which did lend materials, 56 percent of the requests were filled by lending the library's materials, eight percent by sending photocopies in lieu of loaning them. Even when the requirements of the General Interlibrary Loan Code were interpreted as liberally as possible, less than 58 percent of the requests were accurate and contained the minimum citation components required by the Code. Variation in policies of lending libraries on circulation of serials and dissertations, automatic substitution of photocopy, and verification of citations not found in card catalogs as cited in the requests produced significant variations in percentages of requests filled. Four practices of borrowing libraries were found to be significantly related to the percentage of interlibrary loan requests filled: requesting, photocopy, sending accurate citations, verifying requests, and finding out in advance what library owned the item wanted.

RECOMMENDATIONS: The General Interlibrary Loan Code should urge borrowing libraries to attempt to determine ownership before sending requests. A directory of major libraries indicating their interlibrary lending services and policies, especially with regard to lending serials and dissertations and automatically substituting photocopy, should be made.

367. Waddle, Richard Leo (Ph.D., Washington State University, 1967). **The role of the library in the community college with particular reference to the State of Washington.** 306p. Order no. 67-15,768.

PURPOSE: An investigation of the community college library was made by identifying administrative relations, library budget, library staff, library resources, and library services.

PROCEDURE: The sources for the study were the literature of academic librarianship and data gathered from 10 community colleges in Washington.

FINDINGS: The role of the community college library did not differ greatly from that of other academic libraries. Use of the library was required by 87 percent of 232 faculty; the way the instructors made use of the library molded the role of the library.

RECOMMENDATIONS: Greater faculty involvement with the library can be accomplished by an active library staff working with all types of materials and strongly oriented to service rather than materials.

1968

368. Agli, James Joseph (Ph.D., Ohio State University, 1968). **Evaluative criteria for library resources of doctoral physical education programs.** 156p. Order no. 69-4828.

PURPOSE: The purpose of the study was to establish criteria for evaluating library resources serving doctoral programs in physical education.

PROCEDURE: The writer developed 87 tentative criteria for evaluating doctoral physical education programs and sent these to be preliminarily screened by 12 faculty members in five Big Ten universities. From comments received, 23 of the original tentative criteria were rejected; 64 criteria remained as being most pertinent to the study. These were consolidated into a second list that was sent to a jury of 43 professional people directing graduate physical education programs throughout the United States. From the data received, an evaluative "score card" was constructed.

FINDINGS: By comparing one's library resources and facilities with the criteria, one can determine to what degree(s) his library resources and facilities are compatible with those appearing in the "score card."

369. Aman, Muhammad Muhammad (Ph.D., University of Pittsburgh, 1968). **Analysis of terminology, form and structure of subject headings in Arabic literature and formulation of rules for Arabic subject headings.** 365p. Order no. 69-4099.

PURPOSE: The study analyzed and explained the characteristics of the Arabic alphabetical subject system and decided on the major forms and structure of Arabic subject headings as based on the results of the investigation.

PROCEDURE: The subject headings used by the National Library of the United Arab Republic and by the University of Jordan Library were analyzed so that the construction of each heading could be studied.

FINDINGS: In the Egyptian list, 19 percent of the headings consisted of one word, and 30 percent of the headings of two words. In the Jordanian list, 38 percent of the headings were one word and 39 percent were two words. The majority of the grammatical structure of the two-word headings were nouns followed by adjectives. Few foreign words were used in the lists. Individual names were completely excluded from both lists. The writer felt that there was no justification for inversion of headings or for extensive use of punctuation marks. In the last chapter, a code for Arabic subject cataloging is presented. The rules were tested and applied to a sample list of Arabic subject headings which was supplemented by a classified index.

RECOMMENDATIONS: A unified list of Arabic subject headings should be established. An integrated subject catalog should be developed which includes all works (Arabic and foreign) under one standard Arabic subject heading. Individual names should be included in the subject catalog. There should be a classified index to the subject catalog in order to limit the number of "see" and "see also" references.

370. Carpenter, Raymond Leonard (Ph.D., University of North Carolina, 1968). **The public library executive: a study of status and role.** 189p. Order no. 69-1588.

PURPOSE: The purpose of this research is to describe and analyze the relationships of the chief librarian in the medium-sized public library with groups and agencies external to the library.

PROCEDURE: The literature by and about library administrators and interviews with public library administrators and other library officials were used to determine what the profession, the board of trustees and government officials expect of the library administrator.

FINDINGS: Community apathy, the low status of the library, legal and financial restrictions inhibit the administrator's being an aggressive educational leader. Professional norms are either too weak or non-existent to help the executive. Pressures from local groups are stronger than those of the profession. Interrelationships of the administrator and the trustees are not clearly defined and tension between the two is common. The profession has yet to evolve useful norms that will reduce the stresses of the executive role and enhance the library's goal attainment.

371. Chen, John Hsueh-Ming (Ed.D., Pennsylvania State University, 1968). **A survey of the libraries of selected land-grant colleges and universities.** 236p. Order no. 69-14,495.

PURPOSE: A systematic survey of libraries was conducted in order to determine the effectiveness of library services at selected land-grant colleges and universities. The study also investigated specific features of the libraries in terms of their effectiveness in meeting the needs of the users of modern library services.

PROCEDURES: Questionnaires were sent to the libraries of nine selected land-grant institutions in 1967. The professional librarians and users of the libraries were interviewed by the investigator in 1968.

FINDINGS: There were major differences in library services in the libraries of the nine land-grant institutions studied. There were major differences in readers' services offered and in performance of technical services. Libraries that had stronger financial support had better technical services. Library facilities and library budgets had not grown with the increase in student enrollment. The major cause for many of the weaknesses found was inadequate financial support. Library automation was found to be in its initial stage in most of the libraries.

372. Cox, Carl Thomas (Ed.D., George Peabody College for Teachers, 1968). **The perceived value of library service courses in Tennessee state-supported universities.** 184p. Order no. 69-13,814.

PURPOSE: The value of library service courses required by the Tennessee State Education Department for certification as a school librarian was assessed in this study.

PROCEDURE: Questionnaires, based on required certification courses and topics normally included in these courses, were sent to 474 elementary school librarians and nine library service instructors (292 questionnaires were returned).

FINDINGS: Of seven course areas, six were valued as being of major importance. Of 50 topics, nearly 91 percent were rated as important. When rank order of topics as determined by emphasis received in class was compared to the topic's importance to on-the-job needs and as part of an adequate library service certification curriculum, it was found that five topics had been over-emphasized and 12 topics had been under-emphasized in the library programs.

RECOMMENDATIONS: Three courses now required only for full library certification should be required of elementary school librarians. Certification as teacher-librarians should be discontinued. The required courses in audiovisual materials should be designed specifically for the school librarian. Programs of supervised library practice should be developed at each state supported university. User services should be given more emphasis in class instruction. Faculty involvement in library programs should be strengthened.

373. Cox, Doris Walker (Ph.D., Florida State University, 1968). **The curricular role of the school library: an exploratory study of the perceptions of selected public school personnel.** 141p. Order no. 69-11,289.
PURPOSE: An exploratory study was made to determine factors that compose the perceptions of the curricular role of the school library as a cross section of school librarians, classroom teachers, adminstrators, and supervisors think it should be.
PROCEDURE: Questionnaires were sent to 260 participating educators in five public school systems in Georgia and North Carolina with library services which met state and regional accreditation standards.
FINDINGS: Participants perceived Vivid Relevancy and Structural Dynamism and to a lesser degree Climate as positive factors in the curricular role of the school library. Creativity and Cognitive Experientialism were perceived to be of lesser importance. Respondents with wide experience as educators perceived the identified factors except for Creativity to have a more positive relationship than did respondents with little experience; the less experienced saw Creativity more positively. Educators, whatever type, perceived the same five factors as significant and varied very little in how positively each factor was identified in the total concept of the curricular role of the school library.

374. Crowley, Terence (Ph.D., Rutgers University, 1968). **The effectiveness of information service in medium size public libraries.** 182p. Order no. 68-17,762.
PURPOSE: The purpose of this study was to develop a methodology for comparing the information service available to adult patrons of two sample groups of public libraries in order to test the hypothesis that libraries with high expenditures and high per capita support will answer a larger proportion of information questions than will libraries with low expenditures and low per capita support.
PROCEDURE: By combining the rankings for expenditures and per capita expenditures, six "high" and six "low" New Jersey public libraries were selected. Anonymous proxies asked each of the "high" and "low" libraries a total of 12 questions at a variety of times; half of the questions required some knowledge of current affairs for correct answering and the remainder embodied various elements calling for particular search strategies.
FINDINGS: Although the "high" libraries did answer a higher proportion of questions than the "low" libraries, no statistically significant difference between the two types of libraries could be found.

375. Dale, Doris Cruger (D.L.S., Columbia University, 1968). **The origin and development of the United Nations Library.** 346p. Order no. 72-1,293.
PURPOSE: The purpose of this paper was to examine the historical development and administrative organization of the United Nations Library.

FINDINGS: The first chapter describes the historical predecessors of the Library. Chapter II is concerned with the development of administrative policy in the United Nations Library. The use of interlibrary loans and contractual services, the development of departmental libraries, and the work of library committees are analyzed in Chapter III. Chapter IV is concerned with the implementation of the policies that were established for technical services, public services, and the indexing and bibliographical services of the Library. The divers loci of the Library in the administrative structure of the United Nations are described and analyzed in some detail in Chapter V. The study concludes with a chapter on the physical accommodations of the Library.

376. Divett, Robert Thomas (Ed.D., University of Utah, 1968). **Design of a file structure for a total system computer program for medical libraries and programming of the book citation retrieval module.** 178p. Order no. 69-3498.
PURPOSE: The study tested the concept of use of a third generation computer in the on-line or shared time mode for the total system operation of a medical school library.
PROCEDURE: An inverted file structure utilizing indexed sequential and FORTRAN relative file methods was developed and the book citation retrieval module of the total system was built; the bibliographic section (100 entries selected from the files of the Universtiy of New Mexico Library of the Medical Sciences) was tested for operability. The computer used the IBM System 360 Operating System.

377. Evans, Roy Winston (Ph.D., Southern Illinois University, 1968). **An experimental study to determine the effectiveness of using slides with ninth grade students in randomly selected schools in Southern Illinois to teach library usage.** 121p. Order no. 69-6268.
PURPOSE: An attempt was made to ascertain whether library orientation at ninth grade level could be taught by the conventional lecture method or by a visual approach in which slides were used.
PROCEDURE: This study was limited to ninth grade students enrolled in freshman English classes in six Southern Illinois schools who were randomly placed in either experimental groups (library orientation via slides) or control groups (no visuals in the library orientation). The librarian in each school gave the orientation to all groups. Results of the pre- and post-test were measured by a t-test at the .05 level of significance.
FINDINGS: No significant differences were found in the terminal functional behavior or in the gain scores between the two groups. A significant difference between the gain scores of the males and females in the control and experimental groups was found.

378. Gardner, Richard Kent (Ph.D., Western Reserve University, 1968). **Education for librarianship in France: an historical survey.** 411p. Order no. 69-9342.
PURPOSE: This study presents a survey of library education in France from its scattered beginnings following the French Revolution and the founding of the Ecole des Chartes in 1821 down to the present day.
PROCEDURE: The principal sources for this work have been the archives of the various library schools in France, both extant and defunct, as well as those of the Association des Bibliothécaires française and the Direction des Bibliothéques et

PROCEDURE (cont'd): de la Lecture publique. Interviews were conducted with those librarians having played a major role in the development of library education in France over the past 40 years.

FINDINGS: Although the rudiments of library science were proposed in France as early as 1799, it was not until the founding of the Ecole des Chartes (1821) that continuing education for librarianship was established. The rather stultifying program of the Ecole des Chartes dominated library education until the 1920's. Following World War I, the Paris Library School, operated by the American Library Association from 1923 to 1929, brought a new type of technical training to France. Various forces, principally that of the Association des Bibliothécaires française, brought reform of the official training programs with the institution of the Diplôme technique de Bibliothécaire in 1932 and then in 1950 of the Diplôme supérieure de Bibliothécaire, which was eventually placed under the supervision of the Direction des Bibliothèques. This resulted in the establishment of an Ecole nationale supérieure de Bibliothécaire in 1964. The Direction has also been responsible for the creation of training programs for middle-level positions in libraries.

CONCLUSIONS: The present status of library training in France is that of a vigorous, forward-looking program, providing excellent training at both advanced and middle levels and by both official and private training agencies.

379. Hall, Anna C. (Ph.D., University of Pittsburgh, 1968). **Selected educational objectives for public service librarians: a taxonomic approach.** 189p. Order no. 68-14,862.

PURPOSE: *The Taxonomy of Educational Objectives Handbook I: Cognitive Domain* (developed by the Committee of College and University Examiners in 1956) was used to develop a comparative analysis of need knowledges, abilities, and related education for tasks involving public contact in large public libraries.

PROCEDURE: A preliminary list of library tasks was derived from job descriptions, work sheets and experimental testing of data collection instruments used in libraries. Data were collected from librarians in 13 large public libraries by means of the critical incident technique; knowledge and abilities needed were identified and formulated into a classification called "Taxonomy of Educational Objectives for Public Service Librarians." Curriculum information gathered from 12 ALA accredited library schools and interviews with faculty members teaching courses of interest was similarly analyzed.

FINDINGS: Librarians placed complex abilities of comprehension, application, analysis, synthesis, evaluation and social skills in high priority compared to factual knowledge and vocational skills. Librarians also stressed the value of knowledge in other disciplines. In the education they received, it was found, however, that related disciplines were not generally included. Factual knowledge considered unique to librarianship was adequately taught, but instruction stressed factual knowledge to the relative neglect of more complex objectives.

380. Hassell, Horace Paul, Jr. (Ph.D., Purdue University, 1968). **An analytical design framework for academic library system formulation.** 378p. Order no. 69-7455.

PURPOSE: The research attempted (1) to determine and define the role of the systems designer as a major participant in complex academic library systems; (2) to isolate and define the types of problems that must be resolved by library

PURPOSE (cont'd): systems designers; (3) and to provide a structured approach to aid the systems designed in resolving the problems isolated.

PROCEDURE: Both the research and the presentation fall into two basic parts: the formulation of an analytical framework for design and a verification and extension of the framework through application and applied research.

FINDINGS: A Library/User/Funder/Designer Model was created. In the second part of the research, three specific aspects were treated: (1) development of suitable algorithms for the classification and measurement of "user" needs in terms of required and potential system services; (2) development of a suitable method for transforming the need of system services into subsystem requirements; and (3) illustration of both functional and decisional models to abstractly define the subsystems required. Purdue's Interlibrary Loan Service serves as a field laboratory for the second phase of the research.

381. Helmkamp, John Gerhardt (D.B.A., Indiana University, 1968). **Managerial cost accounting for a technical information center.** 308p. Order no. 68-9179.

PURPOSE: The purpose of the study was to determine relevant cost information concerning the literature searching activities of a NASA Regional Dissemination Center.

FINDINGS: A two-fold solution to the cost information deficiency problem is proposed in this study. Service cost data were computed to aid in the development of a statistical cost model (to be used in lieu of formal cost accounting systems). The managerial cost accounting system consists of a collection of source documents, forms, records, computer programs, computer print-outs, and managerial reports. A computerized data processing function is employed to convert cost data recorded during the production process on various source documents into relevant managerial cost information. The statistical cost system is founded on the theory of statistical quality control. Representative values are established on statistical control charts for the direct search cost mean (X) and the direct search cost range (R). The X chart measures the central tendency of the unit search cost data, and the R chart discloses changes in the dispersion of the unit charges. A random sample of five searches is selected every month for both information services, and the direct costs consumed for each sampled search are registered on a single record. The mean and range are calculated and recorded on the appropriate cost control chart. The null hypothesis which is tested with the sample information is that the direct unit search costs are "in control" when compared with the representative values. Immediate managerial action is required if a value is recorded outside the desirable limits.

382. Houser, Lloyd J. (Ph.D., Rutgers University, 1968). **Indices of effectiveness of public library services: relationship of registrants and financial support.** 74p. Order no. 68-14,249.

PURPOSE: The purpose of the study was to determine if there was a correlation between level of effectiveness as measured by the household indices and the per capita financial expenditure by a library.

PROCEDURE: The study was limited to libraries which served populations ranging from 5,000 to 100,000 persons and looked at 28 of the 329 libraries in New Jersey in 1964.

FINDINGS: The hypothesized relationships between effectiveness measured by the household indices and per capita financial expenditure by a library was rejected

FINDINGS (cont'd): because the relationship of the library population to the municipal population depended upon the distribution of the municipal household income not the amount the library spent on a per capita basis. The validity of the "area served" or "population served" concept on which much public library service is planned was questioned.

383. Intrama, Navanitaya (Ph.D., Indiana University, 1968). **Some characteristics of the literature of public administration.** 109p. Order no. 68-11,391.
PURPOSE: An examination was made of some of the characteristics (form, subject dispersion, title dispersion, time span, and language of the material used) of the research materials used by writers in public administration journals.
PROCEDURE: A systematic sample of 1,542 citations was drawn from five journals (ranked as the most important by 10 experts) issued in 1964-1966.
FINDINGS: Books and pamphlets together were more used than all other forms of publications combined; this is similar to the percentages found by investigators in other social sciences, but different from those in the natural and physical sciences in which periodical references were far more numerous. Over one-third of the materials used were in the Library of Congress classification "J" (political science) and 31 percent were in class "H" (sociology and economics). Approximately one-quarter of all references to journals were made to five frequently cited periodicals. Title dispersion in references to books was higher; only 47 percent of books were mentioned more than once. Ninety percent of the citations were to publications in English and were issued since 1930.

384. Jeffries, John Allison (Ph.D., Indiana University, 1968). **Legal censorship of obscene publications: search for a censoring standard.** 200p. Order no. 69-7,690.
PURPOSE: The primary issue in this thesis is whether the threatened danger posed by allegedly obscene publications is sufficient to warrant use of police and judicial power for its suppression.
FINDINGS: Chapter I describes the evolvement of the idea of censorship from the Old Testament to mid-seventeenth century England. Chapter II deals primarily with religious and political censorship in England. Chapters III and IV are concerned with the legal censorship of obscenity in the United States and England. Chapter V deals with the judicial and legislative attempts to formulate a workable censoring standard. Chapter VI contains criticism of the prurient interest censoring test presently used by the United States Supreme Court. It is found that the empirical data fail to reveal the assumed relationship between exposure to alleged obscenity and behavior, although the data are not conclusive. The so-called "appeal test," proposed by the drafters of the Model Penal Code, is suggested as a possible method of suppressing alleged obscenity without relying on the presumed relationship between obscenity and behavior. In the final chapter, an attempt is made to isolate the various evils at which obscenity censorship is aimed. It is submitted that none of the alleged evils is so significant as to justify the present vague and, hence, sometimes abusive, governmental policy against them. Appendix I contains a breakdown of state obscenity statutes. Appendix II contains a model obscenity statute.

385. Lanier, Gene Daniel (Ph.D., University of North Carolina at Chapel Hill, 1968). **The transformation of school libraries into instructional materials centers.** 271p. Order no. 69-10,179.

PURPOSE: The main objective of this study was to trace the transformation of school libraries in the United States into instructional materials centers.
PROCEDURE: The professional and popular literature was surveyed. The 50 state departments of education in the United States were contacted by letter. The 27 North Carolina demonstration school libraries were available for visitation.
FINDINGS: There was a definite trend toward transforming school libraries into instructional materials centers. The National Defense Education Act and the Elementary and Secondary Education Act greatly helped in modernizing school libraries. Educators, students, and librarians were in large part convinced that the IMC arrangement is the most practical and useful. A majority of the state departments of education in the United States accepted the IMC concept. Many schools had indexed all media in the library card catalog. National professional organizations had adopted the IMC concept. Many names were applied to the place in the school where instructional materials were stored and distributed.

386. Littleton, Isaac Thomas (Ph.D., University of Illinois, 1968). **The bibliographic organization and use of the literature of agricultural economics.** 231p. Order no. 68-12,153.
PURPOSE: The paper attempted to describe the characteristics of the literature of agricultural economics produced in the United States, to analyze the extent to which publications produced by agricultural economists are indexed and abstracted, to compare indexing rates by form and source of publications, and to compare the usefulness of various types of publications to agricultural economists.
PROCEDURE: An analysis of 7,624 publications produced by agricultural economics in the United States during 1961-1963 was made. A 20 percent stratified sample was checked in eight indexing and abstracting services. A questionnaire on the use of the literature was sent to a representative national sample of agricultural economists.
FINDINGS: Research is published primarily in monographs, bulletins, and conference proceedings. Serials are indexed at higher rates than separate publications; research publications at higher rates than informal publications; U.S. government publications and national and regional organizations have higher indexing rates than those of local and state organizations. Less than one-half of the total number of publications are listed in one or more of the eight bibliographical services. The most inclusive of the services is *The Bibliography of Agriculture*. Only minimal indexing coverage is given to separate talks and papers and separate research papers. Agricultural economists find informal contacts with their colleagues and the direct consultation of the professional publications of their own field of greater use than the use of bibliographical services. *The Bibliography of Agriculture* is the most frequently used indexing service. There is greater dissatisfaction with promptness of reporting research than with the thoroughness of reporting in indexing service.

387. Lloyd, Helen Ditson (Ph.D., University of Oklahoma, 1968). **Perceived changes in school library programs following an NDEA institute.** 270p. Order no. 69-1988.
PURPOSE: The changes in the functioning of 15 school libraries in Oklahoma following an NDEA institute held at Oklahoma State University during the summer of 1966 were charted in this study.

PROCEDURE: Two instruments based on qualitative criteria from AASL "Standards for School Library Programs, 1960" were designed for the study. One was used to evaluate each library before and after the institute. The other was used by librarians and administrators to rate their libraries as perceived before and after the institute.

FINDINGS: All libraries made improvements in programs following the institute, but there were variations. Little correlation was found between improvement made and size of collection, size or level of school. Significant correlations between improvement and final "high" ratings and between improvement and number of books per pupil were found. Aspects of the program emphasized during the institute were found to be improved in most libraries studied. Librarians showed a changing self-image in areas of leadership, cooperation with teachers and administrators, service as a non-book materials specialist and operation outside the library. After the institute, administrators gave a more realistic appraisal of the libraries based on a better understanding of library potential.

388. McCabe, James Patrick (Ph.D., University of Michigan, 1968). **Catholic reference sources: a critical study.** 378p. Order no. 69-12,178.

PURPOSE: Since no extensive bibliographic survey of Catholic reference works existed, this dissertation attempted to fill the gap by listing, describing, and evaluating such works.

PROCEDURE: The 792 titles selected were either those that dealt with topics peculiar to the Church or those that dealt with topics such as the social sciences, literature, and the arts on which Catholics have traditionally felt the need to express a "point of view." Excluded are unpublished, rare, or very old works. English language publications are emphasized. The books are not necessarily written by Catholics, but they do deal with the Church exclusively or thoroughly. The five chapters cover: general reference works; theology; humanities; social sciences; history. There are critical annotations.

389. Meyer, Donald Paul (Ed.D., Michigan State University, 1968). **An investigation of perceptions regarding the instructional function of the library among faculty members and librarians at public community colleges in Michigan.** 141p. Order no. 69-5915.

PURPOSE: The purpose of the dissertation was to determine the degree to which community college librarians and community college instructors in transfer programs and occupational educational programs differed in terms of perceptions regarding the instructional function of the library.

PROCEDURE: Questionnaires were sent to faculty members teaching in two curriculum programs (those teaching college transfer programs or occupational education programs) and the community college librarians in 20 Michigan community colleges.

FINDINGS: The three groups differed in their perception of the instructional function of the community college library in four areas: (1) the library's organizational structure; (2) the library's facilities; (3) the use faculty make of the library for class preparation and class assignments; (4) the use faculty make of the library for recreational or avocational purposes. The three groups generally agreed in their perceptions regarding the types of materials that should be available in the library, the responsibilities of teachers and librarians regarding teaching students to use the library, the use students should make of the library, and the services the library should make available.

390. Morris, Junius Hugh (Ph.D., Washington State University, 1968). **The feasibility of using criteria book lists to evaluate junior college library holdings.** 94p. Order no. 68-10,968.

PURPOSE: The study determined the suitability of various criteria book lists for evaluating junior college libraries.

PROCEDURE: Seven book lists were used (none more than five years old) and random samples of from 49 to 64 books were selected from each of the lists. In addition, a list of 53 volumes of modern poetry, compiled by Louis Untermeyer and a list of 25 controversial books compiled especially for this study were used. The lists were compared with the card catalogs of the libraries of 10 community colleges all of which have enrollments between 1,000 and 5,000 students.

FINDINGS: The smaller lists (including the poetry and the controversial books) were no measures of the quality of the junior college library collections since they have been used by the Washington community college librarians as buying guides past the point where the lists could continue to serve as measuring sticks. The *Junior College Library Collection* and *The Julian Street Library* should prove to be acceptable sources for fresh random samples for comparing the library collections of junior colleges. *Books for College Libraries* was found to be an inappropriate list for evaluating the collections of junior college libraries similar to those in this study.

391. Peterson, Kenneth Gerrard (Ph.D., University of California, Berkeley, 1968). **The history of the University of California Library at Berkeley, 1900-1945.** 398p. Order no. 69-3673.

PURPOSE: The study traced the development of the library system at the University of California, Berkeley, in the first half of the twentieth century.

FINDINGS: Providing material resources, facilities and services for its users was the primary goal toward which the University of California's library at Berkeley was directed during 1900-1945. The library evolved as an integral part of the larger intellectual and research-oriented community of which it was a part. Educational, institutional and financial factors encouraged the library's development. Strong administrator-librarians emerged during this period. The "book repository" view of academic libraries commonly held in the nineteenth century was replaced by the mid-twentieth century concept of an information and use-oriented facility.

392. Schneider, Frank August, Sr. (Ed.D., Arizona State University, 1968). **A study of the leadership role of directors of public libraries as reported by selected public library directors.** 186p. Order no. 68-15,015.

PURPOSE: An investigation was made of the leadership role perceptions and role expectations public library directors held for themselves while functioning as the leaders of municipal libraries.

PROCEDURE: Leadership Behavior Description Questionnaires and Library Administrator Questionnaires were sent to 147 public library administrators serving communities ranging from 50,000 to 99,999. Regional, county, privately endowed, and other community public libraries were excluded from the sample. Chi-square and analysis of variance were employed.

FINDINGS: Public library directors do not differ significantly from one another in the perceptions they hold for their role in terms of the "consideration" and "initiating structure" dimensions of leadership behavior, but they do in the

FINDINGS (cont'd): expectations they hold for their role. Older librarians have greater expectations regarding "initiating structure" and librarians holding only the Bachelor degree generally have greater expectations under "consideration" than younger library directors.

393. Skelley, Grant T. (Ph.D., University of California, Berkeley, 1968). **The Overland Monthly under Millicent Washburn Shinn, 1833-1894: a study in regional publishing.** 348p. Order no. 68-13,959.

394. Stone, Elizabeth W. (Ph.D., American University, 1968). **A study of some factors related to the professional development of librarians.** 479p. Order no. 68-13,067.
PURPOSE: A study was made of some of the factors that motivated librarians to engage in professional improvement activities and formal course work.
PROCEDURE: Questionnaires were sent to 138 librarians chosen by a stratified random sample from the 1956 and 1961 graduates of accredited American library schools.
FINDINGS: The librarians engaged in professional development activities for reasons that were concerned primarily with the content of the opportunity and its relation to the work process (e.g., ability to use new knowledge in the job situation). Librarians did not participate in activities for reasons that dealt primarily with factors that were peripheral to the content or with contextual elements (e.g., time, location). Age, number of years between the Bachelor's and M.L.S. degrees, the Professional Index Score, the Degree of Aspiration Score and population density of the area where the respondent lived were the variables most closely associated with motivation for professional development. The respondents felt that library management did not support their activities related to professional development and had a responsibility to create conditions that are conducive to professional development.

395. Studer, William Joseph (Ph.D., Indiana University, 1968). **Computer-based selective dissemination of information (SDI) service for faculty using Library of Congress Machine-Readable Catalog (MARC) records.** 263p. Order no. 69-7119.
PURPOSE: From November 1966 through June 1968 the Library of Congress conducted a pilot project involving the weekly distribution of its traditional 3x5 catalog cards in machine-readable form. The MARC records provided a search data base for an experiment in current awareness service designed to furnish faculty with bi-weekly lists of bibliographic notices of new monographs in their specified fields of interest.
PROCEDURE: Forty faculty were chosen in proportion to the number of faculty members in each department or school. An "interest" statement from each faculty member was translated into both Library of Congress classification numbers and subject heading terms. The "interest profiles" were recorded on punched cards for computer matching with subject headings and class numbers of MARC records. The weighted term search strategy was used in comparing profiles with MARC records. Each profile was assigned a "cutoff weight" or "hit level" of 6. Three computer programs were employed in producing the SDI lists: Program Extract, Program Retrieve, and Program Print.

FINDINGS: Subject headings proved to be more effective in searching the MARC file mainly because multiple subject headings could be assigned to each record, whereas there was only one class number. The SDI system performed well in selecting relevant records and overall evaluations were highly favorable. All faculty expressed a desire to have SDI services continued.

396. Vaillancourt, Pauline Mariette (D.L.S., Columbia University, 1968). **Bibliographic control of the literature of oncology, 1800-1960.** 330p. Order no. 71-17,627.
PURPOSE: The study of the development of the bibliographic control of recorded knowledge in the field of oncology from 1800 to 1960 was undertaken to determine when and how the bibliographic tenchiques and devices were brought to bear on the problems of oncology.
PROCEDURE: The methods used included a historical survey of bibliographic control media of the literature of oncology, a descriptive study of the various bibliographic tools of the underlying fields, and a documentary analysis of the devices used in all bibliographic control media.
FINDINGS: While oncology began its independent bibliographies in 1895, it was in the late 1940's that this speciality began to develop leadership in bibliographic control by using Hollerith punch cards for compiling medical data and establishing a photographic semi-mechanized system of producing an index (1954), by utilizing specialized unique indexes, and by originating priority indexing (1960). It was found that the time lag for oncology to adapt bibliographic devices of other fields was not as long as had been anticipated.

397. Verschoor, Irving Alton (D.L.S., Columbia University, 1968). **Tasks and training of personnel in community libraries in New York State, 1958-1966.** 238p. Order no. 69-9225.
PURPOSE: An analysis of the activities necessary for good library service was made in this study.
PROCEDURE: Information on 112 activities was obtained by personal interview from 30 small public libraries in New York State and recorded on a checklist. The results were translated into curricula for training community librarians. Six years later a restudy of 23 of the original 30 libraries was made to determine the effect of the training or lack of training on the librarians with respect to the activities most frequently performed and those judged most difficult to learn on the job.
FINDINGS: There was very little difference between the activities performed in non-system community libraries (although they performed more activities concerned with cataloging and classification) and system-related libraries. The activities most frequently performed by the community librarians were not the most difficult to learn. Not all of the activities of community librarians can be covered by organized training courses. The need for training in the activities performed by community librarians and the reported difficulty of performing the activities was less for librarians who had taken training courses than for those who had not.
RECOMMENDATIONS: Evaluation research should be conducted on the curriculum. The training courses should incorporate a greater degree of material designed for independent study by the community librarian. The methodology of the dissertation should have given greater weight to the effect of the librarians trained as

153

RECOMMENDATIONS (cont'd): teachers in the application of the curricula and the real impact of the growth of the library systems.

398. Winckler, Paul Albert (Ph.D., New York University, 1968). **Charles Clarence Williamson (1877-1965): his professional life and work in librarianship and library education in the United States.** 594p. Order no. 69-11,776.
PURPOSE: A study was made of the professional life and work of Dr. Charles Clarence Williamson: his place, influence, and impact on the history and development of American library education and librarianship.
FINDINGS: Williamson's Report of 1923 (*Training for Library Service*) was his most influential work; it changed the concept of library training from an on-the-job vocational task to a profession. Thus, he can be considered the "father of professional librarianship." He was a man of many interests, deeply involved in his professional career and work. Among other positions, he worked as a teacher, principal, secretary, economist, associate dean, author, editor, bibliographer, compiler, researcher and consultant.
CONCLUSIONS: His many contributions have earned him a place as one of the "greats" in the field of librarianship.

399. Winkelman, John H. (Ph.D., University of Chicago, 1968). **The Imperial Library in Southern Sung China (1127-1279).** 175p.
PURPOSE: This dissertation investigated the purpose, buildings and grounds, personnel, collections and users of the Imperial Library in Southern Sung China during 1127 through 1279.
FINDINGS: The Imperial Library was the agency in the government of Southern Sung China charged with the conservation of documents and scholarly works for the purposes of promoting administrative efficiency and fostering the pursuits of scholarship in the empire. Its activities were carried on in a well-conceived building complex by a staff selected and organized to foster the satisfactory operation of this agency. The Library's holdings, reconstituted in large part from private sources, but continually supplemented by governmentally sponsored compilations, grew to be the largest one in society at the time. Its chief users were probably the staff of the Imperial Library and associated scholarly agencies and in all likelihood scholars engaged in private studies.

400. Woodworth, Mary Lorraine (Ph.D., University of Wisconsin, 1968). **School librarians' opinions on research and research needs in school librarianship.** 238p. Order no. 68-5370.
PURPOSE: The study investigated the differences of opinion on research and research needs between "school library leaders" and "practicing school librarians." The relationships between these opinions and the participants' age, sex, marital status, accreditation status of degree granting program, experience, participation in professional organizations, contributions to professional literature, and receipt of professional honors were also examined.
PROCEDURE: Questionnaires were sent to 308 randomly selected "school library leaders" and "practicing school librarians."
FINDINGS: Significant differences in opinion were found on all topics between the leaders and librarians. The leaders generally placed more emphasis on research. No significant differences were found in opinions when subjects were divided

FINDINGS (cont'd): according to biographic categories. All subjects felt that research was needed in the areas of instruction, services, publicity, accessibility, use and budget.

CONCLUSIONS: There is a need for increased recognition of the role of research and the importance of research needs by school librarians. Additional attention should be given to research in the educational preparation. Active participation in professional organizations can contribute to personal growth of school librarians.

401. Zachert, Martha Jane Koontz (D.L.S., Columbia University, 1968). **Objectives and patterns in undergraduate library science education.** 234p. Order no. 69-13,009.

PURPOSE: Variations in the objectives of undergraduate library science programs were studied.

PROCEDURE: In 1961-1962 data were compiled from U.S. Office of Education sources about selected characteristics of the 563 institutions that offered library science in 1956 and gathered from administrators of undergraduate library science programs in 173 sampled institutions.

FINDINGS: Undergraduate programs were located in liberal arts institutions as well as teachers' colleges. The majority of programs offered more than the minimal introductory courses. Privately controlled institutions formed a significant segment of undergraduate library science education. There was a relationship between the objectives of the undergraduate library science programs and (1) the type of parent institutions and (2) the school library certification requirements. The program objectives involved three career patterns: preparation for minimum certification, preparation for continued study in graduate library schools and preparation for sub-professional library positions. The objectives also involved one non-career pattern: preparation for personal academic work.

1969

402. Baumann, Charles Henry (Ph.D., University of Illinois, 1969). **The influence of Angus Snead Macdonald and the Snead Bookstack on library architecture.** 374p. Order no. 70-787.

PURPOSE: This study examines the role of Angus Snead Macdonald and Snead and Company in shaping library architecture, particularly after World War II.

PROCEDURE: Using the historical method, the writer examined published and unpublished records of Snead and Company, the papers of Angus Macdonald, library archives, and the correspondence of librarians and architects.

FINDINGS: There was a clear change in library design after World War II. Prior to the War, the reader was frequently separated from the books; because of the restricted stack area and the heavy dependence on natural light and ventilation, these libraries lacked flexibility. After the war the multi-tier stack was generally replaced by free-standing book cases and an intermingling of books and readers. Macdonald was one of the major forces helping to bring about this important change. Although

FINDINGS (cont'd): Macdonald, and Snead and Company had a vested interest in multi-tier stacks, Macdonald raised objections to what he considered the faults of the traditional library building. Snead and Company then introduced the Convertible Stack as one means of attaining greater flexibility. Still not satisfied, Macdonald advocated a "modular" library, one made up of low-ceilinged, equal units of space which could serve as reader, office or book-storage space with a minimum of modification. Snead and Company lost its manufacturing facilities in 1946 and ceased doing business after August 1952. Before that time, however, it did have an opportunity to build some of these new modular libraries.

403. Carroll, Carmal Edward (Ph.D., University of California, Berkeley, 1969). **The professionalization of education for librarianship with special reference to the years 1940-1960.** 464p. Order no. 69-18,892.

PURPOSE: The forces and events which contributed to the professionalization of library education, particularly those that were operative between the years 1940 and 1960, are investigated in this dissertation.

FINDINGS: Prior to 1940, three major forces did much to upgrade library education: the Williamson Report (1923), the founding of the American Library Association Board of Education for Librarianship (1924), and the establishment of the Graduate Library School at the University of Chicago (1926). Between 1940 and 1950 the profession defined the content of professional-graduate library education. The acceptance of the five-year basic program as the norm of professional preparation eventually led to the demise of undergraduate programs and put all accredited library schools on a graduate basis. The founding of the *Journal of Library Education* and the establishment of Beta Phi Mu, a professional fraternity, were further indications that by 1960 library education had been professionalized. The reluctance of the profession to recognize the value of doctoral study in library science is seen as a deterrent to professionalization.

404. Caruso, Dorothy Elaine Furner (Ph.D., University of Pittsburgh, 1969). **An experiment to determine the effectiveness of an interactive tutorial program, implemented on the time sharing IBM system 360, Model 50, in teaching a subject-oriented user to formulate inquiry statements to a computerized on-line information retrieval system.** 191p. Order no. 70-2051.

PURPOSE: The study investigated the possibility of creating an on-line interactive retrieval program that would allow flexibility of search strategy and be used by an untrained individual without intervention or instruction by a trained operator.

PROCEDURE: An experimental test was conducted using 37 randomly chosen subjects from a beginning group of library science graduate students on the tutorial program. The remaining 50 members of the class constituted a control group receiving training in the same skills and concepts in a classroom lecture situation.

FINDINGS: No significant differences were found in the effectiveness of the two methods. Almost all of the subjects were able to enter the search program and, using assigned pre-searched questions, create 92 symbolic statements that were executable by the search program. Of these, 48 achieved precision/recall ratios of 1:1.

405. Clark, Harry (Ph.D., University of California, Berkeley, 1969). **The production, publication and sale of the works of Hubert Howe Bancroft.** 290p. Order no. 69-18,999.

PURPOSE: The study explores in detail the participation of Bancroft and his associates in the production, publication and sale of his *Works* and estimates the success of their efforts.

FINDINGS: In 1859 Bancroft began collecting books and manuscripts on the West; by 1871, he decided to write a history of the area. While he continued to search for material, the *Works* was being written by hired writers, who produced about 29 of the 39 volumes. The first five volumes were published by Appleton and sold by canvassers; Bancroft assumed publication of the history in 1882. To aid sales, Bancroft personally solicited endorsements from New England literary leaders and used these to establish the reputation of his history. He later attracted subscribers by placing their names in biographical footnotes in the *Works*. In 1886 his business and publishing house was destroyed by fire, and to recover capital, Bancroft planned a set of biographies, *The Chronicles of the Builders of the Commonwealth*, as a sequel to the *Works*. Subjects were charged $1,000 or more for a biography and portrait. The *Chronicles* hurt the *Works* through association.

CONCLUSIONS: Bancroft showed a genius for improvisation rather than methodical planning. The content of the *Works* was influenced by subscription publishing demands. The result was a set of annals by many hands, a storehouse of information rather than an interpretive history—a condition arising from the pressures of its production, publication, and sale.

406. Comaromi, John Phillip (Ph.D., University of Michigan, 1969). **A history of the Dewey Decimal Classification: editions one through fifteen, 1876-1951.** 463p. Order no. 70-14,490.

PURPOSE: This is a history of the Dewey Decimal Classification through its first fifteen editions (1876-1951).

PROCEDURE: The sources for the study were the correspondence and papers found in the Melvil Dewey Collection at Columbia University; the files of Forest Press, publisher of the DDC; the editorial files at the Decimal Classification Division of the Library of Congress; librarianship periodicals current for the period of this study; and the first 15 editions of the DDC.

FINDINGS: The outline of the first edition of the DDC was drawn from a scheme done by William Torrey Harris; Dewey and several members of the Amherst College faculty provided the 1,000 headings that composed the classification. After the second edition, harsh criticism was levied upon the system, but increasing numbers of American and foreign libraries adopted the scheme. After the fourth edition, Dewey yielded editorship to May Seymour, but he retained control of the DDC until his death in 1931. After his death and the retirement of Seymour's successor, Meannie Dorkas Fellows, the editorial continuity was broken in 1937 and a crisis occurred that culminated in 1951 in the unsuccessful fifteenth edition. The fifteenth edition, nevertheless, made possible some necessary modernizing.

407. Davis, Charles Hargis (Ph.D., Indiana University, 1969). **An approach to automated vocabulary control in indexes of organic compounds.** 133p. Order no. 69-14,700.

PURPOSE: The purpose of this study was to demonstrate the feasibility of using a well-designed authority list and an appropriate computer program to reduce automatically the scattering of index terms that results from the use of synonymous organic compound names.

PROCEDURE: Nomenclature rules, similar to but more consistent than those now used by *Chemical Abstracts* in its subject indexes, were set forth for various types of compounds. An authority list based on these rules was developed and built into a computer program as a dictionary look-up routine. The 741 organic compound names from a recent issue of *Index Chemicus*, which is computer-produced but has no vocabulary control, were selected as input. As each name was read by the computer, it was sent through the dictionary look-up procedure to determine whether it was present in the authority list. If the name is not present in the list, then it is deemed suitable for the index and is printed out in its original form. If the name is found in the list, then it is converted to the preferred index term before being printed out with the information associated with it.

FINDINGS: Of the 741 entries, 71 or 9.6 percent were converted. The entire procedure, run on an IBM 7040 digital computer with 32K of core storage, required 9 minutes 1.4 seconds (this included processing, execution and leading). The cost was $22.56. Since this test was made on a bimonthly index, one could project that the total annual cost would be roughly six times this amount, or $135.36.

CONCLUSIONS: The approach is feasible not only for indexes of organic compounds, but for any indexes where semantic ambiguity is minimal.

408. Evans, Charles Whitney (D.L.S., University of California, Berkeley, 1969). **The attitudes of adults toward the public library, and their relationship to library use.** 246p. Order no. 70-13,004.

PURPOSE: This study was conducted to determine whether or not a significant difference exists between the attitudes of those who use their public library and the attitudes of those who do not, which might account for non-use of the library by individuals within the latter group.

PROCEDURE: A 16-statement Likert-type attitude questionnaire was sent to 4,000 registered voters in Oceanside, California, in July 1967. There were 525 usable responses: 367 from users (used the Oceanside Public Library at least once within the preceding 12-month period) and 153 from nonusers.

FINDINGS: Chi-square tests showed that the two groups differed significantly in education, sex, use of other libraries, and duration of residence in Oceanside; the two groups did not differ significantly in age, income, marital status, race, occupation or in the distance of their homes from the library. Using t-test analysis, it was found that in attitude, public library users were more favorable to the library than were nonusers. The difference between the attitudes of the library users and nonusers was independent of the other significant differences detected between the user and nonuser groups.

CONCLUSIONS: Less favorable attitudes toward the public library may discourage library use. Therefore, it may be possible to increase the number of library users within a community by creating a more favorable attitude toward the library within the community.

409. Evans, Gayle Edward (Ph.D., University of Illinois, 1969). **The influence of book selection agents upon book collection usage in academic libraries.** 167p. Order no. 70-845.

PURPOSE: The purpose of the research was to determine what differences exist in the use of books selected by different methods (librarian, faculty, blanket order-approval plan) in academic libraries.

PROCEDURE: Four unmatched university libraries were studied; each institution used at least two of the three selection methods. Random samples of titles (500 or more) were drawn for each method of selection used at each institution. The physical books were examined to determine whether or not they had circulated in the first year they were available to the public. Chi-square analysis was used on the data. Information was gathered on the number of contacts the selectors had had with patron or potential patron and others that could influence the use of materials. FINDINGS: There was a significant difference in the pattern of use of current imprint English language materials. The analysis of the data regarding contact with patrons indicated that librarians came into contact with more real and potential patrons than did either the faculty or the book jobbers. Public service librarians tended to select a higher percentage of titles that circulated than did technical service librarians.

410. Evraiff, Lois Ann L. (Ed.D., Wayne State University, 1969). **A survey of the development and emerging patterns in the preparation of school librarians.** 273p. Order no. 70-19,055.
PURPOSE: The background out of which the curricula of school librarians had developed from 1887 to 1969 was traced in this paper.
PROCEDURE: The chief sources of data were the publications of professional organizations, selected writings from books and journals dealing with the preparation of librarians and 1967 college catalogs describing the library education programs of 35 ALA accredited master's degree programs, 32 non-accredited master's degree programs, and a representative sample of 27 undergraduate library science programs.
FINDINGS: Library standards and accreditation practices have affected both school library education training programs and the pattern of preparation of school librarians. Public school personnel and library school personnel disagree about the educational preparation needed for school librarians. There is no significant pattern of differences between ALA accredited and non-accredited master's degree programs. The professional role of the school librarians should be that of a materials specialist according to standards and library educators, but this isn't substantiated by a review of the library school catalogs. School librarians are the only librarians likely to have supervised field experience as part of their training.

411. Gerulaitis, Leonardas Vytautas (Ph.D., University of Michigan, 1969). **The Venetian incunabula: printers and readers.** 478p. Order no. 70-4085.
PURPOSE: This study looked at the people who bought and presumably read the books printed during the last three decades of fifteenth century Italy, with Venice, the largest center producing incunabula in Europe, chosen for study.
FINDINGS: Venice was eminently suited to attract printing. Printers in general were not subsidized by private patrons or institutions. Ecclesiastical and civil censorship was almost totally lacking. The main interest of the incunabula publishers was to make the largest profit possible; they preferred to produce books likely to appeal to the public. These books, therefore, can be assumed to represent faithfully the reading public's taste. Humanism, traditionally regarded as the very core of the Italian Renaissance, could never have involved more than a rather small minority. The reading public, which clearly represented the higher strata of society, failed to generate enough demand to make the publishing of humanistic writings

FINDINGS (cont'd): a profitable undertaking. The greatest demand was for
university textbooks and professional literature.

412. Graham, Robert James (Ed.D., University of Michigan, 1969). **The impact
of Title II of the Elementary and Secondary Education Act of 1965 on
selected Michigan high schools.** 187p. Order no. 70-21,669.
PURPOSE: The purpose of the study was to determine the extent of use of the
instructional materials center in selected Michigan high schools as related to financial grants under Title II of the Elementary and Secondary Education Act of 1965.
PROCEDURE: Based on money received from ESEA II during the combined years
1966, 1967, and 1968, the 19 senior high schools with the greatest totals in Michigan were selected for study. In each of the schools, opinionnaires were sent to all
school librarians, all English, mathematics, science, and social studies teachers,
and two classes of students.
FINDINGS: The relationship between the three-year infusion of Title II funds to
the instructional materials program and increases in teacher and student use of
materials was not great enough to be considered statistically significant. When
total Title II receipts, state equalized valuation of the district, and per pupil expenditures were used as a basis for analysis, per pupil expenditures made the
greatest difference in influencing the use of materials in teaching and learning.

413. Hannigan, Jane Anne Thérèse (D.L.S., Columbia University, 1969). **Reading,
viewing, and listening characteristics of academically talented students.** 740p.
Order no. 72-19,062.
PURPOSE: The purpose of the dissertation was to describe the reading characteristics and patterns of academically talented students during their senior year in high
school and to describe the nature and extent of use made by these students of
audio-visual materials.
PROCEDURE: Data from 117 academically talented students (65 boys and 52
girls) from 12 high schools in the New York metropolitan area that provided programs for such students were collected during two eight-week periods during
the 1963-64 school year through questionnaires, checklists, diary records, and
interviews.
FINDINGS: Although reading had a major place in the students' allocation of
time, most students did not have as much time available for free reading as they
would have liked. Free reading consisted primarily of reading newspapers and
periodicals, although the students were interested in and enthusiastic about contemporary literature. They read few items in conjunction with research for term
papers. Materials used for assignments and free reading were generally not obtained
from libraries. The influence of the teacher had the greatest effect on their selection of reading materials. They opposed all forms of censorship.

414. Harris, Jessica L. (Ph.D., Columbia University, 1969). **Subject headings:
factors influencing formation and choice; with special reference to Library
of Congress and H. W. Wilson practice.** 296p. Order no. 70-6991.
PURPOSE: The influences of several administrative factors on selected types of
subject headings were studied.
PROCEDURE: Most of the study was based on analysis of a 10 percent sample of
the seventh edition of the Library of Congress subject heading list.

FINDINGS: For the L.C. subject headings, there is a positive correlation between the number of subdivisions and the number of titles entered under a given heading, indicating that part of the reason for introduction of aspect subdivisions is to reduce the length of undifferentiated files. The choice between inversions and direct entry of adjectival phrases in which the adjective denotes a national, linguistic, ethnic, or geographic distinction is strongly influenced by which of the two words in the phrase better specifies the subject. Inversions and subdivisions of headings are used to produce a classified subarrangement. The size of the library for which cataloging is designed does not affect the relative scope of the headings used. A reasonable computer arrangement can be produced using only the characters actually appearing in the entry. For certain types of headings a general policy of cross referencing from some point other than the entry word is perfectly conceivable. In L.C., from many parenthetical expressions and from words following "and," there is a tendency to make cross references.

415. Held, Charles Holborn (Ph.D., Wayne State University, 1969). **The status of library technicians in the United States.** 233p. Order no. 72-16,212.
PURPOSE: The purpose of this study was to determine the status of library technicians in the United States, with particular emphasis on the history, education, status, attitudes of professional librarians toward library technicians, and the policies of the individual states toward these employees.
PROCEDURE: A historical and literary search was coupled with three surveys.
FINDINGS: The idea of the library technician is nearly as old as professional library education itself. The number of training institutions for library technicians is large; these generally are found in two-year training institutions. Over 90 percent of library technician curricula have been founded since 1960; 75 percent since 1965. More diversity is found in library technician curricula than in professional library education. Over 90 percent of the library technician students are female. Over 75 percent of the instructors have professional degrees. There is overwhelming acceptance of the idea of the library technician at all levels of the library profession. Over 66 percent of all states and provinces have contemplated or are contemplating a written policy concerning these technicians. There is still considerable controversy over the details of their training and their position within the structure of librarianship.

416. Highfill, William Carl (Ph.D., University of Illinois, 1969). **The relationship of indexing depth to subject catalog retrieval effectiveness.** 287p. Order no. 70-13,351.
PURPOSE: The study investigated the relationship between the frequency with which references to works were selected during subject searches of the subject component of a library catalog and the number of subject headings assigned to those works, and the effect of user selection criteria upon this relationship.
PROCEDURE: Three samples were taken: random sampling of the shelf-list, systematic sampling of subject entries in the card catalog, and subject entries selected by catalog users during subject searches.
FINDINGS: The mean number of subject headings for the shelf-list sample was found to be significantly smaller than either of the means of the subject catalog samples. No difference was found between the means of the subject catalog samples. The user-generated sample was examined to determine if criteria used by the patron

FINDINGS (cont'd): in selecting entries from a subject heading file could account for the difference between the adjusted user-generated sample mean and the adjusted systematic sample mean. Publication date, title, connotation, and position of entry were especially evident as selection criteria. Publication date and title connotation were also found to be non-randomly distributed on the variable "number of subject headings." No significant difference in subject catalog user behavior was observed. An association was found between the user-generated entries and the summer circulation record of central stack materials on the distribution of cases among the various classification categories.

417. Huang, George Wenhong (Ph.D., University of Idaho, 1969). **Public secondary school library programs in Idaho.** 198p. Order no. 70-10,793.

PURPOSE: The study examined and determined the adequacy of the public secondary programs in Idaho compared with the school library standards adopted by Idaho, the Northwest Association of Secondary and Higher Schools and the American Library Association. In addition, the size of a school and the school district's financial resources were analyzed in relation to the existing library programs.

PROCEDURE: Questionnaires were sent to 186 public secondary schools listed in the *Idaho Educational Directory, 1967-68*; responses were received from 156 schools.

FINDINGS: A large percentage of secondary school libraries in Idaho were below the state, regional, and national standards. Financing for these libraries has progressed slowly; per pupil expenditure was $2.70. Neither size of a school nor general fund expenditures of a school district were found to be significantly related to adequate school library programs.

CONCLUSIONS: Factors other than school size and district finances are influencing school library programs in Idaho.

418. Khurshid, Anis (Ph.D., University of Pittsburgh, 1969). **Standards for library education in Burma, Ceylon, India and Pakistan.** 752p. Order no. 70-213.

PURPOSE: The purpose of the dissertation was to develop a common set of standards for library education in Burma, Ceylon, India, and Pakistan. The study was primarily concerned with post-Bachelor courses offered by the universities during the period from 1915 to 1966.

PROCEDURE: Questionnaires went to 34 schools, 25 library experts from Australia, Canada, Denmark, the United Kingdom, and the United States who had had assignments in the area, to 114 librarians who did not have any direct connection with the training programs, and to S. R. Ranganathan.

FINDINGS: There were 30 schools in India and four in Pakistan; Burma and Ceylon did not have any graduate programs. These schools offered programs for a Ph.D., M. Lib. Sc., and/or Diploma of B. Lib. Sc. There were inadequate resources and facilities in most schools. The curricula were not balanced. Elective courses were too limited. Admission requirements were not uniform. There were a large number of part-time faculty. The leadership of the schools was by university librarians.

CONCLUSIONS: A mechanism for accreditation by the appropriate university organization in each country was proposed. The proposed standards are qualitative and quite similar to those used in the United Kingdom, the United States, and Latin America.

419. Kunkle, Hannah Josephine (Ph.D., Florida State University, 1969). **A historical study of the extension activities of the California State Library with particular emphasis on its role in rural library development, 1850-1966.** 365p. Order no. 70-3821.

PURPOSE: The purpose of the paper was to trace the evolution of the California State Library as an agency aloof from the educational needs of the people into a strong force for library adult education.

FINDINGS: Until 1850 the Library served only the legislators. The first move toward extension began with W. Perkins (1890-1898). James L. Gillis (1899-1917) implemented the philosophy that the State Library should serve all the people of the state equally. He established the county library system. Under Mabel R. Gillis (1930-1951) federal aid came to California libraries. Mrs. Carma R. Leigh was appointed State Librarian on September 16, 1951. She encouraged the systems concept of library development and worked with the California Library Association to establish minimum standards. Mrs. Leigh's great achievement was her legislative program.

CONCLUSIONS: The California State Library has made important contributions to library adult education. Its main influence has been its philosophy that the Library should serve all the people, the establishment of the county library system, and its legislative program for state aid.

420. Lilley, Dorothy Brace (D.L.S., Columbia University, 1969). **Graduate education needed by information specialists and the extent to which it is offered in accredited library schools.** 264p. Order no. 69-15,693.

PURPOSE: The purpose of the paper was to compare the patterns of organization and the activities of scientific information centers and university libraries with the education needed and offered in accredited library schools.

PROCEDURE: A survey of 10 scientific information centers, two university libraries and five accredited library schools was supplemented by data from five officers of relevant professional organizations and 19 faculty members who were also interviewed.

FINDINGS: Three different patterns of organization of the scientific information centers were found, but these differences did not appreciably affect the activities performed or the kind of education needed by information specialists from pattern to pattern. However, differences in organization of information centers and libraries were related to differences in the kind of education needed by personnel in the two types of institutions. Basic in the graduate program for information specialists should be: uses of reference works, collecting information for answering questions immediately, structure of publishing, information system design, retrieval by logical operations, research in information problems, information center administration, coordinating elements of information systems, developing terminology authority, cost analysis, preparation of current awareness tools, comparison and evaluation of information systems and cataloging. Library schools offer all these areas of knowledge.

RECOMMENDATIONS: Library school students should be screened for personality characteristics as well as academic background. Inquiry should be stressed in courses. Reference and related areas should be subject oriented. Provisions should be made in the curriculum for anticipating future developments in the information field.

421. Litofsky, Barry (Ph.D., University of Pennsylvania, 1969). **Utility of automatic classification systems for information storage and retrieval.** 507p. Order no. 69-21,394.

PURPOSE: This dissertation represents an attempt to solve the problems that large-scale, on-line information storage and retrieval systems face.

PROCEDURE: The methodology on which this solution is based is that of a *posteriori* automatic classification by two independent methods, one manual and one automatic, of a file of 50,000 document descriptions.

FINDINGS: It was shown that the advantages were not dependent upon the indexing method used. Among those automatic classification algorithms studied, one particular algorithm, CLASFY, consistently outperformed the others. This algorithm produced classifications at least as good, with respect to the measures established in this dissertation, as the *a priori* manual classification system currently in use with the documents file.

422. McEowen, James Royce (Ph.D., University of Pennsylvania, 1969). **PAL: a design for a personal automated library.** 300p. Order no. 69-21,398.

PURPOSE: This dissertation provides an overall system design of a self-contained *personal automated library* for the organization, storage and retrieval of papers, books, articles, reports, notes, memoranda, letters, and the like.

FINDINGS: Some of the salient features of the design are: data storage based on a single serial file; auxiliary data structures that can be specified by the user concurrently with the formation of any number of personal data formats; a semi-automatic hierarchical classification process allowing a hierarchy of the items on file to be formed, augmented and modified automatically, interactively or with a user-proportioned mixture of both techniques; a simple yet effective automatic indexing routine with an ability to work with Boolean expressions; and cross referencing among item records on file.

423. McLaughlin, Richard Clarke (Ph.D., Syracuse University, 1969). **Interest profiles for information dissemination.** 149p. Order no. 70-10,367.

PURPOSE: This study investigated the use of a semantic differential procedure for constructing profiles of individual users' interests to be matched with documents for selective dissemination by a computerized current awareness information system. Additionally, this study examined the grouping of users into behaviorally-defined interest clusters for the construction of group profiles.

PROCEDURE: The subjects in the five interest clusters that were constructed were assigned among five treatments: three based upon information from the semantic differential procedure and two control treatments. One cycle of a selective dissemination of information systems was simulated, using the five-profile construction methods to provide input data. The system generated a list of descriptors and corresponding abstracts that were sent to each subject for evaluation. The descriptors and the abstracts were rated "of interest" or "not of interest" by 227 respondents.

FINDINGS: Significant differences were found on all three evaluation criteria among the profile construction methods used and on two of the three criteria among the interest obtained.

CONCLUSIONS: The results indicate that the semantic differential technique is capapble of providing an effective means for initial profile construction. Those

CONCLUSIONS (cont'd): systems now operating or contemplating operating on a group profile basis should additionally consider the use of cluster analysis for the establishment of common interest clusters having group profiles.

424. Magrill, Rose Mary (Ph.D., University of Illinois, 1969). **Occupational image and the choice of librarianship as a career.** 201p. Order no. 70-13,404.
PURPOSE: Graduate students who enter library schools within a year after receiving an undergraduate degree were studied to determine if they held a more favorable image of librarianship than comparable graduate students who entered related graduate fields. The relationship to the image of librarianship of certain background factors—view of possible library work activities, reactions to library work experience, reactions to experiences with libraries and size of hometown—were also investigated.
PROCEDURE: Data were collected from 70 library school students in three representative library schools and from 114 first-year graduate students in education, political science, journalism and sociology in the same large state university as one of the library schools. Data collection instruments included a set of occupational stereotype scales based on the semantic differential, a library work activities checklist, a form for ranking of occupational values and a short questionnaire. Chi square, Kolmogorov-Smirnov and t-test analysis were employed.
FINDINGS: The library school students and non-library school students differed significantly on each of the occupational stereotype scales and on responses to 80 percent of the library work activities. Among those students with library work experience, those who rated the experience as valuable showed a tendency to hold a more favorable stereotype of librarianship than those who rated the experience as less than valuable. Reactions to experiences with both public and academic librarians showed a tendency to be related to stereotypes of librarianship.

425. Manheimer, Martha L. (Ph.D., University of Pittsburgh, 1969). **The applicability of the NASA Thesaurus to the file of documents indexed prior to its publication.** 205p. Order no. 70-10,555.
PURPOSE: The objective of the dissertation was to determine the applicability of the NASA *Thesaurus* to a file of documents indexed prior to its publication by using another authority list, the NASA *Subject Authority List.*
PROCEDURE: An analysis was made of the differences between the forms of the terms in the two authority lists, the *Thesaurus* and the *Subject Authority List.* The second part of the study considered the effect of the change in terminology upon the empirically developed strategies used to search the file during one retrospective search period.
FINDINGS: The two authority lists represented two different systems for the analysis of information. Although the *Thesaurus* was usable to some extent with the file indexed prior to its publication, it did not describe the retrospective file as represented by the empirically developed strategies used originally to search the retrospective file.

426. Nagar, Murari Lal (D.L.S., Columbia University, 1969). **Public library movement in Baroda 1901-1949.** 382p. Order no. 69-17,609.
PURPOSE: The purpose of the study was to trace the development of the public library movement in Baroda, the first territory in India to develop a free public library system.

FINDINGS: His Highness Maharaja Sayajirao III, Geokwar of Baroda (1862-1939), invited William Alanson Borden (1853-1931) to Baroda in 1910 to expand a library movement that had originated in 1906 as a people's movement in the form of Mitra Mandal (Society of Friends) libraries. Borden planned a comprehensive network of libraries: a state central library, district, town and village libraries. His successors, Kudalkar, Dutt and Waknis, brought the movement to a high level. However, the system ultimately declined because of lack of adequate organization, steady finances, social and economic conditions in Baroda, the failure on the part of the libraries to provide enough books to challenge the varied interests and intellectual demands of the people, and the integration of Baroda into Bombay, a state that did not pursue the public library philosophy of Baroda.

CONCLUSIONS: The movement was not too narrowly dependent upon the personality of the Maharaja. It lived even beyond his death; the post-Sayajirao government was equally interested in the development of libraries. The pioneer public library movement in Baroda exercised a wholesome influence on many of the regions of India.

427. Picache, Ursula de Guzman (Ph.D., University of Illinois at Champaign-Urbana, 1969). **Some effects of summer institute participation on school librarians' provision of services and on their attitude toward the instructional materials center concept.** 173p. Order no. 70-13,443.

PURPOSE: The effects of summer institute participation on school librarians' library programs and on their attitudes toward the instructional materials center concept were studied.

PROCEDURE: Fifteen school librarians who had attended six 1965 NDEA summer institutes and a corresponding group who had not were studied using an observation/interview guide and a form of Osgood's semantic differential. The data were analyzed by the Wilcoxon matched pairs signed-ranks tests and the students' t-test.

FINDINGS: School librarians who participated in NDEA summer institutes were found to have provided a significantly greater number and variety of services for students and for teachers than comparable school librarians who did not participate in such institutes. Institute participation seemed not to have exerted much influence on the attitudes of school librarians toward concepts related to the instructional materials center idea.

428. Plate, Kenneth Harry (Ph.D., Rutgers University, 1969). **Middle management in university libraries: the development of a theoretical model for analysis.** 109p. Order no. 70-10,094.

PURPOSE: The paper attempted to develop a methodology for the description of middle management personnel in university libraries and to identify the backgrounds, mobility, role perceptions and attitudes prevalent among middle managers.

PROCEDURE: Questionnaires and interview schedules (based on Robert Presthus' model of patterns of accommodation to bureaucratic milieu) were completed by 77 middle managers in 15 northeastern university libraries that belonged to the Association of Research Libraries.

FINDINGS: The ideal-type middle manager in university libraries exhibits characteristics consonant with upward-mobility (the managers are local, avoid controversies, prefer subordinates who conform, are satisfied with their positions, have high career aspirations, are conservative, and view subordinates in detached terms).

RECOMMENDATIONS: A new model consisting of three new ideal-types (the Specialist, the Executive, and the Technocrat) was constructed; this model should be regarded as theoretical since it has not yet been tested.

429. Price, Samuel Timothy (Ed.D., University of Pittsburgh, 1969). **The development of a thesaurus of descriptors for an information retrieval system in special education.** 473p. Order no. 70-4538.
PURPOSE: The study describes a methodology for the design and development of an improved thesaurus for use as the terminology control mechanism in an information retrieval system.
PROCEDURE: The words and language, identified through a five-year retrospective search of the professional literature of the field, were classified according to their meaning for the field of special education. This was done by assigning each term to its appropriate position on a specialized graphic paradigm of special education patterned after a taxonomy of special education so that all known taxonomic parameters of the field were included. The system groups the terminology of a given subject matter field into taxonomically related sub-sets called taxons. The terms within each taxon are subsequently rearranged hierarchically within the taxon. The thesaurus which results from the execution of this methodology is printed in alphabetical order.
FINDINGS: The differences between the meanings associated with the experimentally derived taxons and the meanings associated with the taxons by experts in the field of special education are not significant. It is very likely that the thesaurus is highly representative, insofar as word meaning is concerned, of the field of special education.

430. Ramer, James David (Ph.D., Columbia University, 1969). **Fifteenth-century Spanish printing.** 732p. Order no. 72-19,085.
PURPOSE: A study was made of the typographic history of the fifteenth century and of the roles of emigrants and native-born in printing activities.
FINDINGS: The church and crown were the most frequent sources of outside financial support for fifteenth century Spanish printing. Indulgences, liturgical works, laws, ordinances, translations and writings of late medieval and early Renaissance Spanish writers were numerous among the imprints of the early Spanish presses. Of these, an unusually high number were in the vernacular. Because the evidence was too circumstantial to settle the question conclusively, the first Spanish city in which the art of printing was practiced was not determined. Emigrant printers were found to be more productive, better craftsmen and dominated more of the presses in Spanish cities for which there are extant incunabula than their native colleagues.

431. Reeling, Patricia Ann (Ph.D., Columbia University, 1969). **Undergraduate female students as potential recruits to the library profession.** 256p. Order no. 70-7053.
PURPOSE: The purposes of the dissertation were (1) to evaluate the relative effectiveness of selected library recruitment activities in stimulating undergraduate female students to consider a career in librarianship; (2) to isolate and define certain measurable characteristics that typify undergraduate female students who are potential recruits to librarianship; and (3) to identify those factors that have influenced

PURPOSE (cont'd):undergraduate female students to consider careers in librarianship. PROCEDURE: Experimental design, standardized tests, questionnaires and interviews were used to study 650 undergraduate female students attending Our Lady of Cincinnati College on a full time basis during 1965-66.
FINDINGS: Library science was preferred less and rejected more than other graduate fields of study. The recruitment tea was the most effective means of inducing more positive attitudes toward library careers. It was found that potential library recruits had parents with a lower terminal educational level, obtained higher scores on the Scholastic Aptitude Test, obtained higher scores for "order" and lower scores for "autonomy," "heterosexuality" and "economic and political values," received higher grades, were more likely to have majored in education and taken a library science course, liked to read and use libraries, and had more part-time library work experience than those who had rejected library science as a career. Students were deterred from library careers primarily because of the negative image they had of librarians whom they frequently confused with clerical workers. The students were for the most part untouched by any library recruitment publicity.

432. Rettenmayer, John William (Ph.D., University of California, Berkeley, 1969).
      The effect of file ordering on retrieval costs. 154p. Order no. 70-14,321.
PURPOSE: This study proposes and investigates file ordering and retrieval techniques which, it is hypothesized, will (1) reduce the average cost of retrieving records which satisfy a query, and (2) increase the rate of retrieval in the initial portion of the response period.
PROCEDURE: A self-adaptive version of the k-centroids algorithm of MacQueen is used to detect clusters of records, where a member of a cluster is more similar in key content to the other records in the cluster than to records which are not in the cluster. A file, which is usually sequenced in an arbitrary fashion that is neither intended nor expected to affect the retrieval costs, is reordered so that the records in a cluster are assigned to adjacent storage locations.
FINDINGS: Experiments on both artificially generated files and small sample files drawn from the 1960 census file indicate that hypothesis (1) is generally accomplished but hypothesis (2) is consistently not supported. The mean retrieval cost per record is decreased, on the average over several queries, by approximately 10 percent, with savings up to 30 percent occasionally obtained.

433. Ribbens, Dennis Neil (Ph.D., University of Wisconsin, 1969). **The reading**
      interests of Thoreau, Hawthorne and Lanier. 527p. Order no. 70-3677.
PURPOSE: The purpose of the study was to determine whether a unifying radix around which almost all of a person's reading centers can be found in the reading of three adults: Thoreau, Hawthorne and Lanier.
PROCEDURE: Personal documents (such as journals, correspondence, personal libraries, records of library withdrawals) and personal testimony were used in the study. The subject content of the books read by Thoreau, Hawthorne and Lanier and the subject contents of what each reader took from his reading were identified, analyzed, categorized by dominant subject content and evaluated. Time categories were also constructed for each reader, thereby enabling comparisons within as well as among the different subject categories.
FINDINGS: Multiple radices for each of the readers were identified. Thoreau's interest in nature and in other manifestations of original conditions provided a

FINDINGS (cont'd): unifying focus for most of his reading. Hawthorne's moral perspective was reflected in much of his reading, but a good deal of his other reading reflected unrelated subject interests and desultory reading. Lanier's philosophy of synthesis, and his interest in belles-lettres in particular, provided a unifying focus for most of his reading.

434. Shearer, Kenneth Decker, Jr. (Ph.D., Rutgers University, 1969). **A comparison of the contents of book selection lists produced nationally and locally for public library use.** 121p. Order no. 70-638.
PURPOSE: The point of the study was to ask if the *adult and young adult portions* of the published book selection lists, "Booklist and Subscription Books Bulletin" and the "Bulletin" of Virginia Kirkus Service, Inc. (with emphasis on the former) could replace the Detroit Public Library's self-produced list of titles recommended for its popular *adult and young adult* collections.
PROCEDURE: A content analysis was made of the Detroit list during January and February, 1964, Booklist during January and February, 1964 and Kirkus from July through September, 1964. Samples taken from these citations were checked against Brooklyn Public Library's catalogs.
FINDINGS: The evidence consistently supported the hypothesis that substantial differences would be found between the adult and young adult contents of book selection lists produced nationally and locally for public library use. The policies, procedures, costs and results of producing Detroit's list are also included in the study as is an annotated bibliography of 130 items related to public library book selection procedures, tools and research.
CONCLUSIONS: It is concluded that a complex book selection process like Detroit's can be streamlined without seriously altering the patterns of selection or eliminating books that reflect the selection policies.

435. Shipps, Harrold Southard, Jr. (Ph.D., University of Denver, 1969). **Evaluation of United States Air Force base libraries supporting undergraduate and graduate education programs in collaboration with civilian colleges and universities.** 391p. Order no. 70-6688.
PURPOSE: The adequacy of base library service and collections to support the undergraduate and graduate study programs undertaken on U.S. Air Force installations by officers and airmen, through civilian institutions, during off-duty hours was evaluated.
PROCEDURE: During the academic term of 1967, resources and services of 71 base libraries in the continental U.S. were studied.
FINDINGS: In general, Air Force base libraries were found to be inadequate insofar as their capacity to support off-duty educational programs of undergraduate and graduate curriculum. Contributing factors to this lack of curriculum related library resources included: inadequate communication between base librarians and representatives of the educational institutions, and inadequate personnel authorization and levels of expenditures.
RECOMMENDATIONS: Contractural agreements between the Air Force and civilian educational institutions sponsoring off-duty educational programs should clearly reflect consideration of requirements for library service. Special budget assistance and increased professional staff authorization should be provided to base libraries.

436. Spence, Paul Herbert (Ph.D., University of Illinois, 1969). **A comparative study of university library organizational structure.** 149p. Order no. 70-988.

PURPOSE: Max Weber theorized that as organizations increase in size, there is also an increase in organizational complexity, in the occupational specialities and pro-fessionalization of the staff, in the percentage of personnel in administrative posi-tions, in the average span of control at each level of the administrative hierarchy, in the written rules and regulations governing operations, in the impersonality of decision making, and in the career stability of employees. This study is an attempt to test Weber's theory by the use of Peter Blau's measurement methodology to see if it applies to American university libraries.

PROCEDURE: The 62 American university libraries which were members of the Association of Research Libraries in 1964-65 were studied. Rank correlations were computed by Spearman's formula for determining coefficients of rank correlation.

FINDINGS: Weber's theory of organizations was not supported. There was a signifi-cant correlation between all measures of size, but there was no significant correla-tion between the size of the library and any of the other components of the theory. The correlations between age and the bureaucratic organizational attributes studied were insignificant or small.

437. Storhecker, Edwin Charles (Ph.D., University of Michigan, 1969). **American juvenile literary periodicals, 1789-1826.** 330p. Order no. 70-4203.

PURPOSE: The dissertation provides a review and compilation of the juvenile liter-ary periodicals published in the U.S. from 1789-1826, the "formative years" of the juvenile literary periodical.

PROCEDURE: Histories of American periodicals and children's literature were searched for reference to the periodicals. The holdings of various libraries were verified in *The Union List of Serials of the United States and Canada*. Excluded from coverage were four publications which had been circulated strictly for religious instruction and eight titles which were no longer extant.

FINDINGS: The tone of the literature for the young person suggested a change from the purely didactic editorial policy to one of instructive entertainment. Juvenile lit-erature began to demonstrate and improve in quality. Children welcomed reading material which extended beyond the textbook realm and parents willingly paid the subscription, and so assisted in the creation of a reading public for a richer juvenile literature. The third part of the dissertation includes: bibliographic data of the extant and non-extant titles; a register of editors, printers and/or publishers and engravers; a chronological and geographical listing; and indexes to cited sources and signed articles and illustrations.

438. Ting, Lee-Lsia Hsu (Ph.D., University of Chicago, 1969). **Government control of the press in modern China, 1900-1949; a study of its theories, operations, and effects.** 448p.

439. Ward, Pearl Lewis (Ph.D., University of Southern California, 1969). **Federal aid to school libraries; a study of the Title II, Phase II program in California, 1965-66.** 246p. Order no. 69-17,894.

PURPOSE: The purpose of the study was to determine the effect of federal aid on library programs by investigating the Title II, Phase II program in California.

PROCEDURE: Questionnaires were sent to principals and librarians in the 48 pilot

PROCEDURE (cont'd): project libraries which received grants in 1965-66. Interviews were conducted in 26 of the libraries.

FINDINGS: The largest percentage of grants was made to elementary schools. The greatest values gained from Phase II were increased use of library materials, improvements in the schools' instructional program, and better working relationships between the library staff and the teachers. The greatest problems were insufficient staff, facilities and time for selecting materials.

CONCLUSIONS: Federal aid results in enrichment of library programs and promotion of the media center concept. Phase II programs encouraged new elementary school libraries and expansion of existing libraries.

RECOMMENDATIONS: The Phase II program in California should be continued, but review and evaluation should be continuous. The program should work to develop outstanding model libraries and provide funds to develop new elementary school libraries. Continuing grants should be made to districts which have given substantial support in personnel, facilities and equipment to their libraries. Case studies of individual Phase II libraries should be made.

440. Weinberg, Paul Richard (Ph.D., University of Pennsylvania, 1969). **A time sharing chemical information retrieval system.** 154p. Order no. 21,452.

PURPOSE: An application of the principles of general purpose time sharing systems to the design of an information retrieval system is described.

PROCEDURE: An information retrieval system was constructed following the design principles of general purpose time sharing systems.

FINDINGS: The information retrieval system's component parts, including scheduling algorithms, are described and justified in terms of analogies to time sharing. The benefits resulting from this approach stem principally from the control of resources inherent in a time sharing system, and its ability to process requests from a number of terminals simultaneously.

441. Wright, Herbert Curtis (Ph.D., Case Western Reserve, 1969). **Metagraphy and graphic priority; a discursus for catalogers.** 348p. Order no. 70-26,012.

PURPOSE: This study posed two questions: (1) Why transliterate? (2) How can bibliographical confusion be eliminated in transcription?

PROCEDURE: The first question was analyzed in terms of cultural pluralism and the need for consistency in the identification and indexing of bibliographical terms; the second question in terms of the separate realism of spoken and written language and the graphic nature of bibliography.

FINDINGS: Native documents written in foreign scripts, when rendered in English, require transcription as well as translation. Proper nouns, for example, must be transcribed because they are not class abstractions with meaning but labels in the identification of unique entries. Graphic priority of phones and graphs is necessary because transcription involves the antithetical claims of spoken and written utterances. The priority of graphs over phones must be asserted in transliterating the data of bibliography.

CONCLUSIONS: The principle of graphic priority, with its corollaries of protographic fidelity and graphemic reversibility is seen as the means of solving the problems of bibliographical transcription.

442. Abrera, Josefa B. (Ph.D., Indiana University, 1970). **Bibliographic and information control requirements of the small/medium sized public library.** 140p. Order no. 71-12,441.

PURPOSE: The principal objective of the study was to determine the bibliographic control requirements of a small/medium sized public library from the point of view of the expressed needs of the library patron through telephone and catalog reference as well as the needs of the professional librarian in identifying, recording, and processing materials.

FINDINGS: Present bibliographic information in a catalog record provides sufficient information to support users' needs. There is no immediate need to expand access beyond the present levels provided in a library catalog. The primary deterrent to effective bibliographic services is the low level of subject specificity in indexing.

443. Allen, Kenneth William (Ed.D., Southern Illinois University, 1970). **An investigation of student and faculty attitudes and their utilization of the community college library in three selected colleges within Illinois.** 195p. Order no. 70-25,511.

PURPOSE: This study investigated student and faculty attitudes and utilization patterns in community college libraries.

PROCEDURE: Questionnaires were sent to 1,312 students in randomly selected classes, 194 full time faculty, and 4,657 students and faculty as they entered the library at three community colleges in Illinois.

FINDINGS: The majority of the students reported that library utilization related to academic success, that the library resources met their needs, that they used the library primarily to study and that they consulted the librarian for assistance. The majority of the faculty indicated that teaching techniques were affected by a lack of library materials, that they required students to use the library and that they had materials on library reserve. In addition, it was found that full time students depended upon the library more than part time students. Students enrolled in the transfer, general studies and occupational curricula varied greatly in their attitudes and utilization patterns from the unclassified students. Neither the courses taught by faculty nor the educational level of the faculty have much importance in reflecting attitudes or utilization patterns.

444. Amick, Daniel James (Ph.D., University of Pittsburgh, 1970). **Information processing in basic and applied science: an exploratory study at the interface of the sociology of science and information science.** 155p. Order no. 71-10,544.

PURPOSE: The study is an attempt to develop a theoretical model of the means by which individuals process information in connection with their occupational roles. The sociology of science provides a context in which the role of the scientist is investigated.

PROCEDURE: Scaling techniques (modifications of the basic Thurstone) were

PROCEDURE (cont'd): used to rank scientists on a continuum from basic to applied according to their reading habits of professional periodical literature. The scientist's scale score or rank was conceived as his scientific mission and the variance about that score was taken to reflect the diffuseness of his interests. Correlation and partial correlation techniques were used to analyze subject's ratings of scientific communication media.

FINDINGS: The scale scores approached a normal distribution on the continuum. Scientists with more basic research interests define their interests more narrowly. There was a distinct tendency for elites to cluster at the basic sector of the continuum. Elites have more narrowly defined, less diffuse interests and significantly greater professional involvement and visibility than non-elites. Needs act as a catalyst to procurement except for the case of accidental acquisition of information. Scientists get the largest amount of their information from sources which are easiest to use and most accessible. A large amount of information is procured from sources where there is little time investment (e.g., reviews, abstracts, etc.). The basic group was found to be significantly different from the applied group because of their greater preference for non-personal, literature oriented methods of information procurement.

445. Anderson, Carolyn Joyce (Ph.D., University of Oregon, 1970). **Role expectations of the high school librarians as perceived by librarians, principals and teachers.** 220p. Order no. 71-10,684.

PURPOSE: This paper attempted to identify the way that high school librarians view their position, the way they perceive the views of teacher and principal populations and the actual views of teacher and principal populations.

PROCEDURE: Data were collected from 151 librarians, 145 principals and 492 teachers in Oregon high schools. A role norm inventory consisting of 60 normative statements was analyzed using means, measures of ordinal consensus and the Kolmogorov-Smirnov two-sample test of significant differences.

FINDINGS: Librarians were in higher agreement regarding their own views than regarding their perceptions of the populations of teachers and principals. Librarians were in higher agreement regarding their roles as administrator, technical processor and teacher; they were in lower agreement regarding their roles as materials specialist, curriculum developer and clerical aide. Statistically significant differences occurred for a majority of the norms in comparing the librarians' expectations with the principal and teachers' expectations for the librarians' role. Librarians perceived more differences than actually existed between their views and the views of others. Teachers and principals were found to have significant differences in expectations for the librarians on a majority of the normative statements.

CONCLUSIONS: The role-defining groups of teachers, principals and librarians do not hold similar expectations for the role of the librarian.

446. Anderson, James Doig (D.L.S., Columbia University, 1970). **A comparative study of methods of arranging Chinese language author-title catalogs in large American Chinese language collections.** 151p. Order no. 72-33,402.

PURPOSE: Four fundamentally different methods used to arrange the author-title catalogs of the 13 Chinese language collections in the United States and Canada having more than 100,000 volumes (alphabetical arrangement on the basis of their Romanization, numerical arrangement, character by character arrangement by the alphabetic position of a character's Romanization and character by character

PURPOSE (cont'd): arrangement by the radical of a character) were compared on the basis of the amount of information required to locate entries in catalogs arranged by these methods.

PROCEDURE: The catalogs at Princeton University's Gest Oriental Library, Columbia University's East Asian Library and the East Asiatic Library of the University of California at Berkeley were examined. Catalog users were surveyed.

FINDINGS: In spite of the enormous differences in the number of potential filing positions provided by these arrangement methods, the amount of information required by these arrangement methods to locate entries did not differ by more than approximately 15 percent. Users of Chinese language catalogs obtained bibliographic information only in Romanized form about 25 percent of the time; users with only Romanized bibliographic information found catalogs arranged on the basis of Chinese characters difficult if not impossible to consult.

CONCLUSIONS: The results of this study reinforce the current trend toward the strictly alphabetical arrangement of Chinese language library catalogs on the basis of Romanized entries.

447. Anderson, LeMoyne W. (Ph.D., University of Illinois, 1970). **Delinquent borrowers in an academic library.** 196p. Order no. 71-5027.

PURPOSE: The purpose of this research was to study the delinquent borrowers' habits of sharing resources, including their responses to an academic library's efforts to stimulate behavior.

PROCEDURE: Five hundred undergraduates at Colorado State University were selected randomly and assigned to a control or treatment group. The experimental groups were treated either by a telephone call or mail notice during 11 weekly intervals during the Spring quarter of 1968. A sample of 210 subjects was also drawn in order to determine the causes for delinquency. These patrons were sent questionnaires; 129 were used in the final analysis.

FINDINGS: There was a statistically significant relationship among the various treatments applied to undergraduate borrowers and their response rate. The most immediate reactions to treatments occurred soon after the treatment. The most personal treatment produced an even significantly greater response. There were no relationships found between rates of responses and point-of-time in an academic term, severity level of the delinquency, in subject content of delinquent materials, or the undergraduate's sex, major field of study or university status. The primary cause for the delinquency was forgetfulness. There was no evidence that borrowers were delinquent because they wanted to defy regulations, keep materials from fellow students or rebel against insufficient loan periods.

448. Berner, William Sherman (Ph.D., University of Illinois, 1970). **The influence of pre-voting activity on the outcome of selected library bond referendums.** 254p. Order no. 71-5043.

PURPOSE: The general purpose was to identify factors related to the outcome of library bond issue referendums.

PROCEDURE: Data and information were gathered on nine library bond referendums held in Illinois cities and villages between January 31, 1967 and October 8, 1968 which had a 1960 population of at least 10,000. The referendums involved either bond issues to finance construction of new library buildings or additions to existing libraries. Of the nine referendums, five were approved and four defeated.

FINDINGS: Several of the nine selected variables accurately predicted the outcome of at least one of the referendums studied while predicting none of the outcomes inaccurately. If the library building existing at the time of the referendum was adequate, the bond issue was defeated, accurately predicted the defeat of one bond issue. A level of high opposition accurately predicted the defeat of three bond issues. A high level of past political activity of campaign leaders accurately predicted the success of one bond issue. In a special election, high voter turnout accurately predicted the defeat of two bond issues.

CONCLUSIONS: Two factors appear to be very important in influencing the outcome of the referendums: opposition to the bond issue manifested during the pre-referendum campaign and the turnout of voters at the referendum.

449. Berry, June (Ed.D., Brigham Young University, 1970). **A comparative analysis of ratings of library concepts given by college freshmen and those given by librarians.** 123p. Order no. 71-8855.

PURPOSE: The purpose of the study was to determine the differences in ratings of library concepts by professional librarians and freshmen students.

PROCEDURE: A semantic differential questionnaire was sent to 100 freshmen students and 25 librarians. The means for the two groups were compared by use of a t-test.

FINDINGS: Significant differences were found between the mean ratings of professional librarians and freshmen students on the following concepts: library profession, librarians, circulation, reserve books, periodical indexes, card catalogs, and university libraries. All of the students' means except one were less favorable than the librarians' and the concept rated as least favorable by the students was "library profession."

450. Bertram, Sheila Joan Kelley (Ph.D., University of Illinois, 1970). **The relationship between intro-document citation location and citation level.** 235p. Order no. 70-20,925.

PURPOSE: The objective of the study was to determine if, in journal literature of original scientific research, the level (or amount) of material actually cited by the source article would vary significantly with the section of the source article in which the citation occurred.

PROCEDURE: Three levels (the whole of the cited article, a part of the cited article, and word/words from the cited article) and three sections (title/introduction, results/discussion, and experimental) were identified in the original research literature of organic chemistry.

FINDINGS: Using a chi-square test, a significant relationship between citation level and section was obtained. When parts from the experimental section of the cited article were added to the word/words category, the chi-square doubled. Neither the gross self-citation distribution nor the gross same journal citation distribution varied significantly with the section at the .05 level.

CONCLUSIONS: The reason suggested for the existence of a relationship between citation level and section was that the properties of citations in general tend to vary with the section, and citation level is a measurable property of citations. A more general reason for the differences in the various citation property distributions with section might be that the three sections represent three different stages in research: title/introduction, results/discussion, experimental. It was therefore suggested

CONCLUSIONS (cont'd): that these findings might have implications for indexing policies.

451. Bingham, Jane Marie (Ph.D., Michigan State University, 1970). **A content analysis of the treatment of Negro characters in children's picture books 1930-1968.** 218p. Order no. 70-20,437.

PURPOSE: Children's literature published between 1930 and 1968 was analyzed in order to ascertain the treatment of the American Negro in the illustrations of children's picture books.

PROCEDURE: Forty-one books found on recommended book lists used by librarians, teachers and children's literature specialists were grouped into four historical periods and analyzed.

FINDINGS: Negro characters were depicted with a variety of skin colors, hair textures, hair styles, nose, lip and eye formations and body builds in all periods. There was a paucity of interior and exterior situations portrayed in the four periods. There were more Negroes in work roles in the first two periods (1930-44; 1945-54) than there were Caucasians in the last two. More Negro than Caucasian home roles were shown, with more mothers than fathers being present. The interaction among a variety of characters did not differ markedly from period to period. However, the variety and type of interaction did differ during the four historical periods. The amount of physical interaction increased from period one to period four (1965-68), most probably reflecting the greater amount of interaction which was being encouraged in society as a whole.

452. Bolvin, Boyd Micael (Ph.D., University of Southern California, 1970). **A survey of mechanization and automation in large university libraries.** 362p. Order no. 70-16,853.

PURPOSE: Large university libraries were surveyed in order to determine the effect technology has had on service to the user, the institution, intellectual and physical access to information, cataloging and classification systems.

PROCEDURE: Questionnaires were sent to the 68 university libraries which were members of the Association of Research Libraries and which, during 1967-68, had book collections in excess of 500,000 volumes and budgets of more than $500,000.

FINDINGS: Nearly 90 percent of the libraries had begun mechanization/automation; all but one library had plans to mechanize at least one function within the next three years. Three-quarters of the libraries had plans to mechanize one or more functions. Accounting was the function most mechanized, followed by circulation control. The functions least mechanized were document and data retrieval. Library mechanization programs were too new to determine their effectiveness.

RECOMMENDATIONS: Systems analysis and the total systems approach should be used in the development of library automation/mechanization programs. Library holdings should be converted into machine readable form. Suggested order of automation: acquisitions, circulation, cataloging, serial records and reference/reader's services.

453. Bose, Anindya (Ph.D., University of Pittsburgh, 1970). **Information system design methodology based on PERT/CPM networking and optimization techniques.** 226p. Order no. 71-1774.

PURPOSE: This dissertation attempts to demonstrate that the Program Evaluation and Review Technique (PERT)/Critical Path Method (CPM) or some modified

PURPOSE (cont'd): version thereof, can be developed into an information system design methodology.

PROCEDURE: The methodology utilizes PERT/CPM which isolates the basic functional units of a system and sets them in a dynamic time/cost, precedence and dependency interrelationship network. The methodology applies Assignment and Sequencing algorithms.

FINDINGS: By providing the means to control the time, cost, assignment, and sequencing of the activities of the basic functional units in a continuous manner, and a way to network them into the desired system, the methodology fulfills the need for a continuous monitoring information system design methodology. An interactive mode PERT Computer Program has been written in PIL/L which runs on the IBM 360/50 Pitt Time Sharing System using the 2741 Terminal.

454. Brundin, Robert Eliott (Ph.D., Stanford University, 1970). **Changing patterns of library service in five California junior colleges, 1907-1967.** 303p. Order no. 71-12,866.

PURPOSE: This study is a history of the development of library services in five California public junior colleges from 1907-1967: Fullerton Junior College, Long Beach City College, Los Angeles City College, Modesto Junior College and Pasadena City College.

PROCEDURE: College catalogs, student handbooks, library handbooks, student newspapers, annual reports of librarians, reports of accrediting agencies, reports of library committees, articles in local newspapers, published writings of college officials and interviews with various library staff members were used to elicit information for the study.

FINDINGS: From 1907 to 1967 there was a change in the libraries from single to multipurpose collections. The primary role of the librarian shifted from caretaker to educator and the library changed from an archives into an educational laboratory. The most significant influences promoting progressive change in the five junior colleges, apart from accreditation requirements and available resources, were the individuals directly involved with providing library services.

455. Bryson, Ernest Ronald (Ph.D., University of Kentucky, 1970). **A theory of librarianship.** 99p. Order no. 71-8577.

PURPOSE: The purpose of this study was to develop a comprehensive theory of librarianship.

PROCEDURE: The procedure followed in this study was (1) to utilize three laws from the field of sociology (communications-need, organization-development, division-of-labor), stating these laws as postulates of the theory and developing from them theorems which were appropriate for the field of librarianship; (2) to validate the theory by demonstrating that it conformed to the norms of correspondence, coherence and function customarily followed by social scientists in such validation; and (3) to present the theory in the form of an interpretative model.

FINDINGS: Libraries develop as organizations designed for the purpose of satisfying subject oriented information needs felt by the parent institution. Librarians develop internal functions which satisfy the information needs felt by the parent institution. Libraries utilize individuals who perform tasks which complete the library functions and thus satisfy the information needs felt by the parent institution.

456. Cagan, Carl (Ph.D., Washington State University, 1970). **An automatic probabilistic document retrieval system.** 243p. Order no. 70-16,800.
PURPOSE: This paper describes a computerized document retrieval system implemented with a subset of the medical literature.
PROCEDURE: With the exception of the development of a dictionary used to delete common words from text, all system operations are completely automatic.
FINDINGS: The connectivity maintained in the files obviates both the need for a thesaurus and the need for query expansion by elaboration. A user may associate with each query term to degree of association desired between the term and retrieved documents. A powerful and selective retrieval capability results.

457. Childers, Thomas Allen (Ph.D., Rutgers University, 1970). **Telephone information service in public libraries: a comparison of performance and the descriptive statistics collected by the State of New Jersey.** 157p. Order no. 71-3037.
PURPOSE: The study investigated the relationship of financial support, personnel, type of materials, circulation, hours of operation and population served to public librarians' response to telephone information requests.
PROCEDURE: Twenty-six questions of the simple factual type were telephoned to the sample of 25 public libraries in New Jersey. Responses were judged for correctness on each of five different scales, including two correct/not correct dichotomies and an attempt/no attempt dichotomy. Analysis of variance and stepwise linear regression analysis were used to measure the relationships.
FINDINGS: Approximately 64 percent of the attempt answers were correct. When no-attempt responses were scored zero, the percentage of correct answers dropped to approximately 55. There was no relationship between attempting to find an answer and success in responding correctly. There was a significant association between the correctness of response and the status of total expenditures.
CONCLUSIONS: The data lent substance to Beasley's hypothesis that the quality of a library's reference service is directly related to a combination of the number of professional personnel and the size of the book collection.

458. Crawford, Susan Young (Ph.D., University of Chicago, 1970). **Informal communication among scientists in sleep and dream research.**
PURPOSE: The study investigates how scientists at the frontiers of an active field of science (sleep research) communicate with each other informally concerning their work.
PROCEDURE: All scientists (618) who had written in the field, held membership in the Association for Psychophysiological Study of Sleep, or received grants for sleep research during the four years preceding this investigation, were contacted. There was a 69 percent response rate; of these, only 218 (51 percent of the respondents) indicated they were still participating in projects in sleep research. These scientists were studied.
FINDINGS: An informal communication network was identified which included 73 percent of the scientists. Within the network was a core group of scientists who were the focus of a disproportionately large number of contacts and who were differentiated from others by greater productivity, higher citation record and wider readership. Information transferred to these scientists is so situated that it could be transmitted to 95 percent of the network scientists through one intermediary scientist or less.

459. Crum, Mark L., Jr. (Ed.D., Western Michigan University, 1970). **What does the public library user REALLY want? The accuracy of library personnel, library educators, and library board members in perceiving the library-related wants of public library patrons.** 135p. Order no. 70-19,181.

PURPOSE: The purpose of the study was to determine the accuracy of library personnel, library educators and library board members in perceiving the library-related wants of public library patrons.

PROCEDURE: Questionnaires with 225 user reported wants were sent to 403 patrons of three medium sized public libraries, to obtain measures of the frequency of mention and relative importance value ascribed to each item. A smaller number of items (for which user measures had been obtained) were sent to 101 librarians, 27 graduate library school faculty and 70 public library board members to obtain measures of the accuracy of these establishment groups in estimating the frequency of mention and importance values reported earlier by users.

FINDINGS: Librarians had a greater error of perception of frequency of mention than either faculty or board members. All groups were relatively unsuccessful in estimating frequency of mention. Users ascribed greater importance values to their wants than were estimated by others in all categories except materials.

CONCLUSIONS: Change in library recruitment criteria, library school curricula and public library service might be more sound if it were based upon surveys of the preferences of the public than if it were based upon the perceptions of the library establishment.

460. Denis, Laurent-Germain (Ph.D., Rutgers University, 1970). **Academic and public librarians in Canada: a study of the factors which influence graduates of Canadian library schools in making their first career decision in favor of academic or public libraries.** 275p. Order no. 70-10,057.

PURPOSE: The purpose of this study was to identify and to describe the environmental and personality factors which influence the graduates of Canadian library schools in making their first career decision in favor of academic or public libraries.

PROCEDURE: Allport-Vernon-Lindzey *Study of Values*, the Kuder Preference Record-Vocational, and the Edwards Personal Preference Schedule were used to measure personality factors. Questionnaires were set to 648 librarians who graduated during 1960-1967 from one of the five Canadian library schools and who accepted their first position in an academic or a public library.

FINDINGS: Librarians who accept their first professional position in an academic library are not greatly influenced by personal contacts, but rather are moved by their interest in students and faculty, liking for campus life, their conviction of the importance of academic librarianship, and their familiarity and previous use of academic libraries. Those who select public libraries do so because that type of library affords them opportunities to meet and serve people and because they have used and worked in these libraries before.

461. Donohue, Joseph Chaminade (Ph.D., Western Reserve University, 1970). **A method for the analysis of a subject literature.** 126p. Order no. 71-1683.

PURPOSE: Selected information scientific techniques (the epidemic theory of literature, the Bradford distribution, Booth's law, citation tracing and bibliographic coupling) were integrated into a general method for the analysis of subject literatures.

PROCEDURE: This integrated method was applied to a subset of the literature of Information Science itself, and generalizations were drawn as to the method's applicability to the basic problems of libraries with respect to literature management.

462. Ebrami, Hooshang (Ph.D., University of Pittsburgh, 1970). **Catchword indexing, subject headings and chain indexing; the formulation of rules for subject analysis in Farsi.** 300p. Order no. 71-14,486.
PURPOSE: The objective of this study was the formulation of rules for the subject analysis in Farsi (Iran).
PROCEDURE: A random sample of 220 microfilmed title pages, both in English and Farsi, was put in the Miracode Retrieval Machine. Four different alphabetical lists were prepared for English and Farsi subject headings and chain indexes. Equal numbers (42) of Farsi and English speaking persons volunteered for the experiment. Every experimenter had a set of 10 title pages and, depending on his group, a list of alphabetical subject entries. By using codes for the subject analytic system either the image on the screen matched the photocopy of the title page or there was no matching. The statistical t-test was used to determine significant differences.
FINDINGS: The chain indexing (both in Farsi and English) is superior to the subject heading method except for "unwanted materials." Farsi has a framework that is well suited for indexing terms.
CONCLUSIONS: The bases for the code of Farsi indexing include: a subject entry must be related to a notation; the terminology of a subject entry should be refined for the title or the subtitle; a subject entry must be retained in natural form morphologically and syntactically. On these bases, four fundamental principles and 26 rules were formulated for subject analysis in Farsi.

463. Elliott, Clark Albert (Ph.D., Case Western Reserve University, 1970). **The American scientist, 1800-1863; his origins, career, and interests.** 383p. Order no. 71-1,685.
PURPOSE: The objective of the study was to chronicle the history of American scientists: their geographic and socio-economic origins, educational preparation, career patterns and areas of scientific interest.
PROCEDURE: Using the first series of the *Royal Society Catalogue of Scientific Papers* (1800-1863), a list was compiled of 538 names of Americans who wrote three or more articles in American science journals. For 503 of the authors, biographical data were collected, analyzed and tabulated.
FINDINGS: American scientists in the first half of the nineteenth century came from a rather narrowly defined segment of the population: the Northeastern part of the country. Their fathers were usually members of the professional, commercial or public service classes. Their education was usually in a college or a medical school. Their occupations were in most cases at least related to science. There was increasing professionalization and differentiation of the science researcher during this period. The social structure of science did differ according to the science-interests of the scientist.

464. Fasick, Adele Mongan (Ph.D., Case Western Reserve University, 1970). **A comparative linguistic analysis of books and television for children.** 144p. Order no. 71-1,687.
PURPOSE: The vocabulary and sentence structure of books and television for

PURPOSE (cont'd): children were compared in this study.

PROCEDURE: The language of five children's picture storybooks and three children's television programs was analyzed. Twelve items of vocabulary and sentence structure which have been associated with language maturity were chosen as measures of the verbal content of the books and television programs.

FINDINGS: The sentences used in the books proved to be more complex than those used on the television programs. The vocabulary items tested did not reveal a striking difference between the two media. The three television programs studied were more similar in their rankings on the various tests than were the books; the five books ranged from very simple to quite complex.

CONCLUSIONS: Among the possible reasons for television's lack of impact on children's language when compared with books are the social context of reading in the home, the appropriateness of the books to the language level of the child, the degree of repetition in book language and the effect of rereading books to children. The relative importance of these factors can only be determined by further research.

465. Fortin, Clifford Charles (Ph.D., University of Minnesota, 1970). **The relation of certain personal and environmental characteristics of school librarians to their life values and work satisfaction.** 124p. Order no. 70-27,116.

PURPOSE: The study was designed to determine if school librarians had an identifiable set of values and satisfactions in their work which relate to education, teaching role or experience.

PROCEDURE: The Allport-Vernon-Lindzey *Study of Values* (1960 revision) and a seven part questionnaire were sent in 1966 to 787 Wisconsin public school librarians; 77 percent returned the questionnaire and 65 percent the *Study of Values*. Chisquare and one way analysis of variance were used to test relationships between the variables and job satisfaction.

FINDINGS: More than 90 percent of the respondents liked their positions. They were committed to providing appropriate library materials and services to students, and to working with faculty to achieve school objectives. Responses to the *Study of Values* showed religious, aesthetic and social values somewhat more prominent than the economic, political and theoretical. No relationships were found when degree, professional role, or major or minor fields of study were related to the six value scales. No differences were found when job satisfaction was related to degree and certification status. Librarians with more training were better satisfied with service rather than administrative aspects of school librarianship. Respondents preferring junior or senior high school libraries were more satisfied with administrative activities than the elementary group.

CONCLUSIONS: School librarians were generally satisfied with their work but somewhat disenchanted with working conditions. School librarians differed most over satisfactions with administrative and service aspects of the work. The impact of the library on the educational program rests with the satisfied librarian.

466. Friedlander, Janet Morgan (Ph.D., Western Reserve University, 1970). **Physician use of a medical library.** 152p. Order no. 71-1691.

PURPOSE: The study attempted to describe the population of users and the kinds of sources they used in an information search and to identify some of the factors which influenced their choice of kinds of sources.

PROCEDURE: A questionnaire was sent to clinicians affiliated with a teaching hospital.
FINDINGS: The most frequently sought information was about a specific disease; a high use was made of informal sources in seeking this information (particularly talking to a man in the same subject area). The major source which provided information was journal articles, especially in xerox copy form. There appears to be a connection between experience/type of work and type of source used. Sources which are accessible and easy to use were used more often than other sources. Most respondents found the information they sought themselves rather than relying upon library services. Telephoning was widely used as a means of contacting the library. Of those who went to the library, more than half used indexes or browsed on the shelf; few used the card catalog.
RECOMMENDATIONS: Journals should be shelved accessibly with *Index Medicus* nearby. Books might be shelved less accessibly. Telephone access to the library and adequate xerox facilities are of major importance.

467. Hamil, Betty Caldwell (Ed.D., University of Georgia, 1970). **The critical requirements for open elementary school library programs as defined by selected seventh grade pupils in the Fulton County, Georgia school system.** 143p. Order no. 71-13,064.
PURPOSE: The problem of the study was to identify the critical requirements for open elementary school library programs based upon an analysis of meaningful opportunities as perceived by selected seventh grade pupils in the Fulton County, Georgia school system.
PROCEDURE: The respondents were 180 seventh grade pupils randomly selected from nine elementary schools having an open library program for pupils grades four through seven. The critical incident technique was employed to gather data. The chi-square test was used to investigate relationships between the critical requirements for open elementary school library programs and certain control data on the respondent and his school situation.
FINDINGS: Six major areas as critical requirements emerged: facilities, activities, organizational framework, personnel, skills acquired through direct library-classroom instruction, and objectives. Significant relationships were found to exist between the six major areas and the respondent's years of participation in an open elementary school library program, the horizontal organizational patterns of the respondent's grade, the number of employed elementary school library personnel in the respondent's school, and the index of social position of the respondent's school community.

468. Harmon, Elmer Glynn, Jr. (Ph.D., Western Reserve University, 1970). **Human memory as a factor in the formation of disciplinary systems.** 143p. Order no. 70-25,872.
PURPOSE: The study explored the relationships between short term memory limitations and the formation and transformation of disciplinary systems.
PROCEDURE: The investigation employed a systems analysis of the evolution of several disciplines, starting with relatively small systems within mathematics and physics and proceeding to successively larger systems.
FINDINGS: In accordance with the notion that human short term memory can effectively encompass approximately seven items, the cases analyzed revealed that roughly seven ideas coalesced to form sub-subsystems or sub-systems; seven

FINDINGS (cont'd): sub-systems coalesced to form a system; seven systems tended to form into a sub-suprasystem. Man's knowledge consists of approximately seven major subdivisions. Hence, man's short term memory limits appear to be reflected in his organization of knowledge. Information science should reach a stage of relative maturity as a disciplinary system during the 1970's. A possible long range role for information science could be as a catalyst in the formation of a complete suprasystem of knowledge which would unify the arts, sciences and professions.

469. Heckman, Marlin Leroy (Ph.D., University of Chicago, 1970). **Abraham Harley Cassel: nineteenth century American book collector.** 212p.

470. Hess, Edward Jorgen (Ph.D., University of Southern California, 1970). **A study of human response to California library organization and management systems.** 253p. Order no. 71-12,393.
PURPOSE: The purpose of this study was to explore the nature of the library as a human organization.
PROCEDURE: Questionnaires, chiefly derived from Likert's "Profile of Organizational Characteristics" were sent to a nonprobability sample of 582 individual respondents in 98 academic and 90 public libraries.
FINDINGS: "Consultative" practices generally prevailed in the California academic and public libraries studied. Some use of participative practices was evident in communication, motivation, decision-making, interaction-influence, and control, but participation was not dominant in any one aspect. Authoritarian practices, while not abundant, did occur in motivation, decision-making, control and training. Decision-making tended to be concentrated at or near the top of the organizational hierarchies.
RECOMMENDATIONS: Organizational productivity could be improved by initiating training programs leading to the development of work groups capable of more effective participation in the management of the library, creating a more supportive atmosphere within the groups and delegating more responsibility to lower hierarchial levels.

471. Heussman, John William (Ph.D., University of Illinois at Urbana-Champaign, 1970). **The literature cited in theological journals and its relation to seminary library circulation.** 267p. Order no. 71-5125.
PURPOSE: The investigation was undertaken to describe the library sources used in theological study, teaching and research and to determine if there is a positive relationship between theological literature and the materials circulated in a seminary library.
PROCEDURE: Three samples were drawn: (1) 4,453 citations from the 1965 volumes of seven English language theology journals; (2) 3,644 items from two Lutheran theological seminary libraries' circulation records; (3) 1,035 items selected randomly from a standard comprehensive theological bibliography to provide comparable groups of cited and uncited works which could be compared on the basis of circulation and used in tests of hypotheses.
FINDINGS: The literature of theological research was largely monographic concentrated in relatively few titles, written in English, relatively stable (50 percent of the literature is about 15 years old; the mean age is 34.5 years) and concerned with theology. Of the material which circulated, nearly all was monographic, in

FINDINGS (cont'd): English, relatively stable (the mean age was 20.4 years) and theological in nature. Direct comparisons of the citation and circulation samples indicated a considerable degree of commonality on a number of variables.
CONCLUSIONS: A cited item is more likely to circulate than an uncited item and the greater an item's citation frequency the greater will be its circulation frequency.

472. Huq, A. M. Abdul (Ph.D., University of Pittsburgh, 1970). **A study of Bengali Muslim personal names to ascertain the feasibility of application of a mechanistic role for their arrangement.** 93p. Order no. 71-14,487.
PURPOSE: The study attempted to ascertain the feasibility of application of a mechanistic rule for rendering Bengali Muslim names.
PROCEDURE: Name arrangements of a sample of over 7,000 names were analyzed to see if these names could be arranged from the position of their elements. All names were keypunched onto IBM cards and computer systems were used to generate alphabetical indices of each of the fields, to rank the order of each of the elements in the data fields and to compile a master index of all the elements in alphabetic sequence showing the frequency of occurrences of each element.
FINDINGS: The study showed that it was not possible to have a mechanistic role in arranging Bengali Muslim names.
CONCLUSIONS: A set of rules for rendering Bengali Muslim names in the existing catalog codes was suggested based on the findings. Enter these names under last element provided it is not an honorific, nor a name title, nor an element with a frequency of over one million, nor a bound morpheme. If it does not meet the criteria, the penultimate element is considered the same way. Should the penultimate not meet the criteria, the ante-penultimate is then considered for entry. The study contains a list of name elements with an estimated frequency of over one million for the entire Muslim population in East Pakistan. Name Authority Files must be maintained.

473. Immroth, John Phillip (Ph.D., University of Pittsburgh, 1970). **An analysis of vocabulary control in Library of Congress classification, indexes and subject headings and the formulation of rules for chain indexing of Library of Congress classification.** 368p. Order no. 71-3,522.
PURPOSE: This study was designed to investigate the relationship control of the vocabularies used in the process of subject cataloging at the Library of Congress.
PROCEDURE: The vocabularies considered were the classification, indexes and subject headings of the Library of Congress. Samples of each of these three vocabularies were taken.
FINDINGS: Individual indexes vary in fullness and are both inconsistent and incomplete. Approximately 50 percent of the schedule terms are indexed in the individual indexes. Only one-fourth of the subject headings tested graphemically match perfectly with both the classification and index headings. The morphological-syntactical analysis showed a single noun in mass form to be the only recurring perfect match. Twenty-six rules for chain indexing were generated and tested; the chain index headings generated by these rules show 90 percent direct indexing and a predictable number of subheadings. Further, a predictable morphology resulted in these headings.
CONCLUSIONS: The use of chain indexing could unify the vocabulary of the Library of Congress' subject cataloging so that an alphabetical array of the

CONCLUSIONS (cont'd): classification will be a list of subject headings and that a classified array of subject headings will be the classification schedule.

474. Jay, Hilda Lease (Ed.D., New York University, 1970). **Increasing the use of secondary school libraries as a teaching tool.** 134p. Order no. 70-21,163.
PURPOSE: The study attempted to identify deterrents to the use of secondary school libraries as a teaching tool and to use this information to increase the use of the instructional materials already owned by the schools.
PROCEDURE: Questionnaires received from 88 teachers and 1,240 students were used as a basis for making the following changes: modifications of the pass system, cataloging of non-book materials for the main card catalog and re-emphasis by principals of the role of the school library in daily teaching. Reassessment questionnaires were used six months later to determine the effect the changes and modifications had on the use of library materials.
FINDINGS: It was found that there was increased use of library materials, per capita average of book borrowing, use of non-book materials, and teacher use of special library services.

475. Jussim, Estelle (D.L.S., Columbia University, 1970). **Photographic technology and visual communication in the nineteenth century American book.** 632p.

476. Marchant, Maurice Peterson (Ph.D., University of Michigan, 1970). **The effects of the decision making process and related organizational factors on alternative measures of performance in university libraries.** 325p. Order no. 71-15,228.
PURPOSE: The purpose of this study was to determine the relationships between professional library staff participation in decision making and a set of performance measurements.
PROCEDURE: All professional staffs and a sample of faculty at 22 universities whose libraries were members of the Association of Research Libraries were surveyed. Likert's "Profile of Organization Characteristics" formed the questionnaire. Regression and correlation analysis were used to measure relationships.
FINDINGS: Significant relationships were found between professional librarians' perception of involvement in the decision making process and/or the librarians' perception of the participative nature of the library's managerial style in general and: staff satisfaction, uniformity of staff evaluation of library quality, and uniformity of evaluation between top management and faculty. A near significant relationship was also found with uniformity of staff evaluation of library importance. Staff satisfaction and collection size were significant factors in affecting faculty evaluation. Circulation per student was shown to be significantly related to faculty evaluation.

477. Massman, Virgil Frank (Ph.D., University of Michigan, 1970). **Responsibilities and benefits of faculty status for librarians: a review of related literature and a survey of librarians and faculty members in nineteen state colleges and universities in Michigan, Minnesota and Wisconsin.** 319p. Order no. 71-4674.
PURPOSE: The study attempted to determine whether librarians met the requirements to receive the benefits of faculty status.

PROCEDURE: In the fall of 1969, 281 librarians (79.1 percent response rate) and 339 faculty (60.5 percent response rate) in six state colleges in Minnesota and 13 state universities in Michigan and Wisconsin were sent questionnaires.

FINDINGS: Librarians had less formal education, lower educational aspirations and published less than faculty members. Nearly 93 percent of the librarians had faculty rank; however, this was not full faculty status because: (1) their average salaries were lower; (2) a smaller proportion were in the higher academic ranks; (3) they were less likely to receive research funds; (4) one-third were on 12 month appointments. Differences between faculty and librarians relating to sabbaticals, tenure and voting privileges were not significant. When educational and scholarly activity were considered, the librarians in general received equitable treatment.

CONCLUSIONS: These findings agree with sociological theory that educational requirements are consistently and closely related to the status of a profession. These librarians received rewards commensurate with their credentials. They had full faculty status when it was measured both by its responsibilities and benefits.

478. Moloney, Louis C. (D.L.S., Columbia University, 1970). **A history of the university library at the University of Texas, 1883-1934.** 404p. Order no. 71-17,525.

PURPOSE: The dissertation investigated the development of the library at the University of Texas at Austin in terms of personnel, financial support, library government, collection development, organization of materials, services, facilities and cooperation.

FINDINGS: Although service was offered in 1884, the library did not move into the mainstream of college library development until the tenure of Benjamin Wyche (1897-1903). He expanded the collection, started the newspaper collection, the Texas collection and introduced the Dewey Decimal Classification. Under Phinease Lawrence Windson (1903-09), the library prepared to support research. Philanthropy was responsible for the development of extensive collections in Southern history. Ernest William Winkler (1923-34) expanded departmental library organization. In 1945 a large new facility was provided and Donald Coney was appointed to the directorship with a charge to coordinate and centralize.

CONCLUSIONS: There was always a high degree of interest in and financial support for the library. There was greater concern with the library's resources than services. Research use was given priority over non-research use. The lack of adequate building facilities had a definite effect on the extent to which collections and services were decentralized.

479. O'Neill, Edward True (Ph.D., Purdue University, 1970). **Journal usage patterns and their implications in the planning of library systems.** 419p. Order no. 70-18,704.

PURPOSE: The study investigated some of the effects that the division of literature by disciplines had on its accessibility and examined the disciplines, the interdisciplinary relationships and the scattering characteristics as they were revealed by journal usage patterns. These results then were applied to the problem of planning and designing library systems.

PROCEDURE: A "discipline wheel" was proposed as a conceptional framework to view the different disciplines, to measure the breadth of a discipline and to measure the similarity between two disciplines. The Bradford, Ule, Borel, Fisher and other distributions of title dispersion were fitted to over 50 groups of productivity data

PROCEDURE (cont'd): from various sources. The application of productivity functions in the operational design and evaluation of library systems was considered. The concepts were applied at Purdue. Complete records of the University Libraries' journal holdings and nearly 25,000 citations from 752 Ph.D. dissertations written in technical fields at Purdue University were collected. The similarity between the different scientific disciplines and different libraries, the breadth of the discipline, and differences between the journal usage patterns and the system's holdings were investigated. Alternate library system configurations were proposed and evaluated through the use of comprehensiveness functions.

CONCLUSIONS: It is possible to quantitively measure such concepts as title dispersion, breadth of a discipline, the similarity between disciplines, and others.

480. Palmer, Richard Phillips (Ph.D., University of Michigan, 1970). **User requirements of a university library card catalog.** 323p. Order no. 70-21,751.

PURPOSE: A study was made of those who use the card catalog, for what purpose, and with that success to determine how items on a catalog card are used and whether a hypothetical five item computer catalog (author, title, call number, subject headings, and date) would meet their requirements.

PROCEDURE: An eight week questionnaire survey of 5,067 users of the University of Michigan General Library card catalog was conducted during the Fall of 1967.

FINDINGS: Graduate students were the major users of the catalog. Nearly 85 percent of the users found what they were seeking. The catalog was used primarily for class assignments, research and then personal use. Seventy percent used the catalog for known item searches; 30 percent for subject searches. Less than two out of ten users were seeking foreign language materials; only 17 percent were seeking works published before 1900. Only author, title and call numbers were used heavily by patrons. As educational level of users rose they conducted more known item and fewer subject searches, they used slightly more catalog card items, more foreign language materials, older publication dates and desired more items in the hypothetical computer catalog.

CONCLUSIONS: Of those who were successful in their use of the card catalog, 84 percent would have found a five item computer catalog sufficient. Thus, most users of card catalogs would be successful with reduced computer catalogs.

481. Pfister, Frederick Charles (Ph.D., University of Michigan, 1970). **School district professional libraries in Michigan.** 243p. Order no. 71-4705.

PURPOSE: The purpose of the study was to provide information on the status and function of the district professional libraries in Michigan public school systems.

PROCEDURE: Questionnaires were sent to (1) 125 Michigan school districts (90 responded, 32 supplied information on a district professional library) and (2) 1,054 school personnel in two large, two medium and two small districts selected by the investigator (84 percent responded). Interviews were conducted with personnel responsible for the professional libraries in 26 districts. Bivariate frequency distributions were compiled and chi-square tests of association applied to them.

FINDINGS: Staff, budget, and collection size corresponded directly with district size. Most library personnel felt responsible for linking school personnel to all information services, but locally available sources were used more than non-local sources (e.g., ERIC). Major use of the professional libraries was made for curriculum study and development, personal professional growth and graduate study requirements.

FINDINGS (cont'd): Traditional print formats were used more than non-print or microforms. The modal use of the libraries was 3 or 4 times a year. Only a minority of the librarians gave a rating of "excellent" to their district libraries. School personnel who used the libraries tended to be older, in a system-wide position, have had more experience and have a more advanced academic degree than non-users.

482. Rosenberg, Victor (Ph.D., University of Chicago, 1970). **Statistical technique for computer-aided indexing.** 183p.
PURPOSE: The purpose of this study was to develop a statistical measure for predicting the terms from a restricted vocabulary that will be used to index a document, given that one of the index terms is known. A methodology is also presented for evaluating indexing resulting from two different indexing procedures.
FINDINGS: The results indicate that a large proportion of terms can be predicted using co-occurrence data and that the best method of ordering the terms ranks them first in descending order of co-occurrence frequency and then breaks ties in descending order of total frequency. The central assumption is that data from a previously indexed collection can be useful in predicting the terms to be assigned to a new document. The evaluation of the two different indexing procedures was accomplished by asking a panel of judges to rate the indexing for a given document on a five point scale. The ratings were made on the basis of (1) appropriateness of the terms to the documents and (2) usefulness of the terms as access points for the documents. Results of an experiment using this evaluation method were presented.

483. Rowe, Howard Marshall (Ph.D., University of Southern California, 1970). **California public libraries and the cooperative systems concept: a study with recommendations.** 221p. Order no. 70-26,531.
PURPOSE: The purposes of the study were (1) to report the developmental, legislative and administrative aspects of the systems concept in California; (2) to discuss the role of the California State Library in the systems concept; (3) to analyze federal and state financial aid; (4) to investigate emerging organizational patterns of systems; (5) to analyze the relative effectiveness of library systems; (6) and to offer recommendations which could aid in the further development of cooperative library systems in California.
PROCEDURE: Documents relating to the formation and operation of cooperative library systems and state and federal financial programs were studied. Interviews were conducted at 13 jurisdictional cooperative library systems and 7 single unit library systems. An "input-output" model was designed to measure the relative effectiveness of the cooperative library systems concept.
FINDINGS: From 1963 to 1968 California received nearly 20 million dollars in federal grants to expand the cooperative library systems concept. The lack of adequate financial assistance from the state has placed a greater burden on the local political subdivisions to support state wide system activities. Library systems are relatively effective.
RECOMMENDATIONS: A Department of Libraries should be established at the state level. The State Library Consultants should help to solve problems in specialized areas. The State Librarian should conduct a study to determine the feasibility of establishing as few as three well located acquisition and processing centers in the state to accommodate all library systems and should establish a pilot demonstration on the use of electronic data processing equipment.

484. Roxas, Savina A. (Ph.D., University of Pittsburgh, 1970). **Library education in Italy: an historical survey.** 372p. Order no. 71-15,951.
PURPOSE: The investigator undertook a comprehensive historical survey and studied library education programs from the unification of Italy in 1870 to 1969.
PROCEDURE: The investigator spent four months in Italy in 1969 visiting universities with postgraduate programs for library education, doing research at various Italian libraries, and interviewing library officials and educators. Questionnaires were sent to library school directors and a selected number of large libraries to study the current status of library education.
FINDINGS: Postgraduate library schools in Italy combine theoretical and practical library training. The majority of students enroll for several subjects in preparation for the civil service examinations but with no intention of earning the diploma. Although formal library training provisions were a part of the 1869 public library law, the concept of apprenticeship training in Italy prevailed until very recently.
RECOMMENDATIONS: An undergraduate degree for librarians should be established, instead of the present postgraduate diploma. This undergraduate degree should be made mandatory for admission to the civil service examinations and to the profession. Civil service ratings for librarians should be upgraded. A professional register for librarians should be established. The curriculum should be up-dated by adding courses in public librarianship and information retrieval.

485. Rupert, Elizabeth Anastasia (Ph.D., University of Pittsburgh, 1970). **Pennsylvania practicum program for school librarians; an appraisal.** 158p. Order no. 70-21,940.
PURPOSE: The practicum and student teaching experience provided the student-teacher-librarian who graduated in the Spring or Summer, 1968 by the eight state affiliated Pennsylvania colleges offering undergraduate training in school librarianship was analyzed and evaluated.
PROCEDURE: Questionnaires were completed by 165 (92.7 percent) of the students contacted. A follow-up interview was conducted with 63 respondents.
FINDINGS: The practicum-training programs did not offer sufficient opportunity for the student to perceive and practice the differentiated roles of the school librarians specified in the job descriptions. The practicum-training programs gave little evidence of unity of purpose and consistency of plan. The practicum-training programs were judged by the respondents to be more traditional than innovative.
RECOMMENDATIONS: A state commission should be appointed to design a state-wide library practicum program. The Pennsylvania Division of School Libraries should assume a leadership role by designing workshops for cooperating librarians.

486. Saracevic, Tefko (Ph.D., Case Western Reserve University, 1970). **On the concept of relevance in information science.** 355p. Order no. 71-1744.
PURPOSE: The past views, trends, theories, definitions, hypotheses and experimental results related to relevance are synthesized and the hypothesis that relevant answers at a source and at a destination in a communication process are distributed in accordance to the Bradford law of literature scatter is tested.
FINDINGS: Both the distribution of relevant answers as retrieved by an experimental information retrieval system (source) and as judged by users (destination) who posed queries were found to be Bradfordian. Formal relationships between a quantity of retrieval and a quality of relevance judgment were derived through the

FINDINGS (cont'd): properties associated with Bradford distributions. Implications of the experiment were related to theory, experimentation and practical applications.

487. Schulzetenberge, Anthony C. (Ed.D., University of North Dakota, 1970). **Interests and background variables characterizing secondary school librarians who work with teachers in curriculum development and improvement of instruction.** 119p. Order no. 72-16,372.

PURPOSE: The study proposed to identify the interests and background variables characterizing secondary school librarians who worked with teachers in curriculum development and improvement of instruction, and to determine which variables served as predictors of success in this working relationship.

PROCEDURE: Questionnaires were sent to all secondary school librarians who served as head librarians during the 1969-70 school year in Minnesota public high schools and their principals. The librarians were also given the Strong Vocational Interest Blank. A return of 114 completed sets (91 percent) was reported. The data were analyzed by stepwise backward elimination procedures and t-tests.

FINDINGS: Significant correlations between personal and school background variables and success in the working relationship were found for: level of training, number of curriculum courses, working preference, years in library work within present district, type of materials program, number of professional and clerical assistants, size of teaching staff and school, and school organization. The best set of predictors were, in order: type of materials program, undergraduate major and working preference. Librarians who worked with teachers were characterized by a diversity of interests, interests similar to their male or female counterparts, and a tendency toward extroversion and social service.

CONCLUSIONS: Basic interests of librarians who work with teachers have little predictive value based on their correlation to success. Occupational interests are not as good predictors as differences in educational preparation.

488. Scott, Edith (Ph.D., University of Chicago, 1970). **Hanson and his contribution to twentieth-century cataloging.** 695p.

489. Sharma, Om Prakasi (Ph.D., University of Chicago, 1970). **Forces behind the Indian movement, 1858-1892.** 335p.

490. Shaughnessy, Thomas William (Ph.D., Rutgers University, 1970). **The influence of distance and travel time on central library use.** 244p. Order no. 71-3100.

PURPOSE: This study was an attempt to evaluate one aspect of public library systems effectiveness, namely the direct use of central libraries by persons living within a system's service area.

PROCEDURE: The usage patterns of 20 central libraries in New Jersey, New York and Pennsylvania were studied through questionnaires sent to 10,857 users and interviews with 121 users. The usage data were cross-tabulated by consecutive distance intervals. Stepwise regression analysis was used to examine relationships.

FINDINGS: To a limited extent central libraries were effective in providing direct service to residents of library systems. A distance of 10 to 15 miles generally marked the practical limit of a central library's range. No differences in the nature of central library use were found when examined in the context of distance traveled.

FINDINGS (cont'd): Trips to central libraries were often made in connection with the use of other near-by facilities. Local libraries of some strength located in trading centers 15 miles or more from the central libraries were sometimes utilized as unofficial central libraries for their immediate regions. A significant difference was observed between the usage rates of these units and official central libraries. The rate of central library attendance by persons living within specific distance intervals was found to be significantly related to certain aspects of a library's strength. In suburban areas, the pattern of central library use becomes uneven and blurred.

491. Shirey, Donald Lamar (Ph.D., University of Pittsburgh, 1970). **Mensuration in the request-document image space of an information retrieval system.** 125p. Order no. 71-16,203.

PURPOSE: The study was conducted to determine the effect that matching weighted request descriptors with a subset of weighted document descriptors had on the recall and precision of the system.

PROCEDURE: A request-document image space was constructed in which request image vectors were matched with document image vectors and their "closeness" in this semantic space determined. Each requester was asked to weigh the descriptors with regard to their importance to him in characterizing his needs. Next document image vectors were derived from the textual representations of the documents. These units were weighted so that each descriptor reflected its relative importance in the document. The predictive validity of the procedure was evaluated by selecting a new sample of documents, weighting their image vectors, locating them in the image space, predicting their relevance, and comparing the predictions with the actual relevancy judgments that had been made on the documents by their requester.

FINDINGS: Image vectors formed from the abstract and the index terms predicted relevancy significantly better than predictions based on the unweighted retrieval system currently employed on the unweighted NAS document field. Image vectors formed from the text of the first and last paragraphs of the documents, however, did not predict significantly better than the unweighted system. The location of the group centroids in the space were according to expectation, but the dispersion of individual documents around each centroid was such that there was considerable overlap precluding effective separation.

CONCLUSIONS: Searching the weighted text of document extracts gave slightly more precision than did searching the weighted descriptors from abstracts or index terms, while highest recall came from searching index terms. Matching schemes are more effective if based on fewer matches of highly weighted terms rather than on a large number of matches with low weighted terms. Optimum retrieval is effected when profiles are updated frequently, ideally just prior to each search.

492. Sinclair, Dorothy Melville (Ph.D., Case Western Reserve, 1970). **Growth patterns in multi-library systems for public service.** 154p. Order no. 71-1750.

PURPOSE: The purpose of the study was to provide an in-depth historical study of the development of multi-library systems.

PROCEDURE: A model of library development is presented in six phases, each of which is represented by a triangle. Each triangle shows a situation, problems inherent in it and their solution. The solution of each phase becomes the situation of its successor. These sequential triangles trace the development from the small,

PROCEDURE (cont'd): inadequate independent library to the multi-type-of-library system with a research component and a complex organizational structure. A second type of triangle shows the process by which development has occurred within each phase. The triangles' sides represent respectively the identification of problems, recommendations for their solution and acceptance (or rejection) of the recommendations. Three case studies, from California, Texas, and Ohio, illustrate the application and possible uses of the design.

493. Sineath, Timothy Wayne (Ph.D., University of Illinois, 1970). **The relationship between size of research library collections and the support of faculty research studies.** 104p. Order no. 71-14,951.
PURPOSE: This preliminary study was concerned with the relationship between the research collection of large university libraries and the conduct of research using these collections. Can the characteristics of size of the collection, in volumes, be acceptable as a general indicator of the ability of the collection to support research?
PROCEDURE: Citations were randomly sampled from the published research articles of the faculties of two universities with libraries of more than 2.5 million volumes. The titles were then checked in the official catalogs of the library at which the research was done, the other large library and a third, smaller library (whose collection was somewhere between 500,000 and 1 million volumes). Ownership of a large proportion of these titles constituted research support. The results were tabulated and the Difference-of-Proportions test was applied.
FINDINGS: There was a statistically significant difference in the ability of both large university library collections and the medium sized collection to support faculty research studies; the two large university library collections were able to support equally well the research of each other's faculty.

494. Slanker, Barbara Olsen (Ph.D., University of Illinois, 1970). **Administrative structure of public library systems and its relationship to the level of service offered by member libraries.** 291p. Order no. 71-5239.
PURPOSE: The effect of different types of administrative structures of public library systems on the level of service offered by the members of libraries of the systems was investigated.
PROCEDURE: Questionnaires, checklists, a performance test and structured interviews were used to collect information from nine library systems in metropolitan areas with populations of 100,000 to 500,000. The data were analyzed statistically using one-way analysis of variance.
CONCLUSIONS: In this sample, public libraries that belonged to systems provided a higher level of service than public libraries which did not belong to systems. There was a moderate amount of evidence to suggest that members of consolidated systems provided a higher level of service than members of cooperative systems.

495. Slote, Stanley James (Ph.D., Rutgers University, 1970). **The predictive value of past-use patterns of adult fiction in public libraries for identifying core collections.** 160p. Order no. 71-3104.
PURPOSE: The purposes of the study included: (1) exploring the possibility of using past-use patterns as the basis for objective weeding criteria for adult fiction collections; (2) determining if "shelf-time" period of a book is a better predictor of future use than "the most recent imprint date;" (3) developing a model for the core

PURPOSE (cont'd): collection of each library in the sample; and (4) determining
if the pattern of current use of books circulating is as valid a predictor of future
use as historical reconstruction of circulation over longer periods of time.
PROCEDURE: Five public libraries having segregated adult fiction collections and
using book cards which recorded previous use, were selected. A sample was taken of
the books circulating for seven days. The distributions of the use-patterns were used
to predict patterns of future use. Systematic samples were made of the total fiction
collection to predict the percentage of the present collection which would be
represented in the core collection. A use prediction was made in one library, based
upon shelf-time period. Seven weeks later, a new circulation sample was taken and
compared with the prediction.
FINDINGS: Past-use patterns were highly predictive of the future use of fiction
volumes. Shelf-time period was a predictor of a "better" core collection than "the
most recent imprint date." An individual model of a core collection was required for
each individual library. The pattern of use of the current circulation created use-
patterns which were as valid for predicting use as any method of history reconstruction tried.

496. Smith, Richard Daniel (Ph.D., University of Chicago, 1970). **The nonaqueous
deacidification of paper and books.** 310p.
PURPOSE: This study relates the concepts of paper durability and permanence. It
reports data which indicate that books published between 1900 and 1960 will be
difficult if not impossible to rebind before they are 60 years old and potentially useless before they are 100 years old.
FINDINGS: The principal cause of deterioration is identified as the acid-catalyzed
hydrolysis of cellulose in paper fibers. The acidic condition of most library paper
materials is caused during the manufacture of the paper and by the natural degradation
processes or by absorption of air pollutants during library storage. The existing
methods of protecting cellulose from acid attacks are unsuitable to preserve paper and
books or prohibitively expensive. The cost of dismantling, deacidifying, and rebind-
ing currently averages from $50 to $80 per book. In this study a new method of protecting cellulose materials from acid attack is developed and evaluated. This novel
nonaqueous deacidification process consists of impregnating paper and books with
a nonaqueous deacidification solution containing an organic solvent and a benign
alkaline deacidification agent. The experimental data indicate that the potential
benefit of nonaqueous deacidification varies according to the condition of the
cellulose in the treated articles. However, the new process appears to be more
generally applicable and less costly than the deacidification methods heretofore
available, perhaps 100 times less than aqueous deacidification methods in the case of
whole books.
RECOMMENDATIONS: The deacidification solution should be composed of an
alkali metal or alkaline earth metal alkoxide dissolved in a chlorofluorohydro-
carbon solvent containing methanol as a solubilizing agent for the alkoxide. Mag-
nesium methoxide is selected as the preferred deacidification agent.

497. Stenstrom, Ralph Hubert (Ph.D., University of Illinois, 1970). **Factors
associated with membership and non-membership in public library systems
in Illinois.** 229p. Order no. 71-14,958.
PURPOSE: The purpose of this study was to investigate some of the factors

PURPOSE (cont'd): associated with public libraries' decision to join or not to join library systems in Illinois.

PROCEDURE: Approximately 500 libraries were investigated to see if the time when they joined systems was associated with any of 11 characteristics: population served, assessed valuation, tax rate, hours open per week, number of volumes, volumes added, circulation, income, expenditures for salaries and materials and total expenditures. The libraries were then stratified by size; three libraries were selected from each of the size groups and within these groups one from each of the time-of-joining groups. Librarians and trustees from these libraries were interviewed.

FINDINGS: Libraries ranking high on the characteristics constituted the group with the highest percentage of its members among the early joiners, followed by the medium and low ranking categories. Among the middle joiners, the low ranking category constituted the highest percentages followed by the medium and high categories. No consistent pattern was visible among the late or non-joiners. A local orientation on the part of the librarians and trustees was associated with greater resistance to systems. The librarians and trustees' most commonly expressed objection was the fear that systems would interfere with local autonomy. The system feature which received the most direct criticism was the requirement of reciprocal borrowing. The most important advantage was declared to be the supplementary collections of materials which the systems could make available. An important factor in the decisions made was the leadership provided by the librarians and trustees.

498. Stevenson, Henry Gordon (Ph.D., Indiana University, 1970). **The classified catalogs of German university libraries, in theory and practice, between 1900 and 1970.** 208p. Order no. 71-6912.

PURPOSE: The study traced the development of classified catalogs in Germany between 1900 and 1970.

FINDINGS: Until the early 1940's, there was no difference between the classification system used for books and for catalog entries. There were only hand-produced book catalogs. Between 1945 and 1960, new classified catalogs were started. Flexibility was achieved by the introduction of the card catalog and the separation of catalog-entry classification from systems of book shelving. Shelf classification was abandoned. The only move to standardization was the adoption of the Eppelsheimer or the Universal Decimal Classification. The alphabetical subject heading catalog continued, as it always had been, to be supplementary. After 1960, a new period in German classified catalogs started. Books were shelved in open stacks and shelf classification was reintroduced. Computers began to produce book catalogs. By 1970, of the 23 university libraries in West Germany, 17 had classified catalogs, four had introduced alphabetical subject heading catalogs, one had no subject catalog and one used the shelflist as a subject catalog.

499. Thomas, Bruce Wallace (Ph.D., Ohio State University, 1970). **Selection of professional staff in a group of college libraries.** 161p. Order no. 71-7580.

PURPOSE: The study compared the staff hiring processes in small and medium sized academic libraries with those developed and in wide use in several other fields.

PROCEDURE: Questionnaires were sent to 89 libraries serving private, four-year

PROCEDURE (cont'd): liberal arts institutions, with three to nine professional librarians (78 percent response rate).

CONCLUSIONS: The libraries surveyed were not making full use of the tools and resources available to them in the procurement and selection of professional personnel. Candidates and potential candidates were too often not supplied with enough information to enable them to make an intelligent job choice.

RECOMMENDATIONS: Advertisements should not be restricted in length. Recruiters should concentrate their efforts on a few productive library schools. Unsolicited applications should be treated seriously. Interviewers should be trained. Tests for career aptitude, interests and general intelligence should be administered before entrance to library school. Reference checks should be made through conversation. Job descriptions should be available.

500. Vignone, Joseph A. (Ph.D., University of Pittsburgh, 1970). **An inquiry into the opinions and attitudes of public librarians, library directors, and library board members concerning collective bargaining procedures for public library employees in Pennsylvania.** 204p. Order no. 71-13,224.

PURPOSE: The study attempted to empirically discern the opinions and attitudes of library directors, librarians and library board members concerning a model of collective bargaining procedures for public library employees in Pennsylvania.

PROCEDURE: The model was influenced by the work of the Hickman Commission, Sinicropi, Heisel and Hallihan, Doherty and Oberer, and Warner and Hennessy. Data were collected by questionnaires sent to 308 individuals and follow-up interviews with 37 of the original respondents. Analysis of variance followed by Scheffe Test comparisons enabled the investigator to measure relationships.

FINDINGS: Library directors and librarians were more in favor of the collective bargaining model than were trustees. There was no significant difference in the response pattern by variables of sex, experience level, professional affiliation, and size of population served by classes of libraries. Differences were found on the basis of age and educational level.

501. Vorwerk, Richard James (Ph.D., Indiana University, 1970). **The environmental demands and organizational states of two academic libraries.** 200p. Order no. 71-17,458.

PURPOSE: Two libraries were examined with respect to the demands made upon them by their respective environments, the organizational responses to these demands, and the organizational fit between each library's demands and responses.

PROCEDURE: Data were collected by interviewing and by questioning the chief administrators and major department heads of two libraries. The environment of each library was divided into three subenvironments: a scientific sector, a techno-economic sector, and a market sector. Each of these three subenvironments was measured along a certainty-uncertainty continuum. The organizational responses for each unit were measured for the degree of differentiation and integration. The organizational fit between the environmental demands and the organizational responses was then determined for each library.

FINDINGS: Library Alpha fit in eight of 16 possibilities; Library Beta in seven of the 16. Implementation of the changes indicated for the two libraries should bring about a closer fit between the environmental demands and the organizational responses of the libraries causing, according to the Lawrence and Lorsch

FINDINGS (cont'd): "contingency" model of organizations, the two libraries to perform more effectively.

502. Weinstein, Frederick Daniel (Ph.D., Columbia University, 1970). **Walter Crane and the American book arts 1880-1915.** 275p. Order no. 71-17,558.
PURPOSE: The principal purpose of the study was to focus upon the book designs of Walter Crane and to attempt to document the influence these works had upon the visual atmosphere of the late nineteenth and early twentieth century American book arts.
FINDINGS: Crane's book arts were related to Blake, to pre-Raphaelitism, to the Arts and Crafts movement, to Art Nouveau itself, as well as other social, artistic, and commercial influences and pressures acting upon them. The essence of the Crane Manner lies in the fact that Crane decorated rather than depicted his texts. Crane was very popular in America. His influence is visible in such vehicles as *The Knight Errant, The Chapbook* and *St. Nicholas* and in the designs and illustrations of Edwin Austin Abbey, George Wharton Edwards, Lucy Fitch Perkins, Will Denslow, Louis Rhead, Will Bradley and Howard Phyle.

503. Weintraub, D. Kathryn (Ph.D., University of Chicago, 1970). **The syntax of some English relative clauses.**
PURPOSE: This study was undertaken as part of a larger concern with a problem of bibliographic organization. The third and major portion of the study consists of a detailed linguistic analysis of a particular syntactic construction.
FINDINGS: The preface outlines a problem of bibliographic organization. The first part of the study outlines the linguistic model used for this analysis. The model is a form of faceted classification, but it is different in form from most (if not all) faceted classifications.

504. Wert, Lucille Mathena (Ph.D., University of Illinois, 1970). **Library education and high school library services.** 364p. Order no. 70-21,083.
PURPOSE: The purpose of this study was to determine the relationship between the amount of library education of high school librarians and the programs of reader services which they developed.
PROCEDURE: Eight high school libraries in Illinois were used in the study. The librarians of four of the libraries had Master's degrees in library science; the remaining four had undergraduate minors or less in library science. The schools were matched on length of time the librarians had been at the schools, the schools' enrollments, and annual per pupil expenditures of the school districts. Data were collected by means of a daily record of library activities kept by the librarians; a checklist of reader services; questionnaires on library use distributed to students and teachers; interviews with the librarian, teachers and administrators of each school; and observation of each library program.
FINDINGS: The group of librarians with the larger amount of library education developed more extensive programs of reader services than did the group of librarians with less library education. A similar pattern was found in the data on teacher and student use of the libraries. Likewise, a larger percent of the students in the schools which employed librarians with Master's degrees in library science used the library to do class assignments and used materials related to class assignments than did the students from the other group of schools.

505. Whitbeck, George Walter (Ph.D., Rutgers University, 1970). **The influence of librarians in liberal arts colleges as demonstrated by their role in selected areas of decision making.** 299p. Order no. 71-12,283.

PURPOSE: The purpose of this study was to examine the influence of librarians in small liberal arts colleges in key areas of decision making. The perceived role of the librarians, as seen by themselves and faculty members and administrators, is also given attention.

PROCEDURE: Data were collected at 10 randomly selected liberal arts colleges having an enrollment of between 800 and 2,000 students in New York, New Jersey, and Pennsylvania. Personal interviews were conducted with 183 academic deans, chief fiscal officers, librarians and faculty members at each college.

FINDINGS: The librarian occupies a distinctly marginal position in regard to the key areas of decision making. They exhibited a significantly lower degree of knowledge and interest in curricular issues than did faculty members. Like faculty, librarians occupied a peripheral role in the budgeting process; unlike faculty, they were not involved in key appointments. The majority of college librarians saw their role as part of faculty rather than as administrators or as a separate group on campus. Approximately half the faculty and administration also saw the librarians' role as that of a faculty member.

1971

---

506. Altman, Ellen O. (Ph.D., Rutgers University, 1971). **The resource capacity of public secondary school libraries to support interlibrary loan: a systems approach to title diversity and collection overlap.** 279p. Order no. 71-20,040.

PURPOSE: This study explored the feasibility of establishing interlibrary loan networks among public secondary school libraries to increase the quantity and diversity of resources for independent study beyond those available in each school.

PROCEDURE: Thirty-one schools in two New Jersey counties which most nearly approximated state norms were chosen for the sample along with the four area reference libraries in those counties. Teachers and librarians in the schools were asked by questionnaires to identify topics on which students had done independent work. The 12 most frequently mentioned topics were selected for collection sampling.

FINDINGS: Unique titles represented 48.1 percent of all titles in the school (refuting the assumption that school library collections are basically similar). In addition, 31.4 percent of school titles were not owned by any of the public libraries. The hypothesized net title increase of 700 percent and the projected net volume increase of 1,200 percent was validated. Schools holding the largest number of titles overall had weaknesses in certain areas. Thus, even large libraries could strengthen certain portions of their collections by pooling. Data indicate that pools of 40 to 50 libraries constitute an optimum secondary school library system.

CONCLUSIONS: Calculations for library systems of any size with probabilities based on sample titles may be made from the equations developed in this study.

507. Amundson, Colleen Coghlan (Ph.D., University of Minnesota, 1971). **Relationships between university freshmen's information-gathering techniques and selected environmental factors.** 248p. Order no. 71-28,205.
PURPOSE: Several questions were asked in this study: what sources of information do university freshmen use to become informed and where do they go to get them? Do students classified variously use different techniques and how do students get to the sources and agencies used?
PROCEDURE: Students relied more on impersonal sources (particularly books and magazines) than on interpersonal sources; librarians were the least used source. In their bibliographies, students rarely cited interviews or non-print media. Campus residents chiefly used university libraries and commuters used public libraries in their research. Prior library instruction did not differentiate students on library skills' tests or in approaches to information gathering. In various phases of preparation, the academic group of students were more discriminating in their use of selected sources; the nonconformist students were more involved with a variety of information sources and the collegiate students delayed work; the vocational students were singularly nondescript.
CONCLUSIONS: Students do not take much advantage of librarians or official library resources. Students had difficulty recognizing bias, authority, appropriateness, availability and sufficient use. Librarians and teachers have to define "good information" and determine their responsibilities for helping students gather it.

508. Armstrong, Charles Wesley (Ph.D., University of Pittsburgh, 1971). **Role of information resources in national development: a descriptive study and analyses of library resources in West Africa.** 654p. Order no. 72-18,291.
PURPOSE: The major purposes of the study were to investigate the role and influence of information resources in national development and the problems of information resources and their organization in certain academic libraries in selected West African countries.
PROCEDURE: Data were collected by analyzing the relevant literature, visiting 12 academic libraries in five West African countries between January 6 and April 11, 1969, and sending questionnaires to 12 academic librarians and heads of Technical Services.
FINDINGS: The libraries had common problems: lack of trained and experienced personnel, lack of space, and lack of funds.
CONCLUSIONS: There is a need for information in national development; the flow of information was hindered by the lack of transportation, manpower, funding and electricity. The plans for organizing and administering library resources and the library budgets are inadequately conceived.
RECOMMENDATIONS: In the study a plan for a national documentation and information services program for the organization and administration of information resources within an academic library center was developed.

509. Barth, Edward Walter (Ed.D., George Washington University, 1971). **The relationship between selected teaching structures and the activities of media centers in public senior high schools in the State of Maryland.** 220p. Order no. 71-22,413.
PURPOSE: In this study an attempt was made to identify and analyze selected teaching structures and activities of media centers and to determine if a relationship existed between them.

198

PROCEDURE: Questionnaires were sent to 24 school systems in Maryland. There was a 77 percent response rate.

FINDINGS: Although there were fewer staff members in media centers of schools with fewer of the selected teaching structures, they provided as many services as the larger staffs. Regardless of the teaching structures, the staffs of media centers acquired similar instructional materials and budgeted their funds with similar percentage levels. Media centers in schools with fewer teaching structures had approximately the same seating capacity as media centers in schools with a higher number of selected teaching structures. However, the latter media centers had a greater number of activity areas.

RECOMMENDATIONS: Para-professional personnel should be employed in one librarian media center. More funds should be made available to purchase both print and non-print material. There should be more cooperation and communication between the librarians and the faculty. Students should be given more of an opportunity to participate in materials selection and to advise the center in its program of services.

510. Baughman, James Carroll (Ph.D., Case Western Reserve University, 1971). **A model for establishing a curriculum and its core literature source.** 191p. Order no. 72-6,272.

PURPOSE: The purpose of the investigation was to develop a general method for establishing a curriculum and its core literature source by using a mathematical approach. The theoretical aspects of the study centered around the structure of knowledge, of a subject literature and of a curriculum.

PROCEDURE: The *Standards for School Media Programs* (1969) and specific journals selected from *Education Index* from 1966-67 through 1969-70 were the source, and the resulting curriculum document was the outcome. The dynamics and statics of the literature were studied in order to make a prediction for the growth of knowledge.

CONCLUSIONS: The structure of a subject literature provides understanding of literature forms and processes, as opposed to the understanding of the literature's intellectual content. It offers a method for talking about a literature in order that relationships and other characteristics of the literature may be recognized which may ultimately lead to the establishment of an effective communication process and system. Thus, a meaningful and economic information transfer scheme can be realized.

511. Blazek, Ronald David (Ph.D., University of Illinois, 1971). **Teacher utilization of nonrequired library materials in mathematics and the effect on pupil use.** 283p. Order no. 71-21,079.

PURPOSE: The purpose of this study was to examine the effects on pupils' use of library materials of a teacher who utilized these materials as part of his teaching routine. The nature of the task was optional rather than required and focused on supplementary materials in mathematics.

PROCEDURE: The study employed the experimental method. In the experimental group, the teacher provided bibliographic awareness and encouragement to use mathematics materials which had been placed on reserve. The control group was not provided with any information except for a remark at the outset that there would be materials on reserve. Circulation records were kept in the library prior to, during,

PROCEDURE (cont'd): and after the test period for comparison. Data on pupils' attitudes toward the teacher, mathematics and library materials were obtained through interviews. Chi-square, Mann-Whitney U, and matched pairs techniques were used to analyze the data.

FINDINGS: Results of the pretest and posttest periods showed no real differences in either number of users or number of circulations between groups. During the test period, however, the experimental group far outdistanced the control group in use of mathematics materials and in total use as well. Teacher utilization was shown to be positively and significantly related to the use of library materials.

CONCLUSIONS: Teacher influence was the most tenable explanation of why pupils followed the teacher's suggestion in using nonrequired materials.

512. Bommer, Michael Roger William (Ph.D., University of Pennsylvania, 1971). **The development of a management system for effective decision making and planning in a university library.** 340p. (To order copies contact author at: 200 Shisler Avenue, Aldan, Pennsylvania 19018.)

PURPOSE: The study attempted to develop an improved management system to provide guidance to university library administrators for making decisions and formulating plans. The system was designed to be applicable in any university library.

PROCEDURE: First, an investigation was made of the hierarchy of library objectives, and it was concluded that the one objective which satisfies a set of specified criteria was the maximization of expected future exposures of university community members to documents given current and anticipated future expenditures. A measure of performance utilizing the concept of item-use-days was developed to evaluate the degree of attainment of this objective. The Planning-Programming-Budgeting System and benefit-cost analysis were discussed. Analytical models were developed to provide guidance to library administrators in decision making and planning processes for selected subprograms: overall library performance, determining the number of multiple copies of a title to purchase, determining the number of new titles to purchase for a subject area, deciding on the number of copies of a title to place on reserve, and predicting the demand rate for circulation use of titles. These models were listed and verified and relevant parameters estimated as applied to a departmental library at the University of Pennsylvania. Guidance was offered for the development of a statistical information system to support the decision making and planning process.

513. Broderick, Dorothy M. (D.L.S., Columbia University, 1971). **Image of the black in popular and recommended American juvenile fiction 1827-1967.** 543p.

514. Brown, Jovana J. (Ph.D., University of California, Berkeley, 1971). **The faculty library committee in the university.**

515. Bullock, Penelope L. (Ph.D., University of Michigan, 1971). **Negro periodical press in the United States, 1838-1909.** 450p.

516. Bush, Nancy Wagoner (Ph.D., The Florida State University, 1971). **Investigation of the relationship between two teaching methods and attitude modification.** 300p. Order no. 72-16,572.

PURPOSE: The object of this study was to determine the relationship between lecture and problem solving teaching methods and attitude modification.

PROCEDURE: The attitude level of Master's degree candidates in Library Science at Florida State University enrolled in the courses Information Resources in the Social Sciences and Basic Reference Sources in Winter 1971 were measured at the beginning, middle and end of the courses. Computation for each subject's and each group's pre-check, midcheck and postcheck were completed and followed by ANOVA for all the variables in combination.

FINDINGS: Neither the lecture method of instruction nor the problem solving method influenced attitude change. The combination of the two teaching methods did, however, influence attitude change. Active learning was correlated with positive attitude toward a reference course. A formal reference course background which dealt with reference services paralleled a negative student attitude. No formal reference course background was preferable to a service course background.

517. Busha, Charles Henry (Ph.D., Indiana University, 1971). **The attitudes of Midwestern public librarians toward intellectual freedom and censorship.** 175p. Order no. 71-29,561.

PURPOSE: This research investigated (1) the extent to which librarians accepted the intellectual freedom principles of the *Library Bill of Rights* and the *Freedom to Read* statement; (2) the attitudes of librarians toward censorship; (3) the relationship of librarians' censorship attitudes to their attitudes toward selected authoritarian beliefs; and (4) the relationship between librarians' intellectual freedom and censorship attitudes.

PROCEDURE: Data were collected by means of a questionnaire containing an intellectual freedom test, a censorship attitude scale, and the F scale on authoritarianism sent to a random sample of 900 librarians stratified by state and size of community selected from 3,253 public librarians in Illinois, Indiana, Michigan, Ohio, and Wisconsin (69 percent of the questionnaires were used in the study). Cronbach alpha coefficients, standard errors and population parameter estimates for each attitude test were determined.

FINDINGS: Significant correlations were found between censorship and authoritarianism scores, between intellectual freedom and censorship scores, between librarians' personal characteristics and censorship and between librarians' personal characteristics and authoritarian beliefs. The attitudes of 14 percent of the librarians were predominantly sympathetic toward censorship (22 percent expressed strong anti-censorship attitudes). Librarians who agreed with authoritarian beliefs also tended very strongly to approve of censorship measures.

518. Carter, Esther May (Ph.D., Indiana University, 1971). **The organizational structure for state school library supervision and the functions, duties, and activities of state school library supervisors.** 225p. Order no. 71-29,562.

PURPOSE: The purpose of this study was to determine whether a direct relationship existed between the hierarchical level of the positions of state school library supervisors in the organizational structure of state departments of education in the 50 states and the range and type of activities that supervisors performed.

PROCEDURE: State constitutions and statutes of the 50 states were examined to determine the organizational structure for school library supervision within the state departments of education as of December 31, 1968. The hierarchical level was

PROCEDURE (cont'd): then ascertained and questionnaires sent to 126 state school library supervisors (67 percent response).
FINDINGS: The primary activities of state school library supervisors in 1968 were service and regulatory activities of a consulting nature. Developmental activities appeared to be gaining in importance. Public support and cooperation activities were viewed as marginal. The supervisors in the upper middle hierarchical level were able to perform a wider range of activities than those supervisors at either the lower middle or lower hierarchical levels.

519. Cole, John Young, Jr. (Ph.D., George Washington University, 1971).
Ainsworth Spofford and the "national library ." 170p. Order no. 72-8994.
PURPOSE: The purpose of this study was to trace the effect that Ainsworth Rand Spofford (1825-1908) had on the transformation of the Library of Congress from a small legislative library (71,000 volumes in 1861) into a library of national significance (246,000 volumes in 1872).
FINDINGS: The idea of a national library in the United States had many advocates before Spofford, including New England intellectual Rufus Choate and Smithsonian Institution Librarian Charles Coffin Jewett. Immediately after the Civil War, the elements necessary for the establishment of an American national library were present at the Library of Congress. Its Librarian, Ainsworth Spofford, was well prepared for his task; he had worked earlier as a bookseller, publisher, cultural entrepreneur, editorial writer and political correspondent for Cincinnati's leading newspaper. The growth of other federal institutions during this time aided Spofford in his undertaking. Important aid came from Joseph Henry. Spofford secured legislation which ensured the place of the Library as the national library. The Copyright Law of 1870, which centralized all U.S. copyright activities at the Library and brought in two copies of each copyrighted work, also helped the transformation. The change was completed when Spofford, in his 1872 annual report, presented a plan for a separate Library of Congress building.

520. Cookston, James Sanders (Ph.D., Louisiana State University and Agricultural and Mechanical College, 1971). **Development of Louisiana public school libraries, 1929-1965.** 335p. Order no. 71-29,355.
PURPOSE: This study traced the development of Louisiana public school libraries from 1929 to 1965. The study primarily encompassed the activities of the Louisiana State Department of Education in the development of the State's public school library program.
PROCEDURE: Primary data came from the official files of the Louisiana State Department of Education, the Louisiana Library Association, interviews and letters. Secondary data included theses, dissertations, books and periodicals.
FINDINGS: Early educational efforts in Louisiana did not include school libraries. It was not until 1908 that serious consideration was given to these libraries; State Superintendent of Education, Thomas H. Harris encouraged local school boards to establish and promote school libraries, but little was accomplished. In 1929 the first State Supervisor of School Libraries was appointed (Lois F. Shortess) and the school library picture rapidly improved. The third State Supervisor of School Libraries, Lena deGrummond, stimulated rapid growth in centralized libraries. The number of institutions offering library education programs increased, book collections in schools improved, and the competencies of school librarians were upgraded through frequent workshops and conferences.

521. Cooper, Michael David (Ph.D., University of California, Berkeley, 1971). **Evaluation of information retrieval systems: a simulation and cost approach.** 222p. Order no. 71-25,445.

PURPOSE: Two specific approaches to evaluating an information retrieval system were explored in the dissertation: a mathematic model for use in studying how to minimize the cost of operating mechanized retrieval systems and a simulation model. PROCEDURE: The cost model divided the costs of a retrieval system into two components: systems/costs and user costs. The simulation program created a well specified collection of documents and analyzed the effect of changes in query file characteristics on system performance. A thesaurus of term relations was generated. Routines generated pseudo-documents and pueudo-queries which, using the thesaurus, were compared to see the effect of various query file parameter changes on the quantity of material retrieved. FINDINGS: Evaluation of the simulation output indicated that there were small differences between the results of the experimental runs. CONCLUSIONS: One method for generating pseudo-queries was not clearly better than another. The simulation model as an approach to the evaluation of retrieval systems seemed to provide a limited but useful framework for the evaluation of retrieval systems.

522. Davis, Lattice Rucker (Ed.D., George Washington University, 1971). **Public elementary school media centers in Baltimore County, Maryland, as compared with "The Standards for School Media Programs,"** 1969. 140p. Order no. 71-22,419.

PURPOSE: The extent to which public elementary school media centers in Baltimore County, Maryland met the "Standards for School Media Programs" was studied in this dissertation. PROCEDURE: A 100 percent response was received on the questionnaires sent to 103 elementary school media specialists in Baltimore County, Maryland. Selected central office personnel were interviewed to obtain data on each school not included in the questionnaire. FINDINGS: More than half of the centers provided most of the qualitative services recommended in the Standards. The services most frequently not provided were supplementary materials production, curriculum planning, dissemination of recent trends and information on in-service education and committee membership. The media programs were understaffed and nearly half of the specialists were not certified. Central processing was provided, but not for non-print or independently ordered materials. The budgets were below standard. RECOMMENDATION: There should be increased budget, in-service education, central processing of materials, improved facilities for the media centers, increased emphasis of non-print materials and better liaison between the Office of Library Services and the Instructional Materials Center staff.

523. Deligdisch, Yekutiel (Ph.D., University of Wisconsin, 1971). **The reading comprehension of adult new readers in relation to their ethnic backgrounds.** 176p. Order no. 72-406.

PURPOSE: The study was concerned with the problem of identification of characteristics of materials needed for Adult New Readers who are making the transition from functional literacy to the regular use of print.

PROCEDURE: The sample included forty Black and forty Mexican-American Adult New Literates, whose comprehension of reading selections was tested at the levels of literal, implied and applied meaning. For each group, comparisons were made of the mean scores on the two literatures at each level of comprehension.

FINDINGS: Each group scored considerably higher on applied meaning for its own culture-related material than on the material related to the other culture. The Mexican-Americans scored on all three levels of meaning consistently higher on their own material than on the Black material; the Blacks scored higher on the literal and implied meanings on the Mexican-American material than on the Black material.

CONCLUSIONS: Publications centering around culture themes of ethnic groups may improve the Adult New Reader's ability to apply and use what he reads.

524. De Pew, John (Ph.D., University of Pittsburgh, 1971). **Business and economic publications in four Pittsburgh libraries: a study of coverage, duplication and omission.** 248p. Order no. 72-2,140.

PURPOSE: This study was conducted to (1) test the hypothesis that four libraries in Pittsburgh (the libraries of Carnegie-Mellon University, Duquesne University and the University of Pittsburgh, and Carnegie Library of Pittsburgh) should have strong collections in business and economic materials because of the continuing contribution the geographic area makes to the economy, and (2) to provide a vehicle which could be used to develop library collections on a systematic basis individually or cooperatively.

PROCEDURE: The Harvard University Library was used as a source of comparison. An acquisitions decision model was developed in order to check whether each library in the study was justified in acquiring or rejecting each title on the check-list for its collection. A total of 1,291 business and economic works published in 1966 and reviewed by journals published in the United States were selected for the checklist. The titles were analyzed by type of publication, country of publication, subject subdivision covered within business and economics, and tone of review.

FINDINGS: The Pittsburgh libraries collected 88.14 percent of the titles and Harvard held 89.93 percent. The Pittsburgh group duplicated 77.78 percent of the titles among themselves. The decision model revealed that several of the titles should not have been duplicated as extensively by all of the four institutions, while all but one of the 1,291 titles should have been held by one or more of the libraries.

CONCLUSIONS: The business and economic collections in Pittsburgh were not as strong as the percentages of holdings would indicate; the decision model would be useful in developing each library's collection individually or in cooperation with other institutions.

525. Donnelly, Sister Francis Dolores (Ph.D., University of Illinois at Urbana-Champaign, 1971). **The National Library of Canada: forces in its emergence, and in the identification of its role and responsibilities.** 443p. Order no. 72-12,380.

PURPOSE: This study was undertaken to locate and describe the forces which operated both positively and negatively in the emergence of Canada's National Library in 1953 and to trace the interaction of internal and external factors contributing to the ultimate identification of the Library's role.

FINDINGS: Canada's first Prime Minister introduced the idea of a National Library

FINDINGS (cont'd): for Canada in the House of Commons as early as 1883. The idea was not realized until 70 years later. The development of the National Library reflects the major influences which were at work in the realization of cultural, educational and informational goals during Canada's first 100 years. At first the Library's activities were restricted to its basic responsibilities (a national bibliography, the national union catalog and limited reference service). A new National Library Act, passed in 1969, provided a wide latitude for the National Library's interaction with other Canadian and international information agencies and allocated to the National Librarian responsibility for coordinating all aspects of library resources and services at the federal government level.

526. Dosa, Marta Leszlei (Ph.D., University of Michigan, 1971). **Scholarship, libraries, politics in the life and work of Georg Leyh (Volumes I-III).** 952p. Order no. 71-740.
PURPOSE: This study was designed to portray Georg Leyh's professional activities and his major contributions to the literature of librarianship. Primarily, it explored the psychological causes of some of Leyh's professional actions. Secondarily, it investigated the influences of politics on librarianship. No attempt was made to present a comprehensive biography of Leyh or a critical evaluation of his published work.
PROCEDURE: The Leyh Archives in the Manuscript Division, State Library of the Foundation for Prussian Cultural Property in West Berlin and papers in the possession of the Leyh family in Lubeck formed the principal source of research. The study is based mainly on an analysis of Leyh's voluminous correspondence and to a lesser extent on printed materials and personal interviews with Leyh and persons who knew him.
CONCLUSIONS: The study concludes that Georg Leyh's distinguished career and leadership were marred by tensions and problems caused, to a great extent, by the conflict of professional commitments and the political environment.

527. Downen, Thomas William (Ph.D., Florida State University, 1971). **Personal reading interests as expressed by children in grades three, four, and five in selected Florida public schools.** 140p. Order no. 72-13,502.
PURPOSE: This study was designed to identify the personal reading interests of third, fourth, and fifth grade students and to determine if significant differences in reading interest categories existed by sex, grade level, ability, sex and grade level, and sex and ability.
PROCEDURE: Questionnaires were given to approximately 1,100 children from 14 randomly selected schools in Florida. For each interest category represented in the instrument, an interest score was computed for each student. Analysis of variance and multiple-range tests were used to analyze the data.
FINDINGS: Sex was the best predictor of reading interest. At the .01 level of significance, boys were more interested than girls in books of Adventure, Tall Tales, Historical Non-fiction, How-To-Do-It, Sports, and Science; girls were more interested than boys in Animal, Fairy Tales, Modern Fantasy, Children of the United States, and Children of Other Lands. Fewer differences were found between the reading categories and grade level, ability subgroup, sex and grade level, and sex and ability.

528. Duncan, Elizabeth E. (Ph.D., University of Pittsburgh, 1971). **Development of a decision model for acquisition of current periodical titles based on usage of periodical literature by chemical personnel.** 117p. Order no. 72-2050.

PURPOSE: The aim of this study was to develop and test a decision model for the acquisition of chemical periodicals. The interactions of the model were to be based on the decision processes of individual chemists as they used the periodical literature for current awareness.

PROCEDURE: *Chemical Condensates*, a magnetic tape variation of *Chemical Abstracts*, was searched weekly for 15 weeks against the profiles of Pittsburgh chemists at the University of Pittsburgh's Chemical Information Center (PCIC). The individual chemists informed PCIC of alerts relevant to their interests (hits). There were 2,822 hits selected by University of Pittsburgh chemists during the test period. In addition, there was a study of three industrial firms and a five week study of the use of current issues of *Chemical Abstracts* at the University of Pittsburgh's Chemistry Library.

FINDINGS: Of the 2,822 hits, 1,235 were unavailable in the Chemistry Library. Not one of the unavailable articles was requested by interlibrary loan. There were 138, 108 and 33 hits for the three industrial firms; each company borrowed only one of these hits by interlibrary loan. There was no use of *Chemical Abstracts* in conjunction with *Chemical Condensates*. A partial analysis of the University of Pittsburgh hits is made to demonstrate how information on periodical usage might, with the Bradford-Zipf Distribution, be used as the basis of an acquisition policy. The characteristics of the *CA Condensates* service are compared with what is known about scientists' use of their literature.

CONCLUSIONS: The study did not show that chemists were using *CA Condensates* as an approach to the periodical literature or to abstracts in *Chemical Abstracts*. Since the research did not disclose what periodical literature the chemists were reading for current awareness, the data necessary for the development of a decision model were not obtained.

529. Edwards, Ralph (D.L.S., University of California, Berkeley, 1971). **The role of the beginning librarian in the University of California libraries.**

PURPOSE: The purpose of the study was to investigate the way the roles of beginning librarians are being defined in practice in university libraries. A further concern was with the attitudes of beginners, their supervisors, and employers about what beginners are doing and what they ideally should be doing.

PROCEDURE: The data were collected from interviews conducted in the eight general libraries of the University of California. The interviewees included 58 beginning librarians, 45 departmental supervisors, and 12 library administrators. The beginning librarians were asked to complete a checklist to indicate which tasks were performed.

FINDINGS: Both the beginning librarians and their supervisors indicated in the study that they believed beginners were asked to perform tasks which were less than professional in nature. This situation was not attributed by the supervisors to any inadequacy in the professional preparation of the beginners but to organizational problems that resulted in not enough non-professional personnel to carry out the non-professional tasks. The library administrators indicated they wanted the professional positions to be redefined and upgraded so that the professional librarians would be relieved of non-professional tasks. In this process, the number of

FINDINGS (cont'd): positions for which beginning professionals would be eligible would be reduced.

CONCLUSIONS: The findings indicated that in spite of the widespread interest in redefining the role of professionals, there seems to be little agreement as to what constitutes professionalism in librarianship. Nor was there a widely shared understanding of what the professional role of the beginning librarian should be.

530. Fidoten, Robert Earl (Ph.D., University of Pittsburgh, 1971). **An organizational analysis of the impact of computers and automation on the management of Engineering Index, Inc., a case study.** 593p. Order no. 72-13,429.

PURPOSE: A case history of the impact of computers and information technology on the management system and organization of Engineering Index, Inc., is presented and analyzed. The study covers the period 1960 through 1971, with emphasis on the years 1968-1971.

PROCEDURE: Data were collected from depth interviews with the president, executive director and management staff of Engineering Index, Inc., the National Science Foundation, users of COMPENDEX, as well as the internal records of the organization.

FINDINGS: Secondary abstracting and indexing services have severe financial problems that transcend the issue of the degree to which they use computers and automation. The availability of machine readable data bases has brought into being a set of complex relationships between information generators, information analysis centers, information dissemination centers and users that require new methods of financing and marketing. Significant development progress with respect to computers and information technology in the not-for-profit secondary abstracting and indexing services are extremely difficult to achieve without large subsidies. Methods used for training incumbent employees to become effective in the use of computers and information technology are inadequate. The users of computerized data bases show a high concern for the quality of the file's content and the time lag between the availability of source material and its appearance in the data base. The potential market for machine-readable data bases that require elaborate computer software and personnel expertise for system operation appears quite limited.

CONCLUSIONS: The Tripartite Committee's effort to form a united engineering information center/system failed primarily because of socio-political reasons, not due to technological shortcomings. The engineering professions are probably too fragmented to support a discipline-oriented national information system.

531. Field, Oliver Thoburn (D.L.S., Columbia University, 1971). **Acquisition and control of books and periodicals in federal research libraries.** 196p. Order no. 72-15,572.

PURPOSE: This dissertation studied the acquisition and control of books and periodicals in the research libraries of the United States government.

PROCEDURE: The material was drawn in part from the findings of the Brookings Institution survey of federal libraries of 1958-59, regulations put in force since that year, and questionnaires sent in October 1967 to a sampling of librarians who responded to the survey.

FINDINGS: There was greater dissatisfaction with acquisition regulations in military research libraries than in civilian ones and in larger, rather than smaller, libraries. There was widespread ignorance among librarians of available remedies to these dissatisfactions and an ignorance of these remedies or an unwillingness to make

FINDINGS (cont'd): use of them on the part of federal procurement officers.
RECOMMENDATIONS: In the short run, the Federal Library Committee should act as a clearinghouse for federal librarians' inquiries concerning procurement. Current restrictions on binding should be revised. The General Services Administration should implement existing laws which permit libraries to have standing orders, etc. The Federal Supply Service should enlarge looseleaf handbooks on laws and legislation pertaining to federal libraries and establish short courses in library procurement. Ultimately, library materials should be taken out of local procurement channels used for other materials and placed in charge of personnel informed about library requirements. Procurement activities for small libraries should be centralized in the General Services Administration; large federal libraries should be authorized to perform their own procurement.

532. Foos, Donald D. (Ph.D., Florida State University, 1971). **The role of the state library in adult education; a critical analysis of nine Southeastern state library agencies.**
PURPOSE: The purpose of the study was to investigate the involvement of the state library agency in the development of adult education programs at the state, regional, and local levels. The study also considered the involvement of the state library agency in a supportive role, where the agency lends assistance and support in developing programs within other adult education agencies.
PROCEDURE: The descriptive case study method was used to investigate the role of the state agency. The investigator used records, files, published and unpublished reports, brochures, pamphlets, proposals, correspondence, and archival material. The states involved were Alabama, Florida, Georgia, Kentucky, Mississippi, North Carolina, South Carolina, Tennessee, and Virginia.
FINDINGS: All of the agencies were founded prior to 1930, and some were established before 1910. Most, however, did not become operational until the late 1940's because of inadequate funding in the early years. Six of the agencies are self-governing, one is semi-autonomous, and two are legally structured within departments. The biggest influence on adult education participation was the American Heritage and Library Community Project, administered by the American Library Association. The current trend in adult education at the state level is the development of programs for the disadvantaged, but state funds are not involved. Eight of the agencies were active in workshops and institutes.
CONCLUSIONS: The following conclusions were offered: (1) the emphasis of the state agencies has been on the development of statewide general library service, rather than specific programs such as adult education; (2) the availability of state financial support did not affect the number of adult education programs conducted by the state library agencies, nor did it foster the agencies' involvement in adult education; (3) the role of the state library agency in adult education can be defined as one of passive support.

533. Franklin, Hardy Rogers (Ph.D., Rutgers University, 1971). **The relationship between adult communication practices and public library use in a Northern, urban, Black ghetto.** 176p. Order no. 72-9621.
PURPOSE: This study identified and described the prevailing communication practices of Bedford Stuyvesant in Brooklyn, New York to determine the relationship between communication practices and use of the public library.

PROCEDURE: The sample consisted of 340 Blacks, 40 Puerto Ricans, 19 whites and one Cuban. Analysis of data was limited to the 340 Blacks (158 males and 182 females). Data for the study were collected by means of a profile form of local branch library resources and services, a community survey, and a Communication Practices Index scale. Chi-square tests for independence and for differences between relations were used.

FINDINGS: Significant relationships were found between the use of the library and age, sex, marital status, education and income. Also, significant relations were found between communication practices and sex, education, income, employment and frequency of use of the public library.

534. Goheen, Patricia Ann (Ph.D., Case Western Reserve University, 1971). **A method for increasing the efficiency of instruction.** 292p. Order no. 71-22,804.

PURPOSE: The basic problem of this study was to develop a method for increasing the efficiency of the instructional process at the introductory level.

PROCEDURE: An experimental approach was used. Control groups did the outside of class assignment in the conventional manner. The experimental groups did the outside of class assignments by attending a learning station. The major statistical test used was the Mann-Whitney U.

FINDINGS: The experimental groups achieved significantly higher scores, took less time to complete the outside of class assignments and had a more favorable attitude toward the outside of class assignments than did the control groups. There was no significant difference between the achievement scores on the course test between control and experimental groups.

535. Goodell, John Silas (Ph.D., The Florida State University, 1971). **A case study of catalogers in three university libraries using work sampling.** 180p. Order no. 72-10,002.

PURPOSE: The activities of university catalogers were studied using work sampling to investigate the problem of how university library catalogers spend their time with respect to specified activity categories.

PROCEDURE: A work sampling study was performed in three university libraries. The subjects were the professional catalog librarians. Chi-square and binomial tests for differences were employed.

FINDINGS: The observed percentages of time university catalogers spent in specified activity categories corresponded closely for all libraries studied. Neither the catalogers nor the directors' estimates of the observed percentages corresponded closely with the observed percentages.

536. Gorcheis, Clarence Clifford (D.L.S., Columbia University, 1971). **Land-grant university library; the history of the Library of Washington State University, 1892-1946.** 424p.

537. Haas, Joyce H. (Ph.D., Rutgers University, 1971). **Ethnic polarization and school library materials: a content analysis of 1,939 fiction books from 30 New Jersey school libraries.** 211p. Order no. 72-830.

PURPOSE: The investigation dealt with two questions: Do the fiction books provided by school libraries present an overall picture which supports our polarized

PURPOSE (cont'd): society: Does the ethnic view of society presented in school library fiction collections vary in schools of varying ethnic enrollments? PROCEDURE: Content analysis of a sample of characters and communications in each chapter of a systematic sample of 1,939 fiction titles from 30 New Jersey elementary schools stratified by "ethnic minority" enrollment was employed. Fifty-one coders identified the content data which was then tabulated and "scored" by computer.

FINDINGS: European-American and European characteristics in American and European settings overwhelmingly predominated. "Ethnic minority" characters tended to be pictured separately and differently than "ethnic majority" characters. "Integration" was typically an adult/child relationship. Contemporary stories and more recently published stories indicated a tendency toward fewer "minority" characters. There were no statistically significant correlations between the ethnic characteristics of the fiction collections and the ethnic enrollment of the schools. There were correlations between the ethnic characteristics of the collections and ethnic characteristics of the counties in which the collections were located.

CONCLUSIONS: The overall picture presented in the study offers little opposition to the ethnic polarization in American society and does not support any trend toward a more integrated or less polarized society. The ethnic content of a school library fiction collection may be so strongly related to factors outside the school (e.g., national and regional patterns of publication/distribution) that variation of content characteristics with individual school characteristics is not possible.

538. Harkin, Willard Dwight (Ed.D., Ball State University, 1971). **Analysis of secondary school library media programs in relation to academic success of Ball State University Students in their freshman and sophomore years.** 129p. Order no. 72-7,508.

PURPOSE: Using college grade-point averages as the measure of academic success, this study was designed to determine whether or not a high media-student ratio contributed markedly to the formal education of students.

PROCEDURE: Data were gathered from SAT Mathematics and English scores and from questionnaires sent to a sample of 200 students representing 20 Indiana secondary schools; 10 of the schools had a high media-student ratio and 10 had a low media-student ratio according to the means of the "Individual School Evaluation and Report-Instructional Materials Program."

FINDINGS: The comparison of the high media-student ratio group and the low media-student ratio group did not indicate any marked differences in the academic records when the criteria of accumulated average grade-point was applied as a measure of success. No marked differences were found, either, in opinions and values of the two groups. The availability of a high media-student ratio group did not appear to reflect any marked differences in the academic successes of the high media-student group in comparison to the low media-student group.

539. Harris, Michael Hope (Ph.D., Indiana University, 1971). **The availability of books and the nature of book ownership on the Southern Indiana frontier, 1800-1850.** 307p. Order no. 71-25,345.

PURPOSE: This study presents a description of the availability of books and the extent of book ownership in Southern Indiana, 1800-1850.

PROCEDURE: Data were collected from newspaper advertisements, diaries, letters,

PROCEDURE (cont'd): general store ledger books, county probate records and other business records. Nearly 3,000 inventories located in 16 selected Southern Indiana counties produced descriptions of more than 500 libraries.

FINDINGS: Indiana's early residents could have acquired, if they so desired, large numbers of books in considerable variety from several outlets. Most of the collections were small and narrowly religious in nature, with larger libraries tending toward the utilitarian. A few men—those with both the means and the inclination—built large, balanced libraries.

CONCLUSIONS: The findings call into question the widely held opinion that books were generally inaccessible in most frontier areas. An analysis of the private libraries shows that the pattern of book ownership was not startlingly different from that revealed by similar studies of book ownership in the American colonies.

540. Hatchett, Harold William (Ph.D., East Texas State University, 1971). **A proposed computer-controlled random access storage and retrieval system for monochromatic moving pictorials.** 158p. Order no. 72-10,798.

PURPOSE: The purpose of this study was to propose a computer-controlled random access and storage retrieval system for monochromatic moving pictorials through an investigation of selected hardware components, component functions and related subsystems.

PROCEDURE: Initial plans included the utilization of a digital computer facility for the development of a prototype system. However, vendors and manufacturers hesitated to allow their components to be shipped to the test location. Definition of the system without actual testing became necessary. From a detailed study of components for the computer-controlled system, requirements of the prototype system were defined.

FINDINGS: A digital computer could be used as a major component of a digital random access storage and retrieval system for moving pictorials. Utilization of modified subsystems was not found to be as satisfactory as utilization of separate components. Procedures were available for the transformation of motion picture film and video tape recording into a format which was compatible with digital storage and transmission. Conversion of analog television signals to digital signals and reconversion of digital signals to analog permitted the utilization of conventional television receivers for image display.

CONCLUSIONS: A computer-controlled random access storage and retrieval system for monochromatic moving pictorials could be accomplished, although expanded inclusion of a large number of motion picture segments would put a high demand on existing memory devices.

541. Holzberlein, Deanne Bassler (Ph.D., University of Michigan, 1971). **The contribution of school media programs to elementary and secondary education as portrayed in professional journals available to school administrators from 1960 to 1969.** 262p. Order no. 72-14,896.

PURPOSE: This was an analysis of the school media center's contribution to the educational program from Kindergarten through twelfth grade in terms of the general philosophy and specific standards expressed in *Standards for School Library Programs* of 1960 and *Standards for School Media Programs* of 1969.

PROCEDURE: The contents of 14 national periodicals available to school administrators were examined.

FINDINGS: The philosophy and objectives of the media programs were adequately described in the literature only through 1966. Articles concerning the media staff were accurate only when written by media personnel or involved administrators. In the early 1960's secondary facilities were stressed; by 1969 it had shifted to elementary. The professional collection was covered adequately, although not abundantly. The cause and effect between the resources necessary for a good media program and the relationship to good services was omitted. The school media program's relation to other educational programs outside the normally structured curriculum was rarely covered. There was a trend to neglect the continuing financial needs of media centers, and to concentrate attention upon expensive facilities. The number of education articles mentioning media programs declined from 224 in 1954-55 to 61 in 1969. The number of media articles increased from 13.9 articles yearly from 1945 to 1955 to 23.1 articles a year from 1960 to 1969.

542. Horrocks, Norman (Ph.D., University of Pittsburgh, 1971). **The impact of the Carnegie Corporation of New York on library development in Australia: a study of foundation influence.**

543. Hyman, Richard Joseph (D.L.S., Columbia University, 1971). **An inquiry into the validity of the direct shelf approach as a concept for the organization of library materials, with special reference to browsing.** 598p. Order no. 71-23,598.
PURPOSE: The study attempted to examine the direct shelf approach of organizing library materials, with special reference to browsing.
PROCEDURE: Questionnaires were sent to 152 practitioners and teachers of librarianship throughout the U.S. and Canada.
FINDINGS: Respondents were ambivalent toward the role of classification in the direct shelf approach. The majority agreed that shelf classification was more valuable as a locational device than as a means of systematic subject approach and that open shelf policy was a library's educational responsibility. Respondents supported the principle of direct access and browsing. Many, however, did not accept browsing as non-recreational or essential for advanced research.
CONCLUSIONS: Preference of the American librarian and patron for the direct shelf approach was unmistakable, though how to implement it remained problematical.

544. Kanasy, James Emery (Ph.D., University of Pittsburgh, 1971). **Citation characteristics and bibliographic control of the literature of microbiology.** 168p. Order no. 71-22,682.
PURPOSE: The objectives of the study were to examine some of the more significant characteristics of the research literature of microbiology and to evaluate three major bibliographic services: *Biological Abstracts, Chemical Abstracts* and *Index Medicus*.
PROCEDURE: A random sample of 2,073 citations was extracted from the 1967 issues of six journals and their characteristics were recorded on a coding sheet for each citation. The bibliographic services were evaluated by checking 1,382 citations from the main sample through each of the three sources.
FINDINGS: There was considerable interdependence and interaction between microbiology, general biology, physiology, biochemistry and medicine. Over 73 percent of the cited references were originally published in U.S. journals. The useful

FINDINGS (cont'd): life expectancy of microbiological literature is relatively short. *Biological Abstracts* was the most comprehensive in its coverage. *Chemical Abstracts* provided the most timely reporting. The *Biological Abstracts-Index Medicus* pair had the highest number of entries in common; the rate of duplication was lowest in the *Chemical Abstracts-Index Medicus* pair.

545. King, Donald Ross (Ph.D., Rutgers University, 1971). **An inverted file structure for an interactive document retrieval system.** 255p. Order no. 72-9634.
PURPOSE: This study proposed to use binary vectors for the storage of the document number references.
PROCEDURE: Two model systems were prepared to contrast the use of the binary vectors with the standard inverted file.
FINDINGS: The binary vector was applied in a working document retrieval system. The size of the binary vector file was reduced significantly by the use of a compression algorithm. The search time for the binary vector file in the study ranged from .79 to 9.72 seconds (compared to .15 to 202.98 seconds for the standard file). Search time for the binary vector file and the number of index terms in the queries had a correlation coefficient of .96 with a significance of .001; search times for the standard inverted file and the number of postings in the terms in the queries had a correlation coefficient of .98 with a significance level of .001.
CONCLUSIONS: The narrower range of search times for the binary vector file and the greater ease of predicting search times for binary vector file provide an advantage over the standard inverted file as the basis for on-line interactive document retrieval systems.

546. King, Geraldine Beaty (Ph.D., University of Minnesota, 1971). **Attitudes of library school students towards reference librarians and library information service.** 181p. Order no. 72-14,327.
PURPOSE: The purpose of the paper was to supply information on the attitudes of library school students towards library information service. The components of the attitude were tentatively seen as aligning with Herzberg's Motivation-Hygiene theory of job attitude.
PROCEDURE: Questionnaires were given to 132 graduate and upper-division undergraduate students at the beginning and end of their Reference I course in the University of Minnesota Library School from January through August 1970. Factor analysis was applied to the results.
FINDINGS: No significant differences were found between population means for the pre- or post-surveys. When the subjects were grouped by personal characteristics, those variables which resulted in the most significant differences in factor scores were (in descending order) library work experience, teacher of the course, career choice of librarianship, sex, career choice of reference librarianship, completion of additional library science courses and age. In descending order, most significant differences in scores were found for sex role, outgoing personality, job content, and professional job. Subjects ranked using the library to complete assignments, the instructor, and observing reference librarians at work, in that order, as most influencing their attitudes towards library information service.
CONCLUSIONS: The factors, or components of the attitude, seem to fit the characteristics of the female semi-professional rather than the more general motivation-hygiene theory. The sub-group scores indicate that library work experience along

CONCLUSIONS (cont'd): with professional education promotes a more positive attitude. The image of the librarian/information specialist is related to sex role stereotypes in the library profession; however, there is some indication that those stereotypes are beginning to be rejected.

547. Kraft, Donald Harris (Ph.D., Purdue University, 1971). **The journal selection problem in a university library system.** 304p. Order no. 71-20,488.
PURPOSE: This dissertation is concerned with the problem of selecting the proper journals to be acquired by a university library.
PROCEDURE: A general model is formulated as a zero-one linear programming problem with an objective function that evaluates various selection policies in terms of the net worth of selecting specific journals and rejecting others. Journal usage is adopted as the better measure of journal worth, using a modified Markovian approach to describe expected usage patterns over time. The constraints are primarily related to cost restrictions that arise due to budgetary controls. The optimization of the journal selection model is considered from two different approaches since its large size does not allow for a fit to one of the now existing computational algorithms for zero-one linear programming problems. A Lagrangian formulation gives an upper bound on the optimal value of the objective function and also generates several near-optimal solutions, some of which may be feasible.
FINDINGS: A small example problem, illustrating how the algorithms operate, is presented and discussed. The computational results show that a solution can be generated in a reasonable amount of time and computer storage space, for at least small and medium sized problems.

548. Lamb, Gertrude Houser (Ph.D., Case Western Reserve University, 1971). **The coincidence of quality and quantity in the literature of mathematics.** 89p. Order no. 72-66.
PURPOSE: The purpose of the study was to determine whether quality articles are imbedded in the journals which can be identified for a subject field as the most productive.
PROCEDURE: The articles indexed and abstracted in *Jahrbuch über die Forschritte der Mathematik* and *Mathematical Reviews* for 1934-1954 are considered a quantity bibliography. The benchmark of quality is a bibliography of the articles published by mathematicians in residence at the Institute for Advanced Study.
FINDINGS: Sixteen percent of these articles are cited at least once 10 or more years after publication. A Bradford distribution identifies the most productive journals in each of these bibliographies. A comparison of the productivity of the quantity and quality bibliographies show that the 15 titles of the nucleus and two zones of the general bibliography include seven of the nine most productive titles in the quality bibliography. Similarly, the six titles of the nucleus and two zones of the Institute for Advanced Study bibliography include four of the six most productive journals in the general bibliography. Moreover, an approach to mathematics, through any one of 26 subject headings by which *Jahrbuch* and *Mathematical Reviews* are indexed for 1934-1954, may start with the most productive journals of the general bibliography.
CONCLUSIONS: There is a possibility that if a bibliography of provable quality is available for a given subject, a Bradford distribution of its journals gives the same assurance as a complete search in reducing the uncertainties inherent in a limited search.

549. Lawson, Abram Benable (D.L.S., Columbia University, 1971). **Reference service in university libraries, two case studies.** 359p. Order no. 72-10,443.

PURPOSE: The purpose of this study was to determine the range and frequency of activities performed by the reference service in two university libraries, to relate these activities to the objectives and functions of the service, and to isolate factors influencing their fulfillment.

PROCEDURE: Data were collected through study of the records and reports, interviews with the directors and reference librarians, work diaries, reference inquiries collected, questionnaires completed by reference personnel, and personal observation at two university libraries.

FINDINGS: Though the two universities selected for study were quite different, their libraries and reference services were found to have many similarities. Neither library had written objectives for reference service, but they generally felt that support of university instruction and research was the primary objective; this received the majority of staff time. Less than half of the work time of the professional reference staff required professional competence for performance. Direct reference assistance was largely instructional or directional in nature.

CONCLUSION: There needs to be a reappraisal of reference service to establish its proper objectives and to determine the legitimate role of the experienced reference librarian in university library reference service.

550. Lickteig, Mary Jane (D.Ed., University of Oregon, 1971). **A comparison of book selection preferences of inner-city and suburban fourth- and sixth-graders.**

551. Longsdorf, Homer Howard (Ph.D., Michigan State University, 1971). **The development and testing of a slide-audio tape program designed to teach the use of the ERIC system of information retrieval.** 143p. Order no. 72-16,471.

PURPOSE: This study includes the development and testing of a slide-audio tape program designed to teach the skills and knowledge necessary to perform a search of the ERIC system.

PROCEDURE: The recorded script was 2,012 words in length and required 17 minutes, or 12 minutes in compressed version playback time. Identical sets of the 61-slide visual portion of the program were then combined with both normal and compressed versions of the audio script. A third instructional treatment consisted of a printed adaptation of the recorded script with no visual supplements. Testing was done in six learning carrels set up on the Michigan State University Instructional Resources Center. An experimental population of 81 volunteers from education and environmental courses were randomly assigned to one of three experimental or one control group. A one-way analysis of variance was performed.

FINDINGS: No significant difference was found between groups in the time required to complete some form of search. There were statistically significant differences obtained on the *successful completion* and *score* variables. The combined mean recall test scores for subjects receiving slide-audio tape programs was significantly greater than the combined mean test scores for subjects receiving printed materials and no formal instruction.

552. McAllister, Caryle (Ph.D., University of California, Berkeley, 1971). **A study and model of machine-like indexing behavior by human indexers.**

553. McCauley, Elfrieda B. (D.L.S., Columbia University, 1971). **The New England mill girls; feminine influence in the development of public libraries in New England, 1820-1860.** 355p.
PURPOSE: This historical study deals with the relationship of the industrial revolution in cotton—which brought into the New England textile manufacturing centers large numbers of young women as operatives—and the development of public libraries from 1820-1860 to which all members of the community, including women, had access.
FINDINGS: In nine of the ten villages studied, public library collections evolved by way of three earlier types of library organization founded and promoted as measures for maintaining and improving the moral and educational environment of the heavily female mill communities: Sabbath School libraries, mechanics' libraries, and counting house libraries. In an era which denied women fundamental rights and opportunities for higher education and vocational choices, the pre-Civil War mill villages offered certain liberating advantages which women had never experienced before. For many young women the mill village experience was preparation for participation in the women's rights, suffrage, temperance, abolition, and other social reform movements of the second half of the nineteenth century.

554. Maxwell, Margaret Nadine Finlayson (Ph.D., University of Michigan, 1971). **Anatomy of a book collector: William L. Clements and the Clements Library.** 429p. Order No. 72-4931.
PURPOSE: The purpose of the study was to show how Clements (1861-1934), a modestly wealthy collector, was able by intelligent concentration in a limited area and time period to create a collection which could function independently as a research library and how, under the terms of the Clements' gift agreement for the establishing of the Clements Library in 1923, the University of Michigan agreed to accept the responsibility for financing the continued conservation and growth of the library.
PROCEDURE: The William L. Clements Papers in the Clements Library were used as the principal primary source, supplemented by the William Warner Bishop Papers in the General Library and the resources of the Michigan Historical Collections at the University of Michigan.
FINDINGS: Clements started his collection in 1903, shortly after he graduated from the University of Michigan. Two book dealers, Harper and Stevens, and three bibliographer-librarians, Winship, Ford and Brigham, influenced the next 20 years of Clements' collection building. In 1923 Clements gave his library and a building to house it to the University of Michigan. During the following decade, Clements began to acquire manuscripts pertaining to the American Revolution. After his death in 1934 the University purchased these papers.
CONCLUSIONS: Clements was the last of the great "classic" collectors of Americana.

555. May, Frank Curtis (Ph.D., University of Denver, 1971). **The California school library program funded through the Elementary and Secondary Education Act, Title II, Phase Two for 1965-66; an evaluation of selected criteria.** 602p. Order no. 72-4197.

PURPOSE: An evaluation was made of the Elementary and Secondary Education Act, Title II, Phase 2, in California for 1965-66 to determine the success of the program in achieving the objectives of the individual schools and the overall objectives of the California State Department of Education.

PROCEDURE: Official documents were examined and 48 project schools were visited.

FINDINGS: The programs were successfully operated under the objectives and guidelines set down by the California State Department of Education. The evaluation process initially used by the Bureau of Audio-Visual and School Library Education to select schools was adequate, but a more exact methodology of initial evaluation was needed. The results of the Activities Checklist for secondary schools as developed by Graver and Jones bore a close relationship to the final evaluation of the project libraries. The project library programs were excellently coordinated with other state and federal programs, but only minimally involved with schools operated by other public or private agencies. The program was highly successful in encouraging school districts to improve library service in schools which did not receive grants. Most librarians felt that the project had been successful, but most also found deficiencies, primarily of local origin.

556. Miller, Laurence Alan (Ph.D., Florida State University, 1971). **Changing patterns of circulation services in university libraries.** 188p. Order no. 72-10,058.

PURPOSE: The study traced the evolution in function and staff of the university library circulation department in this century.

PROCEDURE: Questionnaires were sent to principal libraries in 126 institutions graduating 30 or more Ph.D.s per year (90.5 percent were returned).

FINDINGS: In the mid-1920's there was very little administrative or functional distinction between the circulation and reference departments; interlibrary loan, assistance to readers in the use of the card catalog, library instruction, etc., were in the circulation department. These functions were gradually transferred to separate departments. In the 1970's a typical circulation department included only reserve books, the handling of direction and incidental information inquiries, shelving and stack maintenance. While most professional functions have been taken from circulation services, professional librarians are still widely employed in this department, even in the absence of any professional functions.

CONCLUSIONS: Automation, systems analysis, reader services, divisions and stack access had no relationship to the functional evolution of the circulation department. In the absence of these elements as significant causal factors, the most likely alternative explanation is the growth of libraries as organizations and the dynamics that become operative under these circumstances.

557. Miller, Russell Raymond (Ph.D., University of Chicago, 1971). **An investigation concerning the influence of continuing education on prescribing of drugs by physicians.**

558. Nelson, Jerold A. (Ph.D., University of California, Berkeley, 1971). **Communication between reference librarians and the faculty in selected California State Colleges.**

PURPOSE: The purpose of the study was to determine the degree to which the faculty were aware of eleven reference services offered by their college library reference department.

PROCEDURE: A survey of 694 faculty members, comprising about 20 percent of the faculty population of six colleges in the California State College system, was utilized. In addition, 62 reference librarians (almost 100 percent of the population of reference librarians) were interviewed.

FINDINGS: The average faculty member was aware of barely half of the services actually available. Faculty members in the sciences were less aware than faculty members in other teaching areas. Awareness varied directly with academic rank, experience at the college, membership on committees dealing with library affairs, and reported library and reference use. Communication between faculty members and most reference librarians was found to be infrequent and of a low order. Librarians seldom initiated communication.

CONCLUSIONS: More effective communication is possible when the library environment provides the reference librarian with time and opportunity for meaningful contact with the faculty, when the reference librarian feels strong support for his activity from the leadership of the library, and when the library defines and supports the goal of providing service at a level that is worth promoting.

559. Nemeyer, Carol (D.L.S., Columbia University, 1971). **Scholarly reprint publishing in the United States.** 463p.

PURPOSE: The purpose of the study was to discover the size of the U.S. reprint industry, and to identify and describe the particular characteristics of this sector of the publishing industry.

PROCEDURE: The survey was conducted by means of documentary analysis, personal interviews, and questionnaires.

FINDINGS: Almost 300 U.S. reprint publishers were identified in the study. No standard bibliographic service in this country receives all bibliographic information for all titles published by the reprint houses. Most of the publishers, however, recognize this problem, and see the need to improve. The majority of the firms do issue catalogs or lists of their reprints, and make these available on request.

CONCLUSIONS: There is a likelihood that the world of reprinting will shrink, both in numbers of publishers and numbers of titles. Future success of the industry would seem to depend on a carefully researched plan of publishing, rather than the haphazard, title-by-title approach which has often been the procedure in the past. There is a close relationship between the industry and librarians, and both must recognize their interdependence.

560. O'Loughlin, Sister M. Anne John, O.P. (D.L.S., Columbia University, 1971). **The emergence of American librarianship: a study of influences evident in 1876.** 273p.

PURPOSE: The dissertation studies American librarianship from the Convention of 1853 through the 23 years which followed it and changed the course of American library history.

FINDINGS: The author emphasizes the influencial men in the fields of publishing and libraries: Melvil Dewey, Lloyd P. Smith, William F. Poole, Charles A. Cutter, Justin Winsor, Frederick Leypoldt, and Richard Rogers Bowker. The accomplishments of 1876 are also described: the publication of *The American Library Journal,*

FINDINGS (cont'd): *The Report on Public Libraries in the United States* (Special Report of 1876), Dewey's *Decimal Classification*, Cutter's *Rules for a Printed Dictionary Catalogue*, and the establishment of the American Library Association at the Philadelphia Convention of 1876.

CONCLUSIONS: In a period when the formal organization of people having like interests was a regular occurrence, the librarians felt the need for communication with their colleagues on a formal basis. Pooling information and experience for the good of all was recognized as a necessary service to the whole profession.

561. Orgren, Karl Franz (Ph.D., University of Michigan, 1971). **Preferences in learning under two strategies of computer-assisted instruction for a basic reference course in library school.** 147p. Order no. 71-23,839.

PURPOSE: An attempt was made to determine whether one type of programming for computer-assisted instruction (drill exercise instruction) is better than another (simulating library reference situations) in preparing students to answer reference questions.

PROCEDURE: Twenty-four students who had enrolled in the basic reference course at the University of Michigan were assigned randomly to the two experimental groups. Over a three week period the two groups received the two different types of instruction designed by Thomas Slavens. Pre-tests and post-tests were administered. Information was also gathered from student records and interviews.

FINDINGS: The two different approaches to computer-assisted instruction were not different in their ability to prepare students for either factual questions or questions requiring behavior more complex than recall of facts. Both methods did produce measurable learning of both simple and complex nature. Characteristics of the population did not seem to be very important in determining usefulness of computer-assisted instruction. Group use of computer terminals is a feasible method of cost control.

562. Pannu, Gurdial Singh (Ph.D., Indiana University, 1971). **Cataloging efficiency and its relation to individual work, group discussion and selected student characteristics.** 338p. Order no. 72-6821.

PURPOSE: The purpose of the dissertation was to study the relationship between the method of instruction and selected student characteristics with cataloging accuracy and speed.

PROCEDURE: Two studies were conducted: one at the School of Library Science of the University of Alberta; the other at the Graduate Library School of Indiana University. All students attended lecture-discussion periods together, but for the laboratory sessions, they were randomly divided into two sections: the Individual Section and the Discussion Section. The scores of all the students on cataloging were regressed onto the scores of their personal characteristics (Otis-Lennon Mental Ability Test; Minnesota Clerical Test; Strong Vocational Interest Blank).

FINDINGS: During the laboratory sessions, students working in small discussion groups cataloged library materials with a significantly higher degree of accuracy than students working individually, but with no significant differences in speed. On subsequent tests, there was no significant difference in accuracy or speed. The results of several regression analyses revealed that intelligence was most frequently the best predictor variable to account for accuracy and speed in cataloging.

563. Patterson, Charles (Ph.D., University of Pittsburgh, 1971). **A graphemic, morphological, syntactical, lexical, and contextual analysis of the Library of Congress music subject headings and their relationship to the Library of Congress Classification Schedule, Class M, as determined by a comparative sampling of their two vocabularies.** 256p. Order no. 72-7,564.

PURPOSE: This study was undertaken to investigate the degree of relationship existing between three vocabularies: the Library of Congress *Subject Headings Used in the Dictionary Catalog of the Library of Congress* (1966), the Library of Congress *Classification, Class M, Music and Books on Music* (1917, reissued, 1968), and the Index to the *Classification, Class M.*

FINDINGS: The analysis and manipulation of data revealed a 68 percent graphemic correlation between the subject headings and the index headings, and a 51 percent correlation between the subject headings and the classification headings. Morphological and syntactical analysis revealed that the mass noun appeared most frequently and the adjectival noun was second in frequency. The terms existing in the three lists were identical or nearly identical and it was possible to combine the terms to form a single list. The lexical and contextual analysis revealed that 66 percent of the total of 73 subject headings fell within groups of lexical synonymity; there was a high degree of lexical and contextual synonymity among the three vocabularies.

564. Pope, Shirley Elspeth (Ph.D., University of Pittsburgh, 1971). **The immediacy of cataloging information for newly acquired books.** 255p. Order no. 72-16,142.

PURPOSE: The primary concern of this study was the problem for libraries caused by the time lag between the publishing of an American trade book and the availability of the cataloging information for that book.

FINDINGS: The methodology of the Cataloging-in-Source project of 1958 showed only slight modification from the Cataloging in Publication program of 1971. The time lag existing between the date of publication of a monograph and the date on which the cataloging information is available to libraries significantly increased over the past 10 years in spite of the multiple programs at the Library of Congress. Descriptive cataloging prepared by publishers for their trade catalogs could be accepted by the Library of Congress on the same basis as Shared Cataloging; a comparison of publishers' pre-publication cataloging with the printed Library of Congress card showed a very high correlation.

CONCLUSIONS: Time lag increased in the past because the programs at the Library of Congress were not sufficient. The new Cataloging in Publication program follows the same methodology as previous programs. The solution to the problem must be found in the earlier cooperation between publishers and the Library of Congress.

565. Roper, Fred Wilburn (Ph.D., Indiana University, 1971). **A comparative analysis of programs in medical library education in the United States, 1957-1971.** 191p. Order no. 72-10,002.

PURPOSE: The purposes of this study were to determine the nature and distinguishing characteristics of the 16 specialized programs of education for medical librarianship which have been offered in the U.S. since 1957, to examine the characteristics related to the graduates of these programs, and to compare these characteristics with those of a group of practicing medical librarians who were not graduates of the special programs.

PROCEDURE: Questionnaires were sent to the program directors, the graduates of the programs (more than 70 percent response rate), and to the comparison group of practicing medical librarians.

FINDINGS: Eight degree programs and four internship programs were available. Emphasis in many of the programs was on preparation of management personnel. The degree program trainees were younger and held more undergraduate degrees in the natural sciences than did the interns. The comparison of the former trainees with the non-trainees did not indicate significant differences between the two groups in areas related to professional activity. However, the comparison did indicate that a different type of career track may be emerging; approximately 40 percent of the former trainees were in non-administrative positions that carried high salaries and a high mean score on the Index of Job Tasks.

566. Schlachter, Gail Ann (Ph.D., University of Minnesota, 1971). **Professional librarians' attitudes toward professional and employee associations as revealed by academic librarians in seven Midwestern states.** 431p. Order no. 72-5,575.

PURPOSE: The purpose of this dissertation was to explore the type of associational representation desired by Midwestern academic librarians (in comparison to that currently experienced) and to investigate predictors of librarians' interest in such militant action as collective bargaining, striking and union membership.

PROCEDURE: The data were collected through questionnaires sent to 884 professional librarians employed at a stratified random sample of 164 academic institutions in Iowa, Kansas, Minnesota, Nebraska, North Dakota, South Dakota, and Wisconsin (81 percent return), all (35) employee associations to which the surveyed librarians belonged (100 percent return), and the 16 professional organizations in which at least one percent of the surveyed librarians were members (100 percent return). Multiple stepwise regression analysis was used to analyze relationships at the .025 level.

FINDINGS: The surveyed librarians would like to see their professional societies adopt more aggressive economic orientations than pursued by their societies in 1970. In order to obtain desired benefits, nearly 62 percent of the surveyed librarians agreed that some type of association representing librarians should engage in collective bargaining. Approximately two-fifths of the librarians supported strikes by their association to obtain benefits and would be willing to join a union. The majority (63 percent) preferred that their employee association take the form of an economic-oriented, independent local organization open to all library employees, and, possibly, faculty members. Only politics, sex and supervisory responsibility proved to be significant predictors of the librarians' attitude toward all three types of militant action.

567. Sternberg, Virginia Ashworth (Ph.D., University of Pittsburgh, 1971). **Use of federally supported information analysis centers by special libraries in large companies.** 509p. Order no. 72-7565.

PURPOSE: This study was made to determine the extent of use of federally supported information analysis centers by special libraries in large companies.

PROCEDURE: Questionnaires were sent to more than 500 special librarians inquiring about the libraries' use of 113 Centers.

FINDINGS: Only 26 percent of the special libraries used the Centers and these

FINDINGS (cont'd): were the large libraries. The user ratings of the Centers and their specific services were high. Users indicated that only a minimal amount of money, time, and staff is saved as a result of using the Centers. They used the Centers to supplement their own services and to utilize unique publications. Other libraries did not use the Centers because they did not know about them or because the information was available elsewhere.

568. Stueart, Robert D. (Ph.D., University of Pittsburgh, 1971). **The area special-ist bibliographer; an inquiry into his role.** 210p. Order no. 72-1115.
PURPOSE: The purpose of the study was to describe the role and functions of the area specialist bibliographer.
PROCEDURE: Analysis of qualitative data, the non-scalable portion of the descriptive profile of the area bibliographer, was performed. Non-parametric tests were used.
FINDINGS: There was no significant relationship between the education, experience, and language knowledge of bibliographers and the expectations of faculty and administrators toward those variables. There existed within the faculty-administrator-bibliographer interaction a substantial number of practices which may cause role strain within the organization. There also existed some expectations which were shared by all three groups. The area bibliographer was essentially a generalist working in a special area.

569. Svenonius, Elaine Fackenthal (Ph.D., University of Chicago, 1971). **Effect of indexing specificity on retrieval performance.** 418p.

570. Vavrek, Bernard Frank (Ph.D., University of Pittsburgh, 1971). **Communications and the reference interface.** 136p. Order no. 72-4247.
PURPOSE: The purpose of this study is to discuss the dynamics of reference service—not in the sense of books or other sources of information—but as a responsive, interactive user-oriented system. Reference work is considered to be an interface between the patron and the library's file of information.
PROCEDURE: The data base was 300 reference inquiries collected from three research libraries in the Pittsburgh area during May to October, 1969. Reference inquiries were collected and analyzed in two parts, i.e., the initial statement of the patron's needs and the negotiated question. Content analysis was used to compare the structure of these questions. The data were also analyzed as search strategies using Boolean logic as the framework. The search strategies resulting from the questions collected for the research libraries were compared with an equal number of questions collected from the Chemical Information Center of the University of Pittsburgh.
FINDINGS: Interpersonal communication can provide a theoretical basis from which to analyze the reference interface. Insight into the internal structure of reference inquiries can be provided by the systematization inherent in Boolean logic. Although depth of analysis is an inherent problem shared both by the traditional library and the mechanized information center, the library is less suited to the development of the reference question as a complex search strategy than is the mechanized information center. The average number of search terms in the library question was 2.8 per strategy; for the information center it was 8.6 terms per strategy.

571. Watson, Lynn Allen (Ph.D., Pennsylvania State University, 1971). **A comparison between elementary school libraries of selected non-urban Appalachia counties in Northeastern Pennsylvania and selected non-Appalachia counties in Southeastern Pennsylvania.** 129p. Order no. 72-19,398.
PURPOSE: This study was undertaken to compare elementary school libraries in Appalachia counties in Northeastern Pennsylvania with elementary school libraries in non-Appalachia counties in Southeastern Pennsylvania to determine the extent to which elementary libraries exist, the quality of existing elementary libraries, the extent of expenditures of Elementary and Secondary Education Act Title II monies, and the effect Title II of the ESEA of 1965 had upon library development in the two regions.
PROCEDURE: Questionnaires and interviews were used to study 46 randomly selected public school districts in Northeastern and Southeastern Pennsylvania counties. Five interval scales were developed to measure five quality characteristics: staff, facility, library program, collection size and collection quality. Chi-square was used to test the quality characteristics by comparing schools within the two regions.
FINDINGS: Elementary school libraries in the non-Appalachia Southeastern Pennsylvania region were significantly better than those in the Northeastern Pennsylvania Appalachia region on each quality characteristics. By 1970, about half the elementary schools in the Northeast sample had libraries compared to 85 percent of the schools in the Southeast. Based on money per pupil expenditures, a gradual change had taken place so that in recent years the expenditures in each region were similar.

572. White, Marilyn Domas (Ph.D., University of Illinois at Urbana-Champaign, 1971). **Communications behavior of academic economists.** 171p. Order no. 72-12,432.
PURPOSE: An analysis was made of the communication behavior of academic economists during three stages (the problem stage, the methodology stage, and the presentation stage) of a research project.
PROCEDURE: Questionnaires were sent to a sample of economists on the faculties of 10 universities with doctoral level programs in economics.
FINDINGS: Significant variations in stage behavior were found in the occupation, geographic location, and institutional affiliation of the information source, the recommender, the researcher's purpose in looking for information, and the dominant method of receiving it. The pattern of information gathering behavior that evolved was essentially curvilinear with the major variations occurring in the methodology stage, traceable to the respondent's behavior in gathering data.

573. Wilkinson, Billy Rayford (D.L.S., Columbia University, 1971). **Reference services for undergraduate students: four case studies.** 520p.
PURPOSE: The major purpose of this study was to identify and evaluate reference services for undergraduates on university campuses—both in the undergraduate and main university libraries.
PROCEDURE: The University of Michigan with its Undergraduate and General Libraries and Cornell University with its Uris and John M. Olin Libraries were contrasted with the libraries at the liberal arts colleges of Swarthmore and Earlham. Reference desk activity was monitored at selected times during September-

PROCEDURE (cont'd): December, 1969. Undergraduate users were interviewed during five-day periods at Michigan and Cornell.

FINDINGS: The Michigan and Cornell undergraduate libraries both experienced an increase in the number of substantial reference questions during their first years. However, more recently, the quantity of reference questions had declined. Communications between the staff in undergraduate libraries and university faculty concerning reference services for students were minimal when contrasted to liberal arts college librarians and faculty. No effective means of stimulating use of reference services had been developed by undergraduate libraries; Earlham librarians, however, had developed extensive programs of library instruction. Among the more substantial reference questions, bibliographical assistance with the library's own catalogs and holdings was the most numerous type of question. Unassisted use by undergraduates of the union catalog increased use of the main library and decreased use of the undergraduate library. Librarians rarely initiated reference encounters. Evening hours were busier than afternoon hours at the undergraduate library reference desks. Informal personal instruction to students in the use of the library constituted only a small part of reference services.

CONCLUSIONS: Full advantage has not been taken of the opportunities afforded by the creation of undergraduate libraries. Librarians in the Michigan and Cornell undergraduate libraries have not closed the gap between class instruction and reference services.

574. Willis, H. Warren (Ph.D., Catholic University of America, 1971). **The reorganization of the Catholic University of America during the rectorship of James H. Ryan (1928-1935).** 359p. Order no. 72-15,962.

PURPOSE: The purposes of this study were (1) to examine the administration of James H. Ryan as fifth Rector of the Catholic University of America; and (2) to examine in detail his structural reorganization of the University.

FINDINGS: The study shows that Monsignor Ryan organized a College of Arts and Sciences as an independent unit which would include all the undergraduates not in professional schools, and a Graduate School of Arts and Sciences, closely connected with the College, independently established but cooperating with it. The professional schools were considered as units independent of one another and independent of the College and Graduate School of Arts and Sciences. The influence of the newly developing accrediting agencies on the University is described. Schools and departments that were either instituted or were especially prominent during Ryan's administration are given individual attention.

CONCLUSIONS: Ryan gave the Catholic University of America a needed scholarly revitalization and thrust which propelled it forward for many years. Many of his problems would have been alleviated and many more of his goals achieved if he had had the necessary means.

1972

575. Avant, Julia King (Ph.D., Indiana University, 1972). **Extending library service to rural areas in Louisiana, 1956-1969.** 265p. Order no. 72-19,490.
PURPOSE: Demonstrations of public library service conducted in Louisiana by the Louisiana State Library between 1956 and 1969 and the response to these 20 demonstration libraries by the people within the 22 parishes served were studied. FINDINGS: Parishes with low socio-economic levels predominated. These socio-economic conditions were not found to be negative correlates of the per capita measures of library use; for some measures of library use (e.g., per capita reference questions) they even tended to be positive correlates. A strong positive relationship existed between expenditures per capita and the amount of library use per capita. Strong interrelationships existed between the three broad groupings of library use measures: circulation, number of reference questions answered and library usage. Family income, occupation and adult educational level were related to the percentage of favorable vote for financial support for libraries. Only one of the 22 parishes failed to vote approval for the continuation of the parish library beyond the demonstration period.

576. Ballard, Robert Melvyn (Ph.D., University of Michigan, 1972). **A follow-up study of the academic record and career experiences of students enrolled for the A.M.L.S. degree at the Department of Library Science, The University of Michigan, 1960-1961.** 218p. Order no. 73-6782.
PURPOSE: The purpose of the study was to investigate the relationship between undergraduate academic performance and graduate academic achievement for students admitted during one class year to the Department of Library Science at The University of Michigan.
PROCEDURE: Data were obtained from the files of the Department of Library Science and a questionnaire survey of 75 students admitted to the Department during the 1960-61 academic year for whom addresses could be located.
FINDINGS: Undergraduate grade point average was only moderately successful in predicting which students would rank highest in library school academically. Best predictors of degree completion appeared to be resident or campus status, age at entry and full-time enrollment; full-time, on-campus students under 25 years of age were most likely to complete their degrees. Respondents who were identified as having been high achievers in the subsequent development of their careers tended to have earned average GPA's as graduate library school students, came from families which were not quite as high on the socio-economic scale as the norm of their library school classmates, were a little older than the class median at entry, and possessed unusually heavy family responsibilities. High achievers began their professional careers within a fairly large library system, remained in that system while rising in the administrative hierarchy and made at least two position changes since completion of their degrees.
CONCLUSIONS: In addition to GPA, the applicant's non-academic responsibilities and obligations should be considered in admissions to graduate school. When

225

CONCLUSIONS (cont'd): analyzed on the basis of undergraduate or graduate grade point averages, career patterns of respondents to the questionnaire did not vary significantly. High achievers were the students whose backgrounds gave evidence of perseverance and who were willing to change positions and geographical locations when necessary, for more responsible positions.

577. Bates, Marcia J. (Ph.D., University of California, Berkeley, 1972). **User success in generating headings for catalog searches.**

578. Beasley, Gary Fred (Ph.D., Ohio State University, 1972). **An assessment of an instructional unit for preparing users of the Educational Resources Information Center (ERIC) system.** 144p. Order no. 73-1937.
PURPOSE: This study sought to assess the instructional outcomes achieved through using a preliminary version of the instructional unit. The modules of the unit cover instruction on: (1) An Introduction to the ERIC system, (2) *Abstracts of Research* and *Abstracts of Instructional Materials on Vocational and Technical Education*, (3) *Research in Education*, (4) *Current Index to Journals in Education*, and (5) *Thesaurus of ERIC Descriptors.*
PROCEDURES: The unit was used with 20 participants in a research utilization training program in Portland, Oregon in December, 1971. Pretests and posttests were administered.
FINDINGS: The participants achieved 31 of 42 performance standards for the individual modules, but considerable revision of the instructional unit is needed before national distribution is made.
RECOMMENDATIONS: Recommendations call for modifying the instructional unit by altering the modular format to focus more on retrieval strategies, providing more hands-on experiences with the information retrieval indexes, and improving the visual aids. The unit should be made for use in individual as well as group study.

579. Becker, Dale Eugene (Ed.D., University of Pennsylvania, 1972). **Social studies achievement of pupils in schools with libraries and schools without libraries.** 172p. Order no. 70-22,868.
PURPOSE: Social studies achievement of pupils in schools with libraries was compared to that of pupils in schools without libraries.
PROCEDURE: Two fifth-grade classes in two elementary schools with libraries were used as the experimental group; two fifth-grade classes in two elementary schools without libraries were used as a control group. Both groups were taught the same social studies unit. The skills and content achievement were evaluated in a pretest and posttest plan using sections of the Iowa Test of Basic Skills and a social studies content inventory made up of test items from standardized tests. Analysis of covariance was used to investigate the significance of differences in mean gains.
FINDINGS: The presence of a library and a guidance function of a librarian exerted significant influence on pupil achievement in information gathering skills and in the reading of charts and graphs. No significant difference in the pupil skills in reading maps and globes and on the acquisition of social studies content was found.

580. Bekkedal, Tekla (Ph.D., University of Illinois, 1972). **A study of contemporary realistic fiction for children published in the U.S. since World War II.** Order no. 73-17,114.

581. Boshears, Onva K., Jr. (Ph.D., University of Michigan, 1972). **John Wesley, the bookman: a study of his reading interests in the eighteenth century.** 432p. Order no. 73-11,047.
PURPOSE: The focus of this study is on Wesley's reading interests and his reading advice to courtless numbers of people in the eighteenth century.
PROCEDURE: The study utilizes the sources, principles, and techniques of historical inquiry to determine the reading characteristics of John Wesley. Over 500 reading references plus quotations and allusions are examined.
FINDINGS: Approximately 60 percent of the citations were in subject areas other than formal religion. Frequent references to classical writers reveal that Wesley was grounded in classical literature. He was equally familiar with English poets and authors except for novelists. He read publications in Latin, Greek, Hebrew, French, German, Spanish and some Italian. Historical topics particularly interested him. He was also fascinated with scientific discoveries, especially in the field of medicine. Only philosophical works were least admired. He was concerned that his friends and followers be well read men and women. He popularized literature among a class of people who had previously not been literate. Wesley attached high importance to writing style, good taste and decorum.
CONCLUSIONS: Few eighteenth century men were better read than John Wesley. Popular sterotyped notions that he was only interested in religion have no basis in fact.

582. Boyce, Bert Roy (Ph.D., Case Western Reserve University, 1972). **A literature filter of variable permeability.** 90p. Order no. 73-6274.
PURPOSE:The purpose of this inquiry was to develop an algorithm for the processes of iterative selection which are a prime function of libraries: the initial selection of documents, the selection of classes from the initial selection, the ordering of these classes, and the selection of units from them for presentation to specific users. These processes were viewed as a filtering of the literature of a subject.
PROCEDURE: The specific literature analyzed was that of cardiac arrhythmia. The defined user group was composed of medical students at Case Western Reserve University.
CONCLUSIONS: The automatic indexing techniques utilized resulted in a working definition of a minimal vocabulary for the description of a subject literature.

583. Boyer, Calvin James (Ph.D., University of Texas at Austin, 1972). **The Ph.D. dissertation: an analysis of the doctoral dissertation as an information source.** 131p. Order no. 73-7511.
PURPOSE: The purpose of this investigation was to assess the extent to which the Ph.D. dissertation served as an information source.
PROCEDURE: For the investigation, four disciplines (botany, chemical engineering, chemistry, and psychology) were selected for comparison. Dissertation authors included in the study were asked to provide bibliographic citations to publications they had produced based primarily upon the dissertation. *Science Citation Index*

PROCEDURE (cont'd): was examined to identify citations to dissertations included in the study. Eleven departments in three universities (the University of California at Berkeley, Pennsylvania State University and the University of Texas at Austin) provided data about graduates during the period 1963-67. The name of each dissertation author supplied was checked in *Science Citation Index* to determine if his dissertation had been cited and by whom. Questions were sent to each dissertation author asking him to identify each publication which he had authored based primarily upon his dissertation and to identify each author citing his dissertation.
FINDINGS: Differences of patterns among universities were less varied than differences among and within disciplines with nearly one-third of the dissertations studied yielding no publications.

584. Burt, Lesta Norris (Ph.D., University of Wisconsin, 1972). **Bibliotherapy: effect of group reading and discussion on attitudes of adult inmates in two correctional institutions.** 223p. Order no. 72-31,519.
PURPOSE: This study tested the group book discussion form of bibliotherapy as an effective method for improving the attitudes of adult inmates in correctional institutions.
PROCEDURE: Fifty-nine of the inmates who volunteered for the program were randomly assigned to experimental and control groups in two institutions, the Wisconsin Home for Women and the Wisconsin Correctional Institute for Men. There were two experimental and two control groups, consisting of from six to eight members at each institution, led by a total of eight librarians. Each team of two librarians led one control and one experimental group. Experimental groups met for two hours weekly to read and discuss the same six books consecutively. Control groups met three times during the 12 week period to take part in a reading interest survey. Analysis of covariance was employed to analyze differences in attitude between experimental and control groups.
FINDINGS: At the .01 level there was significant difference between the experimental and control groups on attitude toward "Dope Addiction" and "Stealing," the only behavioral concepts measured. The experimental groups registered a much less accepting attitude. No significant difference between these two groups as a whole was found on attitudes toward concepts relating to persons. There was statistically significant interaction at the .05 level between Race, Number of Months Served or Number of Months to be Served, and Group Treatment. Posttest scores of those in the experimental groups who had over 16 months to serve, had served over 37 months or were Black were higher than their group members and were equal to or higher than all those in the control groups.
CONCLUSIONS: Bibliotherapy may be a helpful adjuvant to the correctional program for improving attitudes related to behavioral concepts for all categories of inmates and related to persons for inmates possessing certain background characteristics. Bibliotherapy may be effectively carried out by librarians when working with small inmate groups who meet the criteria for group book discussion leaders described in this study.

585. Burton, Hilary De Pace (Ph.D., University of California, Berkeley, 1972). **Personal documentation methods and practices with analysis of their relation to formal bibliographic systems and theory.**

586. Cairns, Sister Marie Laurine, O.P. (Ph.D., Florida State University, 1972). **Factors affecting selective admission and retention of students in graduate library programs.** 170p. Order no. 73-184.

PURPOSE: The purpose of the study was to investigate admission policies and procedures of graduate library schools at the master's level, to assess the factors which determine whether an applicant will be admitted or rejected to accredited and non-accredited programs.

PROCEDURE: The study was limited to the 55 ALA accredited library programs and those non-accredited library programs listed in the latest edition of the *American Library Directory* offering at least 30 semester hours of graduate credit. Data were collected from graduate school bulletins, application materials, newsletters and questionnaires sent to directors of graduate library programs. Chi-square analysis, rank sum correlation, coefficient of concordance, and multiple-range comparisons were used in analyzing the data.

FINDINGS: The mean selectivity score calculated for the accredited respondents was significantly higher at the .02 level than that of the non-accredited respondents. No significant differences were found among the selectivity scores for public, private and Canadian institutions or between the accredited and non-accredited programs for the following variables: grade point average, baccalaureate degree, entrance examinations, health, age and library science prerequisites. The difference in overall selectivity was found in these factors: personal interviews, letters of recommendation, foreign language and liberal arts background.

587. Cameron, James Slagle (Ph.D., Ohio State University, 1972). **Automatic document pseudoclassification and retrieval by word frequency techniques.** 172p. Order no. 72-20,948.

PURPOSE: The purpose of the paper was to utilize word occurrence methods to identify a user's topic of interest in order to increase the degree of coincidence between his descriptors and those used to describe the items in the collection.

PROCEDURE: The approach used was to measure the similarity of known relevant documents in order to establish document retrieval criteria, which could then be used to retrieve all documents in a collection falling within the established criteria. The end result of the process is that each document in the collection being searched is classified as relevant or non-relevant to a particular user, a process known as pseudoclassification. The retrieval criteria established were used to pseudoclassify an abstract collection for a group of users and the results were compared with those obtained from index term searches of the same collection.

FINDINGS: The pseudoclassification results obtained with the similarity measures used in this research showed a higher recall but lower precision than the results obtained from the corresponding index term searches. Methods for increasing precision while holding recall constant are discussed, as are possible applications of the system.

588. Chou, Nelson Ling-Sun (Ph.D., University of Chicago, 1972). **A new alphameric code for Chinese ideographs: its evaluation and applications.**

589. Cohn, William Loewy (Ph.D., Florida State University, 1972). **Factors in the career decisions and position choices by the directors of libraries at the state-supported senior colleges of Florida.** 694p. Order no. 73-207.

PURPOSE: This study examined factors which prompted librarians to enter the field and to accept the various positions which culminated in directorships at the nine state-supported senior colleges of Florida.

PROCEDURE: Using a flexible schedule, the nine directors were interviewed for a period of 90 to 120 minutes.

FINDINGS: Prior to making the decision to become librarians, almost all of the directors interviewed had been student assistants in college libraries, had obtained quick access to information about the field, had received encouragement, had not consulted their families (other than wives), had not been exposed to recruitment, and had no clear picture of what a professional librarian did. All would choose the field again. The respondents had chosen library schools on the basis of proximity, previous attendance, low cost, location, or some combination of these. Six of the nine had accepted first positions in technical services. Only one had predetermined that he would become a director. The respondents were strongly motivated by challenge, location, and the opportunity to work on a new campus. None were motivated by money or related fringe benefits. A key factor was timing—the positions were available at the time the individual was considering a change.

590. Davis, Donald G., Jr. (Ph.D., University of Illinois, 1972). **The Association of American Library Schools: an analytical history.** Order no. 73-17,175.

591. Deringer, Dorothy Kiefer (Ph.D., Case Western Reserve University, 1972). **An information retrieval system for a computer center.** 181p. Order no. 73-6287.

PURPOSE: A search strategy for information retrieval, Goffman's Indirect Method, is implemented and tested on the body of literature that describes the use of a computer center's software.

PROCEDURE: The system is tested on titles, abstracts and full text documents.

FINDINGS: Features of the retrieval system are: the user can easily modify the size of the answer set; the system is self-organizing and completely automatic; the query is a document in the set known by the user to be "relevant;" searching is economical because no text is searched at retrieval time. The use of the system is described with instructions for running the programs, program flowcharts and sample input and output.

592. Dorsett, Cora Matheny (Ph.D., University of Mississippi, 1972). **Library technical assistants: a survey of training programs and employment in selected libraries.** 170p. Order no. 73-1260.

PURPOSE: The purpose of this study was to determine what skills are sought and what duties assigned to middle-level library staff members by library directors or personnel officers.

PROCEDURE: Questionnaires were sent to 97 directors of training programs for library technical assistants in two year colleges in the United States (64 percent usable questionnaires returned). A second questionnaire was sent to 120 academic, public, and special librarians in a random sample of cities with populations over 100,000 inhabitants (over 90 percent response rate).

FINDINGS: Opposition remained within the library profession to formally trained library technical assistants. Opposition was based primarily upon the stated belief that clerical workers could effectively perform the tasks that library technical assistants were being trained to perform and that specific in-service was more

FINDINGS (cont'd): efficient than library education in college below the graduate level. Personnel structures in most libraries did not provide a classification for library workers trained in junior colleges. Categories for levels of library employees termed technical assistants were provided; however, these employees were frequently college graduates who were trained on the job. There was disagreement concerning the emphasis in some library technical courses. Library directors called for preparation in specific, practical skills rather than in the theory of librarianship and background information concerning the library profession.

593. Dunlap, Joseph R. (D.L.S., Columbia University, 1972). **The road to Kelmscott: William Morris and the book arts before the founding of the Kelmscott Press.**

594. Ekechukwu, Myriette Revenna Guinyard (Ph.D., University of Washington, 1972). **Characteristics of users and nonusers of elementary school library services and public library services for children.** 216p. Order no. 73-3702.
PURPOSE: This study explored the characteristics of users and nonusers of elementary school library services and public library services for children.
PROCEDURE: Summated rating scales were used in the questionnaires sent to 472 fifth-graders in the regular classes of 19 elementary schools. Spearman rank-order nonparametric correlation techniques were employed as measures of reliability and validity for the attitude scale. Chi-square analysis was used to test the independence of the library use and nonuse characteristics studied.
FINDINGS: Significant relationships were found between: use and nonuse of school libraries and attitudes toward public libraries; sex and favorable attitudes toward public libraries; distance of residence from the public library and public library use/nonuse; distance of residence from the public library and frequency of public library use; distance of residence from the public library and mode of travel to public library. More fifth-graders used school libraries than public libraries. The book collection was the element that fifth-graders liked best about public and school libraries; the most disliked element was the rules and regulations. The major reason for use of both libraries was to borrow books to read outside the library. Use of library materials for school-related purposes was the second most frequently mentioned reason for use of both libraries.

595. El-Erian, Tahany Said (D.L.S., Columbia University, 1972). **The Public Law 480 program in American libraries.** 289p. Order no. 72-31,205.
PURPOSE: The study provides an overall picture of the PL 480 (national cooperative acquisition) program, identifying the problems which have arisen as a result of the implementation of the program and describing the processing of PL 480 materials in the participating libraries.
PROCEDURE: The data were gathered through case studies of three participating libraries and returns from a questionnaire sent to the other participants.
FINDINGS: The PL 480 was mainly concerned with the acquisition of non-western language materials. The Library of Congress and 46 other libraries participated in the program by receiving complete sets of materials published in one or more countries. More than 300 additional libraries also received selective sets from several PL 480 countries. To overcome difficulties in cataloging PL 480 materials, the Library of Congress established in 1962 a centralized cataloging project; in 1968 this project

FINDINGS (cont'd): merged into the National Program for Acquisitions and Cataloging (NPAC). By the end of 1969, LC had cataloged for the participants 77 percent of the PL 480 monographs and 55 percent of the PL 480 serials.

596. Ellison, John William (Ph.D., Ohio State University, 1972). **The identification and examination of principles which validate or refute the concept of college or university learning resources centers.** 265p. Order no. 73-1986.
PURPOSE: The purpose of this study was to identify and examine principles which validate or refute the concept of an integrated learning resources center on a college or university campus.
PROCEDURE: Opinionnaires composed of 35 principles identified by the investigator in the literature were sent to 390 theoreticians of higher education, academic administrators, directors of academic libraries, audiovisual directors, faculty, students and directors of learning resource centers generally selected at random. Three institutions with existing learning resources centers were examined to determine if they embodied the principles identified in the study.
FINDINGS: A majority of the respondents supported the principles stated in the opinionnaire. Thirteen of the principles which support the concept of a learning resources center were statistically significant at the .05 level on the Kruskal-Wallis Test. Using the Mann-Whitney Test it was found that audiovisual directors showed the most statistically significant differences (49) with other individual groups; directors of libraries followed with 22 statistically significant differences. The majority of academic learning resources centers included the library, audiovisual center, graphics department and curriculum center. The directors of learning resources centers fit no single profile. The only similarities identified were 91 percent of the directors reported to academic vice-presidents and all were male. Both the University of Wisconsin at Stevens Point and St. Cloud State College practiced a majority of the principles identified in this study; the philosophy and physical arrangement at Syracuse University did not permit the implementation of many of these principles.

597. Erickson, Wallace Edwin (Ed.D., University of South Dakota, 1972). **Self-perceived needs of media personnel for professional media preparation.** 154p. Order no. 72-32,710.
PURPOSE: The purpose of this study was to determine the opinions of the media personnel employed in public schools of South Dakota regarding their need for knowledge of selected topics dealing with media and education in order to carry out the duties of their present positions.
PROCEDURE: Data were obtained through the administration of an opinionnaire.
FINDINGS: The population of this study was predominantly female, middle-aged, fully certified as teachers, working full time, having more than 10 years of teaching experience, and having a minimum of a four-year college degree. Less than one-fourth of the total had a combined media undergraduate major or minor; the portion holding advanced degrees was much lower. The schools in which the population worked generally were small. Over half of the work day of the population was spent in media related work. The population felt that the following topics should be stressed in a preparation program: cataloging and classification of print and non-print materials; reading, listening and viewing guidance for both adolescents and children; audiovisual equipment; school curriculum; and the supervision and

FINDINGS (cont'd): improvement of instruction. Six topics would not, according to the population, have to be considered in a preparatory program: computer in libraries and education; history of audiovisual; micromaterials; radio and television in education; history of libraries and librarianship; and emerging developments and innovations in technology.

598. Feinberg, Hilda (Ph.D., Columbia University, 1972). **A comparative study of title derivative indexing techniques.** 406p. Order no. 72-20,036.
PURPOSE: The study examined the advantages, disadvantages and effectiveness of four different methods of title derivative indexing, with suggestions for improving this type of indexing.
PROCEDURE: Indexing data in machine-readable form was processed by four different computer algorithms. Differences in the resulting indexes to the same titles were analyzed in terms of index structure and format of the number and types of references appearing at various entry points. The printed indexes were analyzed to determine the effects of normalization of terminology, the effects of entry context on index size and the comprehensibility of entries, and the effect of the provision of secondary arranging elements other than the word following the primary entry word in the normal title order.

599. Fox, Ann Martha Sandberg (Ph.D., University of Illinois, 1972). **The amenability of a cataloging process to simulation by automatic techniques.** 476p. Order no. 73-9934.
PURPOSE: This study attempted to determine whether the human intellectual process of cataloging bibliographic materials using the AA (1967) and ALA (1949) cataloging codes, can be simulated by automatic techniques. The specific cataloging process is that which concerns selection of entry.
PROCEDURE: Directed tree graphs were used to simulate the entry process.
FINDINGS: The assumption that the AA rules of entry are more amenable to simulation than the ALA rules of entry was, in general, not supported. The two sets of rules were found to be highly and equally, or almost equally, accurate and automatic.

600. Fraser, James Howard (D.L.S., Columbia University, 1972). **Resources in the United States for the study of foreign children's literature and other media.**

601. Freudenthal, Juan Rothschild (Ph.D., University of Michigan, 1972). **Development and current status of bibliographic organization in Chile.** 377p. Order no. 72-29,056.
PURPOSE: This dissertation describes Chile's past and present bibliographic organization. Subject and discipline-oriented bibliographical apparatus and services were not covered unless they affected the overall development of Chile's bibliographic organization.
FINDINGS: Notwithstanding the National Library leadership in all bibliographic matters and the emergence of an active library profession in the late 1940's, it was not until the 1960's that the Chilean state became directly involved in the country's bibliographic progress by attempting to plan library and documentation services on a national scale. Although Chile has a strong bibliographic tradition, its overall bibliographic organization is inadequate. The lack of public libraries in Chile has

FINDINGS (cont'd): increasingly damaged the country's entire bibliographic structure. The political and social unrest in Chile also provides an obstacle to an already weak national information pattern.

602. Guise, Benjamin R. (Ed.D., North Texas State University, 1972). **A survey of public school library resources in Arkansas.** 152p. Order no. 73-2904.
PURPOSE: The purpose of this study was an examination of elementary and secondary school libraries in Arkansas to determine the adequacy of their resources as compared with the 1960 and the 1969 national school library standards.
PROCEDURE: Questionnaires were sent to 775 elementary and secondary school libraries in Arkansas (66.1 percent of the total were returned and usable). The data were tabulated, interpreted, and compared with the quantitative tables in the 1960 and 1969 national school library standards.
FINDINGS: In terms of library personnel, facilities, materials, and expenditures none of the libraries met the 1969 national school library standards. In general, the elementary school libraries came closer to meeting the 1960 standards than did the secondary school libraries. When asked to report their greatest needs for improvements, the majority of the librarians listed: central processing, additional staff, better facilities, larger budgets, the combination of print and non-print materials and in-service training.
CONCLUSIONS: Although national school library standards have been purposefully planned to be higher than state and regional standards, Arkansas school libraries are progressing much too slowly to bridge the gap between existing school libraries and the national school library standards.
RECOMMENDATIONS: Additional support is needed from local school administrators, including a minimum local funding increase to six percent of the average per-pupil operational costs for integrated media center operations. School librarians should receive additional education and professionalism. Support is needed from the State Department of Education including in-service programs and regional media centers.

603. Haith, Dorothy May (Ph.D., Indiana University, 1972). **A content analysis of information about educational filmstrips in selected periodicals.** 158p. Order no. 72-30,414.
PURPOSE: The purpose of this investigation was to identify and briefly describe periodicals which contain reviews of filmstrips, to ascertain the reviewing policies of the periodicals and to analyze the quality and content of filmstrip reviews.
PROCEDURE: Of the 98 periodicals reviewing filmstrips, 39 were analyzed. Of the 39 editors sent letters of inquiry, 64 percent responded.
FINDINGS: Only a few periodicals had comprehensive descriptive and critical information about recent filmstrips. Evaluated filmstrips usually received favorable reviews. Descriptive reviews generally did not include release year. Dates given were usually for older filmstrips. Content descriptions were usually longer in critical than in descriptive reviews. Few periodicals had written reviewing policies. Periodicals used a variety of reviewers and criteria for inclusion and exclusion of reviews in their departments.

604. Hall, John Brown (Ph.D., Florida State University, 1972). **Analysis of factors related to channels of patron input and feedback for policy making used by academic library directors.** 228p. Order no. 73-190.

PURPOSE: The purpose of the study was to examine, classify, and analyze what channels of patron input and feedback were used by academic library directors in the library policy making process.

PROCEDURE: Questionnaires were sent to a stratified proportionate random sample of 349 academic library directors (67 percent usable responses). Chi-square contingency tables and Kendall's coefficient of concordance were used to analyze the data.

FINDINGS: Consistent trends in the use of channels were found when the directors were grouped by highest degree awarded, size of institutions with more than 20,000 students, and number of annual terms in committee membership or office in the past five years. Regardless of the grouping of the directors, there was a consistent trend of lower use of informal channels with student patrons than with administration or faculty patrons and there was a strong tendency to agree that "The role of the library patron should be one of an active source of input and feedback concerning library policy rather than a passive acceptor of library policy;" "Library patrons should be more active sources of input and feedback than they presently are;" and "It is the responsibility of the librarian to establish channels and solicit input and feedback."

605. Halsey, Richard Sweeney (Ph.D., Case Western Reserve University, 1972). **A bibliometric analysis of the serious music literature on long playing records.** 406p. Order no. 73-6302.

PURPOSE: The primary intent of the study was to demonstrate that the dissemination of a creative product in this format parallels distribution and dispersion phenomena which have been observed within the periodical literature and that this activity complies with certain mathematical laws.

PROCEDURE: A total population of 42,943 serious music titles issued on long playing records in the United States and added to the *Schwann Long Playing Record Catalog* during 1961 through 1969 was examined.

CONCLUSIONS: A very few serious music works which are audience favorites compete with a vast numerical majority in accordance with the (Zipf) log-log or hyperbolic distribution. Title replication frequencies plot as a straight line on log rank-log percentage. If record companies are grouped so that each set of companies yields the same number of different works by a major composer, the number of labels needed in successive groupings to attain equal increments to the composer's works increases exponentially. Titles with moderately high duplication and low deletion rates include most of the works considered exemplary in structure and content by authorities in the field of musical aesthetics. There has been a direct correlation between musical quality and title longevity on the long playing record market.

606. Hamdy, Mohammed Nabil (Ph.D., University of Pittsburgh, 1972). **The title unit entry: an argument for the rejection of the author main entry in theory and practice.** 298p. Order no. 73-12,369.

PURPOSE: The purpose of the study was to investigate the theoretical and practical foundations of the "main author entry" and the "title unit entry" and to establish, through studying the rules for the choice of entry in the *Anglo-American Cataloging Rules, 1967*, whether or not the main entry should be considered in the design of a

PURPOSE (cont'd): cataloging code to be used in construction of a catalog that serves as a finding tool.

PROCEDURE: Systematic analysis, statistical analysis and flowcharting techniques were used.

FINDINGS: The rules for the choice of entry in *AACR 1967* based on the determination of the main entry, fail to provide an objective means for determining the entry that will preserve the stated objectives of the catalog. The title unit entry, compared to the main entry, is a mechanical approach which can fulfill the same objectives equally well, but with far less decision making, subjectivity and inconsistency.

607. Hazelton, Robert Stafford (Ph.D., Case Western Reserve University, 1972). **Underlying aspects of word frequency distribution.** Order no. 72-26,223.

608. Head, John William (Ph.D., University of Wisconsin, 1972). **The effect of bibliographic format and content on subject retrieval: a comparative study of four cataloging styles.** 130p. Order no. 72-11,242.

PURPOSE: This study was designed to investigate the effect of format and content of library cards on the ability of the catalog user to make relevant selections from the card catalog. Four different cataloging styles were chosen for comparison: author and title only; traditional cards; reformatted cards; reformatted cards with an abstract.

PROCEDURE: Social science and science headings from the subject catalog of the Memorial Library, University of Wisconsin were sampled to produce 107 entries. Four "catalogs" were prepared in the four styles for the 107 documents sampled. A test was conducted with 48 freshmen and sophomores randomly selected from the University's student body. Analysis of variance was performed.

FINDINGS: No significant differences in mean scores were discovered. Thus, none of the cataloging styles used in the experiment could be expected to represent an improvement over traditional cataloging.

609. Henry, Marion (Ph.D., Syracuse University, 1972). **A study of library services in the public schools of Texas.** 237p. Order no. 73-7728.

PURPOSE: This research was conducted in order to determine the status of unified media programs and personnel at the school building level in public schools of Texas.

PROCEDURE: Questionnaires based on the "Media Manpower Job Inventory" (Hamreus, 1970) and "School Library Personnel Task Analysis Survey" (ALA, 1969), were sent to 350 librarians from the southeastern section of Texas.

FINDINGS: The study indicated that 79 percent of the schools had centralized library service, 98 percent of the librarians favored centralized library services and over half considered the quality of their academic library training to be good or very good. Future competencies recommended by the librarians included such specifics as: (1) principles of curriculum development, (2) administration/supervision of media centers, (3) evaluation/selection of non-print materials, and (4) cataloging non-print materials.

610. Hodges, Theodora Long (Ph.D., University of California, Berkeley, 1972). **Citation indexing: its potential for bibliographical control.** 664p. Order no. 73-16,787.

PURPOSE: The purpose of this study is to evaluate on theoretical grounds the principle of access to literature represented by a citation index.
PROCEDURE: The procedures used involved a survey of more than 80 papers, analyses of many writings about writing, and interviews with 42 leading scholars.
FINDINGS: There is a generally accepted "code" governing citation practice. Those interviewed are almost unanimous in believing that the references called for by such a code are not only sound but useful. Access through references differs from that through traditional bibliographical instruments, which in any field are necessarily based on the accepted vocabulary and frame of reference in that field. Work at the forefront of developing knowledge in a field does not fit such a frame of reference, and for it citation connections may provide the only direct access.

611.   Isa, Zubaidah (Ph.D., Indiana University, 1972). **Printing and publishing in Indonesia: 1602-1970.** 217p. Order no. 73-2666.
PURPOSE: The study attempts to trace the development of publishing in Indonesia from the introduction of the printing press in the seventeenth century to the present time, with emphasis on the period since 1949.
FINDINGS: From 1602 to 1942 Indonesia was a colony of the Dutch; the Dutch colonial policy was primarily aimed at exploiting the natural resources of Indonesia and prohibiting the development of local industry—including publishing and printing. Thus, printing and publishing were monopolized either by Indonesian branches of Dutch publishing houses or by Dutch publishers in the Netherlands. The impact of the Japanese occupation (1942-45) on printing and publishing in Indonesia was considerable though not measurable. Indonesians for the first time were given editorial and production experience in publishing. Independence found Indonesia without a healthy publishing industry. Since 1947 the country has struggled to develop a publishing industry that would contribute to the achievement of its national goals in education and economic growth. Three economic-related factors have inhibited the development of a viable publishing industry: chronic paper shortages; high prices of printed material in relation to personal incomes; lack of working capital and high cost of printing equipment.

612.   Jetter, Margaret Ann (Ph.D., Michigan State University, 1972). **The roles of the school library media specialist in the future: a Delphi study.** 172p. Order no. 73-12,746.
PURPOSE: The purpose of the study was to identify viable roles for the school library media specialist of the future.
PROCEDURE: Using the Delphi Technique, 53 leaders in the four professional specializations, nominated by their colleagues as being uniquely qualified to provide significant input, participated in the study. Three questionnaires were sent to the leaders.
CONCLUSIONS: The school library media specialist of the future will function as an instructional development specialist. The participants tended to approach consensus regarding the relative importance of the recommended roles in successive rounds of the study. The members of the four professional specialization groups tended to be more alike than different in their perception and rating of the relative importance of the recommended roles.
RECOMMENDATIONS: It is recommended that programs for preparing the school library media specialist of the future be made interdisciplinary and that the practicing

RECOMMENDATIONS (cont'd): school library media specialist be permitted opportunity to work with teachers and students in non-traditional ways.

613. Kanner, Elliott Elisha (Ph.D., University of Wisconsin, 1972). **The impact of gerontological concepts on principles of librarianship.** 167p. Order no. 72-4281.

PURPOSE: The primary objective of this investigation was to measure the rate which research-based information and ideas were introduced from gerontology to librarianship between 1946 and 1969.

PROCEDURE: Data collected from the literature search were recorded on charts designed to identify all references to sources published between 1946 and 1969. Charts were also coded to distinguish incidence of mention, simplified or amplified mention and level of institutionalization.

FINDINGS: While periods of decline in references to aging in library literature reflect competition with other social issues affecting public libraries, attention to the special needs of an aging population has risen to a point at which a continuing pattern of library development may be predicted. The flow of gerontological information into library literature was followed closely by evidence of direct application to library practice. Incorporation into principles of service was exemplified in the American Library Association's landmark statement of the *Library's Responsibility to the Aging* in 1964.

614. Kosa, Geza Attila (Ph.D., Indiana University, 1972). **Computer-assisted book selecting using machine readable cataloging (MARC II) tapes.** 213p. Order no. 72-19,495.

PURPOSE: A measurement was made of the effectiveness (timeliness and comprehensiveness) of the Library of Congress MARC II tapes when used as a selection aid for current English language monographs by specialist librarians in a large academic library.

PROCEDURE: Six specialist librarians from Indiana University Library participated in the project for 13 weeks in the Spring of 1971. The subject interest profiles of the participants were constructed and a selection of titles was made by the computer from the tapes according to these profiles. The resulting printouts were distributed to the participants for possible final selection. Selection previously done from LC proof slips and the printouts from MARC II tapes were compared.

FINDINGS: The mean difference between the arrival dates of identical entries on the tapes and on the proof slips was about two weeks in favor of the tapes. The tapes' comprehensiveness of subject coverage surpassed that of the proof slips for each participant. The potential effectiveness of the tapes was also considered for foreign language titles. During 1973 when German and Romance language materials will be included on tape, 90 to 100 percent of the participants will be satisfied. The results of the other two measures of effectiveness are assumed to be the same for foreign language titles as for English.

CONCLUSIONS: The tapes are a more effective selection aid than proof slips, but their effectiveness can be fully exploited only when language coverage is extended to German and all Romance languages.

615. Kramer, Dorothy Aristea (Ph.D., Case Western Reserve University, 1972). **Lange's** *Handbook of Chemistry,* **a study of the cultural influences on the**

utility of a data compilation. 236p. Order no. 72-26,174.

PURPOSE: The purpose of the study was to investigate the cultural influences affecting the utility of Lange's *Handbook of Chemistry*.

FINDINGS: The *Handbook* was published by Handbook Publishers from 1934 to 1956 in nine editions and was sold in large numbers to American chemists. The editor, Dr. Norbert A. Lange, was the major influence upon the book. His reliance on scientific handbooks and desire to produce a profitable book led him to design a book of practical utility to chemists and other scientists in every phase of chemical study and activity. The contributors promoted the book's utility through their knowledge of many sciences, their professional status, their awareness of the need for data of various groups, and the provision of useful data of limited accessibility to chemists. The documentary sources promoted the book's utility by reducing its expense, by exhibiting different intellectual and social uses for data, and by giving breadth and impartiality to its contents. The users influenced the book's design through their needs for data which arose from their physical environments, information seeking habits, their diverse scientific interests and occupational activities, and the lack of technical libraries.

CONCLUSIONS: The book's success was due to the satisfaction of the needs and values of its producers and users, and to the editor's sensitivity to prevailing cultural forces.

616. Kunoff, Hugo (Ph.D., Indiana University, 1972). **The enlightenment and German university libraries: Leipzig, Jena, Halle, and Göttingen between 1750 and 1913.** 236p. Order no. 72-30,422.

PURPOSE: The purpose of the study was to investigate the influence the Enlightenment had on the development of German university libraries.

PROCEDURE: Data were collected from general histories, contemporary accounts and histories of the four institutions, government and university reports and the biographies of librarians and university officials.

FINDINGS: The Enlightenment influenced universities primarily by changing the objectives and orientation of universities; the passive universities were transformed into active, progressive, and modern institutions which aimed not only to transmit knowledge but to examine it critically, to present it systematically and to advance it. To realize these aims, professors and students needed large collections of instructional and research materials, particularly recent books and periodicals. They needed easy access to library collections through reliable and complete catalogs and expanded library services, longer opening hours, and more liberal rules of circulation. The Enlightenment also influenced university libraries by accelerating the growth of knowledge by increasing the production of books and by advancing the reading interests of the general public. All four of the university libraries examined in this study recognized the increasing library needs of professors and students and attempted to expand services and collections. However, with the exception of Göttingen, the libraries found it difficult, for lack of adequate funds, to respond quickly and extensively to the needs. The library of Göttingen, the most advanced and best supported institution of the time, could satisfy in large measure the needs of its patrons.

617. Lange, Clifford Elmer (Ph.D., University of Wisconsin, 1972). **Communication behavior and interpersonal coorientation between public library**

directors and their board members. 192p. Order no. 73-9277.

PURPOSE: The purpose of this study was to gather and examine data on the relationship between public library directors and their board members from the point of view of the influence of attitudes and attitude perception on the communication structure existing between them.

PROCEDURE: Interviews were conducted and questionnaires sent to a random sample of 10 Wisconsin municipal public libraries serving populations from 30,000 to 200,000.

FINDINGS: Perceived attitude similarity was found not to be significantly related to director frequency of communication with board members. Perceived influence in the community and the board office of president were found to positively correlate with communication frequency at a statistically significant level.

CONCLUSIONS: To operate successfully, the director must communicate with the president of the library board. A director is motivated to communicate with those board members whom he perceives to be influential in the community because he perceives that this is the most effective way to accomplish his goals and those of the library. The board members represent sources of alternative attitudes from which a director can draw in his attempt to arrive at decisions which will best serve the needs of the library and the community. Where there is frequent communication between director and board, there will be a higher level of accuracy, implying an easier working relationship. One of the major problems in public libraries is the inadequate nature of the communication relationship between director and board members.

618. Little, Robert David (Ph.D., University of Wisconsin, 1972). **A study of the relationship between sources of funds and other selected factors and expenditures for instructional materials in Wisconsin public schools.** 232p. Order no. 72-27,338.

PURPOSE: The purpose of this study was to examine factors that might be related to expenditures for instructional materials (library books and audiovisual materials) in Wisconsin public schools.

PROCEDURE: Wisconsin Department of Public Instruction data from all public school districts in the state for the 1967-68 school year were used. Correlation coefficients were run to examine relationships.

FINDINGS: Statistically significant correlations were found to exist between local, state and federal expenditures for instructional materials and total expenditures for instructional materials. The greatest correlation was found between local expenditures and total expenditures. No significant relationships were found between local expenditures for instructional materials and expenditures from other sources (state or federal) for instructional materials. In general, significant correlations were found between certain selected financial characteristics of public school districts and per student expenditures for instructional materials. No relationships between the tested organizational characteristics and expenditures for instructional materials were found to exist.

619. Long, Lora Alcorn (Ed.D., University of Mississippi, 1972). **The patron of the First Regional Library of Mississippi: his needs, desires and recommendations relating to the public library.** 139p. Order no. 73-1279.

PURPOSE: The study proposed to determine patrons' requirements, opinions and

PURPOSE (cont'd): recommendations concerning the services in the six branch libraries of the First Regional Library of Mississippi.

PROCEDURE: Questionnaires were given by the librarians to each patron, 12 years of age or older, who came to each of the six branch libraries on six selected days. Questionnaires were completed by 639 patrons.

FINDINGS: A very high level of user satisfaction was expressed by the sample patrons of the six libraries. The greater percentage of respondents expressed satisfaction with existing collections. Nearly half of the requests for services were related to fiction materials; only one-fourth were for informational materials. In all six libraries the respondents expressed some interest in new or expanded services. Librarians had partially succeeded in their attempt to inform patrons of the special services which were available. The patrons were interested in helping solve the publicity problem in the library; the newspaper was the favored medium. The patrons of the six separate branch libraries differed little concerning their needs, desires and satisfactions.

620. Lowe, Mildred (D.L.S., Columbia University, 1972). **Government publications and pamphlets in the community colleges of New York State.**

621. Lynch, Beverly Pfeifer (Ph.D., University of Wisconsin, 1972). **Library technology; a comparison of the work of functional departments in academic libraries.** 207p. Order no. 73-9281.

PURPOSE: The purpose of the study was to identify, empirically, the domain of the organizational theory proposed by Charles Perrow and to develop a valid and reliable measure that could be used to compare the technologies of library departments.

PROCEDURE: The study compared 15 departments in three academic libraries on the characteristics of the work done in these departments. A seven-item scale was developed that was a valid and reliable measure of Perrow's construct. The scale does not include measures of task interdependence or overall routineness of work.

FINDINGS: Although the scale was successful in discriminating among the 15 departments as to technology, the differences were small. Generally, predictable events, routine operations, and relatively low knowledge requirements constituted the technologies of all of the library departments participating in this study.

622. McGowan, Frank M. (Ph.D., University of Pittsburgh, 1972). **The Association of Research Libraries, 1932-1962.** 262p. Order no. 73-12,360.

PURPOSE: The purpose of the study was to trace the growth and development of the Association of Research Libraries between 1932 and 1962.

FINDINGS: In 1932, 42 major American research libraries banded together to form the Association of Research Libraries in order to develop and increase by cooperative effort the resources and usefulness of the research collections in American libraries. For 30 years, prior to its reorganization and incorporation in 1962, this association of libraries was essentially an informal discussion group of librarians who had reached the top of their profession. Its policy was to undertake only those few projects that other groups could not, or would not, accept. The Association's major efforts were in the fields of acquisitions and bibliographical control. The Association worked on the Farmington Plan, the Cooperative Acquisitions Project, the Documents Expediting Project and the Public Law 480 Program. They published

FINDINGS (cont'd): such works as *Doctoral Dissertations Accepted by American Universities*, the *Library of Congress Catalog of Printed Cards*, and *Newspapers on Microfilm; a Union Checklist*. The strength of the Association during its first 30 years may be attributed to achieving a successful compromise between talk and action. The Association succeeded for two major reasons: ARL functioned as a structually non-traditional organization and the membership was restrictive, excluding individuals except as representatives of the major research libraries of the country.

623. Maloney, Ruth Kay (Ph.D., Rutgers University, 1972). **An analysis of group profiling for SDI systems in industrial communities.** 188p. Order no. 72-17,853.
PURPOSE: The objectives of this research were to compare the effectiveness of (1) three methods of determining membership in a group for SDI profiling purposes; (2) title searching with titles-and-abstract-text searching.
PROCEDURE: Individual profiles were constructed for 104 chemists from three industrial research laboratories and matched against current issues of machine-readable *Basic Journal Abstracts* (BJA). Users within each company then were assigned to organizational, project and/or interest groups for profiling purposes. The Exact Binomial Test for significance was applied to 36 different comparisons of the performance values of the three methods of grouping.
FINDINGS: Grouping by organizational structure was the least effective method. No statistically significant difference could be established between groupings by project assignment and groupings by self-expressed interest within individual companies; when users of all companies were combined, grouping by project was found to be more effective than grouping by interest. The percentage of retrieval of citations if only titles are searched when compared with searching of titles and abstract text can be expected to fall between 18.2 percent and 35.8 percent with a 95 percent confidence level. The mean of this population was 27 percent. One can expect a higher level in the percentage of retrieval by titles only if only a single term is required for a match than in searches requiring more than one term to be present to constitute a match (39 percent compared with 16.8 percent).

624. Mann, Elizabeth B. (Ph.D., Florida State University, 1972). **The Florida public school library media program, 1969-1970.** 149p. Order no. 72-21,320.
PURPOSE: A study was made of the school library media programs in the 1,803 public schools of Florida during the 1969-1970 school year to evaluate both strengths and weaknesses of the library media centers as a basis for the future development of a statewide program in Florida.
PROCEDURE: Data were secured from accreditation reports filed with the Florida Department of Education, compared to the "Standards for School Media Programs," and analyzed by chi-square, discriminant function, correlation and analysis of variance.
FINDINGS: Size of a school district and establishment of school library media supervision at the district school level were related to staff, financial support and collections of materials and equipment. School library programs were not equally provided in schools with all types of grade grouping organization. The school library media program in Florida public schools generally reflected a unified concept embracing audiovisual and printed resources and services. Florida's public schools generally did not meet the "Standards for School Media Programs."

625. Mathis, Betty Ann (Ph.D., Ohio State University, 1972). **Techniques for the evaluation and improvement of computer-produced abstracts.** 276p. Order no. 73-11,535.

PURPOSE: The purpose of the dissertation was to develop a technique for the computer production of abstracts.

PROCEDURE: An automatic abstracting system named ADAM (which receives journal articles as input and produces abstracts as output) was implemented on the IBM 370. An algorithm was developed which considers every sentence in the input text and rejects sentences which are not suitable for inclusion in the abstract. All sentences which are not rejected are included in the set of sentences which are candidates for inclusion in the abstract. The quality of the abstracts was evaluated by (1) determining the conformity of the abstracts to the defined criteria for an acceptable abstract for the given system; (2) and comparing the abstract with its parent document.

FINDINGS: Based on the results of the evaluation, several techniques were developed to improve the quality of the abstracts. The modifications produce abstracts in which the flow of ideas is improved and which represent a more nearly coherent whole.

626. Maurstad, Betty Louise (Ph.D., Case Western Reserve University, 1972). **Concerning structural properties in the literature of the art historian—a bibliometric study.** 147p. Order no. 72-26,182.

PURPOSE: Inquiry has been made into aspects of the behavior of certain properties of the literature which has been cited by the art historian in a selected group of art-historical publications.

PROCEDURE: The literature analyzed consisted of that cited in nine works by Erwin Panofsky, 1892-1968, and in the *Journal of the Warburg and Courtauld Institutes*, XXX (1967).

FINDINGS: The ratio of change in percentages of works published from 1800 to date cited in a given publication is shown to be a constant of approximately 1.4 per decade, irrespective of when the publication in which these works have been cited was itself published. The chronological behavior of nucleuses of individual authors and specific works was virtually identical to the chronological behavior of the total of this literature. The law of S. C. Bradford was, in general, satisfied. The behavior of the cited literature appeared to satisfy a more "general" law of distribution: that is—in paraphrase of R. A. Fairthorne—hyperbolic distributions are inevitable whenever a group of people form compounds from a repertory of given elements and one aspect of the "cost" of such elements is dominant.

627. Mick, Colin Kennedy (Ph.D., Stanford University, 1972). **Information seeking style in medicine.** 140p. Order no. 72-20,716.

PURPOSE: This study explores the concept of information seeking style, testing the effects of environment and cognitive factors on the way in which medical professionals obtain information from personal sources, other medical professionals, and extra-personal sources such as libraries.

PROCEDURE: Interviews were conducted with 120 medical professionals, ranging from first year medical students to experienced practitioners and researchers. Respondents with similar styles were grouped together using Q-type cluster analysis. Common dimensions in information seeking style were developed using R-type

PROCEDURE (cont'd): factor analysis. The predictive power of both demographic and environmental variables was then tested. Final profiles were composed of use scores on five types of sources: personal notes, personal files, personal libraries, extra-personal sources (library books, journals, etc.), and interpersonal sources (those involving interaction with other individuals). Eight information seeking style groups were differentiated, composed of 66 respondents.
CONCLUSIONS: Distinctive information seeking styles do exist. Information seeking styles change over time. Environmental constraints and demands are dominant factors in determining information seeking style. It is possible for individuals with quite different external attributes to display very similar information seeking styles. Reliance on interpersonal sources does not occur until after the completion of formal medical training.
RECOMMENDATIONS: Recommendations were (1) consider information seeking style when developing sources for specific audiences; (2) offer courses to train medical students in more efficient information seeking techniques and modify the medical school environment to encourage such skills; (3) develop continuing education programs for physicians to improve their information seeking skills; and (4) encourage further study of information seeking using the techniques developed in this study.

628. Miller, Edward P. (Ph.D., University of Oklahoma, 1972). **A method to determine effectiveness of special library operations.** 238p. Order no. 72-22,446.
PURPOSE: A method is developed to determine measures of effectiveness for feasible alternatives of change in influential aspects of library operation.
PROCEDURE: The method combines user opinion and library administration attitudes and expertise in a concert evaluation of library operation.
FINDINGS: Experimental demonstration of the method provides examples of application and amplification of interpretations of the method and its resulting solutions to the decision problem. Other analyses possible with the method outputs are identified using the demonstration experiment.

629. Miller, Rosalind Elaine (Ph.D., St. Louis University, 1972). **Instructional materials centers as related to types of learning: the application of Gagné's learning principles to media stimulus.** 145p. Order no. 72-13,472.
PURPOSE: An attempt was made in this study to formulate criteria other than quantitative for development of instructional materials centers. Gagné's learning principles were used to develop a model of organization and design for instructional materials centers (IMC's).
PROCEDURE: Formulation of Gagné's hierarchical principles revealed a definite model of a learning facility that could be applied to the IMC. Media selection charts were developed from the model that could create learning prescriptions of some exactness. From the model a checklist was devised that would determine if learners' needs were met by IMC's. The checklist was sent to librarians and curriculum directors of IMC's mentioned most frequently in the literature.

630. Montgomery, Kenneth Leon (Ph.D., University of Pittsburgh, 1972). **Factors affecting search time in a document retrieval system.** 214p. Order no. 73-16,338.

PURPOSE: The study investigated factors affecting search time in a document retrieval system.

PROCEDURE: An experiment was conducted using an IBM 360/50 computer system, the Chemical Abstracts Services Condensates tape, and a special purpose retrieval program which is capable of searching both linear and inverted data bases. Three hundred and twenty-one discrete computer searches were run in an operational multiprogramming environment.

FINDINGS: The average search time per question decreased for linear searches as the number of questions increased until 64 questions were searched. For more than 64 questions the average search time per question began to increase. For document files containing more than 512 documents and for searches utilizing 32 questions or more, it was more economical to convert a linear file into an inverted file and utilize inverted search techniques.

CONCLUSIONS: Search and retrieval programs capable of switching between linear and inverted file organizations and search techniques is economically worthwhile.

631. Motley, Drucilla (Ph.D., Florida State University, 1972). **An on-line computer managed introduction to indexing: an individualized multi-media instructional package compared to the traditional method, nine hours of teacher-group contact.** 181p. Order no. 72-18,605.

PURPOSE: An experiment was conducted in order to determine if multi-media instruction was more effective in teaching indexing than teacher-group contact.

PROCEDURE: A systems approach model was used to develop a multi-media instructional package for a three weeks unit on indexing in a graduate library science course. The multi-media instructional package was compared to teacher-group contact in two experiments. The study was replicated to increase the precision of the experiment and to validate a regression equation developed from data obtained in the first experiment.

FINDINGS: The mean scores of the three groups (one control and two experimental) did not differ significantly in regard to achievement or attitude toward the computer managed method of instruction (CMI). In each group a highly significant relationship was found between library science G.P.A. and achievement. The differences in attitude toward CMI (pre- and post-instruction) were consistently related to achievement on the post-test, but directly for experimental and inversely for control groups. In the experimental groups, the number of multi-media lessons not completed accounted for the major portions of post-test score variance.

CONCLUSIONS: Choice of method of instruction should be based on something other than achievement on lecture-based examinations. Greater attention should be given to attitudes and study habits of students since they account for much of the variance in test scores. Students are not handicapped by innovative methods of instruction. More multi-media instruction packages should be developed, possibly as cooperative projects among library schools.

632. Murray, Daniel McClure (Ph.D., Cornell University, 1972). **Document retrieval based on clustered files.** 354p. Order no. 72-23,682.

PURPOSE: This thesis attempts to answer the question "Is a clustered file organization suitable for on-line document retrieval?"

FINDINGS: The proposed organization compares favorably in terms of speed and storage economy; various request document matching procedures, search strategies,

FINDINGS (cont'd): and feedback schemes are easily implemented. Search precision is less, but compensated by a flexible level of recall (low or high). Furthermore, arbitrary accesses for individual records are not required since those records with a high probability of satisfying a request are concentrated in a few disk locations.

633. Ozolins, Karlis Lotars (Ph.D., University of Michigan, 1972). **Book publishing trends in The American Lutheran Church and its antecedent bodies, 1917-1967.** 460p. Order no. 72-29,163.

PURPOSE: The study surveyed book production under the auspices of The American Lutheran Church (1960-) and its antecedent synodical bodies: the American Lutheran Church (1930-1960), the Evangelical Lutheran Church, the United Evangelical Lutheran Church, the Lutheran Free Church, the Evangelical Lutheran Synod of Iowa and the Lutheran Synod of Buffalo.

FINDINGS: Each of the synodical components of The American Lutheran Church began as a specific ethnic background denomination and continued a foreign language publishing program all through the 1920's; their effort for self-preservation and self-defense produced a flurry of publications. When the antecedent bodies merged in 1960, the separate publishing firms (e.g., Wartburg Publishing House of Chicago, The Messenger Press, etc.) eventually conflowed in a greater Augsburg Publishing House. The total output of the publishers within the family of The American Lutheran Church was 1,475 books. A core of publications catering to the basic needs of congregations amounted to 9.5 percent of the total, devotionals 8.8 percent, sermon books 6.2 percent, theological and Biblical studies 20.8 percent, historical and biographical publications 11.1 percent, practical and promotional monographs 5.0 percent, foreign missions 4.9 percent, fiction and poetry 8.5 percent, children's books 24.3 percent and various 0.9 percent of the total.

634. Pao, Miranda Hau-Yung Lee (Ph.D., Case Western Reserve University, 1972). **A general method to establish quality filtering systems for biomedical literatures.** 174p. Order no. 73-6328.

PURPOSE: A filtering system was developed by making use of bibliographic citations in articles published by subject experts. This filtering method is viewed as a partial solution to the problem of the proliferation of literature in terms of both quality and quantity.

PROCEDURE: The method was tested on the literature of the drug therapy of cardiac arrhythmias.

FINDINGS: The result was an information kit or the compilation of a sourcebook on the subject, containing full text of five review articles, and 20 core articles. References to three commonly used textbooks and a list of journals most likely to publish on the subject were also included. A comparison of these references with bibliographic citations of recent texts on the same subject demonstrates that the proposed method of indirect assessment can be used to compile sourcebooks to act as entries to the literature.

635. Patrick, Ruth J. (Ph.D., University of California, Berkeley, 1972). **The development of academic library consortia.** 243p.

PURPOSE: The purpose of the research project was to conduct an exploratory study of academic library consortia. The focus of the study was on guidelines for the development of such consortia.

PROCEDURE: The data were gathered from questionnaires completed by the 125 academic library consortia in existence at the time of the study, and from 15 in-depth case studies.

FINDINGS: Among the findings of the study were the following: (1) the activities in which the greatest number of consortia were engaged in were reciprocal borrowing privileges, expanded interlibrary loan services, the production of union catalogs or lists, and photocopying services; (2) the average funding level of consortia having budgets was $75,000, but over one-half of the consortia reported that they had no formal budget; (3) the use of computer technology was very limited, with only 26 percent of the consortia using a computer; (4) approximately one-third of the consortia had directors, nearly all of whom were full-time.

CONCLUSIONS: The author concluded that academic library consortia are here to stay, and that there will be continued growth in this area. The pattern even suggests the development of consortia of national scope, perhaps under the direction of the Library of Congress or the National Commission on Libraries and Information Science.

636. Pettas, William Anthony (Ph.D., University of California, Berkeley, 1972). **The Giunti: merchant publishers of the sixteenth century.**

637. Plante, Julian Gerard (Ph.D., Fordham University, 1972). **The library of Stift Reichersberg. Portions of text in Latin.** 212p. Order no. 73-1490.

PURPOSE: The study provides a comprehensive catalog of all the extant manuscripts currently housed at Reichersberg, a complete description of another codex originally from Reichersberg but no longer kept there, background information necessary for the understanding of the history of the monastery and its library, and a survey of the contents of the collection prior to its almost total destruction in 1624.

PROCEDURE: The central portion of the study is a comprehensive and analytical catalog of the 13 extant Reichersberg manuscripts which were made available for research through microfilm copies produced for the Monastic Manuscript Microfilm Library, St. John's Abbey and University, Collegeville, Minnesota. A transcription is also included of the text of a Latin-German *Brevis Cronica Reichersbergensis* found in one of the Reichersberg manuscripts and heretofore unpublished. Copies of two early Reichersberg manuscript catalogs, one of 1595 and the other of 1610, were found in a codex now in the possession of the Munich Staatsbibliothek; a microfilm copy of the pertinent portions of this codex was acquired from Staatsbibliothek to determine the Reichersberg manuscript collection as it existed prior to the 1624 fire.

638. Pool, Jane (Ph.D., University of Illinois, 1972). **The selection of science books for elementary school libraries: an analysis of selection from national selection sources and from a local buying list.**

PURPOSE: The purpose of the study was to report the relationship of a local buying list to selection procedures by fourth grade science teachers and librarians, and the resulting elementary school library collections in astronomy and the earth sciences.

PROCEDURE: The data were collected in two cities, from six elementary schools in each city. The collections were compared in terms of selection criteria, selection aids, selection activities, and the quality and adequacy of collections.

FINDINGS: The study revealed no appreciable differences between the city which had the list, and the city which did not, except in four aspects: (1) the schools which use a local buying list held larger percentages of the books recommended for correlation with fourth grade science textbooks; (2) their holdings were, on the average, a year more recent than those in the libraries not using a list; (3) book orders for the schools using the list contained books with more recent publication dates; (4) the schools not using the list received their books quicker.

CONCLUSIONS: There appeared to be no basis for support of the hypothesis that autonomous selection by librarians and teachers is related to better selected and more recent library collections in elementary schools, because selectors who are given more freedom are more involved and adept at selection.

639. Prentice, Anne E. (D.L.S., Columbia University, 1972). **The public library trustee: role perception in relation to performance in obtaining funds for the medium-sized library.**

640. Radford, Neil Anthony (Ph.D., University of Chicago, 1972). **The Carnegie Corporation and the development of American college libraries, 1928-1941.**

641. Raney, Leon (Ph.D., Indiana University, 1972). **An investigation into the adaptability of a domestic approval program to the existing pattern of book selection in a medium sized academic library.** 367p. Order no. 73-9776.

PURPOSE: This study simulated the application of a computerized blanket order approval program to a medium sized academic library for the purpose of determining how closely pre-selections of the approval plan related to the existing pattern of book selection.

PROCEDURE: The participating library was programmed into one of the leading domestic approval programs. A profile depicting the existing pattern of book selection was developed for 10 broad subject areas and submitted to a cooperating academic book jobber where it was entered into a computerized book-screening system and matched against titles treated on approval during an earlier four-month test period. From this operation book forms were generated showing titles which would have been pre-selected for the library by the approval system and those which were considered and rejected by the system. These data were analyzed and compared to actual library acquisitions over the succeeding 21 months. A 2x2 contingency table was used to illustrate the rate of agreement between selections made under the two systems. As a follow-up on actual library acquisitions, faculty members in seven subject areas were asked to review all test titles which had not been acquired or placed on order at the library.

FINDINGS: Out of 4,559 titles treated during the test period, the library and the approval system took essentially the same action on a total of 3,727 titles (82 percent). The library actually acquired a total of 1,504 of the test titles. Analysis of these revealed that 82 percent were pre-selected by the approval system and would have been sent automatically to the library in an operational situation while the remaining 18 percent would have been reported with a notification form only. While the faculty book selectors felt that only approximately 30 percent of the unacquired titles should have been purchased by the library, they chose a much higher percentage of titles pre-selected by the approval system than those rejected (49 percent compared to 25 percent).

CONCLUSIONS: The approval system would have provided an expanded bibliographic base for selection by faculty and librarians. Use of the system would have reduced the time lag in acquiring most new domestic publications by a minimum average of three months.

642. Rickman, Jon Todd (Ph.D., Washington State University, 1972). **Automatic storage and retrieval techniques for large on-line abstract collections.** 119p. Order no. 72-18,482.

PURPOSE: Out-of-context indexing is analyzed and a new indexing technique for on-line interactive retrieval systems is presented.

FINDINGS: The system was found to be superior to several well-known automatic methods. The design of an on-line thesaurus to support interactive browsing is developed. A new method of ordering responses is presented and evaluated. The method of ordering is found to be better than methods which ignore the Boolean logic occurring in a user's query. An experimental automatic relevance feedback technique is presented with test results.

643. Robbins, Jane (Ph.D., University of Maryland, 1972). **Policy formation in American public libraries: effects of citizen participation.** Order no. 73-17,049.

644. Schaefer, Barbara Kirsch (Ph.D., University of Pittsburgh, 1972). **Classification of the literature of mathematics: a comparative analysis of the American Mathematical Society and the Library of Congress schemes.** 141p. Order no. 73-12,373.

PURPOSE: The purpose of this study was to analyze and compare the American Mathematical Society (AMS) and the Library of Congress (LC) schemes for classifying the literature of mathematics.

PROCEDURE: First, the terminology and organizational structures of the AMS scheme (published in 1970) and the 1950 edition of the LC scheme were compared. Next, the two LC editions were compared for additions and changes in the new edition (1970). Finally, the 1970 edition of LC was compared with the 1970 edition of AMS. The similarities and differences between AMS and LC were determined by means of contextual analysis.

FINDINGS: The theories of categorization of AMS and LC were not the same. Terms with the same or similar graphemic structure were classed in entirely different categories in AMS and LC. This is due to the fact that LC arranges topics according to the traditional divisions of mathematics while AMS arranges them by relationships. The extensive additions in the 1970 edition of LC did not bring the scheme into agreement with AMS because the new LC edition has the same organization as the old edition. AMS and LC are both based on the principle of literary warrant rather than on class logic. AMS, however, is based on current journal literature while LC is based primarily on the book form. In addition, AMS and LC differed with regard to (1) the universe of classification, (2) the purpose of classification, (3) the user of classification, (4) the development and revision of classification.

645. Schnaitter, Allene Flora (Ph.D., Indiana University, 1972). **Native and transfer students in one Midwestern university: a comparison of their book borrowing and other library use.** 377p. Order no. 73-2751.

PURPOSE: The study dealt with the use which transfer students made of the library in a four-year university and compared their usage with that of native students.

PROCEDURE: Data were collected for the entire junior class at the University of Missouri at Columbia during the fall of 1968. Questionnaires were sent to a sample of 660 students still enrolled at the University in the spring of 1970 (58 percent of the total were usable). Chi-square and median tests were used to analyze the data.

FINDINGS: For all students, library use was highest for reserve books and personal studying; non-borrowers occasionally used the library, but were exceeded by borrowers in weekly library use; library use in previous years was greater than in the senior year; students owned a variety of books and other materials, with magazine subscriptions purchased by the highest number of students. Analysis of the percentages of student responses about frequency of library use indicated that there was no difference between native and transfer students. Natives in education were found to borrow significantly greater numbers of books than new transfers from both junior and senior colleges. Compared with natives and other transfer groups, junior college transfers had the lowest percentage who never used the library.

646. Schulte-Albert, Hans Georg (Ph.D., Case Western Reserve University, 1972). **Leibniz's plans for a world encyclopaedia system.** 275p. Order no. 72-26,207.

PURPOSE: This is an historical study, bringing together different plans of Gottfried Wilhelm Leibniz for gathering and organizing the recorded public knowledge of his time in an encyclopaedia designed for efficient retrieval of information. The study deals especially with his attempts to systematize the macro- and micro-units of thought and to develop for them a precise, yet flexible classificatory language, his *characteristica universalis*.

FINDINGS: Leibniz's world encyclopaedia was to be a classified, demonstrative work in which propositions were arranged in the order of their dependency. Leibniz never completed his encyclopaedia, but he made important "discoveries" while working on this system and anticipated developments of later centuries. He presented plans for coping effectively with the "publication explosion" of his time and even considered an information rejection system. In his later schemes for the classification of library materials, he expressed clearly the limitation of linearity inherent in library classifications and tried to overcome this drawback. While searching for an ideal notation for his classificatory language, he used and later rejected prime-number coding. Long before Euler he used the so-called Euler diagrams for representing logical relationships now usually displayed by Venn diagrams. He never arrived at a definitive classificatory language, but in the process he invented basic principles of symbolic and mathematical logic. Leibniz even considered building a *machina combinatoria* that would reduce logical operations to a mechanical process, and thus anticipated developments that came to fruition in our generation.

647. Sherrill, Laurence Lester (Ph.D., University of Wisconsin, 1972). **The affective responses of ethnic minority readers to indigenous ghetto literature: a measurement.** 156p. Order no. 73-9292.

PURPOSE: The specific problem of the study was to measure the affective reading

PURPOSE (cont'd): responses of ghetto dwelling ethnic minority adults to samples of indigenous ghetto literature. The underlying purpose of the study was to investigate cultural factors that libraries, especially public libraries, might consider in promoting reading among disadvantaged ethnic minority adults.

PROCEDURE: The data gathering instrument was a testing form consisting of eight passages of literature by four Black and four Puerto Rican authors which depicted personal experience in the ghetto. The respondents were requested to register their emotional responses to each passage of literature on four different semantic differential scales. After pretesting and revision, the testing form was administered to a number of Black and Puerto Rican participants in ABE, GED, and English as a Second Language program in the greater Chicago area. A total number of 193 valid testing forms were analyzed.

FINDINGS: Cultural factors in the observed readers were powerful determinants of the intensity of the affective responses to the literature that they read. Cultural factors constituted a significant element in the process by which the reader evaluated (expressed preference for or aversion to) and interpreted the literature they read.

648. Shoffner, Ralph Merl (D.L.S., University of California, Berkeley, 1972). **Telefacsimile in libraries.**

649. Soper, Mary Ellen (Ph.D., University of Illinois, 1972). **The relationship between personal collections and the selection of cited references.** 208p. Order no. 73-10,059.

PURPOSE: An investigation was made of the effect of physical accessibility upon the selection of cited references. Particular attention was paid to the personal collections of research writers.

PROCEDURE: A nonprobability sample of scholarly articles was selected, and questionnaires sent to the authors to gather data about the references they cited and their personal collections. Telephone interviews were conducted with one-quarter of the respondents, nine personal collections were visited and counted and the location of one-quarter of the references were checked in various institutional libraries.

FINDINGS: Almost all of the respondents had personal collections. Size of the personal collection and age and experience were positively and significantly correlated. There was no relationship between the size of personal collection and: the discipline, the size of the nearby institutional library, the adequacy of the library, or the geographical area. As personal collections increased in size, more of the cited references used were found in them when the articles were written; scientists, however, did not follow this pattern. Fifty-nine percent of all references cited by the respondents came from the personal collections. Eighty-eight percent of the references which were located in the personal collection when cited were also located in the nearby institutional library. The location of a reference was found to be significantly affected by its type and date. Current books and articles which were cited were more likely to be found in the personal collection than in any other location.

650. Stanton, Vida Cummins (Ph.D., Indiana University, 1972). **ERIC newsletters: their content, uses and users.** 202p. Order no. 73-2757.

PURPOSE: The contents, uses and users of the newsletters published by 17 of the 19 clearinghouses operational in 1969 were investigated.
PROCEDURE: Newsletters from the 17 clearinghouses were examined. Questionnaires were sent to a sample of the recipients of the newsletters from 6 clearinghouses (from 36.6 to 70.2 percent of the questionnaires were returned).
FINDINGS: A great variation was revealed in the inclusion of content categories and in the extent of the treatment of the categories in the newsletters. Most respondents were interested in the content categories of the newsletters; they were frequently "scanned." Those categories which dealt with the ERIC system and individual clearinghouses were often disregarded. Many respondents kept files of the newsletters. The respondents' access to other ERIC products varied considerably. The availability of ERIC microfiche collections was quite limited. The respondents did not have extremely negative or positive reactions to the content categories or effectiveness of the clearinghouse newsletters. The respondents tended to be between 36 and 45 years old, have a doctorate and be in teaching or in administration.

651. Stewart, Henry Rotan, Jr. (Ph.D., Indiana University, 1972). **Staff participation in the management of college libraries and its relationship to library performance characteristics.** 163p. Order no. 72-30,451.
PURPOSE: The purpose of this study was to determine whether a relationship existed between the managerial style employed in the operation of college libraries and selected performance characteristics of those libraries.
PROCEDURE: Likert's Profile of Organizational Characteristics was chosen to measure the degree of staff participation. Data were collected at six colleges which were members of the Associated Colleges of the Midwest through interviews and questionnaires with faculty members, library directors and the professional library staff members. A library evaluation form was distributed to a sample of the student body at each college.
FINDINGS: No direct relationship between the degree of staff participation in the operation of the libraries and the performance characteristics was found to exist. Approximately 67 percent of the faculty members favored faculty status for librarians, 73 percent thought that librarians should serve on faculty committees and nearly 79 percent felt that students needed instruction in the use of the library. The most frequently available prerequisites for the library staff members were the same retirement plans as the faculty members, the same sick leave policies and the obligation of participating in formal campus activities. The least frequently available prerequisite was having the same salary scale as the faculty members. Half of the colleges provided their librarians with full faculty rank and responsibilities but did not provide nine month contracts.

652. Sullivan, Peggy A. (Ph.D., University of Chicago, 1972). **Carl H. Milam and the American Library Association.**

653. Suput, Ray Radoslav (Ph.D., Case Western Reserve University, 1972). **The contribution of E. I. Shamurin to Soviet librarianship.** 265p. Order no. 72-26,215.
PURPOSE: The dissertation investigated the contributions of Evgenii Ivanovich Shamurin to Soviet librarianship.

FINDINGS: Shamurin was one of the last great Soviet librarians. He barely fit into the Soviet conformist frame of reference. In the middle 1930's he had to renounce some of his views from the previous decade and in the second half of the 1940's he was subjected to severe ideological criticism which led to his "retirement." Never fully retired, he published in the second half of the 1950's landmark contributions to Soviet and world library literature. He fought for the establishment in Soviet librarianship of the concept of corporate author entries and the adoption of Anglo-American principles of cataloging. He dealt extensively with library classification in a monumental two-volume treatise. He was a true library scientist. He always sought to put the results of his investigations in a theoretical and historical frame of reference.

654. Thompson, Susan Otis (D.L.S., Columbia University, 1972). **Kelmscott influence on American book design.**

655. Tower, Jean DeBroske (Ph.D., University of Pittsburgh, 1972). **A study of changes in children's library services for selected Pittsburgh suburbs related to changes in their population for 1960 through 1970.** 212p. Order no. 73-1653.
PURPOSE: The study provides a critical examination of recent changes in library service for children offered by public and school libraries in a suburban area and evaluates the degree to which this library service has kept pace with the suburb's rapidly expanding population.
PROCEDURE: Data were collected through interviews with staff working with young children in 25 public and school libraries in the 12 school districts in the four areas of the Pittsburgh Standard Metropolitan Statistical Area used for the study.
FINDINGS: The calibre of children's library service improved markedly as population rose. In each element (resources, staff, and budgets) school libraries showed greater change than public libraries. This growth reflects in particular the Pennsylvania school program of mandating school library programs and the fact that Title II Elementary and Secondary Education Act funds were far larger than those available to public libraries through the Library Service and Construction Act Title I.

656. Weech, Terry (Ph.D., University of Illinois, 1972). **State governments as publishers: an analytic study of state government publications.** Order no. 73-17,470.

657. Williams, James (Ph.D., University of Pittsburgh, 1972). **An investigation of a model for a generalized information retrieval program.** Order no. 73-4097.

658. Wilson, Pauline Christine (Ph.D., University of Michigan, 1972). **Information-seeking activity of selected members of community groups seeking social change.** 212p. Order no. 73-6943.
PURPOSE: The problem of the study was to determine if public library service had had an input into presumably important community activities designed to facilitate social change.
PROCEDURE: Groups representing four change issues were included: racism, peace,

PROCEDURE (cont'd): women's rights and environmental problems. The reputational method was used to locate the groups. The method used to study the information seeking system was the critical incident technique. The chunk method was used to identify the information used. Two interviews and a self-administered questionnaire were used. The respondents were compared with the profile of the public library's public as depicted in *The Public Library Inquiry.*
FINDINGS: The respondents were similar to the public library's public, relatively homogeneous, organization joiners, opinion leaders and "communications elite." They used all sources of information, although audio-visual less than printed sources. They were library users. The information seeking system found to have been used in the most recent activities was wholly interpersonal and informal. No library was used in executing the activities studied. The same system was used by all; the system's three components were previous knowledge, organizational contact, and specialty publications owned by the respondents.
CONCLUSIONS: For a public library to have had an input to the social effort represented by these activities, the input would have had to have been to the individual as an individual; it would have had to have been as part of the individual's storehouse of previous knowledge.

659. Wolf, Edward G. (Ph.D., University of Pittsburgh, 1972). **An evaluation of the capability of the Pennsylvania Regional Resource Centers to provide for the availability and accessibility of Pennsylvania social science periodicals.** 231p. Order no. 72-30,777.
PURPOSE: The purposes of this investigation were to: (1) determine the extent to which libraries, organized into systems, collected local or indigenous periodicals for their clientele and made them available to others by means of union lists and (2) to ascertain and then test any discernable principles that could possibly contribute to the resolution and formation of an improved system for their bibliographical control.
PROCEDURE: The four Pennsylvania Regional Resource Centers and three comparable Pennsylvania libraries outside this system were surveyed; the data were collected by personally checking the libraries' performance against a bibliography composed of 442 titles chosen because of their relationship to contemporary developments in Pennsylvania.
FINDINGS: Two-thirds of the periodicals in the bibliography had a life span of 20 years or less. No single resource library and no system of resource libraries had available at least one copy of a complete run of each social science periodical. The incorporation of additional large resource libraries into the present statewide system would result in a far larger proportion of duplication than in extensive additions. More effective collections result when the assignment of responsibilities for securing of given periodicals is made on the basis of place of publication and location of the library rather than by subject interest of the center. No individual library reports its Pennsylvania social science periodical holdings completely and accurately in a union list. The use of regional union lists was substantially more productive than that of national union lists in locating the number of titles held.

660. Wright, Kieth Carter (D.L.S., Columbia University, 1972). **Computer-assisted analysis of a large corpus of current educational report vocabulary.** 526p. Order no. 72-28,114.
PURPOSE: This study of present-day educational research report vocabulary was

PURPOSE (cont'd): conducted in the context of the ongoing research in subject analysis and thesaurus construction and maintenance at Columbia University School of Library Science. It represents an effort to increase substantive information about the linguistic aspects of indexing.

PROCEDURE: The study examined the vocabulary of titles and abstracts from a stratified sample of 300 report resumes taken from the ERICTAPE version of *Research in Education* between November, 1966 and March, 1968. After the removal of function words like articles, pronouns, prepositions and conjunctions, 25,325 word tokens remained representing 4,887 unique word types. The frequency ranks of the sample were compared with the frequency ranks of the same word types found by Kucera and Francis, and with the frequency ranks of word samples from 23 of the ERIC clearinghouses.

FINDINGS: The general growth pattern of new word types added to the vocabulary followed the expected Zipf curve. However, high frequency rank patterns remained stable even when the number of words processed was doubled and proper nouns remained relatively stable in their rate of occurrence as increasing amounts of text were processed. Rank frequency comparisons among the word samples showed an expected similarity between the overall educational research sample and the general American English sample and an expected dissimilarity between the educational research sample and the word samples of the 12 clearinghouses. Words which occurred in the educational research sample 50 or more times were utilized as word pairs in a search of the 300 report resumes for word pair cooccurrences. The expected number of cooccurrences was not found. Word pairs which cooccurred five or more times were found also to be actual indexing terms utilized both in the *Thesaurus of ERIC Descriptors* and in *Education Index*.

RECOMMENDATIONS: The results of the study were used to make specific suggestions concerning the use of computer-assisted text processing techniques similar to those developed in the study as a means both of improving indexing performance and establishing a controlled indexing vocabulary in information center operations.

A STATISTICAL PROFILE OF
LIBRARY SCIENCE DISSERTATIONS
1925-1972

In order to give some perspective to the library science doctoral studies included in this bibliography, a quantitative profile of the dissertations was constructed using five characteristics: completion date, sponsoring school, type of degree received, methodology employed and sex of the recipient. Selected relationships between these characteristics were also investigated.

Completion date

In compiling this bibliography, 660 doctoral studies either accepted by library schools or related to library topics were listed. Annual dissertation production increased from one completed study in 1925 to 86 studies in 1972. In the 47 years covered in this compilation, an average of 14.04 dissertations were completed each year.

An examination of the distribution of listed dissertations revealed three distinct and increasingly active periods of production. Between 1925 and 1955 relatively few dissertations—138—were completed, an average of only 4.45 studies per year. During the next 14 years (1956-1969), total production of library science doctoral studies nearly tripled (303 dissertations) and average annual completion multiplied five-fold (21.64 dissertations). Similar proportional increases in total and average annual production can be found in the dissertations completed between 1970 and 1972. In only three years, 219 library science dissertations were produced, an average of 73 studies per year.

Sponsoring school

The dissertations included in this compilation were completed at 68 private and public institutions of higher learning in all parts of the country. Although a large number of universities were involved, three-fifths of the dissertations were written at only six schools: University of Chicago (16.35 percent), University of Michigan (12.15 percent), Columbia University (11.55 percent), University of Illinois (10.20 percent), Case Western Reserve University (5.40 percent) and Rutgers University (5.10 percent).

Initially, the University of Chicago was primarily responsible for dissertation production; of the 104 dissertations completed between 1925 and 1950 and listed in this bibliography, two-thirds of them were written at the University of Chicago. In recent years, however, the situation has changed. Since 1962, both Columbia (50 dissertations) and the University of Michigan (45 dissertations) have been responsible for twice the total number of studies written at the University of Chicago (22 dissertations).

Degree received

Over three-quarters (76.95 percent) of the doctorates included in this compilation were awarded Ph.D. degrees. The Ed.D. was the next most commonly earned degree (13.20 percent), followed by the D.L.S. degree (8.55 percent).

The Ph.D. has consistently predominated in the degrees earned by the doctorates; in every decade since 1930, the majority of students received Ph.D. degrees. During the 1950's, the smallest proportion of Ph.D.'s (61.38 percent) and the largest percentage of Ed.D.'s (34.70 percent) were earned. Prior to 1950, no D.L.S. degrees were received; since 1950, no more than 12 percent of the earned degrees in any decade were D.L.S. degrees.

Methodology employed

Each of the 660 dissertations was placed into one of seven research categories: citation analysis, experimental design, theory, operations research (systems analysis and all forms of information storage and retrieval), survey research (case studies, mailed questionnaires, interviews), historical analysis (including biography and bibliography), and other (including those dissertations for which insufficient information was available to determine methodology employed).

Of the research methodologies, theoretical (1.95 percent) and experimental design (4.03 percent) were almost never used. Operations research and citation analysis each showed up in approximately 10 percent of the dissertations. Historical analysis (30.00 percent) and survey research (44.25 percent) were employed in a total of three-quarters of the dissertations.

Definite trends in research methodology became apparent when the data were analyzed in 10-year periods (see Table 1). Citation analysis was used to some extent during the 1940's, but since then it has not been employed in more than one-tenth of the studies during any 10-year period.

TABLE 1

Percentage Distribution of
Research Methodology Employed by Date
1925-1972
N=660

Methodology	Date 1925-29	1930-39	1940-49	1950-59	1960-69	1970-72
Citation analysis	0.00	2.00	19.39	10.64	9.65	9.90
Operations research	0.00	3.33	0.00	2.50	6.65	16.72
Survey research	33.33	50.66	57.39	33.71	46.23	53.03
Historical analysis	66.67	25.60	23.32	48.15	33.70	14.26
All other categories	0.00	18.41	0.00	5.00	3.77	6.09

The historical method enjoyed considerable popularity between 1950 and 1959; nearly half of the dissertations employed this methodology. In recent years, however, proportionately fewer doctoral studies have used a historical approach. Between 1970 and 1973, only approximately 14 percent of the dissertations were historical studies.

Survey research proved to be the most consistently used methodology. Except for the 1950's, when historical analysis predominated, approximately one-half of the dissertations written in any decade employed this technique.

Only operations research showed a steady increase in usage, moving from 3.33 percent of those dissertations completed between 1930 and 1939 to 16.72 percent of the studies written during the first three years of the 1970's.

In chi-square analysis, a significant relationship was revealed, at the .05 probability level, between the degree received by the doctorate and the methodology employed in the dissertations. While over 80 percent of the Ed.D. doctoral studies were based on survey techniques, a little less than half of the D.L.S. and only one-third of the Ph.D. dissertations attempted this methodology. Approximately one-quarter of the Ph.D. and the D.L.S. dissertations each used historical analysis; this technique was found in less than 10 percent of the Ed.D. studies. Ph.D. dissertations had almost a monopoly over the employment of operation research techniques. Proportionately, D.L.S. studies used citation analysis procedures twice as often as Ph.D. papers and seven times as frequently as Ed.D. dissertations (see Table 2).

Sex of authors

While women constitute the large majority of practicing librarians, they make up only a minority of the authors considered in this study; 201 of the doctoral studies were written by women.

The number of library science dissertations written by women has increased steadily since 1925. During the first 31 years under study, only 41 dissertations were completed by females. Between 1956 and 1969, twice as many doctoral studies (80) were written by women. The production of female doctorates has so accelerated that in the first three years of the 1970's, the same number of dissertations were completed by women as in the preceding 14-year period.

While the number of theses in librarianship written by women has constantly increased, their proportion of total doctorates in this bibliography has remained constant. Chi-square analysis revealed that since 1925 no significant increase or decrease in the proportion of females to total doctorates occurred. On the average, less than one-third of the studies (31.15 percent) were completed by women in any given year.

Further analysis also showed that no significant differences existed, at the .05 probability level, between males and females and the type of degree they received; approximately the same proportion earned Ph.D. and Ed.D. degrees. Slightly more of the females (12 percent) received D.L.S. degrees than did the males (see Table 3).

Similarly, there was no statistical difference in the research methodologies employed by the two groups; males and females used research techniques with the same frequency. As Table 4 shows, neither sex was significantly more likely to employ any one method.

TABLE 2

**Percentage Distribution of
Research Methodology by Type of Degree
N=660**

Method	Ph.D.	D.L.S.	Ed.D.	Other	Row Total
Citation analysis					
column percent	9.50	15.75	2.26	0.00	
row percent	82.07	14.67	3.26	0.00	
total percent	7.50	1.35	0.30	0.00	9.15
Operations research					
column percent	10.07	1.75	3.39	25.00	
row percent	91.40	1.72	5.16	1.72	
total percent	7.95	0.15	0.45	0.15	8.70
Survey research					
column percent	36.86	47.25	82.49	25.00	
row percent	66.70	9.18	23.82	0.30	
total percent	29.10	4.05	10.95	0.15	44.25
Historical analysis					
column percent	33.25	29.05	0.04	0.00	
row percent	89.72	6.39	3.89	0.00	
total percent	26.25	2.55	1.20	0.00	30.00
All other categories					
column percent	10.32	6.20	11.82	50.00	
row percent	78.25	9.25	6.67	5.83	
total percent	6.75	0.45	0.30	0.40	7.90
Column total	76.95	8.55	13.20	1.30	100.00

X^2 = 74.16
df = 24
Significant at the .05 probability level

TABLE 3

**Percentage Distribution of
Sex by Type of Degree
N=660**

Sex	Ph.D.	D.L.S.	Ed.D.	Other	Row Total
Males					
column percent	69.35	56.00	71.19	100.00	
row percent	77.49	6.63	13.05	0.40	
total percent	55.35	4.80	9.45	0.30	70.90
Females					
column percent	28.12	43.75	28.25	0.00	
row percent	75.48	13.25	13.75	0.00	
total percent	21.60	3.75	3.75	0.00	29.10
Column total	76.95	8.55	13.20	1.30	100.00

X^2 = 5.14
df = 3
Insignificant at the .05 probability level

TABLE 4

Percentage Distribution of
Sex by Research Methodology
N=660

Method	Males	Females	Row Total
Citation analysis			
column percent	8.61	10.20	
row percent	67.20	32.80	
total percent	6.15	3.00	9.15
Operations research			
column percent	8.61	8.67	
row percent	60.70	31.30	
total percent	6.15	2.55	8.70
Survey research			
column percent	43.05	45.90	
row percent	69.29	30.42	
total percent	30.75	13.50	44.25
Historical analysis			
column percent	31.08	26.55	
row percent	73.75	25.37	
total percent	18.75	6.45	30.00
All other categories			
column percent	7.91	7.75	
row percent	69.02	31.08	
total percent	4.65	2.25	7.90
Column total	70.90	29.10	100.00

$X^2 = 4.82$
df $= 8$
Insignificant at the .05 probability level

Summary

A sharp increase in the number of library science related dissertations occurred during the last 12 years; more library science doctoral studies were completed during this period than during the preceeding 35 years of library science production.

When analyzing the dissertations by date, it was seen that the methodology employed and the schools attended changed significantly, while the sex of the recipient and the type of degree received remained constant. Initially, library science dissertations were produced primarily at the University of Chicago. Since the early 1960's, however, Columbia and the University of Michigan have become responsible for the largest number of studies listed in this compilation. Research methodology also underwent changes during the 1960's. Historical analysis, commonly applied before 1960, declined during this last decade. Operations research, on the other hand, experienced a steady increase in usage, particularly in the last 12 years. No change was noticed, however, in either the type of degree received or the sex of the recipient. Since 1925, the majority of doctorates have been awarded to male Ph.D.'s.

No relationship was found between sex and the type of degree earned or the research methodology employed. The proportion of males and females receiving Ph.D. (or other degrees) and using various research techniques was essentially the same.

A significant relationship was found, however, between the type of degree earned and the research methodology employed. Historical methods were principally used in Ph.D. and D.L.S. studies. Survey practices were employed predominantly in Ed.D. and D.L.S. dissertations. Citation analysis was used most frequently in D.L.S. papers and operations research was performed almost exclusively in Ph.D. dissertations.

Using the results of the quantitative analysis it is possible to develop a profile of library science dissertations included in this bibliography. The typical thesis was written for the Ph.D. degree in the last 12 years by a male using historical or survey research methods at one of six major universities in the United States.

AUTHOR INDEX

Numbers in the author and subject indexes refer to entry references, not page references.

Abbott, John Cushman, 154
Abrera, Josefa B., 442
Adams, A. Elwood, 12
Agli, James Joseph, 368
Akers, Susan Grey, 8
Aldrich, Frederic D., 111
Alford, John D., 122
Allen, Kenneth William, 443
Altman, Ellen O., 506
Alvarez, Robert Smyth, 34
Aman, Muhammad Muhammad, 369
Amick, Daniel James, 444
Amundson, Colleen C., 507
Anders, Mary Edna, 175
Anderson, Carolyn Joyce, 445
Anderson, James Doig, 446
Anderson, Le Moyne W., 447
Andrews, Charles Rolland, 343
Archer, Horace Richard, 123
Armstrong, Charles Wesley, 508
Artandi, Susan S., 256
Asheim, Lester Eugene, 92
Autio, Andrew William, 176
Avant, Julia King, 575
Axe, Fred Warren, 40
Axeen, Marina Esther, 344

Badr, Ahmad Aly, 257
Baillie, Gordon Stuart, 226
Baldwin, Ruth Marie, 130
Ballard, Robert Melvyn, 576
Barker, Dale Lockard, 321
Barnes, Eugene Burdette, Jr., 79
Barrilleaux, Louis E., 295
Bartel, Elaine Vetter, 296
Barth, Edward Walter, 509
Batchelor, Lillian L., 116
Bates, Marcia J., 577
Baughman, James Carroll, 510
Baumann, Charles Henry, 402
Beard, John Robert, 297

Beasley, Gary Fred, 578
Becker, Dale Eugene, 579
Bedsole, Danny Travis, 227
Bekkedal, Tekla, 580
Bendix, Dorothy, 298
Berelson, Bernard Reuben, 41
Berner, William Sherman, 448
Berry, June, 449
Bertram, Sheila Joan Kelley, 450
Bidlack, Russell Eugene, 124
Bingham, Jane Marie, 451
Bishop, Martha Dell, 258
Bishop, Olga Bernice, 245
Blazek, Ronald David, 511
Boaz, Martha Terosse, 131
Bobinski, George Sylvan, 322
Boll, John Jorg, 228
Bolvin, Boyd Micael, 452
Bommer, Michael Roger William, 512
Boney, Cecil De Witt, 9
Bonk, Wallace John, 139
Booth, Robert Edmond (Jt. author), 201
Bose, Aninaya, 453
Boshears, Onva K., Jr., 581
Boyce, Bert Roy, 582
Boyer, Calvin James, 583
Braden, Irene Andrea, 345
Branscomb, Lewis C., Jr., 125
Breen, Mary Frances, 126
Broderick, Dorothy M., 513
Brodman, Estelle, 117
Brough, Kenneth J., 93
Brown, Howard Washington, 42
Brown, Jovana J., 514
Brumbaugh, William Donald, 112
Brundin, Robert Eliot, 454
Bryson, Ernest Ronald, 455
Bullock, Penelope L., 515
Bundy, Mary Lee, 202
Bunge, Charles Albert, 346
Burke, John Emmett, 155

Burke, Redmond Ambrose, 83
Burt, Lesta Norris, 584
Burton, Hilary De Pace, 585
Bush, Nancy Wagoner, 516
Busha, Charles Henry, 517
Butler, Helen Louise, 35

Cagan, Carl, 456
Cairns, Sister Marie Laurine, 586
Cameron, James Slagle, 587
Cantrell, Clyde Hull, 203
Carnovsky, Leon, 10
Carpenter, Raymond Leonard, 370
Carrier, Esther Jane, 204
Carroll, Carmal Edward, 403
Carroll, Dewey Eugene, 323
Carter, Esther May, 518
Carter, Mary Duncan, 49
Caruso, Dorothy E. F., 404
Cazden, Robert Edgar, 299
Cecil, Henry LeRoy, 36
Chen, John Hsueh-Ming, 371
Childers, Thomas Allen, 457
Chou, Nelson Ling Sun, 588
Churchwell, Charles Darrett, 324
Clark, Harry, 405
Clarke, Robert Flanders, 259
Clayton, Howard, 300
Coburn, Louis, 229
Cohn, William Loewy, 589
Cole, John Young, Jr., 519
Collier, Francis Gilman, 105
Comaromi, John Phillip, 406
Condit, Lester David, 5
Connolly, Father Brendan, 132
Cookston, James Sanders, 520
Cooper, Michael David, 521
Coryell, Gladys A., 118
Coughlin, Violet Louise, 325
Covey, Alan Dale, 133
Cox, Carl Thomas, 372
Cox, Doris Walker, 373
Crawford, Susan Young, 458
Cross, Neal Miller, 59
Crowley, Terence, 374
Crum, Mark L., Jr., 459
Cyphert, Frederick R., 156

Daily, Jay Elwood, 157
Dain, Phyllis, 326
Dale, Doris Cruger, 375
Danton, Joseph Periam, 21
Davies, David William, 84
Davis, Charles Hargis, 407
Davis, Donald G., Jr., 590
Davis, Lattice Rucker, 522
Dawson, John Minto, 140
De Hart, Florence Elizabeth, 276
Deily, Robert Howard, 43
De Koster, Lester Ronald, 277
Deligdisch, Yekutiel, 523
de los Santos, Alfredo G., Jr., 301
Denis, Laurent-Germain, 460
Denum, Donald David, 206
De Pew, John, 524
Deringer, Dorothy Kiefer, 591
Dickinson, Donald Charles, 278
Ditzion, Sidney H., 69
Divett, Robert Thomas, 376
Donnelly, Sister Francis D., 525
Donohue, Joseph Chaminade, 461
Dorin, Alex, 207
Dorsett, Cora Matheny, 592
Dosa, Marta Leszlei, 526
Dougherty, Richard Martin, 260
Douglass, Robert Raymond, 158
Downen, Thomas William, 527
Drumm, Sister Robert Mary, 302
Ducat, Sister Mary Peter C., 208
Duncan, Elizabeth E., 528
Dunlap, Joseph R., 593
Dyke, James Parvin, 159

Eaton, Andrew Jackson, 63
Eaton, Thelma, 85
Ebrami, Hooshang, 462
Edgar, Neal Lowndes, 303
Edwards, Ralph, 529
Ekechukwu, Myriette R. G., 594
El-Benhawy, Mohamed Amin, 279
El-Erian, Tahany Said, 595
El-Hadi, Mohamed Mohamed, 280
El-Hagrasy, Saad Mohammed, 230
Elliott, Clark Albert, 463
Ellison, John William, 596

Ellsworth, Ralph Eugene, 28
El-Sheniti, El-Sayed Mahmoud, 209
Emerson, Wallace LeRoy, 13
Ennen, Robert Campion, 231
Erickson, Ernst Walfred, 177
Erickson, Wallace Edwin, 597
Evans, Charles Whitney, 408
Evans, Gayle Edward, 409
Evans, Roy Winston, 377
Evraiff, Lois L., 410

Farley, John J., 281
Farley, Richard Alan, 347
Fasick, Adele Mongan, 464
Feinberg, Hilda, 598
Fidoten, Robert E., 530
Field, Oliver Thoburn, 531
Floyd, Grace Hacel, 80
Foos, Donald Dale, 532
Forrest, Earl Arwin, Jr., 232
Fortin, Clifford Charles, 465
Foster, Jeannette Howard, 22
Fox, Ann Martha Sandberg, 599
Franklin, Hardy Rogers, 533
Fraser, James Howard, 600
Freudenthal, Juan Rothschild, 601
Friedlander, Janet Morgan, 466
Fussler, Herman Howe, 86

Galloway, Noel Louise, 304
Gambee, Budd Leslie, Jr., 261
Gardner, Richard Kent, 378
Garrison, Guy Grady, 210
Gelfand, Morris Arthur, 211
Gerulaitis, Leonardas Vytautas, 411
Gleason, Eliza Atkins, 37
Goheen, Patricia Ann, 534
Goldhor, Herbert, 50
Goodell, John Silas, 535
Gorchels, Clarence Clifford, 536
Gosnell, Charles Francis, 60
Goudeau, John Milford, 305
Grady, Marion B., 106
Graham, Robert James, 412
Greer, Roger C., 282
Gribbin, John Hawkins, 178

Grimm, Dorothy Fear, 134
Grotzinger, Laurel Ann, 283
Grunau, Allen R., 306
Grundt, Leonard, 307
Guise, Benjamin, 602

Haas, Joyce H., 537
Hagler, Ronald Albert, 233
Haith, Dorothy May, 603
Hall, Anna C., 379
Hall, James Herrick, 101
Hall, John Brown, 604
Halsey, Richard Sweeney, 605
Hamadeh, Muhammed Maher, 308
Hamdy, Mohamed, 606
Hamil, Betty Caldwell, 467
Hammitt, Frances Eleanor, 87
Hannigan, Jane Anne Thérèse, 413
Harkin, Willard Dwight, 538
Harlan, Robert Dale, 212
Harmer, William R., 193
Harmon, Elmer Glynn, Jr., 468
Harrar, Helen Joanne, 246
Harrington, Father John Henry, 141
Harris, Ira Whitney, 327
Harris, Jessica L., 414
Harris, Michael Hope, 539
Hartin, John Sykes, 142
Harvey, John Frederick, 94
Hassell, Horace Paul, Jr. 380
Hatchett, Harold William, 540
Hazelton, Robert Stafford, 607
Head, John William, 608
Heckman, Marlin Leroy, 469
Heflin, Harry B., 51
Heinritz, Fred John, 262
Held, Charles Holborn, 415
Helfert, Bryan Alois, 143
Helmkamp, John Gerhardt, 381
Hendricks, Donald Duane, 328
Henne, Frances, 95
Henry, Marion, 609
Herald, Homer Wayne, 160
Herdman, Margaret May, 44
Hertel, Robert Russell, 179
Hess, Edward Jorgen, 470
Heussman, John William, 471

Hewlett, LeRoy, 180
Hiatt, Peter, 263
Highfill, William Carl, 416
Hines, Theodore Christian, 234
Hintz, Carl, 113
Hirschstein, Bertha T., 14
Hoage, Alethia Annette Lewis, 235
Hodges, Theodora Long, 610
Hodgson, James Goodwin, 74
Holley, Edward Gailon, 236
Holzberlein, Deanne Bassler, 541
Hopp, Ralph Harvey, 144
Horrocks, Norman, 542
Hostrop, Richard Winfred, 329
Houser, Lloyd J., 382
Huang, George Wenhong, 417
Huang, Theodore Shih-shu, 348
Huq, A. M. Abdul, 472
Hyman, Richard, 543

Immroth, John Phillip, 473
Inada, Hide Ikehara, 349
Intrama, Navanitaya, 383
Isa, Zubaidah, 611

Jahoda, Gerald, 213
Jasenas, Michael, 350
Jay, Hilda Lease, 474
Jeffries, John Allison, 384
Jensen, Elmer A., 52
Jetter, Margaret Ann, 612
Joeckel, Carleton Bruns, 16
Johnson, Robert Kellogg, 161
Johnson, Robert Neil, 351
Jones, Milbrey Lunceford, 284
Jones, Norma Louise, 309
Jones, Robert Corwin, 181
Jones, Ruth Merrell, 119
Jones, Virginia Lacy, 70
Jordan, Alma Theodora, 330
Jussimm, Estelle, 475

Kaldor, Ivan L., 352
Kanasy, James Emery, 544
Kanner, Elliott Elisha, 613
Kaser, David Edwin, 145

Katz, William Armstrong, 310
Kaye, Bernard William, 127
Kelly, Grace Osgood, 17
Kemper, Robert Eugene, 353
Kennerly, Sarah Law, 162
Kephart, John Edgar, 214
Khurshid, Anis, 418
Kidder, Robert Wilson, 215
Kilpela, Raymond Earl Oliver, 237
Kim, Shoong Han, 285
King, Donald Ross, 545
King, Geraldine Beaty, 546
Kittle, Arthur Thomas, 238
Klempner, Irving Max, 354
Knapp, Patricia B., 163
Knox, Margaret Enid, 164
Koepp, Donald William, 331
Koos, Frank Hermann, 2
Kortendick, James J., 264
Kosa, Geza Attila, 614
Kraft, Donald Harris, 547
Kramer, Dorothy A., 615
Kramer, Sidney David, 31
Kraus, Joe Walker, 216
Krause, Carrol Francis, 355
Krikelas, James, 356
Kronick, David, 146
Krummel, Donald William, 182
Kruse, Paul, 183
Kruzas, Anthony Thomas, 217
Krzys, Richard Andrew, 311
Kunkle, Hannah Josephine, 419
Kunoff, Hugo, 616
Kwei, John Chi Ber, 6

Lamb, Gertrude Houser, 96
Lamb, Natalie, 548
Lancaster, John Herrold, 45
Lancour, Harold, 88
Lane, Margaret Elizabeth Bergman, 332
Lane, Robert Frederick, 38
Lange, Clifford E., 617
Lanier, Gene Daniel, 385
LaoSunthara, Maria Eugenia, 147
Larsen, John Christian, 357
Laugher, Charles Theodore, 265
Lawson, Abram Venable, 549

Leidner, Sister M. Dorothy, 32
Lemley, Dawson Enlo, 97
Leonard, August Orin, 107
Leonard, Lloyd Leo, 135
Lesser, Daniel, 266
Lewis, Benjamin Morgan, 148
Lickteig, Mary Jane, 550
Lieberman, Irving, 136
Liesener, James Will, 358
Lilley, Dorothy Brace, 420
Lilley, Oliver Linton, 194
Lincoln, Sister Mary Edmund, 184
Linder, LeRoy H., 185
Linderman, Winifred, 195
Lister, Winston Charles, 359
Litofsky, Barry, 421
Little, Evelyn Steel, 25
Little, Robert David, 618
Littleton, Isaac Thomas, 386
Lloyd, Helen Ditson, 387
Logson, Richard Henry, 53
Long, Lora Alcorn, 619
Longsdorf, Homer Howard, 551
Lowe, Mildred, 620
Lowell, Mildred Hawksworth, 165
Lowrie, Jean Elizabeth, 196
Lynch, Beverly P., 621

McAllister, Caryle, 552
McAnally, Arthur M., 108
McCabe, James Patrick, 388
McCarthy, Stephen Anthony, 46
McCarty, Pearl Sands, 98
McCauley, Elfrieda B., 553
McCoy, Ralph Edward, 149
McCreedy, Sister Mary Lucille, 267
McCrossan, John Anthony, 333
McCusker, Sister Mary Girolama, 268
McDiarmid, Errett Weir, Jr., 18
McEowen, James Royce, 422
McGaw, Howard Franklin, 102
McGowan, Frank, 622
McGrath, Daniel Francis, 334
McGuire, Alice Brooks, 186
Maciuszko, Jerzy Janusz, 247
Mack, Edna Ballard, 166
McLaughlin, Richard Clarke, 423
McMullen, Charles Haynes, 99

McNeal, Archie L., 109
MacVean, Donald Sidney, 187
MacWilliam, Mary Isabella, 150
Maddox, Lucy Jane, 188
Magrill, Rose Mary, 424
Maizell, Robert Edward, 167
Maloney, Ruth K., 623
Manheimer, Martha L., 425
Mann, Elizabeth B., 624
Marchant, Maurice Peterson, 476
Marino, Samuel Joseph, 248
Martin, Lowell Arthur, 71
Mason, Harold Jesse, 335
Massman, Virgil Frank, 477
Mathies, Mary Louise, 360
Mathis, Betty Ann, 625
Matta, Seoud Makram, 312
Maurstad, Betty L., 626
Maxwell, Margaret Nadine F., 554
May, Frank Curtis, 555
Meder, Marylouise D., 286
Mehit, George, 313
Melvin, Sister M. Constance, 249
Merritt, Leroy Charles, 54
Meyer, Donald Paul, 389
Meyer, Floyd Raymond, 168
Mick, Colin Kennedy, 627
Miller, Edward P., 628
Miller, Laurence Alan, 556
Miller, Robert Alexander, 26
Miller, Rosalind Elaine, 629
Miller, Russell Raymond, 557
Minster, Maud, 100
Moid, Abdul, 287
Moloney, Louis C., 478
Monagan, Roger Thomas, 103
Monroe, Margaret Ellen, 250
Montgomery, John Warwick, 251
Montgomery, Kenneth Leon, 630
Morris, Junius Hugh, 390
Morrison, Duncan Grant, 89
Morrison, Perry D., 239
Motley, Drucilla, 631
Muller, Robert Hans, 55
Munn, Robert Ferguson, 252
Murphy, Layton Barnes, 314
Murray, Daniel McClure, 632
Musser, Necia Ann, 361

Nagar, Murari Lal, 426
Nash, William Verlin, 288
Nelson, Jerold A., 558
Nemeyer, Carol A., 559
Niemi, Taisto John, 218

O'Connor, Joel S., 315
Oller, Anna Kathryn, 269
O'Loughlin, Sister Mary Anne J., 560
Olson, Lowell Ellis, 336
O'Neill, Edward True, 479
Orgren, Karl Franz, 561
Ozolins, Karlis Lotars, 633

Painter, Ann Forbes, 270
Palmer, Richard Phillips, 480
Pannu, Gurdial Singh, 562
Pao, Mirando Hau-Yung Lee, 634
Parker, John, 219
Parker, Johnny Robert, 253
Patrick, Ruth J., 635
Patterson, Charles, 563
Penalosa, Fernando, 151
Penland, Patrick Robert, 220
Peterson, Kenneth G., 391
Pettas, William Anthony, 636
Pfister, Frederick Charles, 481
Phelps, Rose Bernice, 61
Phillips, Thomas Edward, 62
Picache, Ursula, de Guzman, 427
Plante, Julian Gerard, 637
Plate, Kenneth Harry, 428
Pool, Jane, 638
Pope, Shirley Elspeth, 564
Poste, Leslie I., 189
Powell, Benjamin Edward, 75
Powers, Sister Mary Luella, 72
Prentice, Anne E., 639
Price, Samuel Timothy, 429
Purdy, George Flint, 27

Qasimi, Abdus Subbuh, 362
Qualls, LeRoy Lillard, 90

Radford, Neil Armstrong, 640
Ramer, James David, 430

Raney, Leon, 641
Rankin, Marie, 64
Ranz, James, 221
Reagan, Agnes Lytton, 169
Reed, Lulu Ruth, 29
Reeling, Patricia Ann, 431
Rettenmayer, John William, 432
Reynolds, Michael M., 289
Ribbens, Dennis Neil, 433
Richardson, Mary C., 33
Rickman, Jon Todd, 642
Robbins, Jane, 643
Robinson, Ruth W., 114
Rockwood, Ruth Humiston, 222
Rogers, Amos Robert, 290
Rood, Helen Martin, 19
Roper, Fred Wilburn, 565
Rosenberg, Victor, 482
Rosenlof, George W., 3
Rothstein, Samuel, 128
Rouse, Roscoe, Jr., 240
Rowe, Howard Marshall, 483
Roxas, Savina A., 484
Ruffin, Mary Beverley, 76
Rupert, Elizabeth Anastasia, 485

Sabine, Julia Elizabeth, 77
Saracevic, Tefko, 486
Schaefer, Barbara Kirsch, 644
Scherer, Henry Howard, 223
Schick, Frank Leopold, 170
Schlachter, Gail Ann, 566
Schmitz, Eugenia Evangeline, 363
Schnaitter, Allene Flora, 645
Schneider, Frank August, Sr., 392
Schulte-Albert, Hans Georg, 646
Schulzetenberge, Anthony C., 487
Scott, Edith, 488
Searcy, Herbert Lyman, 271
Shank, Russell, 337
Sharify, Nasser, 190
Sharma, Jagdish Saran, 129
Sharma, Om Prakasi, 489
Shaughnessy, Thomas William, 490
Shaw, Ralph Robert, 104
Shearer, Kenneth Decker, Jr., 434
Sheil, Marion Dorinda, 316
Shera, Jesse Hauk, 65

Sherrill, Laurance L., 647
Shipps, Harrold Southard, Jr., 435
Shirey, Donald Lamar, 491
Shoffner, Ralph Merl, 648
Shores, Louis, 20
Shukla, Champaklal P., 120
Simonton, Wesley Clark, 224
Sinclair, Dorothy Melville, 492
Sineath, Timothy Wayne, 493
Sisson, Silvanus Hull, 241
Skelley, Grant T., 393
Skipper, James Everett, 225
Slack, Kenneth Thurston, 291
Slamecka, Vladimir, 254
Slanker, Barbara Olsen, 494
Slavens, Thomas Paul, 317
Slote, Stanley James, 495
Smith, George Donald, 78
Smith, Jessie Carney, 292
Smith, Richard Daniel, 496
Smith, Sidney Butler, 81
Smith, Susan Seabury, 152
Snider, Felix Eugene, 318
Soper, Mary Ellen, 649
Spain, Frances Lander, 66
Sparks, Claud Glenn, 364
Spence, Paul Herbert, 436
Spencer, Gwladys, 39
Stallman, Esther Laverne, 56
Stanford, Edward Barrett, 57
Stanton, Vida Cummins, 650
Stenstrom, Ralph Hubert, 497
Stephenson, Harriet Shirley, 171
Sternberg, Virginia Ashworth, 567
Stevens, Norman Dennison, 242
Stevens, Rolland Elwell, 110
Stevenson, Henry Gordon, 498
Stewart, Henry Rotan, Jr., 651
Stewart, Nathaniel, 115
Stieg, Lewis Francis, 23
Stillman, Mary Elizabeth, 338
Stokes, Katharine Martin, 197
Stone, Elizabeth W., 394
Stone, John Paul, 73
Strohecker, Edwin Charles, 437
Studer, William Joseph, 395
Stueart, Robert D., 568
Subramanium, Jonnalagadda Bala, 365
Sullivan, Peggy A., 652

Suput, Ray Radoslav, 653
Svenonius, Elaine Fackenthal, 569
Swank, Raynard Coe, 67
Swarthout, Charlene R., 339
Swindler, Robert Earl, 7

Taam, Cheuk-Woon, 15
Tague, Jean Mary, 340
Tai, Tse-Chien, 1
Tate, Elizabeth Lamb, 272
Tauber, Maurice Falcolm, 47
Thomas, Bruce Wallace, 499
Thompson, Susan Otis, 654
Thomson, Sara Katharine, 366
Ting, Lee-Lsia Hsu, 438
Tolman, Lorraine Enid, 172
Totten, Herman Lavon, 341
Tower, Jean DeBroske, 655
Tracey, Warren, 191
Trueswell, Richard William, 293
Tsien, Tsuen-Hsuin, 173

Upton, Eleanor, 4

Vaillancourt, Pauline M., 396
Vance, Kenneth E., 255
Van Hoesen, Florence Ruth, 91
Van Male, John Edward, 58
Vann, Sarah Katherine, 198
Van Note, Roy Nelson, 243
Vavrek, Bernard F., 570
Veit, Fritz, 48
Verschoor, Irving Alton, 397
Vignone, Joseph A., 500
Villalon-Galdames, Alberto, 199
Voisard, Boyer Warren, 137
Voos, Henry, 319
Vorwerk, Richard James, 501

Waddle, Richard Leo, 367
Wadsworth, Harrison M., Jr. (Jt. author), 201
Walker, Richard Dean, 273
Walther, LaVern Arlene Doubt, 174
Ward, Pearl Lewis, 439

Warner, John Ellsworth, 274
Wasserman, Paul, 244
Watson, Lynn Allen, 571
Webb, David Allen, 275
Weech, Terry, 656
Weinberg, Paul Richard, 440
Weinstein, Frederic Daniel, 503
Weintraub, D. Kathryn, 503
Wellard, James Howard, 24
Wert, Lucille Mathena, 504
Whalen, Sister Mary Lucille, 320
Whitbeck, George Walter, 505
White, Marilyn Domas, 572
Whitten, Joseph Nathaniel, 192
Wilkinson, Billy Rayford, 573
Wilkinson, John Provost, 342
Williams, Dorothy Gwendolyn, 82
Williams, James, 657
Williams, Wiley Julian, 294
Williamson, William Landram, 200

Willis, H. Warren, 574
Willoughby, Edwin Elliott, 11
Wilson, Eugene Holt, 30
Wilson, Pauline Christine, 658
Winckler, Paul Albert, 398
Winger, Howard Woodrow, 121
Winkelman, John H., 399
Wolf, Edward G., 659
Woodworth, Mary Lorraine, 400
Wright, Herbert Curtis, 441
Wright, Kieth Carter, 660
Wu, Kwang Tsing, 68

Yenawine, Wayne Stewart, 138

Zachert, Martha Jane Koontz, 401
Zimmerman, Irene, 153

SUBJECT INDEX

Abstracting. *See* Indexing and abstracting.

Abstracts. *See* Indexes and abstracts.

Academic achievement
and job performance, 226, 576
and library use, 174, 273, 295, 318, 329, 538, 579
and personality characteristics, 30, 226, 239
and reading, 78

Academic librarians. *See* College and university librarians.

Academic libraries. *See* College and university libraries.

Academic status. *See* Faculty status.

Accessibility, 307, 327, 649

Accounting, cost. *See* Cost accounting.

Accreditation, 133, 211

Achievement. *See* Academic achievement.

Acquisitions
academic libraries, 26, 63, 123, 140
approval plans, 641
audio-visual materials, 285, 618
cooperative programs, 63, 595
cost accounting, 26
federal libraries, 531
job analysis, 26
non-western language materials, 595
political science materials, 63
public libraries, 63, 233, 285
research libraries, 140
school libraries, 618
See also Materials selection;
Technical processing.

Administration and organization
academic libraries, 88, 99, 140, 353, 404, 428, 436, 470, 476, 501, 505, 512
community college libraries, 181
library systems, 494
public libraries, 16, 34, 48, 61, 238, 288, 353, 392, 470, 494, 500

Administration and organization (cont'd)
religious libraries, 101, 264, 291
research libraries, 428
school libraries, 36, 100, 103, 118, 135, 353, 518
special libraries, 227
state libraries, 48, 353
theory, 48, 353, 436, 501
See also Decision making.

Administrators
academic libraries, 93, 99, 140, 347, 428, 470, 589
attitudes toward, 135, 370, 399
characteristics, 34, 93, 589
decision making, 604
Library of Congress, 519
public libraries, 34, 48, 220, 238, 288, 347, 353, 370, 399, 470, 494, 500
school libraries, 135, 518
special libraries, 347
their attitudes toward collective bargaining, 500
See also Principals.

Adolescents, 64, 95. *See also* Children; School students.

Adult education, 89, 174, 220, 250, 419, 532

Africa, 508

Aged, 613

Agricultural economics literature, 386. *See also* Economics literature; Social science literature.

ALA. *See* American Library Association.

Alabama, 75, 155, 532. *See also* Southern states.

American Book Publishing Record, 282

American history literature, 7. *See also* Social science literature.

American Home Missionary Society, 361

American Library Association
Bill of Rights, 517
cataloging rules, 272, 362, 599, 606
history, 188, 198, 652
See also Professional associations.
American literature, 142, 282. *See also* Humanities literature.
American Lutheran Church, 633
American Magazine, 82
Annuals, 232, 405. *See also* Serials.
Approval plans, 409, 641. *See also* Acquisitions; Materials selection.
Aquatic science literature, 315. *See also* Scientific literature.
Arabic language and literature, 280, 369
Architecture, 33, 88, 228, 402. *See also* Physical plant.
Archives, 189
Archivo Español de Arte, 224
Arkansas, 602. *See also* Southern states.
Arnold, Matthew, 302
Art. *See* Fine arts literature.
Art Bulletin, 224
Association of American Library Schools, 590. *See also* Professional associations.
Association of Research Libraries, 622
Atlantic Monthly, 46
Audio-visual materials, 106, 341, 377, 413, 631. *See also* Films; Filmstrips; Phonorecords; Slides; Tapes.
Australia, 542
Automatic indexing. *See* Computer produced indexing and abstracting.
Automation
academic libraries, 102, 293, 452, 614
catalog production, 480, 599
materials selection, 547, 614
research libraries, 452
selective dissemination of information, 293, 325, 395, 528, 623
A-V materials. *See* Audio-visual materials.

Ball State Teachers College, 106, 538
Baltimore (Maryland). Public Library. *See* Enoch Pratt Free Library.
Bancroft, Hubert Howe, 405
Baylor University. Library, 240
Bengali Muslim names, 472
Bibliographic control
humanities literature, 6, 67, 350, 626
national, 81, 125, 236, 254, 282, 601
scientific literature, 86, 117, 178, 257, 396, 544, 548, 634
social science literature, 199, 386, 659
Bibliographies
Calvin, John, 277
Gandhi, Mahatma, 129
government publications, 81, 245
Green, Timothy, 286
Holt, John, 314
Hughes, Langston, 278
humanities literature, 4, 25, 108, 142, 219, 334, 343, 350, 437
journals, 148, 153, 303, 437, 615
Muhammad, 308
poems, 343
reference books, 388
Rivington, James, 180
social science literature, 53, 199, 279, 386
translations, 25, 247, 349
Bibliography of Agriculture, 386
Bibliotherapy, 584
Billings, John Shaw, 326
Biological Abstracts, 544
Biology, 144, 309. *See also* Scientific literature.
Bishop, William Warner, 364
Blacks
discrimination in literature, 451, 513
information patterns, 533
library service, 37, 70
reading ability, 523
periodical press, 515
See also Ethnic literature; Minority groups.
Bollettino d'Arte, 224

Bond issues, 210, 448. *See also* Funding.
Book catalogs. *See* Catalogs.
Book lists, 21, 60, 197, 390, 434, 638
Book publishing. *See* Printing and publishing.
Book reviews. *See* Reviews.
Book selection. *See* Materials selection.
Book selling, 139, 151, 180, 405
Books for College Libraries, 390
Botanical literature, 113, 178. *See also* Scientific literature.
Botanists, 113, 158. *See also* Scientists.
Bray, Thomas, 265, 271
Brown University. Library, 20, 216
Browsing, 543
Brush and Pencil, 243
Budgets, 40, 43
Burlington Magazine, 224
Burma, 418
Business and industry, 217

CAI. *See* Computer Assisted Instruction.
California
academic libraries and librarians, 133, 366, 391, 446, 454, 470, 529, 559, 583
administrative practices, 470
community college libraries, 329, 434
cooperative library programs, 366, 483, 492
library collections, 40, 150, 446
library schools, 136
library standards, 150
library use, 408, 558
public libraries, 50, 61, 91, 408, 470, 484, 492
reference services, 61, 558
rural library service, 419
school libraries and librarians, 40, 59, 118, 150, 439, 555
State Department of Education, 555
state libraries, 419, 483

California. State Colleges. Libraries, 588
California. State Library, 419, 483
California. University. Libraries, 366, 391, 446, 529, 583
California. University. School of Librarianship, 136
Calvin, John, 277
Canada
academic libraries and librarians, 47, 342, 460
authors, 290
library collections, 6
library education, 562, 586
national libraries, 525
public libraries and librarians, 49, 233, 297, 325, 460
printing and publishing, 233, 245
subscription libraries, 49
Card catalogs. *See* Catalogs.
Career planning
librarians, 169, 222, 267, 424, 431, 460, 589
scientists, 463
See also Recruitment.
Carey and Lea (Publishers), 145
Carnegie, Andrew, 322
Carnegie Corporation, 322, 542, 640
Carnegie-Mellon University. Library, 524
Carter, Henry, 261
Case Western Reserve University, 340, 582
Cassel, Abraham Harley, 469
Cataloging
academic libraries, 26, 47, 67, 140, 280, 446, 535, 608
ALA code, 272, 362, 599
Anglo-American rules, 606
automated techniques, 480, 599
cooperative programs, 564
cost accounting, 26
educational perparation, 8, 76, 562
foreign language materials, 190, 280, 362, 369, 446
job analysis, 26
main entries, 272, 606
school libraries, 229
USSR, 653

Cataloging (cont'd)
  See also Classification; Dewey Decimal
    Classification; Library of Congress;
    Subject headings; Technical process-
    ing.
Catalogs
  academic libraries, 17, 262, 480, 498
  arrangement, 17, 356, 416, 446
  book catalogs, 221, 262
  computer produced, 480
  cost accounting, 262
  Germany, 498
  government libraries, 17
  public libraries, 312, 442
  union catalogs, 73, 659
  use, 262, 356, 416, 442, 480, 577,
    608
Catholic Church, 72, 83, 132, 388
Catholic University of America, 574
Censorship
  and the Catholic Church, 83, 132
  history, 149, 384
  in Eastern states, 149, 281
  in Midwestern public libraries, 517
  in school libraries, 281
Certification, 372. *See also* Education
  for librarianship.
Ceylon, 418
Chapbook, 615
Chemical Abstracts, 365, 528, 544
Chemical-Biological Coordination
  Center, 260, 528, 570
Chemical literature
  bibliographic control, 86, 178
  dissertations, 583
  document citation and retrieval,
    440, 450
  journals, 144, 321
  reference materials, 31, 213, 365,
    407, 528, 544, 615
  See also Scientific literature.
Chemisches Zentralblatt, 365
Chemists, 86, 167, 528, 623. *See
  also* Scientists.
Chicago. Public Library, 39, 63
Chicago. University, 10, 67, 78
Chicago. University. Library, 17, 93,
  99, 123
Chicanos. *See* Mexican Americans.

Children, 14, 464, 527, 594. *See also*
  Adolescents; School students.
Children's films, 266
Children's literature
  discrimination, 451, 513, 537
  fiction, 513, 537, 580
  in Southern states, 162
  journals, 162, 437
  library collections, 600
  linguistic analysis, 464
  printing and publishing, 162, 205,
    437
  reviews, 205, 304
  values instilled, 19, 162, 186, 451
Chile, 601. *See also* Latin America.
China, 15, 68, 173, 399, 438
Chinese language and literature, 6, 446,
  588
Church libraries, 101, 132, 291. *See
  also* Libraries; Theological libraries.
Church of Jesus Christ of Latter-Day
  Saints, 291
Cincinnati. Public Library, 91
Circulation
  academic libraries, 163, 293, 447,
    556
  automation, 293
  of fiction, 495
  of films, 285
  of theological literature, 471
  public libraries, 285, 495
  seminary libraries, 471
  See also Technical processing.
Civil service, 50
Classification
  academic libraries, 47, 67, 140
  American Mathematical Society, 644
  and retrieval, 421, 543, 587
  educational preparation, 8
  fiction, 22
  foreign language materials, 6, 369
  history of, 47, 406
  Library of Congress, 17, 47, 235,
    473, 563, 644
  mathematical literature, 644
  state libraries, 17
Clements, William L., 554
Collectaneas, 234
Collections. *See* Library collections.

Collective bargaining, 500, 566
College and university faculty
  attitudes toward librarians, 223, 514
  awareness of reference services, 558,
    573
  information gathering patterns, 209,
    558, 572
  in materials selection, 21, 409, 514
  research, 493
  selective dissemination of informa-
    tion, 395
  See also Community college faculty;
    Library school faculty.
College and university librarians
  attitudes toward, 93, 223, 449, 529
  California, 347
  Canada, 460
  career planning, 460, 499, 589
  Colorado, 181
  collective bargaining activities, 566
  Eastern states, 505
  faculty status, 223, 477, 505, 651
  in administration, 93, 347, 428,
    470, 476, 505, 589, 604, 651
  in reference services, 164, 558, 573
  in technical services, 535, 556
  job satisfaction, 476
  materials selection, 21, 409
  Midwestern states, 477, 566, 651
  on-the-job training, 164
  personal characteristics, 93, 164,
    239, 358, 420
  teaching function, 192, 529
  See also Community college
    librarians; Librarians.
College and university libraries
  accreditation, 133, 211
  administration and organization, 88,
    99, 140, 353, 428, 436, 470, 476,
    501, 505, 512, 604, 651
  attitudes toward, 443, 449
  automation, 102, 293, 452, 547, 614
  catalog use, 17, 262, 356, 480, 498,
    608
  collective bargaining activities, 566
  cooperative programs, 63, 289, 366,
    635
  cost accounting, 26, 359

College and university libraries
(cont'd)
  Eastern states, 20, 88, 93, 126, 195,
    345, 355, 366, 446, 505, 512,
    524, 573, 576, 583, 596
  film libraries, 112, 122, 351
  foreign countries, 47, 330, 342,
    369, 498, 508, 616
  funding, 640
  history, 20, 75, 93, 99, 138, 154,
    165, 195, 252, 391, 478, 554, 574
  in land grant colleges, 292, 371, 536
  in teachers' colleges, 3, 187
  job analysis, 26, 358, 529
  learning resources center, 187, 596
  library collections, 3, 53, 60, 63,
    197, 292, 355, 368, 479, 493,
    508, 524, 547
  library committees, 75, 223, 514
  library services, 74, 93, 192, 276,
    549
  library use, 18, 45, 74, 163, 209,
    293, 300, 327, 335, 480, 507,
    558, 645
  Midwestern states, 17, 63, 74, 93, 99,
    106, 123-24, 138, 154, 163, 165,
    177, 187, 197, 225, 293, 340,
    345, 358-59, 366, 380, 443, 477,
    479, 538, 573, 583, 596, 608, 614
  objectives, 163, 192, 616
  orientation programs, 126, 344,
    573
  physical plant, 33, 88, 228
  reference service, 128, 164, 512,
    549, 558, 573
  Rocky Mountain states, 122, 353,
    366, 447
  Southern states, 75, 177, 240, 252,
    289, 345, 366, 478, 583
  standards, 3, 133
  systems analysis, 380
  technical services, 21, 26, 47, 60,
    63, 67, 123, 140, 163, 197, 280,
    293, 359, 409, 447, 495, 535,
    547, 608, 614, 641
  Western states, 133, 327, 353, 366,
    391, 447, 470, 536, 558, 583
  See also Community college librar-
    ies; Libraries.

College and university students
attitudes toward librarianship, 424, 449
Colorado, 447
library use, 18, 29, 45, 163, 273, 327, 480, 507, 538, 645
Midwestern states, 10, 78, 106, 163, 273, 344, 366, 443, 507
reading interests, 10, 78
recruitment to librarianship, 169, 424, 431
See also Community college students; Library school students.
College of New Jersey. Library. *See* Princeton University. Library.
College of Rhode Island. Library. *See* Brown University. Library.
College of the Desert. Library, 329
College of William and Mary. *See* William and Mary College. Library.
Colombia, 311. *See also* Latin America.
Colorado, 181, 226, 353, 366, 447. *See also* Rocky Mountain states.
Colorado. State University. Library, 447
Colorado. University. Library, 353, 366
Columbia. University. Library, 20, 93, 199, 366, 446
Columbia. University. School of Library Service, 311
Communication patterns. *See* Information patterns.
Communications, 41, 510, 570
Community college faculty, 360, 367, 389, 443. *See also* College and university faculty.
Community college librarians, 13, 389. *See also* College and university librarians; Librarians.
Community college libraries
administration, 181
attitudes toward, 443
library collections, 301, 390
library use, 329, 367, 443
objectives, 13, 181, 389
Western states, 181, 301, 329, 367, 390, 454

Community college libraries (cont'd)
See also College and university libraries; Libraries; Vocational school libraries.
Community college students, 59, 329, 443. *See also* College and university students.
Community groups, 658
Company libraries. *See* Special libraries.
Compleat History of Europe, 232
Computer assisted instruction, 344, 404, 561, 631. *See also* Teaching techniques.
Computer produced indexing and abstracting
of Bengali Muslim names, 472
of books and reports, 256, 270
of scientific literature, 407, 456
techniques, 421, 598, 625, 642
See also Indexing and abstracting.
Conferences, 188
Connecticut, 20, 127, 216, 285-86, 548. *See also* New England states.
Continuing education. *See* Education for librarianship.
Cooperative programs
academic libraries, 289, 635
federal libraries, 567
film libraries, 122, 285
foreign countries, 325, 330
parochial libraries, 291
public libraries, 36, 56, 63, 118, 306, 483
school libraries, 36, 56, 118, 306
special libraries, 289, 567
technical services, 63, 246, 257, 564, 595
Western states, 92, 353, 483
West Virginia, 289
See also Interlibrary loan; Library systems.
Copying. *See* Photocopying.
Copyright, 104
Core list. *See* Book lists.
Cornell University. Library, 177, 345, 573

Cost accounting
  in academic libraries, 26, 359
  in school libraries, 40
  of document and information
    storage, 242, 359, 432, 521, 630
  of photocopying, 259
  of reference services, 260, 381
  of technical services, 26, 262, 319,
    328
Crane, Walter, 502
Creativity, 167
Critic, 46
Cumulative Book Index, 282
Current awareness. *See* Selective
  dissemination of information.
Curriculum developments, 137, 152,
  166, 196, 373, 487, 510, 548
Czechoslovakia Socialist Republic, 254

Dalhousi University. Library, 342
Damage, 189, 496
Dartmouth College. Library, 20
Data banks, 206
Data processing. *See* Automation.
Davis, Raymond Cazallis, 154
Deal, 46
Decision making
  academic and research libraries, 353,
    470, 476, 505, 512, 604, 651
  and performance ratings, 476
  government libraries, 353
  patron input, 604, 643
  public libraries, 331, 353, 470
  school libraries, 353
  theory, 201, 353, 512
  See also Administration and organi-
    zation.
Denver. University. School of
  Librarianship, 226
Departmental libraries. *See* Adminis-
  tration and organization.
Department of Commerce. *See* U.S.
  Department of Commerce.
Detroit Book Store, 139
Detroit Gazette, 139
Dewey Decimal Classification, 406.
  See also Classification; Library of
  Congress.

Directors. *See* Administrators.
Discrimination, 37, 70, 451, 513,
  537. *See also* Blacks; Mexican Amer-
  icans; Minority groups.
Dissertations, 67, 110, 259, 320, 583
Doctors. *See* Physicians.
Documentation and citation retrieval,
  206, 348, 450, 545, 630, 632. *See
  also* Inforation storage and retrieval.
Duquesne University. Library, 524

Earlham College, 573
East Germany. *See* Germany.
East Pakistan. *See* Pakistan.
Economics literature, 524. *See also*
  Agricultural economics literature;
  Social science literature.
Economists, 572
Education, adult. *See* Adult education.
Educational literature, 166, 206, 429,
  551, 578, 660. *See also* Social science
  literature.
Educational Resources Information
  Center. *See* ERIC.
Education for librarianship
  academic librarians, 13, 93, 164,
    358
  and job performance, 333, 346
  continuing education, 394, 427
  Eastern states, 33, 397, 485
  foreign countries, 1, 311, 378, 418,
    484, 562
  history, 1, 198, 283, 324, 398, 403,
    410, 484
  information specialists, 420
  library technicians, 415, 592
  medical librarians, 565
  Midwestern states, 546, 561-62
  night courses, 115
  objectives, 379
  public librarians, 346, 379, 397
  requirements, 159, 222, 226
  school librarians, 13, 51, 62, 255,
    372, 410, 485, 504, 597
  southern states, 275, 372, 516
  standards, 418
  teaching techniques, 8, 76, 91, 136,
    164, 346, 516, 546, 561-62, 631

Education for librarianship (cont'd)
undergraduate education, 401, 410
See also Library schools; Library
school students; On-the-job train-
ing; Work-study.
Elementary and Secondary Education
Act of 1965, 412, 439, 555, 571.
See also Library legislation.
Eliot, George, 302
Elziviers, 84
Encyclopaedia Britannica, 183
Encyclopedias, 183, 646
Engineering Index, Inc., 530
England, 4, 24, 79, 113, 121, 185,
212, 219. *See also* Europe.
English literature, 67, 194. *See also*
Humanities literature.
Engraving, 182, 334. *See also*
Printing and publishing.
Enoch Pratt Free Library, 238
ERIC, 551, 578, 650
Escuela Interamericana de
Bibliotecología, 311
Ethnic literature, 14, 278, 523,
647. *See also* Humanities literature.
Europe, 1, 79, 84, 141, 189, 323.
See also names of specific countries.
Evans, Charles, 236
Executives. *See* Administrators.
Experience. *See* Work experience.

Facilities. *See* Physical plant.
Faculty. *See* College and university
faculty; Community college faculty;
Library school faculty; School
faculty.
Faculty status, 223, 255, 477, 505,
651
Farmers, 74, 109, 202
Farsi language and literature, 462
Federal libraries, 17, 353, 435, 531,
567. *See also* Library of Congress;
NASA Regional Dissemination
Centers; U.S. Air Force libraries;
U.S. Army libraries.
Fiction
and their films, 92
attitudes toward, 55, 204

Fiction (cont'd)
best sellers, 94, 131
book reviews, 131, 204-205
children's literature, 64, 513, 537,
580
in journals, 55
in libraries, 22, 204, 495
in paperbacks, 179
set in Southern states, 142
short stories, 247
File structure, 376, 432, 545, 632
Film libraries, 112, 122, 285, 351. *See
also* Libraries.
Films, 92, 106, 266, 285, 540. *See also*
Audio-visual materials.
Filmstrips, 603. *See also* Audio-visual
materials.
Fine arts literature, 224, 243 626. *See
also* Humanities literature.
Finnish Lutheran Book Concern,
218
Florida
administrators, 589
cooperative programs, 366
libraries, 177, 321, 366, 532, 624
library schools, 222, 516
reading interests, 98, 527
See also Southern states.
Florida. State University. Library
School, 222, 516
Florida. University. Library, 177, 366
Fowle, Daniel, 215
France, 79, 113, 185, 251, 261, 378.
See also Europe.
Frank Leslie's Illustrated Newspaper,
261
Fullerton (California). Junior College.
Library, 454
Funding
academic libraries, 640
Australia, 542
Illinois, 90, 448
public libraries, 90, 210, 322, 448,
639
school libraries, 2, 40, 80, 97, 412,
439, 618
Western states, 80, 210
See also Library legislation.

Gandhi, Mahatma, 129
Gazette des Beaux-Arts, 224
Genetics literature, 472. *See also*
Scientific literature.
Geological literature, 147, 178. *See
also* Scientific literature.
Geologists, 147. *See also* Scientists.
Georgia, 75, 155, 177, 373, 467, 532.
See also Southern states.
Georgia. University. Library, 177
Germany, 113, 185, 189, 254, 299,
498, 526, 616. *See also* Europe.
Gerontology literature, 613. *See also*
Scientific literature; Social science
literature.
Gill, Alexander, 130
Giunti, 636
Government documents. *See* Govern-
ment publications.
Government libraries. *See* Federal
libraries.
Government publications
bibliographies, 81, 354
foreign countries, 120, 245
library collections, 620
printing and publishing, 54, 120,
245, 294, 310, 656
G.P.A. *See* Academic achievement.
Grade point average. *See* Academic
achievement.
Gradus Ad Parnassum, 231
Great Britain. *See* England.
Green, Timothy, III, 286
Guidance. *See* Reading guidance.
Handbook of Chemistry, 615
Handicapped, 103
Hanson, J. C. M., 488
Harvard University. Library, 20,
93, 216, 345, 366, 524, 573
Hawaii. University. Library, 327
Hawthorne, Nathaniel, 433
Health information centers. *See*
Information centers; Medical
libraries.
Herbert S. Stone and Co., 31
Hiring, 50, 499
Historical Manuscripts Commission
of Great Britain, 4

Historical materials, 4, 108, 343. *See
also* Humanities; Social science
literature.
*History of the Reign of Queen Anne,
Digested into Annuals*, 232
Holland, 79
Holt, John, 314
Homer, 25
Hughes, Langston, 278
Humanities literature, 153. *See also*
names of specific disciplines.
H. W. Wilson Co., 414

Idaho, 417. *See also* Midwestern
states.
ILL. *See* Interlibrary loan.
Illinois
academic libraries and librarians, 17,
63, 74, 93, 99, 123, 138, 163, 187,
273, 356, 366, 443
funding, 90, 448
library education, 30, 159
library legislation, 87
library use, 273, 443, 511
public libraries and librarians, 27,
34, 63, 74, 90, 288, 436, 448,
497, 517
reading interests, 10, 28, 74, 78,
95, 202
rural library service, 74, 202
school libraries and librarians, 87,
504, 511
students, 10, 78, 95, 163, 258, 273,
344, 366, 443, 511. *See also*
Midwestern states.
Illinois. University. Library, 138,
273, 356, 366
Illinois. University. Library School,
30, 159
Illustrations, 261, 334, 451, 475, 502
IMC. *See* Instructional materials
centers.
Incunabula. *See* Printing and publishing.
Index Medicus, 544
Indexes and abstracts
agricultural economics literature, 386

Indexes and abstracts (cont'd)
historical literature, 4, 343
scientific and mathematical literature,
178, 354, 365, 528, 544, 548
Indexing and abstracting
agricultural economics literature, 386
foreign language materials, 462, 472
government documents, 270, 354
in the U.S.S.R., 354
scientific literature, 213, 315, 348,
407, 421, 425, 491, 530, 587,
610
techniques, 206, 213, 348, 425,
462, 473, 482, 552, 598. *See also*
Computer produced indexing and
abstracting.
Indexing, automatic. *See* Computer
produced indexing and abstracting.
Indexing, computer produced. *See*
Computer produced indexing and
abstracting.
Indexing, machine. *See* Computer
produced indexing and abstracting.
India, 120, 418, 426, 489
Indiana
academic libraries and librarians,
74, 106, 165, 177, 187, 345,
359, 380, 479, 538, 573, 614
automation, 614
censorship, 517
library collections, 27
library education, 562
library legislation, 174, 187, 237
private libraries, 539
public libraries and librarians, 27,
34, 74, 174, 517, 539
reading interests, 74
rural library service, 74, 174
school libraries and librarians,
7, 187
See also Midwestern states.
Indiana. University. Library, 165,
177, 345, 614
Indonesia, 611
Information centers, 260, 354, 381,
420, 530, 567. *See also* Libraries.
Information flow. *See* Information
patterns.

Information patterns
and creativity, 167
Blacks, 533
college students, 507
community groups, 658
farmers, 202
in Europe, 74, 113
in New York, 533
physicians, 466, 627
scholars, 167, 224, 383, 572, 625
scientists, 113, 147, 167, 444,
458, 528
See also Library use.
Information science, 461, 486. *See
also* Librarianship.
Information services. *See* Reference
services.
Information specialists, 420. *See
also* Librarians.
Information storage and retrieval
academic libraries, 340
computer aided instruction, 404
cooperative programs, 246
cost accounting, 242, 359, 432,
521, 630
file structure, 432, 545
for educational literature, 53, 429,
578
for junior college faculty, 625
for scientific and medical literature, 440, 456
medical libraries, 376
personal libraries, 422
simulation models, 521, 657
techniques, 234, 340, 608
See also Documentation citation and
retrieval.
Inmates. *See* Prison inmates.
Inscriptions, 173
Institutes. *See* Education for librarianship.
Instructional materials centers
acquisitions, 618
and learning, 26, 538
attitudes toward, 427, 541
Eastern states, 509, 522, 571
Michigan, 412
personnel, 427, 597, 612
role, 385, 427

Instructional materials centers (cont'd)
Southern states, 385, 624
standards, 522, 541
See also School libraries.
Instructors. *See* College and university faculty; Community college faculty; Library school faculty; School faculty.
Intellectual climate, 46, 79
Intellectual freedom. *See* Censorship.
Interlibrary loan, 125, 366, 506, 567. *See also* Cooperative programs.
Iowa, 1, 27, 135, 187, 268, 566. *See also* Midwestern states.
Iowa. State University. Library School, 1
Iranian language and literature, 190, 462
Italy, 411, 484. *See also* Europe.

Jacob, Louis, 251
Jahburch über del Forschritte der Mathematik, 548
Japanese language and literature, 349
Jesuits, 132
Job analysis, 26, 319, 358, 528
Job evaluation. *See* Job performance.
Job experience. *See* Work experience.
Job performance, 226, 346, 476, 576
Job satisfaction, 465, 476
John Crerar Library, 63
Johnson, Samuel, 302
Jordan, 369
Jordan. University. Library, 369
Journal of the American Chemical Society, 86
Journals
effect on public opinion, 41
for children, 162, 437
history of, 146, 148, 303
humanities literature, 55, 224, 243, 471
in academic libraries, 479, 547
in foreign countries, 153, 321, 323
mathematical and scientific literature, 86, 113, 144, 146-47, 321, 528, 548
photocopying, 259

Journals (cont'd)
printing and publishing, 146, 148, 162, 205, 248, 259, 323, 393, 437, 515
selection, 153, 547
social science literature, 82, 153, 166, 659
use of, 113, 444, 479, 528
See also Serials.
Julian Street Library, 390
Junior College Library Collection, 390
Junior colleges. *See* Community college faculty; Community college librarians; Community college libraries; Community college students; Vocational school libraries.

Kansas, 306, 566. *See also* Midwestern states.
Kelmscott Press, 593, 654
Kentucky, 155, 532. *See also* Southern states.
Knight Errant, 502
Knox College. Library, 163

Labor unions, 298, 566
Ladies Home Journal, 55
Lange, Norbert, 615
Lanier, Sidney, 433
Latin America, 153, 199. *See also* names of specific countries.
Laws. *See* Library legislation.
Learning, 106, 258, 377, 534, 579
Learning resources centers, 596
Legislation. *See* Library legislation.
Leibniz, Gottfried W. Von, 646
Leyh, Georg, 526
Liberty, 55
Librarians, 169, 222, 226, 267, 274, 394, 431. *See also* College and university librarians; Community college librarians; Public librarians; School librarians; Special librarians; names of specific librarians.
Librarianship
and politics, 526

Librarianship (cont'd)
attitudes toward, 424, 449
foreign countries, 526, 653
history, 188, 403, 560
leaders, 125, 198, 200, 272, 283, 364, 398, 488, 526, 652
research needs, 400
theory, 455, 526, 613
See also Information science.
Libraries, 15, 68, 132, 189, 579. *See also* Church libraries; College and university libraries; Community college libraries; Federal libraries; Film libraries; Information centers; Medical libraries; National libraries; Parochial libraries; Private libraries; Public libraries; Regional libraries; School libraries; Special libraries; State libraries; Subscription libraries; Theological libraries; Vocational school libraries; U.S. Air Force libraries; U.S. Army libraries; names of specific libraries.
Library collections
academic and research libraries, 3, 53, 60, 63, 93, 110, 197, 216, 292, 301, 368, 390, 479, 493, 508, 524
Africa, 508
duplication, 63
Eastern states, 93, 524
federal libraries, 435
foreign language materials, 6, 280, 287
literary materials, 204, 495, 600
Middle Atlantic states, 52, 216, 506
Midwestern states, 52, 63, 93, 268, 309, 363, 479
obsolescence, 60
public libraries, 27-28, 63, 204, 495, 524, 659
school collections, 7, 40, 42, 51, 97, 150, 268, 309, 332, 355, 363, 506, 537, 602, 638
scientific materials, 309, 363, 638
social science materials, 7, 63, 368, 524, 551, 659
Southern states, 51, 602

Library collections (cont'd)
standards, 150, 332
subscription libraries, 114
theological libraries, 317
Western states, 40, 150, 301, 332, 390
See also Acquisitions; Materials selection; Weeding.
Library college, 163
Library Company of Philadelphia, 134
Library extension programs, 48, 57. *See also* Rural library service.
Library instruction. *See* Library orientation programs.
Library legislation
history, 87, 111
Midwestern states, 87, 111, 174, 237
public libraries, 174, 191, 237
school libraries, 2, 87, 111, 412, 439, 555, 571
See also Elementary and Secondary Education Act of 1965; National Defense Education Act; P.L. 480.
Library networks. *See* Library systems.
Library non-use. *See* Non-users.
Library of Congress
administration, 519
classification scheme, 17, 47, 235, 473, 563, 644
history, 519
MARC II tapes, 395, 614
subject headings, 17, 157, 194, 282, 414, 473, 563
See also Federal libraries; National libraries.
Library orientation programs, 126, 156, 344, 377, 573
Library resources. *See* Library collections.
Library school faculty, 459. *See also* Faculty.
Library schools
admissions, 586
California, 136
foreign countries, 1, 311, 418, 484, 586
history, 1, 283

Library schools (cont'd)
Midwestern states, 30, 159, 576
New York, 33, 115
physical plant, 33
Southern states, 222, 372, 516
See also Education for librarianship;
names of specific library schools.
Library school students
academic achievement, 30, 576
attitudes, 424, 516, 546
Canada, 562
Midwestern states, 30, 344, 431, 546,
561-62
personal characteristics, 30, 158
recruitment, 169, 431
Southern states, 222
See also Education for librarianship.
Library services
academic libraries, 74, 93, 192, 276,
549
and grade point average, 174, 273
discriminatory practices, 37, 70
Eastern states, 93
federal libraries, 435
in library systems, 494
public libraries, 107, 263, 382, 619
school libraries, 36, 52, 80, 97, 100,
176, 241, 427, 609
Southern states, 253, 609
See also names of specific services.
Library services, rural. *See* Rural
library services.
Library skills, 230
Library systems
administration, 494
foreign countries, 49, 325, 330
history, 492
library services, 494
Midwestern states, 492, 497
Pennsylvania, 659
public libraries, 49, 90, 307, 325, 483,
494, 497, 659
school libraries, 506
Western states, 483, 492
See also Cooperative programs.
Library technical assistants, 415, 592
Library technicians. *See* Library tech-
nical assistants

Library use
academic libraries, 45, 48, 74, 209,
293, 300, 327, 329, 335, 367, 443,
463, 480, 507, 558, 645
Blacks, 533
children and students, 12, 18, 45,
208, 230, 273, 295, 329, 443, 507,
538, 594, 645
Eastern states, 156, 490, 533
factors relating to use, 29, 174, 273,
295, 318, 329, 408, 511, 529, 538,
575
farmers, 74
labor unions, 298
measurement, 18
medical libraries, 466
Midwestern states, 58, 74, 163, 208,
273, 443, 480, 507, 511, 645
physicians, 466
public libraries, 14, 28, 89, 263, 284,
298, 382, 408, 459, 490, 594, 619,
658
school libraries, 12, 29, 58-59, 156,
208, 295-96, 474, 481, 511, 579,
594
Southern states, 575
state libraries, 58, 171
Western states, 329, 408-409, 447,
558
women, 553
See also Information patterns; Non-
users.
Linguistic analysis, 464, 503
List of Books for College Libraries,
21, 60
*List of Books for Junior College
Libraries*, 60
Literature searches. *See* Reference
services.
Los Angeles. Public Library, 50, 61,
91
Louisiana, 75, 155, 171, 305, 575.
See also Southern states.
Louisiana. State Library, 171, 575
Love Story, 55
L.T.A. *See* Library Technical Assis-
tants.
Lubetzky, Seymour, 272
Lutheran Church, 218, 633

Macdonald, Angus Snead, 402
Machine indexing. *See* Computer produced indexing and abstracting.
Magazines. *See* Journals.
Management. *See* Administration and
organization.
Management, participative. *See* Participative management.
Managers. *See* Administrators.
Manuscripts, 4, 23, 141, 637
MARC II. *See* Library of Congress.
Maryland, 84, 238, 509
Massachusetts
academic libraries, 20, 93, 216, 345,
366, 524, 573
censorship, 149
interlibrary loan, 366
public libraries, 61, 91, 307
reference services, 61, 91
state libraries, 17
Massachusetts. State Library, 17
Materials selection
academic libraries, 21, 197, 377,
547, 614, 641
community college libraries, 301
educational preparation, 333
journals, 153, 547
public libraries, 24, 233, 333, 434
school libraries, 119, 339, 638
social science materials, 53, 63, 108
state libraries, 17
techniques, 21, 63, 304, 377, 547,
614, 641
theory, 24, 339
translations, 25
See also Acquisitions; Book lists;
Library collections.
Mathematical Reviews, 548
Mathematics literature, 144, 296, 363,
511, 548, 644. *See also* Scientific
literature.
Mechanization. *See* Automation.
Media. *See* Audio-visual materials.
Media centers. *See* Instructional
materials centers.
Medical librarians, 376, 565. *See also*
Librarians.
Medical libraries, 466. *See also*
Libraries.

Medical literature, 117, 299, 396,
544, 583, 634. *See also* Scientific
literature.
Memory, 468
Mercantilism, 219
Mexican Americans, 523. *See also*
Minority groups.
Mexico, 151. *See also* Latin America.
Michigan
academic libraries and librarians, 124,
154, 187, 197, 358, 389, 477, 573
card catalogs, 480
censorship, 517
faculty status, 477
library collections, 27, 309, 363
library legislations, 237
library schools, 561, 576
library users, 480
printing and publishing, 139, 214,
294
public libraries and librarians, 27,
34, 50, 220, 434, 517
school libraries and librarians, 255,
309, 363, 412, 481
state libraries, 294
See also Midwestern states.
Michigan. State Library, 357
Michigan. University. Department of
Library Science, 576
Michigan. University. Library, 124,
154, 345, 358, 573
Microforms, 559
Middle managers. *See* Administrators.
Midwestern states, 27, 71, 208, 651.
See also names of specific states.
Milam, Carl H., 652
Milton, John, 130
Minneapolis. Public Library, 184, 193
Minnesota
academic libraries and librarians,
187, 507, 566, 596
collective bargaining activities, 566
faculty status, 477
library collections, 27
library school students, 546
library use, 507
public libraries and librarians, 27,
34, 184, 193

Minnesota (cont'd)
school libraries and librarians,
336, 487
See also Midwestern states.
Minnesota. University. Library School,
546
Minority groups, 451, 523, 537, 647.
See also Blacks; Discrimination;
Ethnic literature.
Mississippi, 75, 155, 532, 619. *See
also* Southern states.
Missouri, 28, 52, 61, 103, 645
Missouri. University. Library, 645
*Monthly Catalog of United States
Government Publications*, 81
Mormons. *See* Church of Jesus Christ
of Latter-Day Saints.
Morris, William, 593
Motion pictures. *See* Films.
Muhammad the Prophet, 308
Music, 182, 563, 605. *See also* Fine
arts; Humanities literature.

N.A.S.A. Regional Dissemination
Centers, 381
N.A.S.A. *Thesaurus*, 425
Nation, 46
National bibliographies. *See*
Bibliographies.
National Defense Education Act, 309,
387, 427. *See also* Library legislation.
National Documentation Center, 354
National libraries, 15, 68, 132, 369,
399. *See also* Libraries; Library of
Congress.
National Research Council, 260
National Space and Aeronautics Admin-
istration. *See* N.A.S.A. Regional
Dissemination Centers; N.A.S.A.
Thesaurus.
National Union Catalog, 125, 282
N.D.E.A. *See* National Defense
Education Act.
Nebraska, 168, 176, 351, 355, 566.
See also Midwestern states.
Nebraska. University. Extension
Division. Film Library, 351
Negroes. *See* Blacks.

Networks. *See* Library systems.
Newark. Public Library, 77
Newberry Library, 63
New England states, 69, 172, 228,
434, 553. *See also* names of specific
states.
New Hampshire, 20, 177, 215. *See
also* New England states.
New Hampshire. University. Library,
177
New Jersey
academic libraries and librarians,
446, 505
faculty status, 505
film libraries, 285
library collections, 506
library use, 490
interlibrary loan, 506
public libraries and librarians, 77,
202, 285, 374, 382, 457, 490
reference services, 374, 457
school libraries and librarians, 62,
127, 506
New Jersey. Library Film Circuit,
285
New Jersey. State University. *See*
Rutgers. State University of New
Jersey. Library.
New Mexico, 376
Newsletters, 650. *See also* Journals;
Newspapers; Serials.
Newspapers, 148, 214, 248, 261,
314, 323. *See also* Newsletters;
Serials.
New York
academic libraries, 20, 88, 93, 126,
177, 195, 345, 366, 446, 505,
573, 596
education for librarianship, 33, 115,
397
faculty status, 505
interlibrary loan, 366
library use, 490
parochial libraries, 32
public libraries and librarians, 14,
63, 107, 312, 326, 397, 490, 533
reading interests, 32, 207, 229
reference service, 573
school librarians, 127, 152

New York. Public Library, 107
New York. State University, Buffalo.
Library, 126
New York. State University, Geneseo.
Library School, 33
Non-users, 208, 408, 594, 658. *See
also* Library use.
North American Review, 46
North Carolina, 51, 75, 155, 253, 373,
385. *See also* Southern states.
North Dakota, 566. *See also* Mid-
western states.
Northwestern University. Library, 63
Notre Dame. University. Library, 177
Novels. *See* Fiction.
Nuclear Science Abstracts, 354, 365

Oakland (California). Public Library,
50
Oceanside (California). Public
Library, 408
Office of Technical Services. *See*
U.S. Office of Technical Services.
Ohio
academic libraries, 225, 340, 366, 582
censorship, 517
interlibrary loan, 366
library collections, 27
library legislation, 111, 237
library school students, 431
library systems, 492
public libraries and librarians, 27, 34,
91, 313, 492
school libraries and librarians, 111,
316
See also Midwestern states.
Ohio. State University. Library, 225,
366
O.J.T. *See* On-the-job training.
Oklahoma, 387. *See also* Southern
states.
On-the-job training, 164, 198, 346.
See also Education for librarianship;
Work study.
Oregon, 50, 332, 353, 445
Oregon. State Library, 353
Organization. *See* Administration and
organization.
Overland Monthly, 393

Pakistan, 418, 472
PAL. *See* Personal Automated
Library.
Paleography, 23, 352. *See also*
Manuscripts.
Panjabi language and literature, 362
Paper, 496
Paperbacks, 170, 179
Parochial libraries, 32, 208, 271,
291. *See also* Libraries; School
libraries.
Participative management, 470, 476.
See also Administration and organization; Decision making.
Patrons. *See* Library use.
Pennsylvania
academic libraries and librarians,
20, 504, 512, 524, 583
collective bargaining, 500
faculty status, 505
library education, 485
library standards, 116
library systems, 659
library use, 156, 490
printing and publishing, 145, 182
public libraries and librarians, 490,
500, 655, 659
school libraries and librarians, 100,
116, 156, 249, 485, 571, 579,
655
subscription libraries, 114, 134
union catalogs, 659
Pennsylvania. Regional Resource
Centers, 659
Pennsylvania. State University, 583
Pennsylvania. University. Library,
20, 512
Performance ratings. *See* Job
performance.
Periodicals. *See* Journals.
Persian language and literature. *See*
Iranian language and literature.
Personal Automated Library, 422.
See also Libraries; Private libraries.
Personality, 158, 226, 239, 431. *See
also* Librarians.
PERT/CPM networks, 453
Philanthropy. *See* Funding.

Philosophical literature, 350. *See also* Humanities literature.

Phonorecords, 605. *See also* Audiovisual materials.

Photocopying, 259

Physical education literature, 368. *See also* Educational literature; Social science literature.

Physical plant, 33, 49, 88, 97, 100, 160, 176, 355. *See also* Architecture.

Physical Review, 86, 365

Physicians, 26, 466, 627. *See also* Scientists.

Physicists, 86. *See also* Scientists.

Physics literature, 144, 365. *See also* Scientific literature.

Picture books. *See* Children's literature; Illustrations.

Pittsburgh. University. Library, 524

P.L. 480, 595

Planning, 353, 512

Planning-Programming-Budgeting System, 512

Poetry, 343. *See also* Humanities literature.

Polish language and literature, 247

Political science literature, 63. *See also* Social science literature.

Poole, William Frederick, 200

Portugal, 85. *See also* Europe.

PPBS. *See* Planning-Programming-Budgeting System.

Practical Guide to American Nineteenth Century Color Plate Books, 334

Practicum. *See* Work-study.

Princeton University. Library, 20, 216, 446

Principals, 103, 127, 172, 336, 445. *See also* Administrators.

Printing and publishing
American foreign language press, 218, 248, 269, 299, 633
and cataloging, 564
Asia, 68, 173, 438, 588, 611
Black press, 515
Canada, 233, 245
Catholic press, 72
children's literature, 205, 437

Printing and publishing (cont'd)
Eastern states, 145, 182, 215, 286
encyclopedias, 183
Europe, 11, 84-85, 121, 141, 212, 299, 323, 352, 411
government publications, 54, 120, 245, 259, 294, 310, 656
history of, 5, 11, 31, 38, 68, 72, 84-85, 121, 139, 141, 145, 170, 180, 182, 210, 212, 214-15, 259, 269, 314, 411, 430, 502, 593, 611, 636
impact of photocopying, 259
incunabula, 141, 411
India, 120
manuscripts, 141
Mexico, 151
Michigan, 139, 294
music, 182
national bibliographies, 185
paperbacks, 170, 179
professional association press, 337
reprints, 559
scholarly publications, 38, 84, 259, 559
scientific literature, 146, 337
serials, 146, 148, 214, 232, 248, 261, 314, 323, 393, 405, 437, 515
Southern states, 162
theological literature, 72, 218, 633
typeset, 5
university press, 38, 84, 310
See also Engraving.

Prison inmates, 584

Private libraries, 15, 66, 68-69, 305, 399, 539, 554, 649. *See also* Libraries.

Problem solving. *See* Decision making.

Professional associations, 337, 566, 652. *See also* American Library Association; Association of American Library Schools.

Professors. *See* College and university faculty; Community college faculty; Library school faculty.

Psychological literature, 583. *See also* Social science literature.

Public administration literature, 383. *See also* Social science literature.

Public Law 480. *See* P.L. 480.

Public librarians
  administrators, 34, 48, 220, 238, 288, 347, 354, 370, 392, 470, 494, 500
  attitudes, 204, 500, 517
  Canada, 460
  career planning, 460
  collective bargaining, 500
  Eastern states, 397
  educational preparation, 333, 346, 379, 397
  hiring, 50
  Midwestern states, 34, 220, 517
  perception of patron need, 459
  role, 56, 220, 370, 397
  See also Librarians.

Public libraries
  administration, 16, 48, 61, 331, 354, 470, 494
  adult education, 89, 174, 220, 250
  and state governments, 48, 174
  attitudes toward, 202, 220, 408
  bond issues, 210, 448
  budgets, 157
  catalogs, 157, 312, 659
  censorship, 517
  circulation, 285, 495
  civil service, 50
  cooperative programs, 36, 49, 56, 63, 90, 118, 305, 307, 325, 483, 494, 497, 659
  court decision, 191
  Eastern states, 14, 50, 61, 65, 69, 91, 285, 307, 326, 434, 490, 524-25, 533, 553, 655, 659
  film programs, 266, 285
  foreign countries, 24, 49, 233, 297, 325, 330, 426, 460
  funding, 43, 90, 210, 322, 448, 639
  group discussions, 107
  history of, 44, 65-66, 69, 77, 105, 174-75, 184, 322, 325-26, 426, 436, 553, 575
  library boards, 331, 459, 617, 639
  library collections, 27-28, 63, 204, 495, 524, 659

Public libraries (cont'd)
  library legislation, 174, 191, 237
  library use, 14, 28, 44, 89, 263, 298, 307, 309, 382, 408, 459, 490, 533, 594, 619, 658
  materials selection and acquisitions, 24, 63, 233, 285, 333, 434
  Middle Atlantic states, 69, 77, 202, 285, 298, 374, 382, 457, 490, 618
  Midwestern states, 27, 34, 39, 50, 63, 65, 71, 74, 90-91, 174, 184, 193, 220, 288, 306, 434, 448, 492, 497, 517, 539
  physical plant, 49, 71
  reading programs, 193
  reference services, 61, 128, 346, 374, 457
  Rocky Mountain states, 353
  role, 220, 244
  services to special groups, 37, 56, 74, 174, 202, 284, 306, 533, 575, 613, 655
  Southern states, 37, 61, 66, 80, 91, 109, 175, 305, 492, 579, 619
  Western states, 50, 61, 89, 91, 210, 408, 470, 483, 492
  See also Libraries; Regional libraries; State libraries; Subscription libraries.

Public opinion, 41

Public services. *See* Reference service.

Publisher's Weekly, 282

Publishing. *See* Printing and publishing.

Punched cards, 102

Purdue University. Library, 359, 479

Pushto language and literature, 362

Reader's Digest, 82

Reader services, 196, 504

Reading, 35, 78, 132, 584

Reading ability, 193, 523

Reading guidance, 196, 274

Reading interests
  authors, 433, 581
  California, 59

Reading interests (cont'd)
 children, 14, 64, 95
 farmers and rural inhabitants, 74, 109,
  202
 general population, 22, 28, 35, 55,
  109
 Italy, 411
 Midwestern states, 10, 28, 74, 78,
  95, 202
 minority groups, 523, 647
 New York, 35, 413
 Southern states, 98, 109, 203, 527
 students, 10, 59, 64, 78, 95, 98,
  230, 313, 413, 527, 550
 teachers, 230
Reading programs, 9, 193
Recataloging. *See* Cataloging.
Reclassification. *See* Classification.
Records. *See* Phonorecords.
Recruitment, 169, 431, 499. *See also*
Career planning.
Reference books, 388. *See also* names
of specific reference sources.
Reference services
 academic libraries, 128, 164, 512,
  549, 573
 attitudes toward, 546
 California, 61, 558
 cost accounting, 260
 Eastern states, 61, 91, 374
 educational preparation, 91, 164, 346,
  516, 546, 561
 faculty awareness, 558, 573
 history of, 128
 interface, 570
 Midwestern states, 61, 374, 573
 organization, 61
 public libraries, 61, 91, 128, 346,
  374, 457
 questions analyzed, 91, 570
 research libraries, 128, 260
Regional libraries, 73, 109, 122, 289,
 307, 325, 619. *See also* Cooperative
 programs; Library systems; State
 libraries.
Reprints, 559
Research, 400
Resources. *See* Library collections.
Retarded. *See* Handicapped.

Retrieval effectiveness, 365, 416,
 491, 521, 569
Reviews, 46, 79, 131, 204-205, 304,
 603
Rhode Island, 50. *See also* New
 England states.
Richardson, Ernest Cushing, 125
Rivington, James, 180
Rocky Mountain states, 122. *See
 also* names of specific states.
Roosevelt, Franklin Delano, 82
Rural library service, 74, 109, 111,
 174, 202, 306, 419, 575. *See also*
 Public libraries; Regional libraries;
 State libraries.
Russia. *See* Union of Soviet Socialist
 Republics.
Rutgers. State University of New
 Jersey. Library, 20
St. Louis. Public Library, 61
St. Nicholas, 502
St. Paul (Minnesota). Public Library,
 50
Saturday Evening Post, 55, 82
Saur, Christopher, 269
School faculty, 12, 52, 208, 230,
 336, 445, 481, 487
School librarians
 administrators, 135, 518
 attitudes toward, 255, 336, 445
 career planning, 267
 certification, 372
 Eastern states, 62, 152, 485
 educational preparation, 13, 51, 62,
  97, 255, 372, 410, 427, 485, 504,
  597
 faculty status, 255
 job satisfaction, 465
 library use, 481
 Midwestern states, 52, 103, 135,
  255, 336, 465, 481, 487, 504
 Oregon, 445
 role, 152, 274, 336, 339, 373, 445,
  487, 518, 612
 Southern states, 372-73, 609
 See also Librarians.
School libraries
 administration, 36, 100, 103, 118,
  135, 353, 518

School libraries (cont'd)
and learning, 258, 579
attitudes toward, 127, 135, 166, 172,
467
budget, 40
cataloging, 229
censorship problems, 281
cooperative programs, 36, 56, 118,
307, 506
cost accounting, 40
Eastern states, 32, 100, 116, 127,
156, 207, 229, 249, 281, 571,
579, 655
evaluated, 7, 12-13, 32, 42, 51-52, 58,
80, 97, 100, 103, 116, 143, 150,
168, 172, 176, 207, 284, 316, 412,
417, 555, 571, 624
funding, 2, 36, 40, 80, 97, 412, 439
history, 36, 520
library collections, 7, 40, 42, 50,
52, 97, 207, 309, 332, 355, 363,
506, 537, 602, 638
library legislation, 2, 87, 111, 412,
439, 555, 571
library orientation programs, 156,
377
library services, 36, 52, 80, 97, 100,
176, 241, 387, 427, 609
library use, 12, 29, 58-59, 156,
208, 295-96, 474, 481, 511, 579,
594
materials selection, 119, 339, 638
Middle Atlantic states, 127, 289,
505-506, 509, 522
Midwestern states, 58, 87, 95, 135,
143, 168, 176, 208, 258, 309,
313, 316, 355, 363, 412, 481,
504, 511, 618, 646
New England states, 96, 127, 172
physical plant, 97, 100, 160, 176,
355
reader services, 9, 95, 196, 504
research needs, 400
role, 12-13, 96, 137, 166, 196,
296, 339, 373, 385
standards, 32, 51, 96, 116, 150,
160, 168, 241, 253, 332, 522,
541, 602, 624

School libraries (cont'd)
Southern states, 7, 51-52, 70, 80,
103, 155, 253, 258, 373, 385,
467, 520, 602, 624
teachers' libraries, 481
Western states, 40, 118, 150, 332,
353, 417, 439, 555, 609
West Indies, 330
See also Instructional materials
centers; Libraries; Parochial
libraries; Vocational school
libraries.
School students
attitudes toward library, 467, 594
California, 59
Eastern states, 413, 485
library skills, 29, 230
library use, 12, 29, 58-59, 156,
208, 295-96, 474, 481, 511, 579,
594
Midwestern states, 52, 95, 193,
208, 313, 344, 511
reading interests, 59, 64, 95, 98,
230, 313, 527, 550
Southern states, 98, 467
See also Children.
Scientific and Technical Aerospace
Reports, 354
Scientific literature
bibliographic control, 257, 396
document citation and retrieval,
450
indexing, 213, 365
journals, 86, 144, 146-47
library collections, 363
materials selection, 582, 638
printing and publishing, 146, 337
See also names of specific
disciplines.
Scientists, 146, 167, 444, 458. See
also names of specific disciplines.
SDI. See Selective Dissemination of
Information.
Selection. See Materials selection.
Selective dissemination of information, 293, 315, 395, 423, 528, 623
Self censorship. See Censorship.
Seminary libraries. See Theological
libraries.

Serials, 147. *See also* Annuals; Journals; Newsletters; Newspapers.

Shakespeare, William, 11

Shamurin, Evgenii Ivanovich, 653

Sharp, Katharine, 283

Sheldon, John P., 139

Shinn, Millicent Washburn, 393

Signal of Liberty, 214

Sleep research, 458. *See also* Scientific literature.

Slides, 377, 551. *See also* Audio-visual materials.

Snead and Company, 402

Social libraries. *See* Subscription libraries.

Social science literature, 153, 579, 659. *See also* names of specific disciplines.

Sociological literature, 53. *See also* Social science literature.

South Carolina, 66, 75, 155, 177, 345, 532. *See also* Southern states.

South Carolina. University. Library, 177, 345

South Dakota, 566, 597. *See also* Midwestern states.

Southern states, 37, 70, 75, 142, 155, 162, 175, 203. *See also* names of specific states.

Spain, 85, 430. *See also* Europe.

Spanish Americans. *See* Mexican Americans.

Special librarians, 347. *See also* Librarians.

Special libraries, 217, 227, 289, 330, 347, 381, 567, 628. *See also* Libraries.

Spofford, Ainsworth Rand, 519

Standards

academic libraries, 3, 133, 389

library collections, 150, 332

library education, 418

Pennsylvania, 116

physical plant, 160

school libraries, 32, 51, 96, 116, 150, 160, 168, 241, 253, 332, 522, 541, 602, 624

Southern states, 51, 253, 602

Western states, 133, 150, 332, 417

State libraries

activities, 2, 48, 419, 532

State libraries (cont'd)

administration, 48, 353

California, 419, 483

catalogs, 17

history, 171, 357, 419, 575

library use, 58, 171

Massachusetts, 17

Midwestern states, 58, 357

Southern states, 17, 171, 532, 575

See also Libraries; Public libraries; Regional libraries.

State University of New York. *See* New York. State University, Buffalo; New York. State University, Geneseo. Library School.

Status, 255, 370, 403, 415, 424, 428, 529. *See also* Faculty status.

Stift Reichersberg, 428

Stone and Kimball (Publishing Company), 31

Storage and retrieval. *See* Document citation and retrieval; Information storage and retrieval.

Story, 55

Strahan, William, 212

Strikes, 566

Students. *See* College and university students; Community college students; Library school students; School students.

Subject headings

educational preparation, 8

English literature materials, 194

foreign language materials, 369, 462

formulation, 157, 369, 414

for selective dissemination of information, 395

Library of Congress, 142, 157, 194, 282, 473, 563

retrieval effectiveness, 416

See also Cataloging.

Subscription libraries, 105, 114, 134, 553. *See also* Libraries; Public libraries.

Suez Canal, 279

Supervision. *See* Administration.

Supervisors. *See* Administrators.

Swarthmore College. Library, 573

Syracuse. University. Library, 596
Systems analysis, 380

Tampa (Florida). Public Library, 91
Tapes, 551. *See also* Audio-visual
materials.
Teachers. *See* College and university
faculty; Community college faculty;
Library school faculty; School
faculty.
Technical Abstracts Bulletin, 354
Technical assistants. *See* Library
technical assistants.
Technical libraries. *See* Special
libraries.
Technical processing, 140, 319, 328.
See also names of specific functions.
Telefacsimile, 648
Television, 464
Tennessee, 75, 109, 155, 373, 532. *See
also* Southern states.
Texas
academic libraries, 240, 301, 345, 478,
583
library collections, 301
library education, 275.
library services, 609
library systems, 492
public libraries, 91, 492
school libraries, 80, 155, 609
See also Southern states.
Texas. University, 583
Texas. University. Library, 345, 478
Theocritus, 25
Theological libraries, 264, 317, 471. *See
also* Church libraries; Libraries.
Theological literature, 72, 218, 320,
388, 471, 633. *See also* Humanities
literature.
Thoreau, Henry David, 433
Time and motion studies, 319, 535
Training. *See* Education for librarian-
ship; On-the-job training; Work-study.
Training for Library Service, 398
Transcriptions, 441
Translations, 25, 247, 349, 441
Transliterations, 190, 441
True Story, 55

Union of Soviet Socialist Republics,
257, 321, 352, 354, 653. *See also*
Europe.
Union Theological Seminary, 317
United Arab Republic. National
Library, 257, 321
United Nations. Library, 375
U.S. Air Force libraries, 338, 435.
See also Federal libraries.
U.S. Army libraries, 161, 338. *See
also* Federal libraries.
*U.S. Government Research and
Development Reports*, 354
U.S. history. *See* American history
literature.
U.S. libraries. *See* Federal libraries.
U.S. Office of Technical Services,
270
University librarians. *See* College
and university librarians.
University libraries. *See* College and
university libraries.
Urdu language and literature, 287,
362
Users. *See* Library use.
U.S.S.R. *See* Union of Soviet Social-
ist Republics.

Virginia, 7, 75, 155, 177, 258, 532.
See also Southern states.
Vocabulary, 407, 425, 464, 473,
660
Vocational school libraries, 207. *See
also* Community college libraries;
Libraries; School libraries.
Voting, 448

Wales, 4. *See also* England; Europe.
Washington, D.C. Public Library, 91
Washington (State), 89, 210, 310,
353, 367, 390, 535
Washington. State University.
Library, 535
Weber, Max, 436
Weeding, 60, 495
Wesley, John, 581
West Germany. *See* Germany.

West Indies, 330
West Virginia, 252, 289
West Virginia. University. Library, 252, 289
William and Mary College. Library, 20, 216
Williamson, Charles Clarence, 398
Wisconsin
   academic libraries and librarians, 187, 356, 566, 596, 608
   bibliotherapy, 584
   censorship, 517
   collective bargaining activities, 566
   faculty status, 477
   library collections, 27
   library use, 58
   public libraries and librarians, 27, 34, 517
   school libraries and librarians, 87, 143, 465, 618
   state libraries, 58
   See also Midwestern states.

Wisconsin. State Library, 58
Wisconsin. University. Libraries, 356, 596, 608
Work experience, 30, 239
Work satisfaction. *See* Job satisfaction.
Work simplification, 26
Works Progress Administration, 57
Work study, 485, 561. *See also* Education for librarianship.
World War II literature, 189, 343. *See also* Social science literature.
W.P.A. *See* Works Progress Administration.

Yale University. Library, 20, 93, 216
Young people. *See* Adolescents.

Zeitschrift für Kunstgeschichte, 224